JAZZ

legends of style

AUTHOR: KEITH SHADWICK

JAZZ

legends of style

Eagle
Editions

A QUANTUM BOOK

Published by Eagle Editions Ltd
11 Heathfield
Royston
Hertfordshire SG8 5BW

This edition printed 2001

ISBN 1-86160-355-X

QUMJZZ

This book is produced by
Quantum Publishing
6 Blundell Street
London N7 9BH

Printed in Singapore by
Star Standard Industries Pte Ltd

Photography: Frank Driggs Collection (Pp. 2, 8-11, 14, 16-21, 23-26, 28-33, 35-36, 38-39, 41-43, 46-47, 50, 54-56, 58-59, 62-64, 66, 68-71, 73-76, 80-87, 89-97, 99-103, 105, 112-113, 119, 122-123, 126-127, 132-133, 136, 138, 140, 145-147, 149-152, 154-157, 161-162, 164-65, 167, 169-170, 176-177, 179-180, 182-188, 190-196, 199-202, 204, 208, 210, 212-213, 218, 222-223, 225, 227, 229-230, 232-238, 240-243, 246, 248-252, 254, 256-259, 266-273, 275-276, 280-283, 285-287, 290, 294-296, 298-303, 305-309, 311, 313, 323, 339, 342, 343); **Dat's Jazz Photo Library** (Pp. 15, 27, 37, 40, 44, 45, 48, 51-53, 57, 60-61, 65, 67, 72, 77-78, 88, 98, 104, 108, 109-111, 114-118, 120-121, 124-125, 128-130, 134, 137, 139, 141-144, 148, 153, 158-159, 163, 166, 168, 181, 203, 205-206, 209, 211, 216-217, 219, 221, 226, 228, 239, 244-245, 255, 264, 277-279, 288-289, 292-293, 297, 304, 310, 312, 314-316, 325, 329-330, 332-333, 338, 340, 346, 350), **Peter Symes** (Pp. 172, 189, 322, 328, 331, 341, 344-345, 347, 351), **BMI Archives** (Pp. 135, 324, 335, 336-37, 348-349), **Ray Avery Photo Library** (Pp. 7, 12-13 photo by Bernard Gidel, 197, 207, 214, 220, 260, 265, 274, 317-321, 326-327, 334), **Val Wilmer** (Pp. 22, 34, 49, 79, 106-107, 131, 160, 171, 173-175, 178, 198, 231, 253, 291); **Sony-Blue Note** (Pp. 247, 261). *Every effort has been made to ensure this listing is correct; the publisher and the author apologize for any omissions.*

contents

Foreword and Introduction by Barry McRae 6

The Artists: An A-Z of the Best in Jazz 8

with special features on:

Albert Ayler Louis Armstrong Chet Baker Count Basie Sidney Bechet Dave Brubeck Benny Carter Ornette Coleman John Coltrane Miles Davis Tommy Dorsey Duke Ellington Bill Evans Ella Fitzgerald Stan Getz Dizzy Gillespie Benny Goodman Lionel Hampton Fletcher Henderson Woody Herman Billie Holiday Keith Jarrett Louis Jordan Stan Kenton Gene Krupa Wynton Marsalis Charles Mingus Thelonious Monk Jelly Roll Morton Gerry Mulligan Charlie Parker Bud Powell Max Roach Sonny Rollins George Russell Artie Shaw Archie Shepp Nina Simone Sun Ra Cecil Taylor Sarah Vaughan Fats Waller Mary Lou Williams Lester Young

Index 352

JAZZ A foreword and introduction

This book is one man's Hall Of Fame. It faces the daunting challenge of selecting three hundred musicians who, throughout the twentieth century, have applied their instrumental skills and their creative awareness to the world of jazz. At the same time, they have provided individual inspiration and important stylistic sign posting. Keith Shadwick is a writer well equipped for such a task. His concern is with the music itself and he does not deal in abstract arguments or in the anthropologists' theories of racial origins. He draws attention to the gulf between inspired discovery and applied eclecticism and, in presenting the jazz alumni in alphabetical order he avoids the trap of seeing one era as more significant then another.

He is aware that hearsay must play a part in his evaluations on the music's founding fathers. There are no existing recordings by men such as Buddy Bolden but every effort is made to put into perspective the contribution made by him and by his contemporaries. In terms of the music's earlier years, a conscious effort is made to avoid the regional stereotypes and great care is taken to approach the work of each player on individual merit.

Special emphasis might well be placed on jazz's most influential figures but the loose cannon is not ignored. Shadwick values the music's most creative players on all instruments and, where necessary, points out square, musical pegs in their, nevertheless, round holes. The relationship between composer, arranger and performer is consistently acknowledged although, by the very nature of the music, it is the improvising soloist who is consistently the hero of this book.

The quality of musician's work is diligently assessed in the light of their contemporary situation. Note is also taken of the fluctuation between the organised and the extempore and of the players comfortable in both areas. The fact that a player can be no greater than the best in his era is conceded and care is taken to observe each individual's place in the evolutionary process. In the swing era, for instance, the pre-eminence of the orchestras led by Duke Ellington, Fletcher Henderson and Count Basie is established and, as the reputations of the big bands grew, attention is drawn to the success enjoyed by populists such as Benny Goodman, the Dorsey Brothers and, ultimately, Glenn Miller. The unique position of Stan Kenton, Woody Herman and Shorty Rogers is carefully plotted and their star soloists are given constructive reports.

With the demise of the swing era, the umbilical chord between jazz and popular music was severed and musicians became more specifically categorised. With this polarisation, Shadwick continues to introduce the stylistic areas through their finest protagonists and the long time affect had by Charlie Parker, Dizzy Gillespie, Thelonious Monk and the other great bebop players is strongly emphasised. The reader is invited to trace jazz's search for freedom through the biographies of men such as Sonny Rollins, Charles Mingus and John Coltrane.

The perhaps exaggerated freedom of later masters such as Ornette Coleman and Cecil Taylor is put into perspective and the daunting contribution by Miles Davis is looked at from several standpoints. Jazz has never turned its back on outside musical influences and Davis's role in the rock/jazz fusion of the sixties is outlined clearly. What Shadwick ensures is that the individual developments by the trumpeter's sidemen is also given careful consideration, maintaining balance among all players.

The evaluation of jazz singers is always a contentious issue and, while certain figures qualify obviously, observers continually haggle over the definition of the term. Shadwick's selections in the area show, not only his good taste but also his consistency of motive. A poor singer in front of an outstanding orchestra does not qualify and he is at length to point out why singers as diverse as Billie Holiday and Big Joe Turner are masters of the art, while the likes of talented performers like Tony Bennett just fail to make the sacred three hundred.

Care is taken to ensure that the evolutionary importance of well known majors such as Louis Armstrong and Jelly Roll Morton is not seen as any more significant than that of later figures such as Albert Ayler and Muhal Richard Abrams. Their talented disciples are also chosen with care and the work of men like David Murray, James Carter and Joshua Redman is seen as distinct from the revivalism of Wynton Marsalis and the Lincoln Centre repertory regime. Hip hop and rap is traced through the work of Branford Marsalis, Greg Osby and M-Base stalwart, Steve Coleman, and the small part played latterly by "show biz" is highlighted in the concert spectaculars by the Art Ensemble Of Chicago and the Sun Ra Solar Arkestra.

Important European originals such as John Surman, Jan Garbarek and Eberhard Weber gain entry and the importance of record labels such as Hat Art and ECM, chronicled.

Inevitably, every reader will find reason to carp at the absence of certain personal favourites and might also question the inclusion of mere revivalists such as George Lewis and Chris Barber. The point is that Shadwick is a writer with an historian's attention to detail, coupled with a broad minded attitude toward jazz and an ability to evaluate it within the compass of all world music. He has ended up with a wise, yet challenging selection and it s one that shows his remarkable perception.

By **Barry McRae**, author of *The Jazz Cataclysm (Dent)*, *The Jazz Handbook (Longmans)* and acclaimed biographies of Miles Davis, Ornette Coleman, and Dizzy Gillespie. Barry also writes a regular column on contemporary developments in jazz for *Jazz Journal International* ("Tomorrow Is Now"), as well as contributing to *Music Maker* and *Jazz Forum*. Barry is one of the few European critics to have a biographical entry in the prestigious publication, *The Grove Dictionary of Jazz*.

Muhal Richard Abrams

fact file

BORN 1930

MUSICAL SELECTION
Levels and Degrees of Light
The Hearinga Suite

Muhal Richard Abrams, Creative Band founder and first president of the influential Chicago group, the Association for the Advancement of Creative Musicians (AACM)

Pianist/composer Abrams, born and raised in Chicago, has been a father figure for a number of generations of that city's jazz musicians. His own musical training was undertaken at Chicago Musical College; after four years there, in 1948 he began taking professional jobs around Chicago with a variety of local leaders, including the tough tenors of Gene Ammons, "Lockjaw" Davis, Johnny Griffin, and, later, John Gilmore. Other luminaries such as Roland Kirk, Zoot Sims, Clark Terry, Art Farmer, and Max Roach also used his talents, as well as R&B bands and the singing group Lambert, Henricks, and Ross. By the end of the 1950s Abrams felt the need for something more than freelance work and the vague desire to progress through peer recommendation. In 1961 he formed the Experimental Band, a group that convened whenever possible in the early 1960s to probe new musical areas.

Although hardly a financial goldmine, the Experimental Band became immensely important in its impact on all young local avant-garde musicians, giving them new and rewarding outlets for a mode of radical expression very different from that being formulated in New York and Europe. By the middle of the decade, Abrams's central role and organizational talents had made him instrumental in the formation of the Association for the Advancement of Creative Musicians (AACM), a body which to this day is fundamental to the continuing creative impetus of Chicago music. Abrams was the AACM's first president.

Abrams's own career has waxed and waned: his first album, *Levels and Degrees of Light* (Delmark), appeared in 1967 to a muted reception, and it was to be the 1980s before he began recording regularly with his own groups, although during the 1970s he appeared as a sideman with many, including the Art Ensemble of Chicago. He had moved to New York in 1977, and by the late 1980s his activities with small group and big band had reached an artistic peak reflected in the series of albums for Black Saint, including his masterwork, *The Hearinga Suite* (1989). Abrams continues to pursue a vigorous career, enjoying the fruits of years of effort.

SEE ALSO: Gene Ammons, Eddie "Lockjaw" Davis, Johnny Griffin, Roland Kirk, Zoot Sims, Art Farmer, Max Roach

Julian "Cannonball" Adderley

fact file

BORN 1928

DIED 1975

MUSICAL SELECTION
"Mercy, Mercy, Mercy"

A Florida-born former teacher, Cannonball Adderley became one of the most articulate musicians of his generation, as well as one of the most successful

Adderley's is one of the instantly recognizable instrumental voices of jazz: his warm, friendly tone and ebullient phrasing, plus his adherence to the more traditional elements in modern postwar jazz, eventually made him one of the best-loved and most popular post-Parker leaders.

Adderley was born in Tampa, Florida, and was attracted to jazz while at high school, learning saxophone there and leading high-school bands while living and teaching in Fort Lauderdale during the late 1940s. After a stint in the army, 1950-53, he returned to Florida and his teaching activities, playing in local clubs strictly as a hobby. In 1955 he decided to join up with his cornetist brother Nat (b. 1931), who was already a professional musician and had played in Lionel Hampton's band before settling in New York. A jam session weeks after his arrival landed Cannonball a job with Oscar Pettiford and a recording contract with Savoy, and by early 1956 he and his brother formed the first version of their Quintet. This proved premature for the general public, and the group disbanded in the face of adverse economics. Cannonball joined Miles Davis in the fall of 1957: this quintet quickly became a sextet with the return to Davis in early 1958 of tenorist John Coltrane, and until the departure of Adderley in September 1959 the Davis Sextet was one of the hottest groups in jazz.

Reunited with his brother, Adderley launched another Quintet, this time with pianist Bobby Timmons supplying many of the trademark soul-jazz compositions which were to propel the group to jazz stardom within a year. This band remained the central vehicle for Adderley's music for the rest of his life, occasionally expanding to be a sextet (tenorists Yusef Lateef and Charles Lloyd played with the Adderleys in the early 1960s), and musicians closely associated with the band's success include Victor Feldman, Joe Zawinul, Sam Jones, and Louis Hayes. Zawinul penned their US hit *Mercy Mercy Mercy* in 1967. Adderley, an articulate spokesman and a man of wide interests, busied himself with other projects during the 1960s and 1970s, from big-band albums and "concept" suites through to being a talent scout for labels such as Riverside and Columbia and an album producer for the same labels. He brought the then unknown Wes Montgomery to Riverside and also recorded Bud Powell for Columbia. In the turbulent atmosphere of the late 1960s and early 1970s, Adderley embarked on many programs to help people through music; he remained a tremendously popular figure up to his death, from heart failure, in 1975.

SEE ALSO: Lionel Hampton, Oscar Pettiford, Miles Davis, John Coltrane, Yusef Lateef, Charles Lloyd, Wes Montgomery, Bud Powell

Toshiko Akiyoshi

fact file

BORN 1929

MUSICAL SELECTION
Tales of a Courtesan

Toshiko Akiyoshi, one of jazz's greatest living composer/arrangers, continues to enjoy popularity world-wide

Born in Dairen, China, to Japanese parents, Akiyoshi studied classical piano and theory while in China, turning to jazz only after her arrival in Japan in 1946. By the mid-1950s she was a prominent local player, being discovered in Tokyo by the visiting Oscar Peterson and encouraged to make the journey to America. Three years at Berklee College in Boston prepared her for her US career, and shortly after her graduation from Berklee in 1959 she formed the Toshiko-Mariano Quartet with altoist Charlie Mariano, who by then was her husband. An impressive album from Candid in early 1960 brought her wider attention, and for a while both she and Mariano played with Charles Mingus's ensembles. A second stint in Japan took her away from America in the mid-1960s, but by the end of the decade she had formed a second quartet, with her second husband, saxophonist Lew Tabackin. The exposure this brought allowed them, after a relocation to Los Angeles, to form in 1973 a co-led rehearsal big-band. In this band, which recorded regularly and occasionally played live, she found perhaps her true jazz métier, writing and arranging material with style, aplomb, and a contemporary updated bop feel, combining the power of the Jones-Lewis orchestra with the textural sensitivity of Gil Evans.

During the 1980s Akiyoshi slowly became part of the international jazz touring circuit, appearing often as soloist or leader of different aggregations, while her big-band albums proved consistently popular, especially in Japan, where she was a major musical figure. A move back to New York in 1981 had helped her American profile, and her large groups became consistent poll winners. A sellout Carnegie Hall concert in 1991 (later released on album by Columbia) proved her long-term appeal and the continuing rude health of her creative muse.

SEE ALSO: Oscar Peterson, Charles Mingus, Gil Evans

Henry "Red" Allen

fact file

BORN 1908

DIED 1967

MUSICAL SELECTION
World on a String

Inspired, like every one of his generation, by Louis Armstrong, Henry "Red" Allen in later life became one of jazz's great originals

Allen, born and raised in New Orleans, was taught trumpet by his father, a brass-band leader himself for a number of decades. Allen spent the early 1920s developing his technique, leaving New Orleans in 1927 to join King Oliver's Dixie Syncopators in St Louis.

Traveling with Oliver, he reached New York that same year, making his recording debut with the Clarence Williams. After a return to New Orleans and two years on the riverboats with Fate Marable, Allen landed a contract with Victor, recording four sides with the New York-based Luis Russell orchestra, whom he subsequently joined. Allen, decidedly influenced by Armstrong, was placed in competition with him by record company publicity. Yet Allen was forging his own personal variation on the Armstrong method and he quickly became one of the most distinctive trumpeters in all jazz, often leading small-group dates as well as being lead trumpet for Russell (1929-32), Fletcher Henderson (1933-34) and the Mills Blue Rhythm Band (1934-37). Allen was one of the first New Orleans trumpeters to adapt the newer swing-style playing to his own needs and, prior to Roy Eldridge's emergence, was second only to Armstrong himself as a trumpet stylist, Hot Lips Page and Buck Clayton notwithstanding. Unfortunately, Allen rejoined Russell in 1937, when the band was employed as Armstrong's backing band. Reduced to section work, he left in 1940, spending the next decade in the burgeoning revivalist movement and regaining his profile through his own Sextet, which included Edmond Hall. Kenny Kersey and J.C. Higginbotham. By the mid-1950s established as a regular at New York's Metropole bar, Allen was employing Coleman Hawkins and others and developing his later style, a highly vocalized and dynamic portrait of his complex but sunny creative personality. His group appeared at Newport in 1957 and on the 1958 *Sound of Jazz* TV program, stealing the show on both occasions. Allen continued to base himself in New York though he toured overseas and recorded regularly. His unique mature style was written about by avant-garde trumpeter Don Ellis in the mid-1960s, prompting an overdue reappraisal of his substantial contribution to the music. By late 1966 he was visibly suffering from the cancer which would eventually kill him the following spring.

SEE ALSO: King Oliver, Clarence Williams, Louis Armstrong, Fletcher Henderson, Roy Eldridge, Hot Lips Page, Buck Clayton

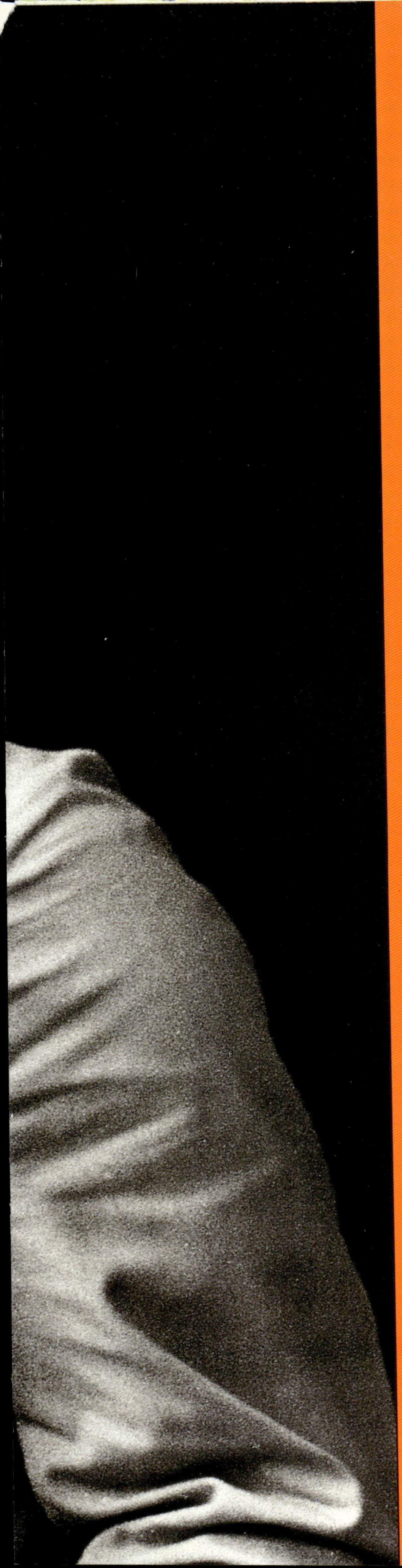

Albert Ayler

Saxophonist Ayler was the most radical jazz innovator of the early 1960s; a primitive playing some of the most sophisticated music of his time, a man who talked of spiritual unity but who created music which often seemed chaotic and pain-filled, a saxophonist possessed of such overwhelming pathos in his balladry that it reached beyond jazz tradition to sentimental "sweet music" and outright bathos.

He was born in Cleveland, Ohio, into a musical family, his father being a violinist and saxophonist, his brother a trumpeter. At the age of seven Albert started on alto sax and by the age of 10 joined his father to play at funerals. He also studied music at the Cleveland Academy. By his mid-teens he was an enthusiastic practitioner of R&B sax in local bands, briefly joining, at 16, blues harpist Little Walter's touring band. He later claimed that he was known in Cleveland at this time as "Little Bird." In 1958 it was his turn for Army service, and he served some of his three years in Europe, playing both alto and tenor in a services band. He emerged in 1961, spending time in Sweden, playing in a somewhat tortured bebop style. A stint with Cecil Taylor in Copenhagen in the winter of 1962-63 led to both men playing together once more on their return to America.

This led to Ayler putting together his first jazz band, with Don Cherry, Gary Peacock and Sunny Murray. In early 1964 they visited Europe, then made a series of recordings which would turn modern jazz on its ear, the most important of these being in a trio without Cherry, *Spiritual Unity* (ESP-Disk). Ayler's extraordinary ferocious hoots, squawks, squeals and long, fractured altissimo glisses ushered into jazz a completely new musical vocabulary, one few commentators were ready for. Drummer Murray's abandoning of a metric beat added to the controversy. Quickly embraced world-wide as a darling of the avant-garde in every artistic discipline, Ayler formed a new group in 1965, bringing his brother Donald in from Cleveland, hiring drummer Milford Graves, and occasionally using fiery altoist Charles Taylor. This band unveiled Ayler's approach to unison playing and melody, sounding for all the world like a Salvation Army band in bleak midwinter, playing simplistic unison themes with uncanny musical relations to spirituals and hymns, then breaking into his ferocious improvisations, sometimes singly, sometimes collectively. An appearance at Town Hall in 1965 became the band's first release, *Bells* (ESP-Disk). By the middle of the next year Ayler's name was consuming more jazz press newsprint world-wide than any other artist; he signed with the Impulse! label, thus availing himself of decent recording budgets and first-class packaging and distribution. His first two albums for Impulse!, *At Greenwich Village* (1966/7) and *Love Cry* (1967) are perhaps his most completely evolved artistic statements on record.

In 1968 Ayler changed direction with the album *New Grass*, introducing Bernard Purdie's boogaloo beat and various other R&B trappings. Few perceive this experiment as successful. Unfortunately, Ayler's records from his last three years continue to dabble with increasingly inappropriate musical settings for his playing, although his live concerts during the same period show him more successfully blending the various inspirations and influences from his complete career. Shortly after his return from a brief European tour in late 1970, Ayler disappeared from his New York home. His body was found two weeks later floating in East River.

fact file

BORN 1936

DIED 1970

MUSICAL SELECTION
Spiritual Unity
Bells
At Greenwich Village
Love Cry

No collection of jazz greats would be complete without Albert Ayler

SEE ALSO: Cecil Taylor, Don Cherry, Milford Graves

Gene Ammons

Son of pianist Albert, Gene Ammons became influential in the jazz scene in the late 1940s

fact file

BORN 1925

DIED 1974

MUSICAL SELECTION
Live In Chicago

Chicago-born like his famous pianist father, Gene Ammons was from the first absorbed by and in music, studying under a Captain Walter Dyett at Chicago's DuSable High School. A prodigy doted upon by his parents and full of self-confidence, Ammons was ready musically to go out on the road at the age of 18 with the King Kolax band, and from there progressed in 1944 to the famous Billy Eckstine Band which proved such a hot-house breeder for the emerging bebop style. Ammons, who was forging a new hybrid from the styles of the two premier saxophonists of that time, Coleman Hawkins and Lester Young, via the ideas of "Chu" Berry and Herschel Evans, stayed with Eckstine until 1947, picking up numerous musical nuggets from other band members as well as less desirable behavior, including a heavy drug habit. After some time out on his own and playing with a range of men, including his father Albert, Dexter Gordon, and others, Ammons replaced Stan Getz in Woody Herman's Herd in 1949, thus helping spread his name internationally. By this time his style was well formed and he had begun in turn to influence a new generation of tenor players, the so-called "Chicago school" which included people like Johnny Griffin, his big sound and aggressive up-tempo playing balanced by the sensual romanticism of his ballads. The roots of the soul-jazz tenor and its logical extensions can be found in Ammons's early recordings.

Following the new fashion for two-tenor "battles" initiated by people like Flip Phillips and Illinois Jacquet, Dexter Gordon, Wardell Gray, and Teddy Edwards, Ammons formed in 1950 a group with Sonny Stitt, thereby helping launch the so-called "tough tenor" school – indeed, he became known as a "boss tenor" during this period. Just as the economic fruits of this new style became reachable, Ammons was incarcerated for drug use (1958-60). His return to active music-making coincided with the arrival of the avant-garde and his soul-jazz rivals were already entrenched. Ammons spent a couple of years attempting to restart his career, but a seven-year jail term (1962-69) for a second drug bust effectively killed it off. A new start in 1970 saw him settle into a regular work pattern using the old tenor approach, but his health had been damaged by years of drug abuse, and his early death, from pneumonia, was mainly due to the weakened state of his body. In the decades since his death, his musical significance has begun to emerge and he is now recognized as a postwar giant.

SEE ALSO: Billy Eckstine, Coleman Hawkins, Lester Young, Albert Ammons, Dexter Gordon, Stan Getz, Woody Herman

Ray Anderson

Trombonist Ray Anderson, possibly the most versatile and exciting player on the trombone today

fact file

BORN 1952

MUSICAL SELECTION
Every One of Us
Azurety

Chicago-born trombonist Anderson has the wide musical interests and stylistic sweep typical of so many musicians of that city. Picking up the trombone at the age of eight, Anderson applied himself to it conscientiously, especially during teen years when he and fellow trombonist George Lewis were pupils together, learning classical techniques before deciding to play music across the board, from classical to jazz, funk, and blues. As interested in Trummy Young and Vic Dickenson as Roswell Rudd and Paul Rutherford, Anderson began applying his technique to his musical imagination in many of these settings, learning from AACM concerts that such wild expressionism, whether humorous or deadly serious, could be musically valid and exciting. After completing his studies, Anderson moved out to California while still a teenager before arriving in New York in 1972.

In New York, Anderson moved primarily with young avant-gardists such as Anthony Davis and his old friend George Lewis, and also managed to sit in with Charles Mingus. A major step forward came in 1977, when he began regular stints with both Anthony Braxton and Barry Altschul as well as continuing a typical New Yorker's freelance life. This led to exposure which brought him international attention, and by the beginning of the 1980s he was able to tour Europe with a group of his own. This in turn led to a rapid acceptance of one of his ventures, Slickaphonics, a Zappa-esque funk band full of wild humor and expressionistic musical color, although largely using acoustic instruments. Since that time Anderson has established himself as the premier young trombonist in jazz, working on a multitude of projects and with a plethora of bands and styles, from duos and trios with people such as Han Bennink through to his Alligatory Band experiences, both live and on record, while Slickaphonics still occasionally comes back to life. Anderson's prodigious technique and big tone are never used garrulously: he can play sweetly with organist Barbara Dennerlein, or full out with his own quartet, but his approach is full of a zest for life and good humor, which makes his ideas doubly attractive.

SEE ALSO: George Lewis, Vic Dickenson, Roswell Rudd, Charles Mingus, Anthony Braxton

Louis Armstrong

Few would dispute Louis Armstrong's position as the most important formative influence on classic jazz and, with Ellington and Parker, the presiding genius of the music up to the 1960s. Armstrong came from New Orleans, his early childhood spent fatherless in the slums and brothels frequented by his mother. His real musical beginnings are to be found in the two or three years after being sent in 1913 to the Home for Colored Waifs, a corrective institute for poor young ne'er-do-wells. In the home he learned the cornet and played in the band, and on his release made his young presence felt among the professional bands of New Orleans. This prodigiously gifted youth quickly overtook most of the cornetists of the day, so that when Joe "King" Oliver left Kid Ory's band in 1919 to take up a job in Chicago, Armstrong was the natural replacement. Within three years Oliver himself was inviting Armstrong to join his band at Chicago's Lincoln Gardens dance hall; in 1923 Armstrong debuted with Oliver's band for Okeh records.

By late 1924 Armstrong had been persuaded by his new wife, the band's pianist Lil Hardin Armstrong, that he was not being best served by staying with Oliver, and in the fall he joined Fletcher Henderson's orchestra in New York. His reputation spread, leading to many freelance recording sessions. His justly famous series of sides with his studio-only band, the Hot Five also began in 1925 when he returned to Chicago. Over the next three years Armstrong (swapping eventually to trumpet) would use this band, the Hot Seven, and other variants to create a body of recorded work unsurpassed in jazz, including the phenomenal "West End Blues" (1923). Outside the studio he continued to play with big bands, including Erskine Tate and Carroll Dickerson, and his repertoire began to shift to popular songs such as "Ain't Misbehavin'." Now backed by the Dickerson band billed as his own "orchestra," Armstrong used his virtuoso trumpet playing and charming singing (as well as his playful scatting) to full effect on the popular tunes of the day, all supported by a respectful big band. The advent of the powerful and ruthless Joe Glaser in 1935 as his personal manager, and the hiring of the Luis Russell band as Louis's support, set the course for the rest of the decade in which Armstrong was transformed from a jazz sensation into a famous popular-entertainment figure.

In 1940 Glaser broke up the Russell-based big band and brought in younger players: this unit was Armstrong's principal support until 1947. The change of that year was presaged by the soundtrack recordings for the film *New Orleans*, in which Louis appeared, and which used small-group renditions of classic jazz repertoire. By 1947, Louis started up his All-Stars, his permanent touring and recording band until his death almost 25 years later, albeit with many personnel changes. The original band featured his old friends and colleagues, Earl Hines and Jack Teagarden, but by 1952 Trummy Young had replaced Teagarden and Billy Kyle had substituted for Hines. By the mid-1950s the band's live sets had become formulaic, but Armstrong's majesty of tone and delivery, and his winning vocals, always communicated, as seen in the film *High Society*. He also embarked on classic co-led sessions such as those with Ella Fitzgerald (1956-57), Oscar Peterson (1957), and Duke Ellington (1961). By this time, he had enjoyed a worldwide hit with his version of "Mack the Knife," and as his trumpet playing faded in the 1960s, another major hit was produced in "What A Wonderful World." Armstrong kept performing until shortly before his death, a venerated musical ambassador.

fact file

BORN 1898

DIED 1971

MUSICAL SELECTION
Louis Armstrong Plays W.C. Handy
Satch Plays Fats
Satchmo Plays King Oliver

Louis Armstrong (here seen performing at the Cotton Club in 1939) was the first great improvisatory genius in jazz

SEE ALSO: Duke Ellington, Charlie Parker, Joe "King" Oliver, Kid Ory, Fletcher Henderson, Clarence Williams, Bessie Smith, Earl Hines, Jack Teagarden

Art Ensemble of Chicago

The Art Ensemble of Chicago, a revolutionary jazz ensemble combining many traditions now in its fourth decade of music

fact file

FORMED 1966

MUSICAL SELECTION
Nice Guys

Formed initially by saxophonist Roscoe Mitchell for a concert in Chicago in December 1966, the band was, until 1969, called simply the Art Ensemble. This innovatory group of musicians was originally made up of Mitchell, trumpeter Lester Bowie, bassist Malachi Favors, and drummer Philip Wilson. Reed-man Joseph Jarman joined in 1967, and occasional 1967-68 participants included drummers Thurman Barker, Robert Crowder, and bassist Charles Clark. Set against the background of New York-led avant-garde styles, most of which stressed dense, high-energy, wildly expressive and iconoclastic approaches to improvisation, the Chicagoans showed an interest in not only the unorthodox sonics of their instruments, but also the sounds of what they called "little instruments" such as bells, shakers, even car horns.

They also took a selective approach to the entire field of previous jazz style, fusing disparate elements together in long collective improvisations which often contained very long periods of near-silence or just a single soloist. Mitchell's compositions at first dominated the group's concepts: with Jarman's arrival, the group became more stylistically diverse and its stage act became increasingly bizarre and ritualized. A move to Paris in summer 1969 saw its name finalized as the Art Ensemble of Chicago, and a year later drummer Don Moye became a permanent member. The Art Ensemble perfected their performing technique so that, by the end of the 1970s, their telepathic collective playing could be adapted to any musical situation. Performances began to be self-edited so that vignettes and one-theme ideas could be expressed.

In the 1980s trumpeter Lester Bowie developed outside projects such as Brass Fantasy and became a popular figure away from the Ensemble, but the music they made continued to challenge, although by now the group had settled into a recognizable style of its own. Sometimes their latter-day music is taken for granted, but its individual components remain potent, and their pioneering importance remains intact.

SEE ALSO: Roscoe Mitchell, Lester Bowie, Joseph Jarman

Mildred Bailey

Mildred Bailey was a unique and brilliant stylist, recording hits with Paul Whiteman and her husband, Red Norvo

Bailey, born Mildred Rinker in a little town near Seattle called Tekoa, had Canadian Indian blood in her veins and was wont to remind people that, due to this, she was more American than most. Given an education in Spokane, Washington, she began singing in local cabarets and doing occasional work in Seattle before venturing down the West Coast and singing on a local Los Angeles radio station. Her introduction to the Paul Whiteman band which would make her a national figure came probably via her friendship with Bing Crosby, a fellow Spokanean, and in 1929 Whiteman asked her to become his first female lead.

Bailey stayed with the band just four years, enjoying in 1932 a major hit with her version of Hoagy Carmichael's "Rockin' Chair." Her striking features and her clear, soft and beautifully melismatic voice made her ideal for the radio and music industries, but her ever-robust figure, denied her any opportunity to move into films. In 1933, however, she left Whiteman's band and married Whiteman's xylophonist, Red Norvo. In 1936 the two launched a band together, but Bailey's desperate insecurities about her weight, plus her feelings of being passed over in favor of the rising stars Ella Fitzgerald and Billie Holiday, led to increasing strain and moodiness. By 1939 she had left the band and the marriage was in trouble: it was dissolved in 1943, by which time Bailey's instinctive jazz singing was in danger of falling out of fashion while her body began to experience the first signs of the diabetes and liver complaints which would ultimately kill her. Her increasingly irascible nature made it more difficult for people to hire her with confidence, and, Bailey withdrew from her old lifestyle. In the early 1940s she moved to the country in upstate New York, but by the end of the decade she was living in a New York apartment. She was found in a state close to death there in 1949, and her hospitalization was presided over by Bing Crosby and Frank Sinatra, but her remaining two years saw little relief, despite a last recording session in 1950. Bailey remains one of a tiny handful of white singers with authentic jazz feeling in everything they did.

fact file

BORN 1907

DIED 1951

MUSICAL SELECTION
"Rockin' Chair"

SEE ALSO: Red Norvo, Ella Fitzgerald, Billie Holiday

Chet Baker

Baker was born Chesney Baker in the farming town of Yale, Oklahoma, but his family moved to Oklahoma City when he was still an infant. When he was ten the family relocated to Glendale, California, as his father chased work; Baker began studying trumpet at junior high, but his acute ear and natural talent made him lazy in his lessons and he remained an ear player for years. At 16 he joined the army, serving in Berlin where he came across live jazz for the first time, and on his return to civilian life in 1948, he spent time checking out LA trumpeters. He re-enlisted in 1950 specifically to intensify his musical training, finding the Presidio Army Band in San Francisco ideal for this purpose. A transfer to Arizona in 1951 quickly cooled Baker's ardor for army life and he faked sufficiently to arrange a psychiatric discharge. Within months he was jamming around LA and by late spring 1952 he had auditioned for and been accepted by Charlie Parker for a West Coast tour which went up into Canada. Bird spread the word about Baker on his return to New York.

Baker was spreading his own waves after he joined the new pianoless Gerry Mulligan Quartet in summer 1952: their first records together, made in the 11 months to May 1953, remain some of the most influential of the period and of the decade, pioneering a melodic polyphony new to postwar jazz. Baker, with his melodic gifts, his extreme good looks, and his easy on-stage personality, soon became a major star in his own right. Mulligan was pulled up on drugs charges in late 1953; in his absence Baker won both the Downbeat Critics' and Readers' polls on trumpet. The group never reconvened, and Baker went out as a leader. He'd also picked up a drug habit, and after a successful European sojourn in 1955-57, he went through rehab and jail sentences in the US before, in 1959, bolting once again for Europe. By this time Baker had made a distinct impact on records as a limited but effective singer as well. Drug addiction continued to catch up with him, however, and he spent 1960-61 in an Italian jail before returning in 1964 to the US and making a string of records exhibiting a stronger, more dynamic approach and greater instrumental control than of yore. A severe drug-related beating in 1968 left Baker with several of his front teeth missing, and in the early 1970s he reached an all-time low, giving up music for a time before a triumphant 1974 comeback at Carnegie Hall, sharing the stage with Gerry Mulligan and Stan Getz. After that he spent much of his time in Europe, making literally hundreds of recordings, many of them live, some of them as good as anything from the 1950s. Baker died in curious circumstances, falling from an Amsterdam hotel window in 1988.

fact file

BORN 1929

DIED 1988

MUSICAL SELECTION
Chet Baker And Crew

The young Chet Baker pictured here in 1956, before "the jazz life" ravaged his features

SEE ALSO: Charlie Parker, Gerry Mulligan, Stan Getz

Chris Barber

fact file

BORN 1930

MUSICAL SELECTION
Mardi Gras at the Marquee

Influential trombonist and band leader Chris Barber in conversation with Otis Spann (left) and Muddy Waters (right) at the Marquee (Oxford Street, London) in October 1963

Barber has been an important figure in the revivalist and traditional jazz of the postwar period. A Guildhall student and an accomplished instrumentalist, he discovered his talents as a leader after forming his first trad band in London in 1948. In the early 1950s he became an established attraction in Britain as trad jazz became a viable alternative for teenagers and dancers to the sugary pop music of the time. An attempted union in 1953 of his talents with the irascible and somewhat doctrinaire trumpeter Ken Colyer was short-lived, and after Colyer went off to form a unit closer to his ideals, Barber and his new trumpeter Pat Halcox worked hard to establish the band as the premier trad unit in Britain. By the end of the 1950s the Chris Barber Band, with the added attraction of hard-hitting vocalist Ottilie Patterson and the occasional inspired vocals of Lonnie Donegan (later to be a skiffle star in his own right), became frequent guests on television and radio, and he had a string of British hits to his name.

Barber was never merely interested in a small repertoire of so-called classic jazz, showing enthusiasm for then contemporary blues and R&B sounds emanating from America as well as the folk music espoused by such artists as Josh White, Sonny Terry, and Brownie McGhee. With the huge explosion of interest in various forms of blues in the 1960s, Barber widened his stylistic ambit to include a range of blues-based material in his on-stage repertoire as well as relocating his jazz timescale to include Ellington, Basie, and others. Barber has continued to prosper across Europe by his judicious mix of musical roots, based on the authority of research and real understanding of the styles he is dealing with, while his US reputation is matched by very few Europeans of any jazz style or period.

SEE ALSO: Duke Ellington, Count Basie

Charlie Barnet

fact file

BORN 1913

DIED 1991

MUSICAL SELECTION
"Skyliner"
"Cherokee"

Saxophonist and band leader Charlie Barnet led one of the happiest and most creative of the swing bands

A New Yorker, born into a wealthy family with high-level social connections, Barnet learned the saxophone from the age of eight onward. In perfect teenage style he bailed out of studying for a legal career by signing on with the SS Republic's orchestra and learned his trade crisscrossing the Atlantic. On his return he found his passionate commitment to jazz at odds with prevailing musical tastes, and after arid trips to Texas and California, in late 1930 he began making the rounds of Harlem, gradually pulling together his own band. In 1932 he landed a residency at the Park Central Hotel. With arrangements culled from many jazz sources, including Horace Henderson, Benny Carter, and Don Redman, and a number of Ellington standards in his repertoire as well (he was a lifetime Ellington devotee), Barnet set about taking jazz to the people: not exactly a fashionable thing to do in pre-Swing America.

Barnet's total commitment to swinging, authentic jazz won him the respect of the best black musicians and garnered for him the ultimate accolade of leading the first white band at Harlem's Apollo Theatre, in 1934, where he proved successful, his Hawkins-inspired tenor leading his fired-up band by example. This reaching across the color bar in America at the time extended to his policy of hiring top black talent for his band such as Roy Eldridge, Charlie Shavers, and Benny Carter. Barnet was never one to compromise, and with his financial security rarely came across a situation where he needed to, but a serious run-in with politicians and the law in New Orleans in 1938 led to disbandment and a career lull for Barnet in Hollywood, where he even appeared in a movie with Alice Faye and Jimmy Durante. Barnet put together a new band which included trumpeter and arranger Billy May, arranger Bill Miller and drummer Cliff Leeman and signed a record deal with Bluebird in January 1939. By July he'd recorded Ray Noble's song "Cherokee" and scored a massive hit, the biggest of the year. From then on Barnet was a musical force to be reckoned with, consistently scoring hits through the war years, landing one of his biggest in 1944 with "Skyliner." He also stuck to his musical principles, upholding his own standards and seeking out the best talent for his group, such as Buddy de Franco, Dodo Marmarosa, and Lena Horne. Barnet's run at the top lasted longer than most: he finally disbanded in 1949, acknowledging the eclipse of swing by bop and R&B. Switching to management and real estate, Barnet stayed in contact with music, wrote an autobiography worth seeking out, and occasionally put together bands to have fun with, on his own terms, as ever.

SEE ALSO: Benny Carter, Don Redman, Duke Ellington, Roy Eldridge, Buddy De Franco, Dodo Marmarosa

Count Basie

William "Count" Basie is for many people the epitome of swing. In every band he led, the prime element was a rhythm section which was as light as a soufflé but that had effortless power at every tempo. All of this was possible due to Basie's own quite revolutionary approach to piano playing, it being as sparse in his accompaniment and soloing as every other pianist's was fulsome and overbearing. That this should have been his trademark is no accident, it being a product of his own inclinations and his background. Basie was born in New Jersey and got his first musical experiences around New Jersey and New York, in vaudeville and clubs, where he saw many of the great Harlem stride pianists, but in 1927 he settled in Kansas City and the following year joined Walter Page's Blue Devils. Late in 1929 he left Page for the Bennie Moten Band, an orchestra whose style presaged much of what Basie would eventually present to the world after 1936. With Moten's death in 1935 and after a period of uncertainty, Basie formed a band largely composed of ex-Moten men and including drummer Jo Jones, Hot Lips Page, Jimmy Rushing, and Buster Smith. A residency at the tiny Reno Club in KC allowed Basie to pull together his first great band featuring Lester Young, Herschel Evans, and, later, Buck Clayton and guitarist Freddie Green.

Nightly radio broadcasts from the club led to jazz-lover John Hammond discovering the band and negotiating its 1937 New York debut: simultaneously, Basie signed an exploitative two-year deal with Jack Kapp's Decca label, which nonetheless established the band as one of the most dynamic and creative blues- and riff-based swing bands of the period. Increased income allowed for an expanded band and in 1938 trombonist Dicky Wells and trumpeter Harry Edison joined. Allowing for personnel changes (Lester Young left for good in 1944, replaced by Buddy Tate) and record company shifts, this band stayed intact until 1950, when economics forced Basie to disband and continue with just a sextet. This band, featuring Clark Terry and (through sheer persistence) Freddie Green, gradually grew in popularity and size, and in 1952 Basie reconvened a large ensemble. He was never again to disband. This new group had a markedly different approach than the prewar group: the emphasis moved from riffs and star soloists to outstanding charts and tunes penned by people such as Neal Hefti, Nat Pierce, Ernie Wilkins, and Frank Foster. Although Basie had hits with singer Joe Williams and a parade of outstanding soloists such as Eddie "Lockjaw" Davis and Thad Jones, the style of the band remained static for the rest of Basie's life in music. Basie enjoyed many awards and honors during his maturity, and toured the world countless times to great acclaim, becoming one of the few jazzmen known to the man in the street. His death in 1984 was mourned by newspapers worldwide.

fact file

BORN 1904

DIED 1984

MUSICAL SELECTION
The Original American Decca Recordings

A brilliant band leader and talent spotter, Count Basie ran bands successfully for 50 years

SEE ALSO: Jo Jones, Hot Lips Page, Jimmy Rushing, Lester Young, Buck Clayton, Harry Edison, Joe Williams, Eddie "Lockjaw" Davis, Thad Jones

Bix Beiderbecke

Bix Beiderbecke was the first Golden Boy of jazz and a man whose cornet playing sounds miraculous even today

fact file

BORN 1903

DIED 1931

MUSICAL SELECTION
"Singing the Blues"
"Sorry"
"Since My Best Girl Turned Me Down"

A native of Davenport, Iowa, a short train ride from Chicago, Beiderbecke had an unerring musical ear, his interest in music awoken early by family piano lessons. He remained largely self-taught on both the piano and the instrument he adopted in mid-teens, the cornet. By this time he had discovered early "hot" music as heard on the first records by the Original Dixieland Jazz Band, and he taught himself "hot" phrasing by playing along with these and other records. Bix's unorthodox brass technique, including his idiosyncratic fingerings, using different valve combinations for notes than those normally taught, helped give him an individuality from the beginning. Abandoning any pretense of a "straight" career, Beiderbecke moved to Chicago in the early 1920s, landing a job with the Wolverines, a mediocre local "hot" band with whom Bix made his debut recordings in 1924.

His reputation burgeoning and his lyrical, beautifully flowing style formed, Bix moved to New York via a stint with Jean Goldkette's band. There he joined up with Frankie Trumbauer, the two of them playing in the latter's band in St Louis 1925-26 until they returned to New York and Goldkette. Goldkette's band provided steady work until it broke up in September 1927, by which time Bix was both a serious alcoholic and a man in the middle of his most sustained creative streak. His finest recordings, with Trumbauer and under his own name, were made between then and the end of the decade, all by pickup groups usually selected from the ranks of the Paul Whiteman orchestra, for whom they all played at one time or another. Tracks like "Singing the Blues," "Sorry," "Since My Best Girl Turned Me Down," and "At The Jazz Band Ball" (the last with Adrian Rollini's bass sax prominent) constitute the core of Bix's improvisatory achievement, showing him a unique stylist, quite different even from Louis Armstrong. His famous piano solo, "In a Mist," shows the influence of classical composers such as Ravel and Debussy and was far ahead of its day, but his cornet playing is where his true genius lies. Bix gradually lost his battle with alcoholism, succumbing to pneumonia in the summer of 1931.

SEE ALSO: Frankie Trumbauer, Adrian Rollini

George Benson

fact file

BORN 1943

MUSICAL SELECTION
Beyond the Blue Horizon
Breezin'
That's Right

Guitarist and singer George Benson, one of the most prodigiously gifted guitarists in jazz history

Pittsburgh-born Benson, though he has achieved worldwide fame as a singer and middle-of-the-road performer, is quite possibly the most gifted mainstream jazz guitarist of his generation. Benson started his musical career while still a boy, singing in clubs before his tenth birthday. Beginning guitar at the age of 11, he quickly moved as a teenager into the rock-'n'-roll/R&B scene, running a group for a while at the start of the 1960s, but as his expertise increased he developed a taste for jazz performance, joining organist Jack McDuff's group in 1962 and recording prolifically with him. At this point Benson had an approach quite close to Wes Montgomery and Grant Green, but the fluidity of his lines and his unique touch were also evident to those willing to listen.

Benson went out on his own in 1965, landing a contract with Columbia and cutting a series of fine mainstream jazz-guitar records which hold up well today. In 1967 he moved to Verve, where producer Creed Taylor saw him as a replacement for Wes Montgomery; he also worked for a while in Jimmy Smith's trio and recorded with many of the music's best talents, including Miles Davis. Moving with Taylor to the CTI label at the beginning of the 1970s, Benson began combining jazz and the rhythms and sounds of rock and funk, thereby reaping considerable popular success. His guitar playing on these records, however, is as sparkling as ever, as *Beyond the Blue Horizon* (1971) attests. Another move, to Warner Brothers, gave Benson his break into serious stardom: the 1975 album *Breezin'* became a bestseller, and his later albums, such as *Live,* usually produced a single, some of which charted worldwide. Benson, however, never abandoned the guitar, and there are always exciting musical moments on all his records. In 1975 he jammed with Benny Goodman, proving more than a match for the clarinetist on a new version of "Seven Come Eleven." Benson's latter-day career continues to combine contemporary sounds with jazz values, as the recent *That's Right* demonstrates. Whatever the context, Benson's innate musicality is irrepressible, and his stage performance continues to bring in the crowds.

SEE ALSO: Jack McDuff, Wes Montgomery, Grant Green, Jimmy Smith, Miles Davis, Benny Goodman

Sidney Bechet

Clarinetist/saxophonist Bechet is one of the great New Orleans classic jazz triumvirate (the others being Armstrong and Morton) who did so much to formulate not only early jazz but much that came after. Bechet, born into New Orleans Creole society from a musical family was decidedly precocious in his assimilation of clarinet techniques and early jazz styles: by 1910 he was already working casually with regular bands. His earliest reputation was created by his playing there up to 1916, when he decided to travel and moved all over the South and Midwest, ending up in Chicago in 1917. There he played with transplanted New Orleans men such as King Oliver and Freddie Keppard, but his next permanent employment came from orchestra leader and composer Will Marion Cook, who hired him to be a member of his concert orchestra for a 1919 tour of Europe. Bechet, a nonreader, had been hired for his improvisatory skills and was featured in a blues which had European critics and musicians in raptures.

Even geniuses have their problems, though, and although Bechet discovered the soprano saxophone with which he would be forever identified in London on this tour, and even played at Buckingham Palace, he was deported from England for a minor affray in 1922. Back in New York, in early 1923 he hitched up with businessman/musician Clarence Williams and recorded with Bessie Smith, later duetting with Louis Armstrong on the classic Clarence Williams Blue Five recordings for Okeh. He also played with Duke Ellington before returning to Europe, where in Paris he played for the Revue Nègre. He also traveled as far as Russia and Germany. Another affray, in Paris in 1929, led to a jail sentence. The following year, on his release, Bechet headed back to New York. He found the scene changed dramatically, and got work where he could, mainly with the Noble Sissle Orchestra, for whom he worked sporadically for many years. Having become something of a back number, Bechet managed some spirited "hot" sessions for Bluebird in 1932 featuring his trumpeter friend Tommy Ladnier, but the 1930s remained a lean time, and for a while Bechet ran a tailoring shop in Harlem. In 1939 he caught the crest of the gathering wave of enthusiasm for the classic jazz styles expressed by young white purists: his "Summertime," cut for Blue Note that year, became a modest hit, and he took up regular work on 52nd Street with his pals such as Ladnier and the irrepressible Mezz Mezzrow. He made a series of classics for both Bluebird and Blue Note, including a famous session with Jelly Roll Morton and a legendary 1940 trio date with Earl Hines and Baby Dodds. He and Mezzrow also made a series of immortal sides for Mezzrow's King Jazz label. Bechet even managed a reunion on record with Armstrong, but prima donna antics between the two made it a muted affair. Bechet eventually found himself spending the latter part of the 1940s in isolation from the revivalist mainstream.

His career was saved by a move to France in 1949, following a triumphant return to the Paris Festival of that year, where he'd even jammed with Charlie Parker and Miles Davis. Bechet used groups of enthusiastic young French traditionalists for musical support and enjoyed acclaim throughout Europe. Moving to Antibes in 1951 and marrying for a second time, Bechet eventually became something of a national hero, and after his death, from cancer in 1959, a large sculpted likeness was erected in Antibes. Nobody in New Orleans at the time had similar ideas.

fact file

BORN 1897

DIED 1959

MUSICAL SELECTION "Summertime"

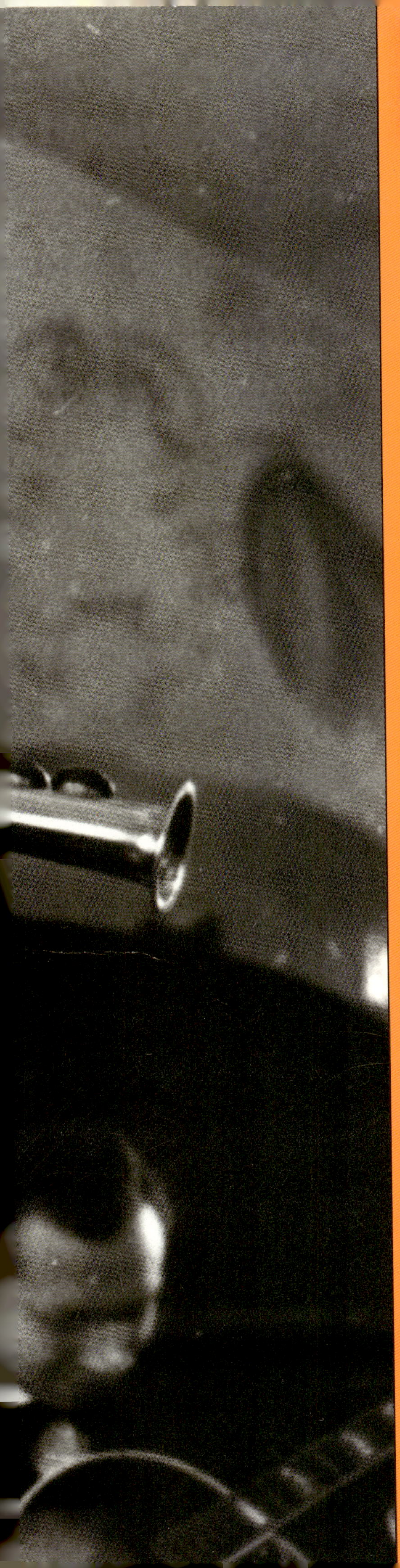

Sidney Bechet in 1938: a commanding leader and inspirational soloist on the brink of a major revival in the 1940s

SEE ALSO: Louis Armstrong, King Oliver, Freddie Keppard, Clarence Williams, Duke Ellington, Tommy Ladnier, Earl Hines, Charlie Parker, Miles Davis

Bunny Berigan

Bunny Berigan, a superb trumpeter and a fatally heavy drinker, led his own bands with distinction in the 1930s

fact file

BORN 1908

DIED 1942

MUSICAL SELECTION
"I Can't Get Started"

Berigan, born Roland Berigan in Hilbet, Wisconsin, was a trumpeter of great power and lyricism and a natural when it came to the most felicitous way to phrase a melodic statement. During the late 1930s he was a serious rival to Louis Armstrong for trumpeting supremacy. He was also, to his misfortune, an alcoholic and a bandleader with no inherent gift for financial matters or for leading men. Learning trumpet as a teenager, Berigan by the age of 18 in 1930 had been hired to tour Europe by Jack Kemp, supplying the "hot" trumpet work with that enormous, clear tone of his, close to Armstrong but with a liquid quality of its own.

Back in New York, Berigan worked in studio outfits and for a while took over Bix Beiderbecke's recently vacated "hot" trumpet chair with Paul Whiteman, and appeared as a session man on a host of different people's records, from Mildred Bailey to Frankie Trumbauer to Lee Wiley and the Boswell Sisters. By 1933 he was sufficiently well known to make some sides under his own name, but in 1935 he joined the Benny Goodman Band just as it was becoming the hottest thing in popular music. Berigan stayed with Goodman for two years, making scores of fine sides with him, the delights of "King Porter Stomp" and "Sometimes I'm Happy" being particular highs. Berigan formed his own band in 1937 after a short stint with Tommy Dorsey. Band members included Buddy Rich and Georgie Auld, and it was a musically rewarding unit. After an early - and massive - hit with "I Can't Get Started" in late 1937, Berigan's utter inability to lead a band or handle money led to the band's eventual demise in 1940. Rejoining Dorsey that year, Berigan was fast disintegrating through his alcoholism and his disappointment with what he saw as his own failures. He didn't last: by 1941 he was leading another band of his own, but his own involvement was fading, his body weakening. He died of complications from alcoholism in the summer of 1942; Tommy Dorsey saw him die in hospital and paid the funeral expenses.

SEE ALSO: Louis Armstrong, Mildred Bailey, Frankie Trumbauer, Lee Wiley, Benny Goodman, Tommy Dorsey, Buddy Rich

Leon "Chu" Berry

fact file

BORN 1908

DIED 1941

MUSICAL SELECTION
Leon "Chu" Berry: 1937-41

The great "Chu" Berry, who came close to challenging Coleman Hawkins for tenor sax supremacy before his untimely death

Leon "Chu" Berry was one of the first and greatest of the Coleman Hawkins school of tenor saxophone to establish his own personality on the instrument and create a lasting body of recorded music. He also went on to influence many players of later generations with his rhythmic drive and robust sound. Berry was born in Wheeling, West Virginia, and learned to play saxophone while in high school, starting out on the alto. By 1929 he was working in Chicago with the Sammy Stewart big band, in 1930 moving to New York to try his luck.

In the next few years he made sufficient impact to appear on a series of top-rate recordings with, among others, Benny Carter and Spike Hughes. Joining Teddy Hill's band in 1933, he continued to develop his playing so that, by 1935, he was in demand with virtually every popular black orchestra of the day, including Ellington and Calloway. He opted for Fletcher Henderson's unit, bringing Roy Eldridge into the band at the same time. The two stayed with Henderson until the leader quit and went with Goodman as an arranger, and Berry moved on to Cab Calloway in 1937. Calloway was well aware of Berry's talent and featured his star heavily in arrangements. Berry was also free to appear on many small group records, such as the Billie Holiday/Teddy Wilson Brunswick sides, and jam sessions, and the tenorist stayed until his death. Berry perished in a car accident, one of the many victims of the road in the music business of the time, where so much of a musician's life was taken up traveling from one one-nighter to the next. Berry's recorded legacy is relatively large for such a short-lived player, for his talent was recognized and rewarded throughout his professional days. This in part accounts for the influence he had on people such as Gene Ammons, Ike Quebec, and Dexter Gordon in the next generation.

SEE ALSO: Coleman Hawkins, Benny Carter, Duke Ellington, Cab Calloway, Fletcher Henderson, Roy Eldridge, Benny Goodman

Art Blakey

fact file

BORN 1919

DIED 1990

MUSICAL SELECTION
"Moanin'"

Drummer and band leader Art Blakey ran his Jazz Messengers for close to four decades, making it a modern jazz finishing school

Few drummers have proved to be enduring bandleaders, but Pittsburgh-born Art Blakey not only led his own bands for over 30 years: he became a mentor to prime exponents of each generation of new jazz talent between 1955 and 1990. The list of people who were part of the Jazz Messengers during this period would fill the rest of this entry, and while Miles Davis could claim an equal track record for nurturing talent, some of Miles's greatest partners, such as Wayne Shorter and Hank Mobley, came to him via Blakey's band.

Blakey came up the hard way, receiving only a basic education and teaching himself piano. By his teens he was working professionally, leading a local big band at the age of 16. Swapping to drums, he schooled himself by hearing the greats of the day, including Big Sid Catlett and Chick Webb. Moving to New York, in 1942 he landed the drum chair with Mary Lou Williams at Kelly's Stable, then went out on the road with Fletcher Henderson's latter-day big band (1943-44). Leaving Henderson, Blakey was a founder member of the exciting new bebop band Billy Eckstine was putting together after his departure from Earl Hines. Blakey stayed until the band broke up in 1947, then led various aggregations, often using the title Messengers. During the early 1950s Blakey spent some time in Africa studying music and culture, and returned to America a convert to Islam. In 1954 he and Horace Silver, after a "live" recording session involving the two of them with Clifford Brown, formed a cooperative group, the Jazz Messengers, bringing in Kenny Dorham, Hank Mobley, and Doug Watkins to complete the quintet. Silver and Dorham left after a relatively short time, and Blakey assumed sole leadership responsibilities. Between them, he and Silver had helped forge the new so-called "hard-bop" approach in modern jazz, one which combined the harmonic sophistication of Parker and Gillespie with the simple elegance of blues and gospel melody and rhythm. Blakey, one of the most powerful drummers in jazz history, rarely strayed too far from this formula in the next 30 or so years as talents such as Donald Byrd, Lee Morgan, Freddie Hubbard, Woody Shaw, Bill Hardman, Chuck Mangione, and Wynton Marsalis - to mention just the main trumpeters - passed through. In latter years Blakey, though no longer in peak health, continued to exude power and authority from behind the drum kit, and was looked upon by all as a patriarch in the music.

SEE ALSO: Miles Davis, Wayne Shorter, Big Sid Catlett, Chick Webb, Mary Lou Williams, Fletcher Henderson

Jimmy Blanton

fact file

BORN 1918

DIED 1942

MUSICAL SELECTION
"Jack the Bear"
"Ko-Ko"

Jimmy Blanton in 1940, already the greatest bassist in jazz and well on the way to revolutionizing the bass's role in the music

Blanton was the first virtuoso bass player in jazz: as such, he has cast a very long shadow, directly or indirectly affecting every jazz bassist since then. As a child he was a violin student, having been born into a musical family in Chattanooga, Tennessee, but while still a college student he switched to the double bass, fitting in valuable vacation experience with the Fate Marable Band in St Louis. Blanton's first fully professional job was with the St Louis-based Jeter-Peters band, but all of this experience pales beside the events of his last three years.

In 1939 Duke Ellington, passing through St Louis, discovered Blanton and hurried him into his band. The reason for this was that Blanton was easily the most complete bassist heard to that date in jazz: his timing was impeccable and his pulse was thrillingly alive, his note choice revelatory, his dexterity simply unprecedented in jazz. He brought a completely new lease of life to the Ellington rhythm section and, in time, Ellington realized that he was perfectly capable of taking the solo spotlight as well. It was noticeable that Ellington always made sure that Blanton's bass was properly represented in all his studio recordings. Band features for Blanton included the excitingly arranged 1940 blues "Jack the Bear" and "Ko-Ko," while he was also involved in duet recordings that year, with Ellington as accompanying pianist, of "Pitter Patter Panther," "Mr J.B. Blues," and "Sophisticated Lady," the last of these an arco excursion - another rarity in the jazz of the day. Blanton succumbed to tuberculosis, leaving the band for a sanitarium in 1941 and dying the following year. His influence on his instrument's importance is still felt.

SEE ALSO: Duke Ellington

Carla Bley

Composer and leader Carla Bley began by writing songs for then-husband Paul, later completing operas and other extended works for medium size ensembles

fact file

BORN 1938

MUSICAL SELECTION
A Genuine Tong Funeral
Escalator Over The Hill

Born Carla Borg in Montreal, Bley learned piano and violin from her piano-teaching father, also gaining experience of music from church singing as a child. Strongly self-determining, Bley taught herself theory and extended her piano technique while a teenager before leaving in 1955 for New York, where she met Canadian pianist Paul Bley and, in 1957, married him. Through his encouragement she began composing, supplying him with material which was to gradually alter his performing career completely: early compositions of hers were used and recorded by the Jimmy Giuffre Trio, of which Paul Bley was a member at the dawn of the 1960s.

Other New York-based musicians began to notice the quality of her work, and people such as Art Farmer and Gary Burton regularly included her songs in their live sets and albums. A member of the ill-fated Jazz Composers' Guild, convened in 1964 and abandoned a year or so later, she and trumpeter/composer Mike Mantler co-led the Jazz Composers' Orchestra (which was incorporated into an Association in 1966) from that time until the end of the decade. By 1967 she was disenchanted with the direction so-called "free jazz" was taking, and turned her creative energies to through-composed music: the result was the acclaimed large-group work *A Genuine Tong Funeral*, commissioned and recorded by Gary Burton and one of the successes of 1967. Encouraged by this, Bley continued to write extended-form works, the next being *Escalator Over The Hill*, an odd amalgam of music and rather self-conscious words, the latter by Paul Haines. The work won many awards at the time of its 1973 release. Since then Carla Bley, by then married to Mike Mantler and co-running Watt Records, has continued to work primarily with large hand-picked bands, touring and recording effectively. In the 1990s she has also gone out on tour with partner Steve Swallow and Andy Sheppard and worked in duets with Swallow as well as continuing to produce large-scale works, some highly serious, some very much with tongue in cheek. She remains undoubtedly one of the leading postwar jazz composers and arrangers to this day.

SEE ALSO: Paul Bley, Jimmy Giuffre, Art Farmer, Gary Burton

Paul Bley

fact file

BORN 1932

MUSICAL SELECTION
Barrage

Canadian-born pianist Paul Bley, pictured here in 1954, would lead small groups with many key avant-garde musicians during his long career

Born in Montreal, pianist Bley came to jazz a thoroughly trained musician, having studied both piano and violin and also taking a course (1950-52) at New York's Juilliard School. While completing his studies Bley began moonlighting in jazz clubs and bars and was quickly picked up by leading musicians, including Oscar Pettiford, Charlie Parker, and Jackie McLean. An album made with Pettiford in 1951 went unreleased for some years, but a trio session for Charles Mingus's Debut label and featuring him with Mingus and Art Blakey in 1953 was released immediately. Moving to LA in 1955, Bley began moving toward more progressive musical ideas, and his late-1950s quintet featured all four members of the original Ornette Coleman Quartet prior to its formation. Moving back to the East Coast, he met and married Carla Borg and she began supplying him with first-rate and unusual themes, some of them being played by various groups Bley appeared in, including the Jimmy Giuffre Trio, a group in which he met bassist Gary Peacock. In the early 1960s Bley also served as a sideman with headlining players such as Sonny Rollins, Charles Mingus and Don Ellis, and was a charter member of 1964's self-proclaimed "October Revolution in Jazz," which led directly to the founding of the ill-fated Jazz Composers' Guild.

At this point Bley flirted seriously with the New York avant-garde, recording *Barrage*, a quintet album of Carla Bley themes which utilized trumpeter Dewey Johnson and the Sun Ra stalwart Marshall Allen, with Milford Graves on drums. This was a one-off, however, and after this Bley turned to a trio-format interpretation of themes by Carla Bley and the younger composer, Annette Peacock, evolving a meter-free approach to theme statement and improvisation to which he largely holds today. A master of melody and of phrasing, Bley spent the years at the beginning of the 1970s experimenting with synthesized sound, appearing live with Annette Peacock and Han Bennink in America and Europe, but by the mid-1970s he returned to acoustic instruments. He has largely plowed a similar path since, although he has developed strongly his own composing talents in the past 15 years. Bley, in his seventh decade, is a master of jazz piano and a unique stylist.

SEE ALSO: Oscar Pettiford, Charlie Parker, Jackie McLean, Charles Mingus, Art Blakey, Ornette Coleman, Sonny Rollins, Don Ellis

Buddy Bolden

fact file

BORN 1877

DIED 1931

MUSICAL SELECTION
No recordings available

Buddy Bolden (pictured here with his own band, circa 1895, back row, second from left) was the first recognized trumpet "king" of New Orleans

Buddy Bolden was the first - and for some years the most flamboyant - jazz legend, a man capable of holding untold amounts of booze, playing around with any number of women, and playing brilliant, forward-thinking music for the day. For a short time in the early 1900s he was also proclaimed the trumpet "king" of New Orleans. As such he was claimed by many classic jazzmen of later generations to be their mentor and best pal, and the progenitor of the classic New Orleans jazz-trumpet style. All this could be done partly because Bolden vanished from the scene a good 10 years before any jazz was recorded, so it was one man's story against another's. Author Don Marquis a decade or more ago established the more prosaic but equally fascinating truth in all this.

Bolden came from the black quarter in New Orleans and adopted the rougher, more carefree style and approach to music of this area, as compared with the Creoles such as Bechet, Tio, and Morton, who combined syncopated rhythms with more refined and elaborate arrangements. Bolden learned cornet as a teenager and began playing in bands as a part-timer in the early 1890s. By 1895 he had formed his own group, taking over leadership of guitarist Charlie Galloway's unit and playing dances, picnics, and private dances. By the turn of the century Bolden's clear, ringing tone and his use of blue phrases and notes in playing the repertoire of the time, plus his undoubted gift for showmanship, had brought him a degree of prominence unmatched by previous small-band leaders. The next five years saw him in his pomp, playing as a full-time professional musician (a rarity at the time in New Orleans) and being a big draw at saloons, dance halls, outdoor picnics in parks around New Orleans, and on the occasional parades his band would be a part of. His style of playing is unlikely to have contained any real improvisation; it is more likely that the band's approaches to the jigs, rags, and quadrilles they played was to heighten their rhythmic and timbral color, and to incorporate occasional melodic embellishments. Eyewitnesses state that Bolden's party piece was to play a slow blues melody with great exaggeration and "dirty tones," which always sent the audiences wild.

Bolden's erratic behavior verging on violence led to his arrest, on Labor Day in 1906, for dangerous mental derangement, possibly exacerbated by his heavy drinking. A year later he was committed by his family to a mental institution in Jackson, Mississippi, where he stayed until his death in 1931.

SEE ALSO: Sidney Bechet, Jelly Roll Morton

Lester Bowie

fact file

BORN 1941

MUSICAL SELECTION
Rope-A-Dope
Serious Fun

Lester Bowie came to fame first as a member of the Art Ensemble of Chicago, then garnered praise with his Brass Fantasy

Born in Frederick, Maryland, trumpeter Bowie came from a musical family (his brother, Joseph, is a fine jazz trombonist) which settled in St Louis while he was still a child after spending a few years in Little Rock, Arkansas. Bowie played trumpet from early boyhood onward, and by his teens was a regular in local youthful St Louis R&B and blues outfits. Military service intervened at the end of the 1950s and after its completion, Bowie, now married to Fontella Bass, moved to Chicago in 1965. Initially he ran the music policy for her band, but quickly fell in with the group of musicians around Muhal Richard Abrams, Roscoe Mitchell, and Joseph Jarman, becoming in 1966 a founder member of the AACM and featuring largely on Mitchell's debut album, *Sound,* a record that announced the arrival of a whole new attitude to modern music.

In 1967 Bowie joined with Mitchell and bassist Malachi Favors to form the Art Ensemble, using his sardonic, blues-based smears, glissandi, and growls to great effect in the long and complex improvisations the three men were creating. The advent of Joseph Jarman expanded the group's reach and creativity further and gave Bowie an important balancing role between the two reed men. He moved to Paris with the Art Ensemble (later called the Art Ensemble of Chicago) in 1969, and returned to Chicago in 1972 when the group came back; by this time his on-stage persona was fully developed, his doctor's white coat ever present, his humor sly and infectious. Bowie has stayed with the Art Ensemble of Chicago up to the present day, but has been very active in pursuing a parallel solo career, initially with his creation of the late 1980s, Lester Bowie's Brass Fantasy, an all-brass group which veers between gentle send-ups of old popular songs and hard-hitting, brilliantly written original pieces. Bowie has also consistently toured internationally leading his own small groups, and has made albums with a huge range of differing personnel, from trios to large big bands. Hardly a great technician or blessed with outstanding beauty of tone, Bowie remains nonetheless one of the great trumpeting originals in contemporary jazz, his interpretation of jazz brass history always worth hearing.

SEE ALSO: Muhal Richard Abrams, Roscoe Mitchell, Joseph Jarman, Art Ensemble of Chicago

Ruby Braff

fact file

BORN 1927

MUSICAL SELECTION
First Set At Wimbledon

Old-fashioned and unconcerned about it from day one, Ruby Braff has created brilliant pre-bop style jazz since the 1950s

Braff is a trumpeter/cornetist who deliberately ignored the revolution wrought by bebop in the 1940s, preferring to develop and perfect an approach deeply indebted to Louis Armstrong and other swing trumpeters but one that quickly matured into one of the most melodic and heartfelt trumpet styles in all jazz. The fact that he did this in the face of contempt from those advocating modernism as the only means of artistic relevance demonstrates his other major quality: remarkable singularity of purpose and determination to see things through his way.

Braff was born in Boston and began finding work in that area in the late 1940s, often appearing at Storyville as the 1950s gathered speed, usually in the company of clarinetist Pee Wee Russell. A move to New York in 1953 brought him the benefit of plenty of recording opportunities (he began with a fine album as support to Vic Dickenson), but club work was hard to find, his style being regarded as passé, and although he often appeared at festivals organized by old Bostonian George Wein, work was sporadic, to say the least. Becoming a charter member (along with Russell) of George Wein's Newport All-Stars in the early 1960s brought him steady work on an international basis and a hitherto undreamed-of profile.

By the 1970s he was able to work as a lead attraction, as well as often working in tandem with guitarist George Barnes, and the work came steadily; during the 1980s, with the rise to prominence of Concord Jazz Records and a new generation of mainstream artists, Braff was often to be found in the company of like souls such as Dave McKenna and Scott Hamilton. Such liaisons have continued into the 1990s, and Braff has also begun making a long series of records in England for Zephyr with Brian Lemon which continue to demonstrate his uniquely treasurable qualities of tone, phrasing, and melodic grace.

SEE ALSO: Louis Armstrong, Pee Wee Russell, Vic Dickenson, Scott Hamilton

Anthony Braxton

fact file

BORN 1945

MUSICAL SELECTION
Three Compositions of New Jazz

Multi-instrumentalist and composer Anthony Braxton is to some the most creative man in jazz today, to others an impenetrable mystery

Braxton is a Chicagoan with a thorough musical training in harmony and theory, as well as tertiary education in philosophy, whose intellectual and artistic concerns are unusually broad. Braxton was serious about music from his earliest studies, and his stint in the US Army (1964-66) served to confirm his chosen path and give him time to settle his musical style. Returning to Chicago in 1966, he was introduced to the AACM by Roscoe Mitchell and became involved in an intensely creative group exercise with violinist Leroy Jenkins and trumpeter Leo Smith. This led to the group's first record, *Three Compositions of New Jazz* (Delmark, 1968), another of the pivotal avant-garde albums to come from Chicago in this turbulent period. At the time, Braxton claimed "Paul Desmond" Ornette, Eric Dolphy, Jackie McLean [and] Karlheinz Stockhausen" as major influences, adding that John Coltrane's lyricism was also influential: "I never felt music could be so beautiful: Coltrane made me believe in myself."

Braxton's highly individual alto style and his compositional abstractions, plus his intense explorations of sonority and musical shapes when playing unaccompanied, often seem to carry few reference points to outside influences; however, in another context, such things as his lyricism and wonderful sense of musical form become very clear: his work with Philly Joe Jones and Archie Shepp in Paris, in 1969, is a case in point. Further defining examples of his work with other leaders came with the adventurous quartet, Circle, led by Chick Corea (1970-71), but in the early 1970s Braxton's solo concerts were the major factor in getting him his own loyal audience. This, plus his regular quartet concerts (often with trombonist George Lewis and bassist Dave Holland) greatly increased his stature: he entered the 1980s as a leading avant-garde figure with immense artistic integrity at a time when the avant-garde was generally regarded as creatively bankrupt.

Since that time Braxton's own creative gifts have become progressively more fleshed out and sharply defined, his concern with aspects of composition and performance revealing him to be primarily a composer rather than simply an improviser. This has presented its own difficulties, with some of his more abstruse musical ideas seeming to leave their inspiration on the workshop floor, and his piano works remaining an acquired taste, but his works for large forces and his intense, characterful reed playing can still cut through any amount of theory and constructs. He remains one of the major musical talents of the contemporary scene to this day.

SEE ALSO: Roscoe Mitchell, Paul Desmond, Ornette Coleman, Eric Dolphy, Jackie McLean, John Coltrane

Michael Brecker

The most influential saxophonist since Wayne Shorter, Michael Brecker is also one of the busiest in jazz today

fact file

BORN 1949

MUSICAL SELECTION
Tales from the Hudson

Philadelphian saxophonist Brecker came from a musical family, his father being a pianist and his elder brother Randy becoming a successful trumpet player. In his late teens he graduated from clarinet and alto sax studies and took on the tenor sax, inspired by his love of the contemporary rock and soul of the time, including King Curtis and Jimi Hendrix. As his interests broadened he came under the influence of hard bop and, as the 1960s drew to a close, John Coltrane. From this mixture he began to fashion his own amalgam and build up a formidable instrumental technique which would eventually bring him as much studio session work as he could handle, including spots on albums by Laura Nyro and James Taylor. He was a member of the jazz-rock group Dreams and in 1973 joined Horace Silver's band. A year with Silver, plus an on-off membership of groups led by Billy Cobham, brought Brecker quick international attention, and by the time he and his brother Randy formed the Brecker Bros group in 1975, much was expected of it. Noted for its consolidation of techniques pioneered elsewhere, this band became important for its successful translation of an often deplored hybrid into an artistically and commercially valid and absorbing entity.

Brecker gained further respect and more widespread fame in his next venture, with the band Steps Ahead, co-led with vibist Mike Mainieri, which became one of the most popular instrumental groups of the 1980s. By the time Brecker left in the late 1980s he was regarded as a leader on his instrument and was being widely imitated by younger players, his combination of Coltrane- and funk-inspired melody, plus his impeccable technique, exerting a universal fascination. Since that time Brecker has been part of many projects, including bands with Herbie Hancock and with his brother Randy, but has preferred in general to move from one thing to another, readily available for any number of recordings and events. His recent album, *Tales from the Hudson* (Impulse!), is a succinct summary of his current prowess.

SEE ALSO: John Coltrane, Horace Silver, Herbie Hancock

Bob Brookmeyer

Valve trombonist and composer Bob Brookmeyer, pictured at Basin St East in 1956, supplied the sparks for Gerry Mulligan, Stan Getz and Clark Terry, among others

A Kansas City native, Brookmeyer is one of very few jazz musicians to have made the valve trombone their instrument of choice. He began musical education on clarinet, moving later to piano and trombone, studying at the Kansas City Conservatory. His initial professional experience was in big bands, including Ray McKinley, Louis Prima, and Tex Benecke, ending up with Woody Herman and Terry Gibbs. In 1952 he decided to concentrate on valve trombone; the following year he joined the Stan Getz group and began to become more widely known. Just a year later, in 1954, Brookmeyer took the place of Chet Baker in the re-formed Gerry Mulligan Quartet (later a sextet) and stayed, on and off, with the baritonist through to 1957, when he moved over to the group led by Jimmy Giuffre. This he left just prior to its appearance at the 1958 Newport Jazz Festival. Brookmeyer freelanced and made records under his own name, such as *Traditionalism Revisited* (with Giuffre's group as sidemen for the day) and *The Ivory Hunters*, a twin piano album with Bill Evans, until the early 1960s, when he joined the new Gerry Mulligan Concert Big Band. While with Mulligan he was under contract to Verve and made some of his best records, the small-group *7xWilder* and the large-group *Gloomy Sunday and Other Bright Moments* included.

Mulligan's band took him to Europe and gave him a new audience. This helped, firstly with the quintet he formed in 1964 with Clark Terry, and then with the Thad Jones/Mel Lewis Orchestra, with whom he played for much of the latter part of the 1960s. Brookmeyer garnered much studio work when he moved to the West Coast in 1968. By the time Brookmeyer returned to New York in the late 1970s, his LA experience had made him a fine writer and player. Reinvolved with the Jones/Lewis band, he began contributing new scores to their book. During the 1980s he spent more time in Europe, especially Scandinavia, moving there in the 1990s, although in recent years he has begun splitting his time between both continents again.

fact file

BORN 1929

MUSICAL SELECTION
Traditionalism Revisited
The Ivory Hunters

SEE ALSO: Woody Herman, Stan Getz, Chet Baker, Gerry Mulligan, Jimmy Giuffre, Bill Evans, Thad Jones

Clifford Brown

fact file

BORN 1930

DIED 1956

MUSICAL SELECTION
Live At Basin St.

The most breathtaking and complete trumpeter to emerge after Dizzy Gillespie, Clifford Brown died tragically young in 1956

Brown, from Wilmington in Delaware, has long been seen as the greatest of all the tragic losses to jazz from the dangers of the road and endless travel between gigs. A trumpeter blessed with imperious technique, astonishing warmth and expressiveness of tone, a beautiful melodic sense on ballads and a hugely inventive vein of improvisation to explore, Brown seemed the complete musician, emerging from the trumpet section of the Lionel Hampton band in the early 1950s and stunning his peers as co-leader of the Max Roach-Clifford Brown Quintet. There is scarcely a trumpeter in subsequent jazz history who has not been touched by his conception.

Brown began private and school trumpet tuition at the age of 13, by 15 doubling these lessons with ones in theory and jazz harmony. Progressing through college, he also studied mathematics, completing studies at both Delaware College and Maryland State University by 1950. Eager to take up the life of a professional musician, Brown sat in with many musicians passing through Philadelphia and became well known to trumpeters such as Dizzy Gillespie and Fats Navarro, both of whom left their mark on the youngster. A near-fatal car crash in summer 1950 kept him hospitalized for the best part of a year, but in March 1952 he was sufficiently recovered to make his recording debut, with the R&B band Chris Powell and his Blue Flames, a band he also gigged with for the best part of a year. Simultaneously, Brown began appearing and recording as a member of Tadd Dameron's band, then in August 1953 joined Lionel Hampton's big band for a European tour. In the company of musicians like Quincy Jones and Jimmy Cleveland, Brown made a number of illicit recordings in Paris and elsewhere and established his European reputation on this tour. Back in New York Brown gigged around in the opening months of 1954, recording live with Art Blakey prior to the formation of the Jazz Messengers, then linked up with Max Roach to form their famous co-led quintet, initially with Harold Land on tenor, latterly with Sonny Rollins. The band swept all comers before it during the two years of its existence, recorded prolifically and toured widely. Brown's artistry was captured in both studio and live settings by the band for EmArcy, as well as a number of successful jam sessions staged with other EmArcy artists. In the early hours of a late June morning in 1956 a car driven by the wife of Bud Powell's pianist brother, Richie, with Richie and Brown as passengers, veered off the Pennsylvania Turnpike. All three in the car were killed.

SEE ALSO: Lionel Hampton, Max Roach, Dizzy Gillespie, Fats Navarro, Tadd Dameron, Quincy Jones, Art Blakey

Marion Brown

fact file

BORN 1935

MUSICAL SELECTION
Afternoon of a Georgia Faun
Vista

Altoist, composer and teacher Marion Brown, a key avant-garde figure of the 1960s and 1970s

Saxophonist Brown was born in Atlanta, Georgia, but moved with his mother to Harlem when just 13. Two years later he volunteered for the army, staying just 18 months before opting to return to Atlanta and attempting to pick up his general education. He studied reed instruments in addition to more common subjects while at Clark College in his home town. A burgeoning interest in the civil-rights movement, as well as marriage, led him to study economics, history, and political science at Howard University, in Washington, DC, where he majored in political science. Off campus, he was attending as many club dates by visiting jazz musicians as he could fit in. In 1962, at the age of 27, he arrived in New York and slowly made his talents known to the city's highly active avant-garde circle of the day. Six months in Archie Shepp's group in 1965 led to his appearing on records for the first time with the same outfit, followed by an invitation to record with John Coltrane on his epic *Ascension* date of mid-1965. From that time on, although work was sporadic, Brown was a "name" and was soon recording albums under his own name, first for ESP-Disk and later for various European labels. Brown, ever a disciplined and organized musician and a fine composer, from the start had his own warm tone and logical style of lyricism, abilities he used in a variety of contexts.

Spending 1968-70 in Europe, first with drummer Steve McCall and later with Gunter Hampel and Karl Hans Berger, Brown developed two parallel musical philosophies, one reflecting Chicago's AACM musicians' fascination with every sound and musical construct made from the use of "little instruments" and nonlegitimate sounds from ordinary instruments (accurately summarized on his *Afternoon of a Georgia Faun* (ECM, 1970)), the other continuing his passion for melody and tone. This led ultimately to recordings with Harold Budd in 1974 and his 1978 Impulse! album, *Vista*, on which, among other things, he performs a moving version of a Stevie Wonder ballad. Brown has for many years now been deeply involved in music education, emerging from long ethnomusicology studies, especially in African music, to teach courses to students at a number of institutions. His talent and its impact are undeniable.

SEE ALSO: Archie Shepp, John Coltrane

Ray Brown

fact file

BORN 1926

MUSICAL SELECTION
This One's For Blanton

Bassist Ray Brown, long associated with Oscar Peterson, has for many years been at the peak of his art leading his own groups

Bassist Brown's name was for many years closely identified with that of his one-time pianist boss, Oscar Peterson, but his long career has been diverse and rewarding in a number of capacities. Born in Pittsburgh, Brown came from a musical family, learning bass in his early teens before arriving in New York in 1945, where his big tone and commanding rhythm quickly made him in demand among the beboppers. He joined Dizzy Gillespie's big band in 1945, staying close to two years before forming his own trio which was used as support for Ella Fitzgerald, whom he married in 1948. The marriage broke down in 1952, a year after Brown had disbanded his trio and joined Oscar Peterson's group.

Strangely enough, Brown might well have become the bassist in an equally famous and even more long-lived small group, the Modern Jazz Quartet, for he knew both John Lewis and Milt Jackson from Dizzy Gillespie days and appeared on 1951 recordings of Jackson's Quartet, which was soon to undergo a name change. But Peterson was the choice, and Brown was his trio's regular bassist for 15 years until 1966. By that time the bassist was by a good distance the most popular bassist in jazz, and his time, tone and note choice was acknowledged as irreproachable by his peers. He also took up the cello, which he has continued to feature to the present day. At the beginning of the 1960s Brown had picked up the threads of his professional friendship with Milt Jackson, and when Brown left Peterson and the MJQ temporarily disbanded, the two formed a quintet with Teddy Edwards on sax. Based in LA, it became one of a number of groups Brown managed in the next decade (the re-formed MJQ being another in the 1970s), in addition to session work. Brown also made an acclaimed duet album in 1972 with Duke Ellington, *This One's For Blanton* (Pablo). A founder member in 1974 of the LA 4, Brown has continued working to the present day, running his own trio in the 1990s with pianist Benny Green and recording prolifically for Telarc.

SEE ALSO: Dizzy Gillespie, Ella Fitzgerald, Oscar Peterson, John Lewis, Milt Jackson

Kenny Burrell

fact file

BORN 1931

MUSICAL SELECTION
Guitar Forms
Ellington is Forever

Smooth but endlessly resourceful guitarist Kenny Burrell has often been a perfect foil for organist Jimmy Smith

Burrell was surrounded by music as a boy in Detroit, his family being amateur musicians; he began guitar just prior to becoming a teenager. Studying at Wayne State University, Burrell spent much time sitting in and gigging locally in Detroit, coming to the attention of a visiting Dizzy Gillespie in 1951, who used him as a sideman on a recording date that year. Burrell continued to play with visiting musicians while he finished his music degree, then in 1955 made the move to New York. Already well known to musicians there through his Detroit activities, Burrell became a fixture on record dates for a number of companies, including Savoy, Prestige, and Blue Note, both as leader and as sideman. His modern combination of a warm tone and good blues feeling was a nicely judged update of the basic Charlie Christian approach. Burrell appeared as sideman with many great players, including Oscar Peterson, Benny Goodman, and, on occasion, Jimmy Smith, but by the close of the 1950s was sufficiently established to run his own trio, periodically expanded to quartet with the addition of saxophonist George Coleman.

An association with Gil Evans led to a mid-1960s album for Verve, *Guitar Forms*. The brainchild of producer Creed Taylor, in many ways it was a prototype for what Taylor was later to achieve with CTI and other labels, but the unique Evans orchestrations gave the music an unusual depth and resonance, while Burrell's own playing is varied and ever tasteful. Burrell has continued to play in many contexts and make many records: in the 1970s a major project was his two-volume *Ellington Is Forever* recordings on Fantasy, again with big band. He has since then included courses on Ellington's music in his teaching at the University of California. Burrell continues to divide his time between live work all over the world, teaching and recording commitments, often with his group Kenny Burrell's Jazz Guitar Band, initially featuring younger players such as Rodney Jones and Bobby Broom and helping each new generation of players as it comes to the fore.

SEE ALSO: Dizzy Gillespie, Charlie Christian, Oscar Peterson, Benny Goodman, Jimmy Smith, Gil Evans, Duke Ellington

Dave Brubeck

West Coaster Brubeck, born in Concord, California, has been the object of much curmudgeonly criticism over the years, especially when he was the leader of probably the most popularly successful small group of the postwar years, the Dave Brubeck Quartet, featuring saxophonist Paul Desmond and, latterly, drummer Joe Morello. Yet with hindsight Brubeck's achievements are not easy to gainsay, and it is tempting to consider whether his supposed shortcomings and lack of originality have been pointed out with such alacrity precisely because he had the wit and talent to take undiluted modern jazz and deliver it to a mass audience.

Brubeck had music in his family, his mother being a pianist, and he received formal musical training from her and others, gigging locally during his teens with various groups while studying for his music major in Stockton. Progressing to Mills College, he received tuition from, among others, composer Darius Milhaud. Two years' war service was spent mostly with service bands, and on his discharge he completed his studies with Milhaud and formed a band that would evolve into the Dave Brubeck Octet and record under that name in 1949. Another venture, started that year, was the Dave Brubeck Trio, featuring Cal Tjader on drums and vibes. Brubeck built a large Californian following due to his intelligent combination of jazz spontaneity and a classical approach to form and harmony, building astutely on this audience by taking his music to the colleges and campuses in California. But his popularity began to skyrocket once a former Octet member, Paul Desmond, made his trio into a quartet. The combination of Desmond's liquid sound and melodic elegance and Brubeck's attack made for exciting listening and the group quickly became a national talking point, even making the cover of Time magazine in 1954. Brubeck kept building on this interest, bringing in drummer Joe Morello and bassist Eugene Wright in 1956 to create the "classic" quartet which would remain intact until 1967. This band toured the world countless times, taking jazz to virtually every country, and Brubeck wrote many compositions for the group based on these travels. In 1959 he brought his interest in unusual time signatures to a peak with the album *Time Out*, which spawned the hit single "Take Five," ironically written not by Brubeck, but by Desmond. Scoring also with "Bossa Nova USA," Brubeck had joined the jazz elite in claiming top-ten pop success.

But his musical interests always ran deeper than chart success, and by 1967 Brubeck was prepared to disband in order to pursue his compositional projects. A trio with Alan Dawson and Jack Six at the end of the 1960s became a sometime quartet with the addition of Gerry Mulligan, but by the 1970s Brubeck was mostly inclined to pace things more slowly and work with his now mature sons, three of whom were professional musicians. Brubeck continues to work and compose, and has received just about every honor jazz can bestow, including command performances at the White House. Of his many fine compositions, the most widely popular are probably "The Duke" and "In Your Own Sweet Way," perhaps because, even now, most jazz musicians would rather not play in 7/4 or 9/8 time.

fact file

BORN 1920

MUSICAL SELECTION
Time Out

Pianist and band leader Dave Brubeck, composer of classics such as "The Duke" and "In Your Own Sweet Way"

SEE ALSO: Paul Desmond, Cal Tjader, Gerry Mulligan

Gary Burton

Vibes player and teacher Gary Burton was a prime mover in bringing jazz and rock together in the late 1960s

fact file

BORN 1943

MUSICAL SELECTION
A Genuine Tong Funeral
Right Time Right Place

Vibraharpist Burton, from Anderson, Indiana, arrived on the jazz scene in a blaze of publicity from his record company at the age of 17. Jazz critics, ever willing to smell a rat in such circumstances, took a number of years to grant him the stature his obvious talent demanded. A student at the famous Berklee College of Music in Boston, Burton quickly transferred to the higher reaches of the jazz world, playing first with George Shearing's quintet, then between 1964 and 1966 with the mercurial Stan Getz. His lack of obeisance to the all-pervading style of Milt Jackson made for a refreshing change from virtually every other vibist's approach. A musician with wide tastes and a desire to be part of contemporary culture, Burton pursued a number of musical paths on his records for RCA prior to his launching a solo career, including exploring the connections between jazz and country music on *Tennessee Firebird* (1967). His departure from Getz's group allowed him to form a quartet which constituted one of the earliest attempts to combine jazz and rock in a musically valid hybrid. With guitarist Larry Coryell, bassist Steve Swallow and a succession of drummers, the band created a distinctive style, based on the unusual and intriguing compositions of all three members, plus composer and close friend Mike Gibbs. A commission from Burton also led to the recording of Carla Bley's first major composition, *A Genuine Tong Funeral,* in 1968, with a band that included the quartet plus Steve Lacy, Gato Barbieri, and Jimmy Knepper.

Burton's career slowed down in the 1970s, even though he was at the helm of a fine new quartet featuring Mike Goodrick: the heavyweights of fusion music pushed his more subtle efforts into the shade. His achievements, however, continued to mount, with fine duet concerts and recordings with Chick Corea and guitarist Ralph Towner, while his Atlantic album with Keith Jarrett is a high point for both men. In the early 1970s Burton joined the teaching faculty at Berklee and teaching slowly became the main focus of his activities. His efforts in this direction have been universally admired, as is his comprehensive knowledge and understanding of jazz forms. Burton continues to make records and perform – as the live duet with Paul Bley, *Right Time Right Place* (Sonet, 1990), demonstrates.

SEE ALSO: George Shearing, Stan Getz, MiltJackson, Larry Coryell, Carla Bley, Steve Lacy, Jimmy Knepper

Jaki Byard

fact file

BORN 1922

MUSICAL SELECTION
Out Front

Pianist Jaki Byard has been the driving force behind many classic "live" and recording groups

The sheer diversity of Byard's talents and interests in music have to some degree mitigated against a larger public awareness of his achievements. A brilliant and original pianist who nonetheless has a comprehensive grasp of jazz piano history, an accomplished composer whose largest works (including operas) remain unrecorded, and a saxophonist all too rarely heard in public, Byard has appeared most often as inspired accompanist to the likes of Charles Mingus, Eric Dolphy, Booker Ervin, Roland Kirk, Don Ellis, Ray Nance, and Sam Rivers, but his achievements as a leader and teacher are also to be reckoned with.

Coming from a musical family, Byard began learning piano and trumpet as a child, starting professional work as a trumpeter in the mid-1930s with a local Worcester, Massachusetts, band. Later he switched to piano in Earl Bostic's postwar group but while with Herb Pomeroy he concentrated on sax. By now a Boston legend, Byard remained based in that city, thus depriving himself of wider recognition, until joining Maynard Ferguson's big band in 1959. His talents were quickly appreciated in New York, and work with Mingus, Dolphy, and others followed in the early and mid 1960s, accompanied by his own recording debut as a leader, with Candid, followed by a string of diverse and fascinating records for Prestige, culminating in a riotous 1968 outing, The Jaki Byard Experience, featuring Roland Kirk in blistering form.

Byard turned to music teaching in the early 1970s, becoming music professor at New England Conservatory from the late 1960s to the mid-1980s. After that he taught at both the Manhattan School of Music and New York's New School of Music. All three institutions sprouted student bands capable of holding down professional gigs in Boston and New York. Byard continues to perform and teach.

SEE ALSO: Charles Mingus, Eric Dolphy, Booker Ervin, Roland Kirk, Don Ellis, Maynard Ferguson

Don Byas

Don Byas, a key transition figure between swing and bop, pictured here in 1940, a member of Andy Kirk's Clouds of Joy

fact file

BORN 1912

DIED 1972

MUSICAL SELECTION
"Byas A Drink"
"Danny Boy"

Tenor saxophonist Byas came to prominence quite late in life, compared with the majority of his peers: he was in his early 30s when he first made his mark in the Count Basie band of the early 1940s. Starting out on alto, Byas, born in Muskogee, Oklahoma, gained initial experience in territory bands, eventually settling in the early 1930s for a while in Kansas City, where he played tenor with Bennie Moten and Walter Page's Blue Devils. A move to California in 1935 led to work with Lionel Hampton, then a relocation to New York in 1937 opened the doors to work with a raft of groups, including Andy Kirk and Lucky Millinder. Byas – whose style was based on Coleman Hawkins's investigation of the harmonic basis of popular songs and who adopted a huge, sensual tone which on occasion could take on a telling rasp – replaced Lester Young in Count Basie's band between 1941 and 1944, a period not well represented on record due to the American Musicians' Union recording ban of the time, and went on to feature in groups led by Coleman Hawkins, Dizzy Gillespie, and Charlie Parker. His inquiring musical mind allowed him to be at ease in the company of the boppers, and for a time he was perceived as perhaps the most gifted of the coming men on tenor sax.

But Byas was not a great leader and his groups tended to have a haphazard nature. He also took the opportunity to move permanently to Europe in 1946 after a tour there with Don Redman, thus removing himself from the New York spotlight. Although high-profile concerts and appearances with touring troupes or bands, plus regular jobs with local musicians, first in France and latterly in Amsterdam, kept Byas in the public eye, his style showed little signs of evolution after the mid 1950s. He remained on his mettle throughout his career, as recordings with JATP in 1959 and 1960s studio dates with Bud Powell and Ben Webster amply demonstrate. Byas appeared in the US in 1970 at the Newport Jazz Festival, but remained domiciled in Europe until his death in 1972.

SEE ALSO: Count Basie, Lionel Hampton, Lucky Millinder, Coleman Hawkins, Lester Young, Dizzy Gillespie

Donald Byrd

fact file

BORN 1932

MUSICAL SELECTION
Black Byrd
Free Form

Trumpeter Donald Byrd's long career has seen him travel from hard bop to funk and back over four decades

In the aftermath of the tragic death in 1956 of Clifford Brown, many jazz observers spent fruitless hours looking for likely "successors," just as they had done when Charlie Parker had died the previous year. There was no shortage of young and brilliant trumpeting talent, and 24-year-old Detroiter Donald Byrd was perceived as first among equals. Byrd had come to New York after completing a Bachelor of Music at Wayne State University, which had been interrupted by army service. He was initially in New York to complete an MA at the Manhattan School of Music, and his beautiful brass tone and elegant musical imagination quickly came to the attention of other musicians and record companies: by September he had made an album under his own name for Savoy and was beginning to rack up sideman appearances on many sessions, including those as a member of George Wallington's Jazzmen. At one point in the late 1950s it seemed there was hardly a small-group date emanating from Prestige that did not have Byrd on it. Byrd came into the Jazz Messengers for a brief time in 1956 after the departure of Kenny Dorham, but by 1958 was co-leading a group with Pepper Adams, which lasted until late 1961 and made many fine records.

The early 1960s saw Byrd make inroads into musical education when jazz courses were still virtually unknown on mainstream campuses and in the average US conservatory. Completing a composition course with Nadia Boulanger in 1963, Byrd embarked on jazz and general music teaching at a succession of prestigious institutions, including Rutgers and Howard University, and eventually became one of the most respected authorities on American music studies. He also tasted commercial success at the beginning of the 1970s with his album *Black Byrd* (Blue Note, 1972). This was a jazz-funk album which in turn launched the group Blackbyrds, made up of his former students, who took the formula further toward chart success. Byrd continued to concentrate on teaching, returning to live work and recordings in the late 1980s, by which time he had reverted to his hard-bop style of the late 1950s. Byrd continues to teach and play.

SEE ALSO: Clifford Brown, Kenny Dorham

Cab Calloway

fact file

BORN 1907

DIED 1994

MUSICAL SELECTION
"Minnie The Moocher"
"Kickin' The Gong Around"

Cab Calloway, the original hi-de-ho man, all smiles as ever

The younger brother of singer and band leader Blanche Calloway (1902-1978), Cab Calloway went on to become a major figure of the Swing Era and a nurturer in his bands of significant jazz talent, including "Chu" Berry, Dizzy Gillespie, Jonah Jones, and Ike Quebec. Calloway also helped make scat singing, brought to jazz by Louis Armstrong, a popular craze of the 1930s.

Born in Rochester, New York State, Calloway was raised in Baltimore, where his family lived and where his sister was born. Calloway was attracted to the entertainment business and music early, first appearing as a singer and dancer in Baltimore clubs before venturing to Chicago. In 1928 he joined the Missourians, appearing with them as a singer and occasional drummer in New York, where he also scored a success in 1929 in the revue Hot Chocolates. Calloway's star was on the rise and the Missourians agreed to record and perform under Cab's name. By 1931 the Calloway band was appearing at the Cotton Club opposite Duke Ellington, so that when Ellington left the club in 1933 to go out on the road, Calloway was perfectly placed to replace him there. Using this as a base and building up a repertoire balanced between vaudeville and disciplined, exciting jazz, Calloway began having hits ("Minnie The Moocher," "Kickin' The Gong Around") which often alluded to nefarious activities, especially dabblings with marijuana, and became popular enough to take his flamboyant act to Hollywood, where he made several cameo appearances in 1930s and 1940s films and became known as the "Hi-De-Ho" man. Calloway kept his band functioning right up to 1948, using his own Pullman railroad car to transport the group around America on the long round of one-nighters which constituted popular success in prewar American music.

As the 1940s faded into the 1950s Calloway scaled down to small groups, then quit regular touring altogether, moving into music theater such as *Porgy and Bess* and *Hello Dolly!*, but his jazz roots were never far away. He made a number of records in the stereo era re-creating his old hits, but it was for his stage act that people loved him, as well as his sartorial keenness – whether it was a white tux or a zoot suit, Calloway always had the flair to carry off the most outrageous stage garb. Calloway remained active right up to his death, aged 86, loved and admired for his contribution to music and entertainment.

SEE ALSO: "Chu" Berry, Dizzy Gillespie, Ike Quebec, Louis Armstrong, Duke Ellington

Betty Carter

fact file

BORN 1930

MUSICAL SELECTION
The Audience With Betty Carter

Singer Betty Carter's unique improvisatory style guarantees her a place in the forefront of jazz singers

Born Lillie Mae Jones in Flint, Michigan, Carter grew up in Detroit, singing in clubs and gradually sitting in with visiting bebop musicians such as Dizzy Gillespie and Charlie Parker. Carter followed in Dinah Washington's footsteps, joining Lionel Hampton's big band in 1948, two years after Washington had gone solo; by this time she was using the stage name Lorraine Carter, which was subsequently altered by Hampton himself to Betty Carter, after his nickname for her, Betty Bop, describing her scatting abilities and her musical preferences. She left Hampton in 1951 and made her way, with considerable difficulty, as a solo, her propensity for vocal improvisation proving difficult for less than attentive audiences. A recording in 1961 of big band-backed duets with Ray Charles remains a popular high point in her career, reaching an audience far beyond that usual for jazz, but after this she went into semi-retirement while she started a family, embarking on only the occasional overseas tour. By the end of the decade she was ready to re-emerge professionally, using her own trio and forming her own record company, Bet-Car Records. In this guise she pursued a performing and recording career which gradually gained momentum and won her sincere praise from her peers and jazz commentators. By the 1980s she was accepted on both sides of the Atlantic and in Japan as one of jazz's premier female vocalists, her highly unusual and risky improvisational style, which had once been a barrier to her audience, now being eagerly embraced by new generations of fans. Her trio has seen a number of first-class pianists brought to maturity, the latest being Cyrus Chestnut. Carter's rearrangement of the melody, harmony, and lyrics of a song are now recognized as a considerable artistic achievement, and her place in the music is assured. Many of her records for her own company have been reissued on CD by major labels.

SEE ALSO: Dizzy Gillespie, Charlie Parker, Dinah Washington, Lionel Hampton, Ray Charles

Benny Carter

Carter has enjoyed one of the longest and most rewarding active careers in jazz, first coming to attention around 1923 at the age of 16 playing in New York bands and still composing, playing festivals and clubs, and directing ensembles in the year of his 90th birthday. A multi-instrumentalist and a gifted composer/arranger, Carter eventually concentrated on the alto sax as his main instrument and became the primary influence, along with Johnny Hodges, on the instrument prior to the advent of Charlie Parker. The possessor of a ravishingly full tone and the combination of a natural symmetry of phrasing and an impeccable rhythmic sense, Carter was for years the ideal alto man, able to bring elegance to every musical context.

Carter was born in New York and was attracted very early to music, playing in a string of bands between 1923 and 1928 around Harlem and emulating his early hero, altoist Frank Teschemacher (also a major influence on Lester Young). By 1928 Carter was a member of Fletcher Henderson's band, arranging for both Henderson and his rival, Duke Ellington. Leaving Henderson, by 1932 he was sufficiently established to start his own big band, a group he ran with typical attention to musical standards, especially when it came to ensemble precision. His band proved a major nurturing ground for talent which went on to greater fame in other groups: alumni included Dicky Wells, Ben Webster, Teddy Wilson, Big Sid Catlett, and "Chu" Berry. During this time Carter would often feature himself on trumpet, an instrument he played with equal facility to his saxophone. In 1934 Carter moved to Europe, working in Paris, London, and Scandinavia, for a time holding down the job of staff arranger to Henry Hall's BBC Dance Orchestra. Sensing the changing political climate, Carter returned to the US in 1938 and started up a new band. Offered a residency at the Savoy Ballroom, he held down a position for his band there until the latter part of 1940, when he disbanded and, after some initial indecision, moved to LA in 1942, where he led a big band that comprised many young players later to make their mark, including Miles Davis and Max Roach, but became increasingly involved in studio session and composition work. Carter's role in opening the doors of the Hollywood studios to black musicians was of the greatest importance for his profession, but the public knew him better in the postwar years as a regular with Norman Granz's Jazz At The Philharmonic tours of America and, later, Europe. Carter joined Granz's record label in the early 1950s and made a string of outstanding small-group sessions as well as putting in an appearance on the famous *Funky Blues* jam-session album featuring him with Johnny Hodges and Charlie Parker.

During the 1950s and 1960s Carter maintained his multidirectional career, though his writing and arranging commitments to other artists forced him to scale down his live work. This imbalance has been addressed in the past two decades, while Carter has also added the role of educator to his portfolio, during the 1970s beginning to lecture at Princeton University, among others. Carter is admired for his arranging skills and is also responsible for at least one jazz standard, written in the 1930s, "When Lights Are Low." He continues to pursue a vigorous career.

fact file

BORN 1907

MUSICAL SELECTION
"When Lights Are Low"

Multi-instrumentalist Benny Carter has been a major force in jazz in every decade since the 1920s

SEE ALSO: Johnny Hodges, Charlie Parker, Frank Teschemacher, Fletcher Henderson, Duke Ellington, Ben Webster, Teddy Wilson, Big Sid Catlett, "Chu" Berry

James Carter

fact file

BORN 1970

MUSICAL SELECTION
Jurassic Classics
Dialogues With The Elders

Saxophonist James Carter has proven to be one of the great talents of the new jazz generation of the 1990s

Carter is one of the most astonishing and individual reedmen to have emerged in the past decade. He is at ease on a range of saxophones, from alto to baritone, and also accomplished on clarinet and bass clarinet. Carter's attack on his instrument ranges from a whisper to a devastating roar. Born and raised in Detroit, Carter was playing alto sax in a youth band at the age of 10, making sufficient progress to be a member of the International Jazz Band composed of members of the Blue Lake Fine Arts Camp which toured Europe in 1985. During the rest of the 1980s he began appearing with different parts of the music establishment, from Wynton Marsalis to Lester Bowie, and became a permanent part of Julius Hemphill's big band. He also became a regular in the Mingus Big Band. By 1991 he was back in Europe touring with his own trio, which by 1992 was a quartet with the addition of Detroit pianist Craig Taborn. This group debuted on the Japanese label DIW in 1993 with *J.C. On The Set*, where Carter virtually exploded out of the speakers on a largely unsuspecting public and immediately established himself among the front rank of the younger generation. This impression was confirmed by *Jurassic Classics*, a 1994 DIW record which was released internationally by Columbia. Since then Carter has been in constant demand as a leader and has signed with Atlantic Jazz, making highly varied albums, the latest, *Dialogues With The Elders*, featuring him in a series of duets with men such as Sweets Edison, Buddy Tate, and Lester Bowie. Carter's career is still in its first flush, and much is expected of him.

SEE ALSO: Wynton Marsalis, Lester Bowie, Charles Mingus

Philip Catherine

fact file

BORN 1942

MUSICAL SELECTION
Transparence

Belgian guitarist Philip Catherine, once a driving force of fusion, now as eloquent on acoustic as on electric guitar

Guitarist Catherine was born in London of an English mother and Belgian father and returned to Belgium as a young boy with his family at the close of World War II. His first inspiration was the sound of Django Reinhardt's records on the radio, and Reinhardt and Belgian guitarist René Thomas were the models for his initial guitar style.

Turning professional at 17, he joined up with organist Lou Bennett, with whom he toured Europe, and gradually modified his style to encompass the various influences of players such as Toots Thielemans, Wes Montgomery, and George Benson. Catherine also claims a considerable influence from pianists such as Erroll Garner and Herbie Hancock and a formative influence from composers such as Ravel, Debussy, and Bach. At the beginning of the 1970s Catherine became intensely involved in both free jazz and fusion, playing extensively with Jean-Luc Ponty and recording with Larry Coryell as well as playing with Charlie Mariano and Jasper van't Hof.

Catherine and Coryell completed two very successful tours of Europe in the late 1970s, adding to Catherine's reputation. By this time the Belgian had recorded his initial album under his own name and was equally prominent on both acoustic and electric guitars. From the mid-1970s onward Catherine also struck up a rewarding creative partnership with bassist Niels-Henning Ørsted Pedersen. Since then Catherine has subtly modified his more aggressive youthful style to reveal an uncommon touch and melodic expansiveness, combined with flawless technique and sufficient rhythmic drive to keep interest up even when he records without a drummer, as he has frequently done.

SEE ALSO: Django Reinhardt, Wes Montgomery, George Benson, Erroll Garner, Herbie Hancock, Larry Coryell

Big Sid Catlett

fact file

BORN 1910

DIED 1951

MUSICAL SELECTION
Satchmo at Symphony Hall

Big Sid Catlett, playing here with Louis Armstrong in 1938, was an influential swing drummer at home with any style

Big Sid was one of the great drummers of the swing period and also one of the few who could happily cross stylistic borders as if they did not exist. He was born in Evansville, Indiana, and learned piano as a child before moving on to playing drums in the school band. He began his professional career in Chicago in the late 1920s before moving on to New York at the onset of the Depression, where he worked initially with Elmer Snowden and then, in 1932, with Benny Carter. From late in 1933 he freelanced assiduously, spending quality time in both the Fletcher Henderson (1936) and Louis Armstrong (1937-41) orchestras as well as making a plethora of recordings with a large range of name bands and musicians.

Catlett became known as the possessor of a light but hard-swinging beat which he would carefully adapt to properly accompany each soloist or band he was playing behind. His style was not overly flash, although his dress sense and visual showmanship certainly were. This brought him the adoration of the fans and the respect of musicians, who could hear that he never compromised his music's character for the sake of shallow effect. As a drummer he was at home with classic jazz players as well as swing and, later, bop musicians: he was one of the first of the older generation of musicians to sit in with Gillespie and Parker and recorded with the latter. Catlett was instrumental in pointing people to the commonalities between all jazz players rather than the petty stylistic differences. His work with various Benny Goodman small groups also marks a high point in small-group swing drumming. Having spent the last few years of his professional life back with Louis Armstrong as a member of the All Stars, he died of heart failure after progressive physical deterioration in health.

SEE ALSO: Benny Carter, Fletcher Henderson, Louis Armstrong, Dizzy Gillespie, Charlie Parker, Benny Goodman

Serge Chaloff

fact file

BORN 1923

DIED 1957

MUSICAL SELECTION
Blue Serge

Baritonist Serge Chaloff, one of the "Four Brothers" and a prodigiously talented player

Bostonian Chaloff came from a musical family, both parents being trained musicians with a classical background and his mother giving private music lessons. Chaloff's chosen instruments as a child were piano and clarinet, but once his interest in jazz was awakened in the 1930s he began teaching himself the baritone sax in emulation of his heroes, Harry Carney, the long-serving baritonist in Duke Ellington's orchestra, and Count Basie's well-respected baritonist, Jack Washington.

Chaloff gained early experience in bands based around Boston before moving to New York and eventually getting a place in the progressive Boyd Raeburn Orchestra in 1945. In quick succession he moved from there to the bands of Georgie Auld and Jimmy Dorsey before arriving, in 1947, in the sax section of Woody Herman's Second Herd. By this time Chaloff's chaotic lifestyle was well entrenched, as was his drug habit, and while he was a supremely gifted musician with a melodic facility and tone others would die for, he was a trying personality to have on the band's books, as even the normally placid Herman discovered. Chaloff's non-appearances and his general lack of discipline left both Herman and Chaloff's next employer, Count Basie, bemused, but his abilities remained undimmed, even after his lifestyle began to seriously affect his health in the 1950s. It was during this decade that his classic album, *Blue Serge* (Capitol, 1956), was made, demonstrating his utter ease with the harmonic language of bop and his expressivity even through the veneer of cool jazz which was then at its peak of fashion. A progressive paralysis of the spine eventually rendered him an invalid and he died in 1957 after a long decline. His popularity among ordinary jazz fans has not lasted well, but his recorded legacy, both with Herman as a member of the famed Four Brothers and as a leader, bears witness to the huge talent that was his.

SEE ALSO: Duke Ellington, Count Basie, Boyd Raeburn, Woody Herman

Ray Charles

Ray Charles aka "The Genius" as his publicity of the 1950s named him, was as adept at jazz as he was with 1950s R&B

fact file

BORN 1932

MUSICAL SELECTION
"What'd I Say"
"Drown In My Own Tears"

Born Ray Charles Robinson in Albany, Georgia, but brought up in Florida, the great singer/pianist lost both his only brother and his sight during boyhood (his family were too poor to pay for treatment of the glaucoma which blinded him). Charles was self-taught at piano, but learned to read music in Braille at the St Augustine School for the Blind. At the onset of teenage years Charles left school and formed his own group, which toured Florida and took him eventually to Seattle, where he decided to settle. At this stage his ambition was to lead a trio in the fashion of the currently popular Nat King Cole, and his earliest records, made at the close of the forties, show a singer and pianist heavily indebted to the Cole formula, with lashings also of the vocal approach and material favored by R&B star Wynonie Harris.

Charles continued in this vein, making little headway, until a good time after he was signed by the Ertegun brothers to the Atlantic label. They were aware of his talents - his piano playing and his way with a saxophone, plus his ability to run a tight band, were already noticeable, on top of that uniquely expressive voice – but no one knew how to bring them out to the best effect. Charles himself claimed in later years that it was the result of a rethink after a period recording in New Orleans, when he decided he wanted to take his music back to its earliest, strongest influences. At this point the gospel and blues elements of his vocal and piano style fused, and Charles began notching a string of massive worldwide hits, including "What'd I Say," "I Believe," "Hallelujah! I Love Her So," and "Drown In My Own Tears." During his time with Atlantic he frequently recorded with big bands (sometimes using Quincy Jones as arranger) and also made two outstanding instrumental small-group dates with Milt Jackson. Charles's affinity with jazz was at its strongest in these years: after his change of record company (he began his own in 1960) he looked for a new, larger audience and began experimenting with combining pop sensibilities through a country-music repertoire. Charles remains a charismatic performer, but his jazz content in latter years is minimal.

SEE ALSO: Nat King Cole, Quincy Jones, Milt Jackson

Don Cherry

fact file

BORN 1936

DIED 1995

MUSICAL SELECTION
Complete Communion
Symphony For Improvisers

Trumpeter Don Cherry (seen here playing his "pocket trumpet") showed the way forward for many brass players in the 1960s

Oklahoman Cherry came to jazz by a similar route to that of his early leader, Ornette Coleman, playing as a youth in R&B and blues groups around his home town of Oklahoma City before moving to LA and meeting Billy Higgins. Through Higgins Cherry met Coleman in 1957 and all three men played, along with Charlie Haden, in Paul Bley's quintet before recording as a separate group without Bley under Coleman's contract with Atlantic records between 1959 and 1961. As a member of this group Cherry came in for close scrutiny and plenty of verbal abuse from critics, the public, and other musicians, Miles Davis being particularly dismissive. But Cherry's fractured and pointillistic improvisations, much less flowing and blues-based than his leader's, served as a rallying point for younger players looking for a post-cool avant-garde style, and Cherry's approach, partly formed by his own admission through being at a loss to know what to do from time to time in Ornette Coleman's music, became massively influential for the duration of the 1960s.

Cherry himself grew in confidence and technical assurance after Coleman disbanded in 1962, joining the famously no-nonsense Sonny Rollins Quartet of 1962-63 before co-leading the New York Contemporary Five in 1963 with Archie Shepp and then leading his own group in Europe, a band which featured Gato Barbieri shortly after his arrival from Argentina. From this band's nucleus came the line-up that made his three classic mid-1960s albums for Blue Note, *Complete Communion, Symphony For Improvisers* (with Pharoah Sanders added) and *Where Is Brooklyn?* A 1968 concert in Berlin with George Russell, later released on MPS/Saba, hinted at the change in direction which presaged Cherry's latter-day consuming interest in world music. During the 1970s and 1980s Cherry energetically followed up on his studies into ethnomusicology, striking up a rewarding partnership with percussionist Collin Walcott and Milton Nascimento. He also ventured into some ill-advised and rather painful attempts at funk and rock albums, perhaps influenced by Coleman's work with Prime Time. A more memorable type of musical recollection was achieved through New and Old Dreams, a quartet of ex-Coleman alumni with Dewey Redman playing sax. In the 1990s Cherry's activities were curtailed by the onset of a variety of ailments, to which he succumbed in 1995.

SEE ALSO: Ornette Coleman, Charlie Haden, Paul Bley, Miles Davis, Sonny Rollins, Archie Shepp, Pharoah Sanders

Charlie Christian

fact file

BORN 1916

DIED 1942

MUSICAL SELECTION
Solo Flight

The man who delivered the electric guitar to jazz, Charlie Christian

Christian, born in Texas but raised in Oklahoma, may not have been the first guitarist to use amplification, but his was the style and conception that affected every subsequent guitarist into the 1960s and, via his successors, beyond. Christian was brought up in poverty but his whole family had musical inclinations, his brothers playing the blues while Charlie showed an interest in many different types of music. His ear, which allowed him, like Bix Beiderbecke and others, to retain complete chord structures from a single hearing, gave him a quick and complete grasp of whatever music he was required to play on local gigs in and around Oklahoma City.

Many touring musicians were aware of Christian's prowess, but it was Mary Lou Williams who tipped off jazz fan John Hammond in the late 1930s to his gifts. Hammond went to Oklahoma City and was immediately convinced of the 23-year-old's prowess. He took him to LA and arranged a rather fraught audition with Benny Goodman. Christian's obvious ability won over Goodman's initial reluctance and the guitarist became a permanent member of Goodman's setup, recording many classic sides with his small groups and big band, including a session made by Goodman and unreleased at the time which combined Christian with Count Basie and Lester Young. Christian's combination of blues phrases with advanced harmonies he later found he shared with Harlem's nascent bop community, plus his enormous verve and drive and his ability to construct well-formed solos, leapfrogged him over every other guitarist of the era and he quickly became the leading influence on his instrument. His love of all-night jam sessions in New York may have given us some fine examples of his extended "live" work from private tapes, but it also exacerbated the tuberculosis diagnosed in 1940. Careless of his health, Christian died of pneumonia brought on by his weakened state in the early spring of 1942.

SEE ALSO: Bix Beiderbecke, Mary Lou Williams, Benny Goodman, Count Basie, Lester Young

June Christy

fact file

BORN 1925

DIED 1990

MUSICAL SELECTION
Something Cool
The Misty Miss Christy
The Song is June!

Emerging from out of the Stan Kenton band of the 1940s, June Christy (pictured here in 1953) went on to become a major solo star in the following decade

Christy came to prominence with the Stan Kenton Band of the late 1940s, then during the 1950s enjoyed popular success as a solo on a series of fine albums combining her with various big-band and orchestral settings. Born Sharon Leslie in Springfield, Illinois, she started out in the late 1930s singing with local groups before venturing out as far as Chicago and singing with, among others, Boyd Raeburn around 1944. Her cool, light voice may have seemed similar to many of the so-called "canaries" fronting many big bands of the day, but she had a quality of her own which was recognized by Stan Kenton, who brought her in as a replacement for the departing Anita O'Day in 1945.

Her success with the public was almost immediate, delivering a string of hit vocal sides for Kenton which helped him establish his special brand of jazz. These singles included "Tampico" and "How High The Moon." Christy stayed with Kenton through the 1940s and was married at the same time to Kenton saxophonist Bob Cooper, but in 1947, she began recording as a solo artist, to considerable success, winning many polls as the most popular female vocalist of the day. She began to use Kenton arranger Pete Rugolo for many of her own recording sessions, but for a few years at the turn of the decade spent most of her time out of the profession. She returned, however, to appear as a solo act and to occasionally meet up with Kenton's band for sessions or live performances. By 1955 her recording career was in full swing and her careful balance between jazz and popular music yielded a number of classic albums, starting with *Something Cool* (Capitol, 1953-55) and continuing with *The Misty Miss Christy* (1955-56) and *The Song Is June!* (1958). These albums remained an artistic peak with her, the Rugolo arrangements perfectly complementing her breathy but oddly pure vocals and lack of overt drama. Christy's career slowed down with the arrival of rock music, but her best efforts remain some of the most perfectly realized vocalizations of the 1950s.

SEE ALSO: Stan Kenton, Boyd Raeburn, Anita O'Day

Kenny Clarke

fact file

BORN 1914

DIED 1985

MUSICAL SELECTION
Bohemia After Dark

Drummer Kenny Clarke, reputedly the first to introduce the use of bass drum "bombs" rather than a steady four-beat pattern

Clarke, born in Pittsburgh, was one of the most important rhythmic innovators at the time of bebop's emergence in the early to mid-1940s. Clarke was conversant with a number of instruments but concentrated on drums before leaving high school, gigging regularly outside of school time with local Pittsburgh units. He first came to wider attention working with Roy Eldridge in 1935 and moved around the Midwest in different groups before landing in New York in 1937, where he joined the Edgar Hayes Band. A tour of Europe with Hayes in 1937-38 gave Clarke a taste of life outside the USA, but on his return he eventually became the drummer in the Teddy Hill Band, which also boasted Dizzy Gillespie. Introduced to the young musicians playing the after-hours Harlem clubs, Clarke rapidly became the drummer of choice at Minton's and Monroe's, playing with Gillespie, Thelonious Monk, and Charlie Christian prior to Charlie Parker's New York arrival. Clarke is often credited with the development of the broken bass-drum beat, emphasizing offbeats once every couple of bars rather than marking a strict four-to-the-bar beat. This in turn led to the moving of time marking to cymbals while other drums marked accents, thus giving a sense of suspended time, an intensifying of the beat, rather than the relaxed, dancing common time marked by swing drummers.

Clarke did time in the army (1943-46), then became a sought-after session drummer and a group leader: in 1951 he was first-choice drummer for John Lewis and Milt Jackson when the Milt Jackson Quartet, the first version of the Modern Jazz Quartet, was formed, but he left in 1955, first to spend time organizing recording dates for Savoy and other labels, but moving eventually the following year to Paris. There he became lionized as the greatest drummer on the Continent, and often appeared with fellow expatriate Bud Powell in Paris.

During the 1960s he formed and co-ran a big band with Francy Boland which plowed a similar musical field to the Thad Jones/Mel Lewis band in New York and provided a very high degree of musicianship during its decade or more of on-off existence. By the time of his death Clarke had become something of an institution in France, admired by all he played with and honored for his youthful innovations.

SEE ALSO: Ray Eldridge, Dizzy Gillespie, Thelonious Monk, Charlie Christian, Charlie Parker, John Lewis, Milt Jackson

Stanley Clarke

fact file

BORN 1951

MUSICAL SELECTION
Journey To Love

Bassist Stanley Clarke exploded onto the jazz-fusion scene in the 1970s with Return to Forever

Philadelphian Clarke emerged in the 1970s as the leading electric bassist in that decade's fusion movement. His background in music prepared him well for this role: as a child he learned to play the principal instruments in the violin family, swapping to electric bass by the time he was in high school and joining local rock and R&B bands. The thrill of the stage led to his abandoning plans for a more academic life and he spent some months in New York with Horace Silver's band in 1970 before, in 1971, moving on to groups led by Pharoah Sanders and Joe Henderson. Word quickly got around about his phenomenal technique and his musicality on an instrument that had not at that time been exactly welcomed by the jazz community. He worked with Stan Getz, Gil Evans, Art Blakey, Dom Um Romao, and many other leading figures before collaborating with the pianist he had met in Joe Henderson's band, Chick Corea. The result of this was the formation of Corea's electric-Latin group Return To Forever.

As Return To Forever became the only serious rivals to Weather Report in the fusion field during this decade, so Clarke's stock as electric bassist par excellence grew, his only real rival in popular affection being Report's Jaco Pastorius. Clarke began making fusion records under his own name in 1974. These showed both the strengths and weaknesses of the genre at this time: mind-boggling technique and powerful rhythmic thrust from all concerned (Clarke pioneered the slapping of bass strings for effect), but little attention to form and a tendency to empty pomp and pretentiousness.

Many fusion stars also thought they could sing. Leaving Return To Forever in 1977, Clarke managed to chart with a couple of singles; in more recent years he has attended a reunion tour of RTF and has continued a solo career, also appearing as guest with many other front-line fusion and jazz artists. His contribution to the popularity of electric bass in jazz cannot be underestimated and his style remains quite distinct in the jazz arena.

SEE ALSO: Horace Silver, Pharoah Sanders, Joe Henderson, Stan Getz, Gil Evans, Art Blakey, Chick Corea

Buck Clayton

fact file

BORN 1911

DIED 1991

MUSICAL SELECTION Buck Clayton's Jam Sessions

Top swing trumpeter Buck Clayton, pictured at Café Metropole in 1954

Clayton is one of the great trumpeters in jazz, a poised and powerful stylist who combined the crisp articulation and big tone of Armstrong with a powerful swing and a lead trumpeter's precision, both in ensemble and improvisation. Born in Parsons, Kansas, Clayton grew up among a musical family and took private trumpet tuition as an adolescent. Moving to Los Angeles as a young man he gained valuable experience in local big bands before being asked in 1934 to form a big band specifically to take it to play in Shanghai, China. This he did successfully, finally returning to LA in 1936. There he led his own band, The 14 Gentlemen from Harlem, as well as continuing to freelance. Making his way east later that year he stopped off in Kansas City and found himself replacing the recently departed Hot Lips Page in Count Basie's band, then resident at the Reno Club. Clayton stayed with the band as it moved to New York in 1937 and became a national name by the time he was drafted into the army in 1943. His involvement in the prewar recording sessions Teddy Wilson organized for Brunswick, especially those involving Billie Holiday, are some of his finest work. Clayton spent most of the war in musical circles at training camps and emerged in 1946 none the worse for the experience, playing an early JATP tour (April 1946) with Coleman Hawkins and Lester Young, for the first concert of which he was still in his army uniform.

Clayton reached perhaps the best form of his career in the decade after WWII, swapping between running his own bands, touring Europe as a solo (initially in 1949), and playing in small groups with pianist Joe Bushkin and Jimmy Rushing. Clayton's swing conception rarely interfered with his acceptance by audiences in this time, as his generosity of spirit and his naturally lithe phrasing made his playing unusually accessible, while his all-round musicianship and his readiness to play with both swing and bop players kept his approach fresh. In the 1950s he made a series of masterful albums under the title of *Buck Clayton's Jam Session* for Columbia, plus some superb small-group dates for Vanguard's John Hammond.

Clayton continued in the 1960s to mix his musical company, playing with Eddie Condon but also running his own groups and arranging for various big bands. His lip began to fail at the end of this decade; after 1979 Clayton concentrated on teaching, arranging, and composition. He wrote his autobiography, published in 1986. He led a big band in the late 1980s before his death, after a long illness, in 1991.

SEE ALSO: Hot Lips Page, Count Basie, Teddy Wilson, Billie Holiday, Coleman Hawkins, Lester Young, Jimmy Rushing

Arnett Cobb

A seminal influence on all post-war Texas tenor players, Arnett Cobb first flew high with Lionel Hampton in the early 1940s

fact file

BORN 1918

DIED 1989

MUSICAL SELECTION
"Flying Home No. 2"

Cobb's saxophone playing was a virtual definition of the term "Texas Tenor": a man possessed of a giant tone and the occasional rasp and honk to boot the rhythm along, Cobb could employ blues phraseology and wild swoops and hollers in his music, bringing his audiences to a frenzy, but he could also play with exemplary restraint, delicacy, and sensuous warmth on ballads and medium-tempo, easy swingers. He was not the first such player, but his style was hugely influential on all who came after him as the swing-style big bands gave way to bop and rhythm and blues.

Cobb was born in Houston, Texas, and was competent on piano, trumpet, and violin before moving to saxophone in late boyhood. His earliest significant experience was with Houston trumpeter Chester Boone between 1934 and 1936, a position he held while finishing his high school studies, while his long stint with Milt Larkin, from 1936 to 1942, gave him the time to develop a consistent approach, learn the ways of life on the road, and to learn from section mates who included Illinois Jacquet and Eddie Vinson. In 1939 he was offered the sax chair in the Basie band vacated by the death of the original Texas Tenor, Herschel Evans, but remained in Houston with his wife and Larkin, who by then was a close friend. Cobb also turned down a 1939 offer to join Lionel Hampton's new big band. Illinois Jacquet took the job instead. Three years later Cobb replaced the by-now famous Jacquet in the Hampton band and in 1944 recorded "Flying Home No. 2" with the band. His wild solo made him a star, as had Jacquet's three years earlier. Cobb stayed with Hampton until 1947, when he took his own small group out on the road and recorded for the Apollo label. Illness and operations kept him from music until 1951, when he formed a new small group, but a near-fatal auto accident in 1956 left him on crutches and kept him from his career until 1959, when he began recording for Prestige and leading bands again. Cobb's fragile health kept him in Houston through the 1960s, but during the following decade he made regular trips to Europe and was given a hero's welcome in France in particular. Swapping between his own groups and projects, often recorded by Progressive Records, and reunion tours with Hampton, Cobb kept up his profile well into the 1980s, still commanding attention with his enormous tone and rich swing-based improvisatory ideas. His health finally gave way as the 1980s drew to a close, and he died in the spring of 1989, a critically underrated but well-loved figure.

SEE ALSO: Illinois Jacquet, Lionel Hampton

Cozy Cole

fact file

BORN 1909

DIED 1981

MUSICAL SELECTION
"Topsy"

Cozy Cole was a band leader, drummer and educator, and is seen here at the Cotton Club in 1939

Cole, born in New Jersey, moved with his family to New York in 1926, where he and his two brothers, also both musicians, began playing freelance engagements as well as taking private musical tuition. Cole took for his initial inspiration in New York the work of Ellington's drummer, Sonny Greer, and secured his first job with a name band when joining Wilbur Sweatman in 1928. His first recordings came in 1930 with Jelly Roll Morton; he joined Blanche Calloway's orchestra the following year. In 1934 Cole moved on to Benny Carter's band, then Willie Bryant and Stuff Smith before joining Cab Calloway in 1938. By this time Cole was widely seen as a brilliant technician, a fine timekeeper and a gifted showman who would attract fans to any group he played in. His successful stint with Calloway lasted until 1942, after which he ran his own groups, worked in radio bands and in Broadway pit bands, and began studying at Juilliard School of Music. In 1944 he began recording as a leader, making sublime small-group swing records for Keynote and Savoy featuring luminaries such as Joe Thomas, Coleman Hawkins, Earl Hines, Ben Webster, Emmett Berry, Frankie Newton, Don Byas, Teddy Wilson, and Earl Bostic.

Cole was a natural for the drum chair in Louis Armstrong's All Stars in 1948 after the death of Big Sid Catlett, staying with the trumpeter until 1953, after which he picked up his freelance way of life and founded a drum tuition school with his old companion Gene Krupa. An unexpected chart success occurred with his group's recording of the song "Topsy" in 1958, allowing Cole to keep a small group going successfully until he took the drum chair in Jonah Jones's quintet in 1969. During his last decade he was regarded as a worthy elder statesman in the music and made appearances on TV and in documentaries.

SEE ALSO: Duke Ellington, Jelly Roll Morton, Benny Carter, Stuff Smith, Cab Calloway, Coleman Hawkins, Earl Hines

Nat King Cole

fact file

BORN 1917

DIED 1965

MUSICAL SELECTION
After Midnight
"Sweet Lorraine"

Nat King Cole was a massively influential pianist and trio leader prior to his crossover into the popular entertainment market

Cole was born in Santa Monica, California, but his family moved to Chicago when he was four, so he began hearing local piano styles at an early age. Cole had three brothers, all of whom became professional musicians, and Nat made his debut on record with his brother Eddie's Solid Swingers in 1936. His early devotion to the keyboard style of Earl Hines helped him form a cohesive trio routine when he moved back to the West Coast in 1937 after a time in a New York theater. Guitarist Oscar Moore joined the first edition of the trio, and Cole gained a residency at Hollywood's Swannee Inn with Moore and with bassist Wesley Prince. This drummerless trio soon became popular with other pianists and in 1940 Cole began clocking up the hits as pianist-singer signed to Decca with his version of "Sweet Lorraine." It was the first of many such single successes, the biggest perhaps being 1941's "Hit That Jive, Jack." Meanwhile he continued to play piano on various dates in the early to mid-1940s, including two separate sessions with Lester Young which rank among his best post-Basie work. Cole moved to Capitol in 1942, scoring a massive hit the following year with "Straighten Up And Fly Right." By this time his burnished baritone vocals were becoming more important than his pianisms, and though he could still hold his own in any company, as he proved at a 1944 JATP concert with Les Paul, Jack McVea, J.J. Johnson, and Illinois Jacquet, he began to move in the direction of more popular material. By 1946 he was beginning to record with orchestra and opt for a considerably less jazz-led vocal style, a process which was never reversed. During the 1950s Cole became a major star with his own television show, appeared in movies, and came off the road to concentrate on other ways of furthering his career. By the 1960s his public jazz ties were nonexistent, though he remained close to old colleagues, and two latter-day albums show his talents were not blunted: 1956's *After Midnight* featuring Willie Smith and Harry Edison and the 1961 with-strings outing with George Shearing's Quintet. Whatever music he chose in his latter years, Cole's early piano stylings have proved influential down to the present day, as was his trio, and for this he has earned a permanent place in jazz history.

SEE ALSO: Earl Hines, Lester Young, J.J. Johnson, Illinois Jacquet, Willie Smith, Harry Edison, George Shearing

Ornette Coleman

Coleman has occupied an unresolved position in jazz since his startling impact on New York in the winter of 1959. Arriving with his style fully developed and his own group attuned to his musical concerns, Coleman demanded of his listeners absolute acceptance or total rejection. Since he has always been content to plow his own musical fields, there have been few opportunities for audiences to find other ways of addressing his music. Consequently, Coleman's freshest, most characteristic and innovatory work was completed within five years of his arrival in New York.

Coleman was born in Fort Worth, Texas, and his early musical experiences revolved around teaching himself the saxophone and playing at school in the marching band and in local blues and R&B bands. Introduced to bebop in the late 1940s by a local musician, Coleman unsuccessfully attempted to inject jazz ideas into his R&B work but more often than not ended up fired for his pains. Moving to LA in 1951 through a tour with Pee Wee Crayton, Coleman spent long periods of the early 1950s working menial jobs while developing his musical knowledge and his own style, moving away from the all-pervading influence of Charlie Parker. By the mid-1950s Coleman had met and played with Ed Blackwell and trumpeter Bobby Bradford, and soon after became a member of Paul Bley's quintet. Here he developed a rapport with the other members to the point where this group, *sans* Bley, became the first Ornette Coleman Quartet. After an introduction to Contemporary records by Red Mitchell, Coleman made two albums in LA before coming under the wing of John Lewis and appearing at the Lenox School of Jazz in summer 1959. This endorsement led to a winter booking at New York's Five Spot, which delivered Coleman and his ideas to a shocked jazz world. Coleman was playing in a pianoless group, and had abandoned conventional key centers and the common popular song structures, relying instead on group intuition and the general patina of blues phraseology to deliver cohesive performances. He was a skilled composer whose memorable themes of this period, such as "Peace," "Lonely Woman," "Ramblin'," and "Una Muy Bonita," have often been recorded by others, but the stark tone and nontempered pitch caught many unprepared, as did his theories of collective improvisation, which, when analyzed, were not dissimilar to those of classic New Orleans polyphony. Coleman released five classic albums between 1959 and 1961 which encapsulated his musical philosophy. After an enforced retirement from performance, he returned in 1965 with live albums from Copenhagen and won numerous awards with his new trio comprising himself, cellist David Izenson, and drummer Charles Moffett. By the end of the 1960s Coleman was working once more with a quartet, using an old friend, tenorist Dewey Redman, as front-line mate, but during the 1970s Coleman saw a need to change his instrumental backdrop. By 1975 he had formed the group Prime Time, against whose often cacophonous-seeming sounds he soloed in his usual manner. Apart from his ventures into completely scored acoustic music written in the European art-music tradition, Coleman has stuck to playing either in the Prime Time format or with acoustic partners. Unfortunately for Coleman, though his promotion of his musical type, which he terms Harmolodics, is unceasing, his own playing has for a long time been stagnant and his role in the music has become that of a representative of the past. This conundrum throws the focus back to his early achievements, which remain among jazz's greatest treasures.

fact file

BORN 1930

MUSICAL SELECTION
"Peace"
"Lonely Woman"
"Ramblin'"
"Una Muy Bonita"

Saxophonist and band leader Ornette Coleman turned jazz on its ear with his arrival in New York late in 1959

SEE ALSO: Charlie Parker, Paul Bley

Steve Coleman

fact file

BORN 1956

MUSICAL SELECTION
Def Trance Beat

M-Base founder and a leading saxophonist and composer, Steve Coleman is also a committed musicologist

Coleman is one of the more formidable of the latter-day Chicago musicians to have made their initial mark in the 1970s and 1980s. Brought up in a musical family and introduced to jazz by his father, Coleman also picked up on blues, soul, and funk at an early age. Choosing the alto saxophone, Coleman brought his broad taste to bear when it came to learning about musical tradition, one of his early role models being Chicago's famous tenor saxophonist, Von Freeman. Unlike hometowner Freeman, however, Coleman left Chicago for New York in 1978 and quickly gained recognition for his high technical and theoretical skills, landing a berth in the Thad Jones/Mel Lewis Orchestra as well as playing extensively with established avant-garde players, Cecil Taylor in particular. He was widely acclaimed for his role in Dave Holland's late 1980s quartet.

Coleman, however, came to a prominent position during the 1980s due to his championing of a new hybrid of jazz and contemporary urban musics which he titled M-Base, a shortening of Macro-Basic Array of Structured Extemporization. These theories were elaborated on albums he and kindred spirits like Cassandra Wilson, Geri Allen, Graham Haynes, and Marvin "Smitty" Smith made on the New York-based label, JMT, which revealed tightly woven musical structures and dense improvisation underpinned by the type of rhythm more often associated with funk and R&B. The M-Base approach established Coleman worldwide as a heavyweight, an impression his subsequent career has done nothing to dispel. Coleman's pure, liquid tone is the perfect vehicle to deliver his logical but highly abstract improvisations, while his compositional talents lie at the heart of much of his achievement. His records and concerts with his band Five Elements, begun in the 1980s and still functioning with an ever-shifting personnel, reveal both a natural complexity of thought and a pleasing ability to communicate directly to his listeners. Of late Coleman has brought a denser rhythmic matrix to his work, making it an even richer brew and one with echoes of many musics, past and present, from around the world.

SEE ALSO: Thad Jones, Cecil Taylor

Eddie Condon

fact file

BORN 1905

DIED 1973

MUSICAL SELECTION
The Original Decca Recordings, 1939-46

Easily one of the greatest raconteurs and band leaders in jazz, Eddie Condon reputedly never took a solo in public on guitar

Condon was not exactly the world's greatest guitarist (or banjoist), and was never heard to play a solo intentionally, but he was an immensely important figure in the establishment and development of the white jazz tradition in Chicago in the 1920s. A born communicator and organizer, Condon not only ran groups comprising most of the best young classic jazz players of Chicago and, later, New York, but also successfully ran a New York bar, Condon's, where good jazz was always on tap to the delight of jazz fans, along with the liquid refreshments so enjoyed by its owner.

Condon was born in Goodland, Indiana, and first became interested in the ukulele before turning to the banjo as a teenager. Freelancing around the Midwest, Condon eventually built up a network of like-minded young musicians. Settling in Chicago for a while, Condon in 1927 formed with Red McKenzie a band called the Chicagoans, which played extensively around the area and made some important early recordings using many of the new young Midwest faces in "hot" music, including Frank Teschemacher, Bud Freeman, and Jimmy McPartland. A move to New York in 1928, although it initially incorporated an unhappy period in Red Nichols's Five Pennies, proved permanent, Condon settling into a series of fine recordings with his old sparring partner, singer/paper-and-comb expert Red McKenzie, using talent such as Gene Krupa, Jack Teagarden, Red Allen, Coleman Hawkins, and Louis Armstrong. Ever the organizer, Condon sat in or played with virtually every small-group star of note during the 1930s, encouraging the career of many such as Pee Wee Russell, Bud Freeman, Max Kaminsky, and Bobby Hackett. Singer Lee Wiley also became a regular at Condon-arranged concerts and on broadcasts. By the end of the 1930s Condon was involved in setting up Milt Gabler's Commodore label, for whom he recorded prolifically in the subsequent decade, and he also settled into a long residency at a mid-Manhattan club, Nick's. During World War II he helped organize a series of Carnegie Hall concerts, many of which were televised, giving him a previously undreamed of profile. Condon capitalized on it by opening his own club in 1945 down in the Village. Condon wrote his witty and incisive autobiography, *We Called It Music*, in the late 1940s and began touring internationally, becoming a celebrity in the process and even making it to Australia in the next decade. By the 1960s, however, a lifetime of heavy drinking was slowing the fast-talking rhythm guitarist down, and he cut back on his commitments, although tours to Japan and Australasia in 1964 were a success. By the early 1970s he was clearly ailing, a Carnegie Hall concert in his honor in 1972 being his last public appearance. He died in hospital the following year.

SEE ALSO: Frank Teschemacher, Bud Freeman, Red Nichols, Gene Krupa, Jack Teagarden, Red Allen

John Coltrane

The impact of Coltrane on jazz in the 1950s and 1960s was all-pervasive: no area of small-group contemporary jazz was left untouched. The intensity, the confessed spirituality, and the dignified solemnity of purpose Coltrane brought to his mature music-making ventures taught a generation of musicians to believe in themselves and their own creative nature.

Coltrane, born in Hamlet, North Carolina, came to professional music late, not learning saxophone until he was 18. Entering military service soon after, he spent time overseas playing alto in a navy band, then with various big bands around Philadelphia on his return before joining Dizzy Gillespie's big band in 1948. Coltrane slowly developed his improvisational style from such models as Dexter Gordon, Charlie Parker, and the more raucous tenors such as Big Nick Nicholas and Sam "The Man" Taylor. When Gillespie disbanded in 1950, retaining a sextet from the old personnel, Coltrane was a holdover. Dropping the alto completely, Coltrane concentrated on tenor but by mid-1951 was out of the Gillespie outfit. By this stage Coltrane was suffering from the drink and drugs problems that beset so many players at this time, and his tenures with Eddie Vinson, Earl Bostic, and Johnny Hodges were blighted by erratic behavior. Withdrawing from an offer to join Jimmy Smith's group in 1955, Coltrane was brought into the new Miles Davis Quintet through Red Garland's recommendation after Sonny Rollins pronounced himself unavailable. Coltrane grabbed this opportunity and, from his first recordings with Davis on the Prestige and Columbia labels, began to make waves. By 1957, however, Davis had tired of his personal problems, and Coltrane left the group. He kicked his drug and alcohol habits that year, began recording as a leader, spent the fall of the year playing with Thelonious Monk at the Five Spot in New York and, as he testified in 1964, experienced a spiritual awakening which pointed the way forward.

Rejoining Miles Davis in 1958, Coltrane remained with the trumpeter for three more years while compiling a massive recorded legacy, firstly for Prestige, then between 1959 and 1961 for Atlantic, for whom he recorded, among others, *Giant Steps* (which included the classic ballad "Naima"), *Coltrane Plays The Blues,* records co-led with Milt Jackson and Don Cherry, and his first hit LP, *My Favorite Things,* on which he deployed his new soprano saxophone. By the time he launched his own group in the midst of this recording activity, he was the coming man in jazz, and the classic John Coltrane Quartet (featuring McCoy Tyner and Elvin Jones) confirmed this impression. Signing a deal with Impulse! records in 1961, Coltrane embarked on an ambitious series of albums, using big bands, live dates (still unusual at the time) with the guest presence of his friend Eric Dolphy, and albums sharing leadership with Duke Ellington and the singer Johnny Hartman. In 1965 Coltrane won virtually every award he was eligible for his album *A Love Supreme.* He used this position of eminence to foster interest in the young players of the emerging avant-garde such as Archie Shepp and Albert Ayler. This led to tensions in his own group and the departure of Tyner and Jones in 1965-66: Coltrane replaced them with his pianist wife, Alice, and drummer Rashied Ali. By now suffering from the liver cancer that would kill him in summer 1967, Coltrane embarked on a number of tours with this group, augmented by saxophonist Pharoah Sanders. His death left a gaping hole in contemporary jazz with no one able to continue the advancement of the type of music he was espousing, as his thousands of imitators, then and later, unhappily proved.

SEE ALSO: Dizzy Gillespie, Dexter Gordon, Charlie Parker, Johnny Hodges, Jimmy Smith, Miles Davis, Sonny Rollins, Thelonious Monk, Don Cherry, McCoy Tyner

fact file

BORN 1926

DIED 1967

MUSICAL SELECTION
Giant Steps
My Favorite Things
A Love Supreme

Sax giant John Coltrane changed the course of jazz in the early 1960s with seminal works such as his timeless Giant Steps

Chris Connor

Singer Chris Connor, seen here at the Newport Jazz Festival in 1957

fact file

BORN 1927

MUSICAL SELECTION
Chris Craft
George Gershwin Almanac

Connor, born in Kansas City, Missouri, came from a musical family and originally trained on the clarinet, though she was first heard publicly as a vocalist, singing with the University of Missouri college band. Connor was an early lover of jazz; while she was still in KC she met up with Bob Brookmeyer and sang locally with his group for a while. In 1949 she moved to New York, shortly after landing a berth in the Snowflakes, Claude Thornhill's vocal trio. After three years with Thornhill, Connor was recommended by the departing June Christy to Stan Kenton as a logical replacement and jumped at the opportunity. She scored a hit with "All About Ronnie," then went out on her own in 1953. She has remained a solo since then, usually leading her own trios. After a series of albums on the Bethlehem label Connor moved in 1956 to Atlantic, where she scored a major hit with "I Miss You So." Her breathy, highly accentuated style, allied to an on-stage persona rare for its heightened concentration on acting out the feelings expressed by the song and lyrics, have brought her both fame and controversy, but Connor is one of a small band of white singers who are incontestably jazz singers, first and foremost. Her lineage is often traced to Anita O'Day, but Connor's musical roots go much further, back through Billie Holiday to Lee Wiley and her era. With Atlantic Connor produced a stream of well-considered and near-faultless albums, all of which won her the praise of critics and fans. *Chris Craft* (1958) found her handling offbeat material with imaginatively varied small-group line-ups; her *George Gershwin Almanac* (Atlantic, 1957), coming as it did in the middle of Ella Fitzgerald's *Song Books*, took rare courage to do, but its artistic integrity is uncompromised and its musical value a lasting one, as its CD reissue a few years ago has proved. Connor has continued her career up to the present day, bringing her unique magic to her projects and still touring internationally.

SEE ALSO: Bob Brookmeyer, June Christy, Stan Kenton, Anita O'Day, Billie Holiday, Lee Wiley, Ella Fitzgerald

Chick Corea

fact file

BORN 1941

MUSICAL SELECTION
Now He Sings, Now He Sobs
Piano Improvisations Vol. 1 & 2
Return to Forever
Remembering Bud Powell

Chick Corea has proved himself a master in both the acoustic and electric jazz contexts

One of the most influential piano stylists, composers, and bandleaders of the past 30 years, Corea was born into a musical family and took music lessons from his father, a qualified professional musician. Before he was 10 Massachusetts-born Corea was proficient on both piano and drums and was developing an interest in jazz. His early heroes included Bud Powell, Horace Silver, Dizzy Gillespie, and Charlie Parker. Later he would become a devotee of Thelonious Monk's compositions. By the early 1960s Corea was the possessor of a formidable technique and a wide interest in various jazz styles, including the Latin influence initially brought into the music by Dizzy Gillespie in the postwar years. His first steady work after arriving in New York in 1962 was with the popular Mongo Santamaria group, but he was soon appearing with many different groups, including Stan Getz, Willie Bobo, Dizzy Gillespie, Herbie Mann, Blue Mitchell, and others, his grasp of the Latin aspect as secure as his technical mastery was now near total.

Talent like his was bound to be noticed. In 1968, when Herbie Hancock decided to leave Miles Davis, the trumpeter brought in Corea as replacement, urging him to explore the possibilities of the then new electric keyboards in a jazz context. As Davis slowly assembled his electric style, Corea experimented as freely as he wished, as can be seen by the progressive loosening up of his playing from *Filles de Kilimanjaro* (1968) to *Live-Evil* (1970). On his own, however, Corea stuck with acoustic, as his stunning 1968 debut album, *Now He Sings, Now He Sobs* (Solid State), made clear. Not only that, but his first venture after Davis was with the avant-garde acoustic trio, Circle, with ex-Davis bassist Dave Holland. Later, reed-man Anthony Braxton pushed the boundaries even further, and the music was in danger of passing over their audience's heads. Corea disbanded Circle in 1971 and recorded his first solo piano efforts, *Piano Improvisations Vol. 1 & 2* (ECM). Corea's journey towards lyricism and massive popularity had been started, although he would always retain an interest in art-music composition, writing chamber music and piano suites frequently in the coming decades. A further ECM album, in 1972 and with Flora Purim, Airto Moreira, Joe Farrell, and Stanley Clarke, carried the title *Return to Forever.* Though a mainly acoustic effort, it led eventually to the forming of the electric Latin-fusion band of the same name which in the mid-1970s became a big enough draw to fill amphitheaters worldwide. Corea, however, never abandoned acoustic music, as his tours duetting with Herbie Hancock in the 1970s and 1980s showed. During the 1980s he formed the Elektric Band and the Akoustic Band, featuring Bob Berg, John Patitucci, and Dave Weckl: these have both toured extensively and often. Corea recently returned to his youth with an impressive sextet album, *Remembering Bud Powell* (Stretch), giving moving interpretations of Powell originals.

SEE ALSO: Bud Powell, Horace Silver, Dizzy Gillespie, Charlie Parker, Thelonious Monk, Stan Getz, Herbie Mann

Larry Coryell

fact file

BORN 1943

MUSICAL SELECTION
Twin House

Guitarist Larry Coryell was a key musician in the marriage of jazz with rock during the late 1960s

Guitarist Coryell, a native of Galveston, Texas, was an important shaping influence on the early course of jazz-rock, but has never enjoyed the popular acclaim ceded to players such as John McLaughlin, George Benson and Al DiMeola. Coryell was largely self-taught on his instrument as a boy and joined a rock-'n'-roll band in his teens, as soon as he was proficient enough to hold down the chords. In the early 1960s he studied journalism at Seattle's University of Washington, leaving university prior to completing the course to pursue his music interests, which were by this time in both the rock and jazz fields. When he moved to New York in 1965 his first important job was that of replacing Gabor Szabo in Chico Hamilton's band, a position made for his dual musical interests. Coryell followed that up with a move in 1966 to set up his own band, Free Spirits, with Bob Moses, but lack of commercial interest led him and Moses to join vibist Gary Burton's new quartet in 1967, a band combining Burton's interests in jazz, rock, and country music. This led to him rapidly becoming perceived as an important new stylist on guitar, and he toured and recorded extensively with Burton until 1969. Then he briefly joined Herbie Mann and went through a number of projects, including an album featuring him with John McLaughlin, before, in 1973, launching Eleventh House, an important jazz-rock band featuring Randy Brecker and Alphonse Mouzon. By 1975 this project had run out of steam and Coryell switched to acoustic guitar, touring widely and appearing with many guitarists, including Philip Catherine (with whom he recorded *Twin House* in 1976), Paco de Lucia, and John McLaughlin. Coryell's career since then has not been along straight lines, and rarely has his path carried the impetus that his talents suggest it should have. Nevertheless, he remains an impressive player. He continues to record and perform, mostly leading his own groups.

SEE ALSO: John McLaughlin, George Benson, Gary Burton, Herbie Mann, Philip Catherine

Marilyn Crispell

fact file

BORN 1947

MUSICAL SELECTION
For Coltrane
Nothing Ever Was, Anyway

Ever a brilliant pianist, Marilyn Crispell has emerged as a major avant-garde figure in the past decade

Crispell is a formally trained and qualified pianist and composer who has adapted her early viewpoints to the musical messages she read in the music of people such as John Coltrane, Cecil Taylor, and Anthony Braxton, the last of whom she appeared with in his mid-1980s quartet. Crispell began piano lessons when still very young in her native Baltimore, completing her studies some years later at New England Conservatory in Boston. Crispell's early performance experience was mostly in the field of music interpretation and in executing her own compositions, but her contacts with avant-garde jazz in the 1970s led her to seek out situations where she could begin developing her improvisational approach. Soon, her improvised excursions, bearing a superficial similarity to Cecil Taylor but in fact quite different in their musical logic, rubbed shoulders with works such as "Ode to Olivier Messiaen," the composer being an early inspiration. Crispell began appearing with Anthony Braxton and performing in his projects of various instrumentation, leading to her regular inclusion in his quartet.

By the end of the 1980s Crispell was appearing as leader of her own trio, touring both the US and Europe with Reggie Workman and Gerry Hemingway and recording a series of fine live albums which were quite ambitious in their scope. Many of them would include compositions by John Coltrane and in fact the 1987 London concert released by Leo records as *For Coltrane* mixes her own tributes to him with new and carefully considered versions of Coltrane classics.

Crispell has continued to mature as an artist and improviser, as her recent ECM debut, *Nothing Ever Was, Anyway* (ECM 1997), a reinterpretation of Annette Peacock's compositions in the company of Gary Peacock and Paul Motian, demonstrates.

SEE ALSO: John Coltrane, Cecil Taylor, Anthony Braxton, Paul Motian

Sonny Criss

fact file

BORN 1927

DIED 1977

MUSICAL SELECTION
Portrait of Sonny Criss

West Coast altoist Sonny Criss, one of the few altoists of the 1940s not to be completely engulfed by Charlie Parker's genius

Alto saxophonist Criss was one of the most talented of the post-Parker generation. Born in Memphis, at the age of 15 he moved with his family to Los Angeles. Studying alto sax while still at high school, he began playing occasional professional gigs while continuing his daytime studies. After finishing school he went professional, playing with a wide range of LA groups, including those of Billy Eckstine while the singer had a residency at Billy Berg's club in Hollywood. Criss also featured in Gene Norman's mid-1940s "Just Jazz" concerts alongside stars such as Stan Getz, Wardell Gray, Dodo Marmarosa, and Howard McGhee. Airshot recordings of these reveal him to be equal to the task. By 1948 Criss had worked with Johnny Otis and was also a member of the JATP tour package which crisscrossed America that year - the one year Granz did not extract performances to release on his fledgling Norgran and Clef record labels in the famous JATP series. Granz did, however, make studio dates with Criss.

Criss continued to base himself in LA, and this undoubtedly held him back. A fiery, imaginative player with a beautiful tone and an intensity alien to the newly fashionable cool scene which predominated there, Criss played in a succession of groups - Howard Rumsey, Victor Feldman, and others - but failed to excite national attention, even when recorded as a leader. Resigned to obscurity in LA, Criss opted for a period in Paris, where he was given due recognition and made some dazzling records for local companies, few of which were released outside France. Criss returned to LA in 1965 for family reasons, but the West Coast still held out little reward. A series of fine mid-1960s albums for Prestige gave him critical acclaim, but he was increasingly dividing his time between music and community projects. An upturn in his fortunes in 1973-74 took him back to Europe and awakened interest in Japan: he was booked for a tour there in 1977 when he took his own life in a hotel room back in the United States.

SEE ALSO: Billy Eckstine, Stan Getz, Wardell Gray, Dodo Marmarosa, Howard McGhee

Bob Crosby

fact file

BORN 1913

DIED 1993

MUSICAL SELECTION
"Christopher Columbus"
"The Big Noise From Winnetka"

Band leader Bob Crosby, brother of Bing, ran a popular and distinctive Dixieland-style band during the 1930s and 1940s

Brother of singer/film star/jazz fan Bing, Bob Crosby ran one of the most authentic and musically excellent Dixieland jazz bands of the 1930s, the Bob Cats, landing one of the biggest hits of the swing era in 1938, "The Big Noise From Winnetka." Bob was a half-decade younger than his brother and was an enthusiast for jazz and the entertainment business although he had virtually no musical training. He specialized in unambitious vocals and fronting bands, getting experience with Anson Weekes and the Dorsey Brothers (1934-35) before being approached to front a band which was being organized around a nucleus of musicians drawn from the old Ben Pollack band. Crosby accepted the offer and found himself in front of players of the caliber of Yank Lawson and Matty Matlock. The driving Dixieland style of the band - a sort of halfway house between the Dorsey Brothers and Eddie Condon - and its small-group spin-off, the Bob Cats, soon became very popular and Crosby himself a star. The band recorded all the usual swing repertoire, including "Christopher Columbus" and "Goody Goody," but with soloists such as Eddie Miller, Irving Fazola, and Billy Butterfield and a rhythm team driven by Ray Bauduc there was little sugaring of the musical content.

In 1942 the band broke up and Crosby took up a career in films and television. He also saw Pacific action in World War II, leading a service band. Crosby's postwar career was for the most part away from jazz, but for the rest of his life he would periodically reconvene a band and go out on a tour or appear on a show with it, playing repertoire from a wide range of periods though always with jazz at the heart of it.

SEE ALSO: Eddie Condon

Tadd Dameron

Composer and arranger Tadd Dameron, seen here with Sarah Vaughan (right) in 1946, was one of the first to bring bop into jazz big band writing

fact file

BORN 1917

DIED 1965

MUSICAL SELECTION
The Gentle Touch
Fontainebleu

Dameron was an important arranger and composer of the 1940s and 1950s whose work has rarely been accorded the recognition it deserves. Born in Cleveland, Ohio - not a noted jazz hotbed at the time - Dameron trained in piano and music theory, then started playing with local Cleveland groups, graduating in his late teens to Cleveland's best of the day in the shape of the Freddie Webster outfit. Moving on to other bands, including that of Blanche Calloway, Dameron settled in New York, where he was hired by Harlan Leonard in 1940 as pianist, arranger, and composer for Leonard's band. Dameron's first four recorded arrangements were made that year with the Leonard group, although some, including "Dameron Stomp," would not be released until the LP era. Dameron was drafted into the war effort, and on his discharge went freelance, writing arrangements for many of the top swing bands, including Lunceford, Basie, Georgie Auld, and Sarah Vaughan, who recorded his beautiful "If You Could See Me Now" in 1946; Coleman Hawkins also used him on occasions. By this time bebop was making itself heard, and Dameron's forward-thinking arrangements fitted effortlessly with the new mood. Compositions such as "Good Bait," "Cool Breeze," and "Our Delight" became regular material for big bands such as Eckstine and Gillespie, while Dameron's arrangement of "Hot House" was a Parker favorite. Dameron was closely associated with the three top young trumpeters, Gillespie, Fats Navarro and Miles Davis: he wrote "Soulphony" for Gillespie's 1948 Carnegie Hall concert, he gigged and recorded extensively with Navarro, and he co-led with Davis the group that appeared at the 1949 Paris Jazz Festival. Unfortunately, Dameron was also prey to the curse of many bop musicians, picking up a heavy heroin habit.

He spent 1951-52 arranging R&B tunes for Bull Moose Jackson, but in 1953 he ran his own band featuring Clifford Brown for a few months in Atlantic City: this band cut four sides for Prestige, including "Dial B For Beauty," but broke up after the season. Dameron's drug problems increased, but he managed in 1956 to record his "Fontainebleu" and five other compositions for Prestige with an octet featuring Kenny Dorham, followed a few months later by a quartet date for the same label featuring John Coltrane. Within two years, however, Dameron was in jail on drug charges, not to emerge until 1961. On his release he arranged for Milt Jackson, Sonny Stitt, and even Benny Goodman, and recorded in 1962 *The Gentle Touch* for Riverside. The following year, however, an abrupt decline in health led to hospitalization with heart problems. In 1964 cancer was diagnosed, and he died in March 1965.

SEE ALSO: Count Basie, Sarah Vaughan, Coleman Hawkins, Billy Eckstine, Dizzy Gillespie, Charlie Parker

Eddie "Lockjaw" Davis

fact file

BORN 1922

DIED 1986

MUSICAL SELECTION
The Lockjaw Davis Cookbooks

Eddie "Lockjaw" Davis, big-toned tenor man, pictured here with the Count Basie Band, 1965

Davis was born in New York and became interested in playing jazz in his teens. Self-taught, he bought his first horn and within eight months was working at Monroe's in Harlem. Davis's early style was derived from the driving tenor work of "Chu" Berry and Herschel Evans, as his first employers appreciated: he worked for Cootie Williams from 1942 to 1943, then with people such as Louis Armstrong, Andy Kirk, and Lucky Millinder. By 1946 he was a big enough name to go out on his own, and gigged and recorded with his own combo from then until 1952, when he joined the revamped Count Basie Band, becoming one of the main musical symbols of its second great period. Davis left Basie in 1955 to run a small combo again, hiring organist Shirley Scott to help create one of the first working tenor-and-organ trios in jazz. The band stayed intact for five years, during which Davis also worked as road manager for Basie on occasions. By 1960 he was looking for a different approach, finding it in the "tough tenors" format of a quartet with Johnny Griffin. This band proved very popular live, its exciting records demonstrating just why. Davis also freelanced extensively in the early 1960s, appearing on many record sessions, but in 1964 returned to Basie, where he stayed until 1973. After this, as an established figure still sporting a swing-based style but with a huge tone and a very well-developed technique, Davis freelanced all over the world, a man constantly in demand for his particular abilities. He recorded prolifically, both as leader and as guest soloist, often returning to the Basie fold for small-group sessions and the like. He died after a short illness in 1986.

SEE ALSO: "Chu" Berry, Louis Armstrong, Andy Kirk, Lucky Millinder, Count Basie, Johnny Griffin

Miles Davis

Davis, due to his sustained leadership and creativity from the 1940s to the close of the 1980s, occupied a position in jazz analogous to that of Armstrong and Ellington of the prewar period.

St Louis-born Davis arrived in New York in 1944 at just 17, recording with Charlie Parker a year later at Parker's famous session for Savoy, where the immortal "Ko-Ko" was cut with Dizzy Gillespie on piano. By 1947 Davis was leading his own session for Savoy, with Parker on tenor, and in 1948 Davis was the figurehead guiding the so-called Birth of the Cool band featuring Gil Evans, John Carisi, and Gerry Mulligan. A 1949 trip to the Paris Festival with Tadd Dameron confirmed Davis's status, but a heroin habit slowed his career to a near stop from then until 1954, when he emerged, "clean," to take on his career again. An appearance with a quartet at the 1955 Newport Jazz Festival announced his return, and a swap from Prestige to Columbia, coupled with the forming of his new Quintet featuring John Coltrane and Philly Joe Jones late that year, ensured a much wider career path in the future. This was confirmed not only by the live dates and record sessions by the quintet, but the series of exquisite and revolutionary big-band records Davis made in tandem with Gil Evans between 1957 and 1960, starting with the *Miles Ahead* classic.

After *Miles Ahead* Davis made the soundtrack to a Louis Malle film, and his "new" sextet of 1958, featuring Coltrane, Cannonball Adderley, and Bill Evans, was briefly the talking point of the music. In early 1959, after both Evans and Adderley had branched out on their own, they returned to record *Kind of Blue.* With the break-up of this group and the departure of Philly Joe Jones and Coltrane in 1960, Davis had a quiet start to the 1960s, but by mid-decade his new band, featuring Tony Williams, Ron Carter, and Herbie Hancock, was startling audiences with their flair. Saxophonist/ composer Wayne Shorter joined in 1965, giving Davis the new material he was desperate for in order to update his sound. Within two years, Davis began experimenting with the combination of acoustic and electric instruments on *Miles In The Sky.* This led to the decade-end triumphs of *In A Silent Way* and the bestselling *Bitches Brew.* Backed up by the powerhouse music on *Jack Johnson,* where guitarist John McLaughlin fulfilled a role Davis had originally dreamed Jimi Hendrix might fulfill, the trumpeter entered the 1970s as the dominant force in jazz. This was confirmed by the increasing radicalism of his music up to 1975, where a type of abstract brutalism kept concert audiences absorbed for hours. Davis's own trumpet style had changed very little after his mid-1960s rebirth.

The second half of the 1970s was a period of grave ill health for the trumpeter. He re-emerged in 1980 with a twin-guitar line-up and for the first half of the decade produced albums such as *Star People* and *Decoy.* In 1985 he came up with an instrumental treatment of Cyndi Lauper's "Time After Time." A switch of record labels (to Warner Bros) began with the bestselling *Tutu,* but his energies rapidly dispersed as the decade wore on. The rest of his career, seen in perspective, was a triumph of artistic will against encroaching physical infirmity. An appearance at the 1991 Montreux Festival was the last hurrah. He died that September.

fact file

BORN 1926

DIED 1991

MUSICAL SELECTION
Kind of Blue
Bitches Brew
Tutu

Miles Davis with members of his first great quintet, in 1955: bassist Paul Chambers and saxophonist John Coltrane

SEE ALSO: Louis Armstrong, Duke Ellington, Charlie Parker, Dizzy Gillespie, Gil Evans, Gerry Mulligan, Tadd Dameron, Sidney Bechet, John Coltrane

Wild Bill Davison

Wild Bill Davison favored this unique sideways approach to trumpet embouchure

fact file

BORN 1906

DIED 1989

MUSICAL SELECTION
Commodore Master Takes

Ohio-born Davison, from a musical family, was attracted to music young, playing banjo and mellophone in his high school band. Swapping to cornet, he first imitated Beiderbecke, but later developed a hard-hitting style. He recorded as an 18-year-old with the Chubb Steinberg Orchestra in 1924. Moving to Chicago in 1927, he gained freelance work in theater bands and began associating with the Condon crowd. In late 1931 he joined up with Frank Teschemacher to run a big band, but the saxophonist's death put paid to the venture. Moving to Milwaukee, Davison ran small groups for the rest of the decade, concentrating on the no-nonsense Dixieland style of the so-called Austin High School gang led by Condon. Davison cut his first 78 release in February 1940 in Chicago then later that year moved to New York, where he became a regular at Nick's. By 1943 he was sufficiently established for Commodore to use him as titular leader on a series of rampaging Dixieland sides featuring Pee Wee Russell, Condon, and the rest, and these forceful performances made his wider reputation. Army duty intervened from 1943 to 1945: on his return he played for a while with Art Hodes, then settled into a long residency with the house band at Condon's in Greenwich Village, taking periodic "vacations" to tour overseas and appear with other old colleagues. A move to the West Coast brought him more varied work and he became a regular with the Jazz Giants in this and the next decade. He worked as a solo in the 1980s, leading from the front as ever, up to his death in 1989.

SEE ALSO: Bix Beiderbecke, Frank Teschemacher, Eddie Condon, Pee Wee Russell

Buddy DeFranco

fact file

BORN 1923

MUSICAL SELECTION
With Art Tatum

Brilliant clarinettist Buddy DeFranco shone as a member of some of the top bands around in the 1940s, including Gene Krupa's and Tommy Dorsey's

DeFranco was born in Camden, New Jersey, into an Italian family with musical connections: his father was a piano tuner and music-lover. He started clarinet at the age of 12, winning an amateur competition in 1937 sponsored by Tommy Dorsey. Quickly working his way up, by 1941 he was a member of Gene Krupa's band, following this in 1943 with a stint in Charlie Barnet's (1943-44), then on to Tommy Dorsey between 1944 and 1946. With Dorsey he was arranging as well as playing clarinet and taking many solos. After his departure from the Dorsey band DeFranco attempted his own large group, but the timing was poor, and the bottom dropped out of the big-band business the following year. From then, DeFranco led various small groups as well as joining for short periods the small groups of Count Basie, Art Blakey, and Kenny Drew. During the early 1950s DeFranco also recorded prolifically for Norman Granz's labels and appeared at many Granz-organized concerts. He won many polls in the early 1950s as the most popular jazz clarinetist of the day. Settling in California in 1955, he dropped from view for the rest of the decade, but in 1960 launched a quartet featuring an accordion player, Tommy Gumina, and once again found considerable popularity. In 1966 he was appointed director of the official Glenn Miller orchestra, leading it until 1974 and raising its standards and profile. Since that time he has run his own small groups and toured widely. He has been a regular visitor to the studio, his fine technique, liquid tone and rhythmic drive quite unimpaired by the years. Still straddling swing and bop, DeFranco is the only living jazz clarinetist with a broad base of popular appeal.

SEE ALSO: Tommy Dorsey, Gene Krupa, Charlie Barnet, Count Basie, Art Blakey, Glenn Miller

Jack DeJohnette

fact file

BORN 1942

MUSICAL SELECTION
Album Album
Tin Can Alley

Drummer and band leader Jack DeJohnette, whose innate musicality enriches any group in which he appears

DeJohnette is one of the most naturally gifted of modern drummers, a man like Elvin Jones blessed with a natural ease of swing even when executing the most complex of polyrhythms. Born in Chicago, DeJohnette studied both piano and drums from early childhood, taking formal lessons on both instruments for a decade and graduating eventually from Chicago's American Conservatory of Music. In high school his main musical interests were contained by rock and blues, but during his teens he discovered jazz and became a quick convert, playing initially in piano trios and sitting in where he could, on one occasion even sharing the bandstand in Chicago with John Coltrane, a man noted for his willingness to let young players sit in with his Quartet. At the age of 24 he decided to make the move to New York, immediately picking up work with a range of players, from Jackie McLean to Big John Patton. However, the breakthrough in his career came with his joining Charles Lloyd in 1966. Lloyd's quartet, with pianist Keith Jarrett and bassist Ron McClure, was the first to broach the barriers between jazz and rock audiences, breaking through at the Fillmore West with its brand of melodic but highly colorful and rhythmic modern jazz. DeJohnette's role was vital, giving the most flexible support to the players in every mood and style, from cod blues to free-form expression. The band was an immense worldwide success, touring constantly until 1969, when the four members went their separate ways. DeJohnette joined Miles Davis, appearing on *Bitches Brew* and staying on until 1971. Since that time the drummer/pianist has run his own exciting and diverse small groups, often playing keyboards as well as drums, and appeared regularly with Keith Jarrett. He has also become one of the most ubiquitous sidemen, on the ECM label and elsewhere, his unmistakable rhythmic patterns enlivening many a disc. DeJohnette has made many records as a leader, with groups such as Special Edition featuring David Murray and others to a recent trio featuring pianist Michael Cain. He remains a key figure in contemporary jazz.

SEE ALSO: Elvin Jones, Jackie McLean, Big John Patton, Charles Lloyd, Keith Jarrett, Miles Davis, David Murray

Paul Desmond

fact file

BORN 1924

DIED 1977

MUSICAL SELECTION
"Audrey"
"Take Five"

Altoist and all-around wit Paul Desmond, a long-term member of Dave Brubeck's quartet

Desmond, a San Franciscan born into a middle-class Jewish family whose father had worked in the music business, studied clarinet while at San Francisco High and San Francisco State College, graduating to local bands after completing his studies and swapping to alto by the late 1940s. In 1948-49 he rehearsed and recorded with the Dave Brubeck Octet but didn't make the subsequent Brubeck trio into a quartet until 1951. The band's success, first local, then national, then international, brought Desmond a degree of the spotlight his generally retiring nature often seemed ill at ease with, but his unendingly melodic, often witty playing, using the most transparent and beautiful of alto sax tones, was the perfect foil for the very full Brubeck piano style. Desmond was also a considerable composer of tunes, contributing the delightful "Audrey" in 1954 (in honor of Audrey Hepburn) and "Take Five" in 1959, a song that brought the Brubeck Quartet massive popularity worldwide. Desmond, as a member, was also part of the unprecedented touring schedule which sustained the quartet's success, right up to its 1967 break-up.

During the Brubeck years Desmond had made the occasional album as a leader, most usually with guitarist Jim Hall as his foil, while his 1964 co-led album with Gerry Mulligan (as opposed to their late 1950s effort together) is one of his finest recorded efforts. Desmond also consistently won popularity polls for alto sax during these years. Once he was cut free from Brubeck the saxophonist led a low-profile professional career, running small groups for specific engagements and indulging in the occasional reunion with Brubeck. He also intended to get down to writing more seriously - a discipline he was also singularly gifted at, judging by the liner notes he wrote for his own records. But Desmond had little remaining time: a heavy drinker and a three-pack-a-day smoker, he succumbed to cancer in the late spring of 1977. More than just a talented sideman, Desmond brought a spark and joy to everything he played.

SEE ALSO: Dave Brubeck, Jim Hall, Gerry Mulligan

Vic Dickenson

Swing trombonist Vic Dickenson, possessor of one of the most conversational styles in jazz

fact file

BORN 1906

DIED 1984

MUSICAL SELECTION
Gentleman of the Trombone

Born in Xenia, Ohio, trombonist Dickenson was the possessor of a distinctly human tone on the instrument and used this to considerable advantage in his mature playing, incorporating many voicelike techniques which imparted to his music a rare degree of humor and conversationalism.

Dickenson had a natural ear for music and learned most of his theory from playing along with records - all the parts, not just the trombone. This alone pointed toward a trombone style immensely more sophisticated than those to be found for the most part in classic jazz. His early experiences were in local and territory bands around Ohio, Wisconsin, and Kansas City, including Benny Moten and Blanche Calloway, the latter up to 1936. From 1936 to 1939 he was a member of Claude Hopkins's band, then for a short time was in Benny Carter's orchestra. A short stay with Count Basie as the new decade began brought him wider recognition, but a period of illness while living out on the West Coast took him out of the business for a while. Back with Eddie Heywood in 1943-45, Dickenson finally headed back east at the war's end and freelanced extensively. He appeared in this time on Commodore record dates with Lester Young in the Kansas City Five, records which cemented his reputation as one of the great swing trombone stylists. For the rest of the decade and well into the 1950s Dickenson concentrated on work around the Boston area. It was in 1953 that he made perhaps his best records, for Vanguard and featuring Ruby Braff. Moving to New York toward the end of the 1950s Dickenson paired up for a time with Henry "Red" Allen and made records under his own name and appeared frequently later with George Wein's All-Stars as well as being a main attraction at Condon's. Dickenson thrived in the small-group context, the band he co-led with Bobby Hacket in the 1960s and 1970s showing him off ideally, although he did also appear with the World's Greatest Jazz Band during the latter decade. A favorite in Europe, he made a number of albums while on tour in the 1970s.

SEE ALSO: Benny Carter, Count Basie, Lester Young, "Red" Allen, Eddie Condon

Johnny Dodds

Innovative New Orleans clarinetist Johnny Dodds, pictured here in 1938

Dodds is a unique and instantly recognizable voice on the clarinet and possibly the most influential of the New Orleans players who came to attention at the very birth of jazz, in the teens. Born in Waverly, Louisiana, but from the first a New Orleans resident, he was part of a musical family (his younger brother, Warren "Baby" Dodds, 1898-1959, was the first great jazz drummer) and sang in the family quartet. He came to clarinet relatively late, at age 17, taking lessons from New Orleans professional Lorenzo Tio, but was playing full-time with Kid Ory by 1911 - a fast rise in a close musical community. Dodds remained a relatively spare player, his technique mostly self-taught. Ory and others, such as Frankie Dusen, provided his employment until he spent some time on the riverboats with Billy Mack around 1918. The following year Dodds returned briefly to Ory before striking out for Chicago, where in 1920 he joined the King Oliver outfit, then one of the hottest acts in the city. Dodds spent four years with Oliver, right through the period when Louis Armstrong came and went, touring and recording with Oliver.

Dodds left Oliver for similar reasons to those of Armstrong - the withholding of due pay. He ran his own bands - very professionally - in Chicago for the rest of the decade and was a constant presence on the scene, appearing on many of the best jazz records of the 1920s. Indeed, some are now regarded as certified jazz classics. His presence on the Armstrong Hot Fives and Sevens is an enlivening and contrasting one to the great trumpeter, his jovial, conversational, deeply bluesy style providing a perfect foil. A similar chemistry is notable with Jelly Roll Morton. Dodds recorded into the 1930s but suffered from the Depression and the change in public taste. Although a shrewd businessman away from music, he spent the 1930s in relative obscurity. He was in the midst of a comeback of sorts at the end of the decade, recording with Charlie Shavers and Natty Dominique, but his health failed and he died of a stroke in summer 1940.

fact file

BORN 1892

DIED 1940

MUSICAL SELECTION
South Side Chicago Jazz

SEE ALSO: Kid Ory, King Oliver, Louis Armstrong, Jelly Roll Morton

Eric Dolphy

fact file

BORN 1928

DIED 1964

MUSICAL SELECTION
Outward Bound
Far Cry
Conversations
Out To Lunch

Multi-instrumentalist (he was adept on alto, flute and bass clarinet, among other instruments) and innovator Eric Dolphy, seen here in 1958

Los Angelean Dolphy was a musician who, as the early 1960s avant-garde made inroads into the jazz audience, seemed most likely to provide a complete and compelling new vision of what the jazz tradition could transmute into. His early death, from complications brought on by undiagnosed diabetes, left his rich legacy to be developed by other musicians instead.

Dolphy, a multi-instrumentalist, began on clarinet while in high school. A serious music scholar all his life, he took a music course at Los Angeles City College and then joined the Roy Porter Big Band (1948-50), playing lead alto. His first records with the band date from 1949, and he can be heard dueling at length with altoist Leroy Robinson on "Sippin' With Cisco." After Army service Dolphy worked around LA with Gerald Wilson, Buddy Collette, and Eddie Beal, but his next step forward came with membership of the Chico Hamilton Quintet in 1958. Hamilton's so-called "chamber-jazz" was very fashionable in cool-conscious jazz circles of the time, and Dolphy became a nationally known sideman, playing in an updated bebop style on alto, flute and bass clarinet. He appeared at Newport 1958 with the band and can be seen in *Jazz on a Summer's Day*. In the winter of 1959/60 he settled in New York, coming into Charles Mingus's orbit by playing at the Showcase with Mingus's band. Becoming a permanent member, he stayed with Mingus until the fall of 1960, making a string of landmark small-group records with the bassist at this time and appearing at the 1960 Antibes Festival with him. He also signed to Prestige in spring 1960 and began making a series of meticulously prepared albums as leader for the label such as *Outward Bound*, *Out There* and *Far Cry*, the last of these made on the same day he participated spectacularly in Ornette Coleman's epochal *Free Jazz* session.

Dolphy freelanced intensely for the next three years, spending September 1961 to March 1962 in the John Coltrane Quintet and embarking on a spring 1964 European tour with Charles Mingus from which he did not return, dying in Berlin. During that same period he recorded and played with both Max Roach and Orchestra USA, and ran two bands of his own, the first with trumpeter Booker Little, the second featuring Herbie Hancock on piano. He also rehearsed intensely with bassist Richard Davis. Dolphy was a composer of considerable originality, as all his studio albums demonstrate, but his greatest impact was as an explosive and often humorous improviser, as can be heard on any of his Prestige albums, his 1963 record *Conversations* and his Blue Note classic of 1964, *Out To Lunch*.

SEE ALSO: Chico Hamilton, Charles Mingus, Ornette Coleman, John Coltrane, Max Roach, Booker Little

Lou Donaldson

The stalwart altoist and band leader Lou Donaldson

fact file

BORN 1926

MUSICAL SELECTION
Good Gracious!
Alligator Boogaloo
Blues Walk

North Carolina native Donaldson, an exact contemporary of Coltrane, took a rather different path to jazz fame. Initially an alto player heavily indebted like most of his generation to Charlie Parker, Donaldson was also steeped in the blues, and as jazz moved closer to rock and funk in the 1960s, Donaldson simplified his style down to the basic bluesy elements, thus enjoying considerable success for a period.

Donaldson grew up the son of a preacher who was also a music teacher, beginning his music studies on clarinet and progressing to alto sax by the time he left the navy. While in the navy he played in a band featuring Ernie Wilkins and Clark Terry. On his demob in 1950 he completed his music education and headed for New York, where he quickly became known in jazz circles. Recording with Milt Jackson and Thelonious Monk in 1952, Donaldson began to make wider circles that same year when he played and recorded with Horace Silver. He and Clifford Brown joined the Jazz Messengers in 1954, consolidating their nascent hard-bop style at the time. Soon after, he signed as a solo with Blue Note and made numerous albums with them over the next decade or so. At the same time, live work in the 1950s was scarce, and Donaldson often had to resort to R&B gigs to make ends meet. During the squeeze on jazz in the 1960s Donaldson opted for a more commercial approach, recording such pieces as "Alligator Boogaloo" and instrumental covers of top-ten funk and Motown hits. This did little for his jazz reputation, but by the late 1970s Donaldson had once again turned to his first love, bop. Since then he has moved consistently further back into the jazz mainstream and, in recent years, his tone more luminous than ever, he has been playing high-quality music both live and on record.

SEE ALSO: Charlie Parker, Milt Jackson, Thelonious Monk, Horace Silver, Clifford Brown, Art Blakey

Kenny Dorham

fact file

BORN 1924

DIED 1972

MUSICAL SELECTION
Una Mas

Trumpeter Kenny Dorham, with Conte Candoli looking on

Dorham, born McKinley Howard Dorham in Fairfield, Texas, was initially known as Kinny Dorham but through sheer pressure of convention accepted the change to Kenny when he began leading his own bands in the 1950s. He was a fine trumpeter, part of the second wave of bop brass players which followed in the footsteps of Gillespie and included Miles Davis and Fats Navarro. More lyrical in conception than Navarro and more boppish than the studied Davis, Dorham managed a degree of popularity but never gained the widespread recognition his talent deserved.

Dorham came from a musical family and learned piano as well as trumpet as a boy. He played in the high school band before going into the army, (1942-43), where he boxed as well as played music. On return to civilian life, he played with the Eckstine and Gillespie big bands before joining the Charlie Parker Quintet in the late 1940s, when the altoist was at a peak of expression. Dorham traveled to Paris to appear with Parker at the 1949 Paris Jazz Festival. Like so many others of this time Dorham battled with drug addiction for years, but in 1954 he appeared on the album Horace Silver and the Jazz Messengers, which was to prove formative for so much of what was to come in the hard bop scene later that decade. Dorham vacillated between the two styles, joining Max Roach after the death of Clifford Brown and making classic bop records as well as leading dates on Blue Note closer to hard bop in style. Dorham perhaps reached a peak in the early 1960s with a quintet including Joe Henderson. This band was extensively recorded. In the jazz downturn of the later 1960s Dorham was a loser, surfacing little after 1967, although for a short time he became a record reviewer for DownBeat magazine, contributing some of the most amusing and incisive reviews of the mid-1960s. His health deteriorating, he became progressively less involved in the scene, dying of kidney failure in 1972.

SEE ALSO: Dizzy Gillespie, Miles Davis, Fats Navarro, Billy Eckstine, Charlie Parker, Horace Silver, Art Blakey

Billy Eckstine

fact file

BORN 1914

DIED 1993

MUSICAL SELECTION
Imagination

Singer Billy Eckstine, seen here performing at Carnegie Hall in 1952

Eckstine was a brilliant and influential bass baritone with a gorgeous dark tone and lazy vibrato way on a ballad, but he was also a gifted instrumentalist with discerning taste to the point where in 1944 he formed the first and possibly the greatest bebop big band of all.

Eckstine was born in Pittsburgh but educated in Washington, DC, latterly at Howard University. After this he worked as a singer and emcee in Buffalo nightclubs, gaining experience, then through the good offices of saxophonist Budd Johnson he was hired as the male vocalist for Earl Hines in 1939. He stayed with Hines until 1943, during which time he became a singer of renown and landed hits such as "Stormy Monday" and "Jelly Jelly" for the Hines band. Leaving Hines, Eckstine, now also a competent trumpeter, formed his own big band in 1944, filling it with the new young players he had tried to get into Hines's outfit, using Budd Johnson as musical director. Musicians passing through this band included Sonny Stitt, Gene Ammons, Dexter Gordon, Leo Parker, Kenny Dorham, Fats Navarro, Art Blakey, Miles Davis and Cecil Payne. The band was a commercial flop, but its music is now looked upon as some of the best of the time.

After breaking the band up in 1947, Eckstine went out as a solo, scoring countless hits in a balladeering style, largely abandoning a core jazz approach by the early 1950s. Eckstine's records fell from favor as the country's mood shifted in the early 1950s, but he remained a strong live act, supported by pianist Bobby Tucker. In the late 1950s and early 1960s he occasionally returned to a jazz setting, including standout sessions with Count Basie and Quincy Jones. His last decades were spent mostly on successful nightclub engagements and on the nostalgia circuit, although his musical standards never slipped.

SEE ALSO: Budd Johnson, Earl Hines, Gene Ammons, Dexter Gordon, Leo Parker, Kenny Dorham, Fats Navarro

Tommy Dorsey

Hard-drinking and irascible, Dorsey produced one of the sweetest and most liquid legato trombone styles of all time. A product of the Dixieland era of jazz, he became one of the biggest and longest-lived big-band stars of the swing era, even holding down a television show up until the time of his death. The stories concerning Dorsey and his band leadership style are legendary in jazz circles, but he was also capable of acts of great generosity toward fellow musicians.

Dorsey was the younger brother of Jimmy Dorsey, the reed player who also ran a successful swing-style band in the 1930s and 1940s and with whom he twice ran a dual-leadership band. Tommy was born in Shenandoah, Pennsylvania, and studied music with his part-time musician father. He and Jimmy co-led in the early 1920s Dorsey's Wild Canaries and Dorsey's Novelty Six, Tommy playing both trumpet and trombone at this stage. He and Jimmy became ubiquitous in New York session work as well as working at various times with Jean Goldkette and Paul Whiteman. Jimmy, although hardly an improviser of stature, was a consummate technician whose style influenced many later players, including Lester Young. Tommy was equally held in awe for his trombone technique. They enjoyed a hit record leading the Dorsey Brothers band with Tommy's feature, "I'm Getting Sentimental Over You," but in 1935 a fistfight on stage between the brothers led to Tommy stalking out of the theater and out of the band. He set up his own outfit in competition, succeeding admirably for close to 20 years, providing hit after hit (including the awful pastiche "Boogie Woogie" in 1938) in his inimitable style and even running a Dixieland-style small group within the larger band, the Clambake Seven, which enjoyed a hit with "The Music Goes Round and Round." Dorsey hired the singer Frank Sinatra in 1940: eventually the singer was more popular than the band and was allowed to go out solo. Dorsey remained highly popular through the 1940s - there was a Hollywood biopic in 1947, *The Fabulous Dorseys*, telling the usual half-truths about the two men's climb to fame and fortune. By 1953 the skids were under the big band business and Tommy once more joined forces with Jimmy to co-lead a band. They landed a TV show which Charlie Parker was watching the night he died in 1955 and which ran up until Tommy's death, in 1956, choking in his sleep on undigested food. Jimmy died the following year after a long illness.

fact file

BORN 1905

DIED 1956

MUSICAL SELECTION
"I'm Getting Sentimental Over You"

Bandleader Tommy Dorsey is credited with having the smoothest legato of all trombonists

SEE ALSO: Lester Young, Charlie Parker

Harry "Sweets" Edison

Trumpeter Harry "Sweets" Edison, seen here in mid-solo

fact file

BORN 1915

MUSICAL SELECTION
Blues For Basie

Edison is one of the great swing trumpet stylists, forming a highly characteristic trumpet language early in his career and largely sticking with it ever since. The durability of that early model is in the fact that, today, he is still capable, in his 80s, of thrilling a crowd of thousands with his playing.

Edison was born in Columbus, Ohio, of Native American mother and black father, though he spent his early years in Kentucky. He came to jazz through hearing Louis Armstrong on Bessie Smith records in the 1920s; moving back to Columbus as a teenager, he gained early experience playing in local groups. After work with some territory bands, followed by stints with Alphonso Trent and Lucky Millinder, Edison joined Count Basie in New York in 1937. His trumpet became an important part of the post-Kansas City Basie sound and he gradually earned star status within the band. He appeared in the famous Gjon Mili short *Jammin' The Blues* in 1944. He stayed with Basie until the demise of the first Basie band in 1950; after that he freelanced successfully across a large range of activities, touring with JATP and recording regularly for Verve, both as leader (most memorably with Ben Webster) and sideman (with his old friend Lester Young). During this same decade he became an in-demand West Coast session man (most notably with Frank Sinatra). This continued through the 1960s and Edison was seen by the jazz world mostly at festivals. In his latter years Edison has returned more vigorously to live playing, both in clubs and on tours to the various festivals of the world. He often appeared with Eddie "Lockjaw" Davis in the 1980s and most recently (1997) has been straw boss of a touring aggregation including Flip Phillips and Harold Land. His on-stage personality still communicates as readily as his warm and engaging trumpet playing.

SEE ALSO: Louis Armstrong, Lucky Millinder, Count Basie, Ben Webster, Lester Young, Eddie "Lockjaw" Davis

Roy Eldridge

fact file

BORN 1911

DIED 1989

MUSICAL SELECTION
Little Jazz
The Verve years

Roy "Little Jazz" Eldridge, fieriest of all jazz trumpeters, pictured here in performing action in 1945

It is often stated that Roy Eldridge is the trumpeting link between Louis Armstrong and Dizzy Gillespie, providing the stylistic and emotional background for Gillespie to nurture into the mature bebop style. Apart from this approach being a tacit put-down of Eldridge's own swing-style trumpeting achievements (as if classic jazz and bop were somehow intrinsically superior to swing), it puts Eldridge in a false position. Eldridge was just six years older than Gillespie but of a completely different generation than Armstrong. Unlike both Armstrong and Gillespie, he was also not an innovator: his only advance in trumpet terms was to play harder, higher, and more passionately than previous musicians. This is not to denigrate his artistic achievements, but to give them their proper form. After all, J. S. Bach was not an innovator either.

Eldridge was born in Pittsburgh and was taught the rudiments of music by his older brother, saxophonist Joe Eldridge. He started out as a six-year-old on drums, but when his professional career started in 1927 he was on trumpet and exhibiting the influence of the first great tenor saxophonist, Coleman Hawkins, whose recordings were already widely heard and whose arpeggio'd approach to improvising proved the basis of Eldridge's style. After a short spell with Fletcher Henderson (Hawkins's band) in the late 1920s he arrived in New York in 1930, finally landing a job with Teddy Hill in 1933. Leaving Hill the following year to work with his brother away from NYC, he returned to New York and Hill in 1935, recording his first sides with the band the same year. His exciting playing quickly drew praise and attention, and he made a regal procession through a number of top swing bands, including Fletcher Henderson in 1936-37, where he met "Chu" Berry. By 1939 he was leading his own band and had a recording contract, but his move to Gene Krupa's band in 1941 gave him unprecedented exposure. The two years with Krupa made him hot property, raising him to the status of hot-trumpet king. As such he went to Artie Shaw's band in 1944, but found the constant racism of many audience members too much after a year. He left and formed his own band again. Engulfed, as were other swing giants, by bebop, the combative Eldridge continued to give as good as he got, but it was Norman Granz, in the shape of JATP and records, who saved his career in the 1950s. With Granz he toured widely, even to Europe and Japan, and often played with his old inspiration, Coleman Hawkins. He was also embraced eagerly by European fans not interested in internecine wars between jazz generations. Eldridge continued to appear and record with players from his generation, including Hawkins, Johnny Hodges and Earl Hines. He also struck up a considerable friendship with Dizzy Gillespie, and the pair often performed and recorded together. By the 1970s Eldridge's style had ossified, but he was as exciting as ever on a good night, and his residency at Ryan's in New York, where he led a traditional jazz band, was never devoid of interest in its decade of presiding. Eldridge returned to the Granz fold in the last two decades of his life, touring worldwide and appearing on numerous Pablo records.

SEE ALSO: Louis Armstrong, Dizzy Gillespie, Coleman Hawkins, Fletcher Henderson, "Chu" Berry, Gene Krupa

Duke Ellington

Edward Kennedy Ellington, born in Washington, DC, known as "Duke" due to his love of elegance, has long been recognized as the most protean creative figure in the first five decades of jazz. As Miles Davis once commented, "Everybody ought to get down on their knees one day and thank Duke." Other players have been as brilliant, innovative, and occasionally influential in any given decade – Davis, Armstrong, Parker, Coltrane – and certainly these players were all greater improvisers than Ellington. But his total achievement consistently evolving from the 1920s to the 1970s cannot be gainsaid.

Ellington grew up in a close family, part of the capital's black middle class. He studied art and music while at Armstrong High and took private lessons as well as watching pianists playing around town. By 1918 he was running small bands for dances and parties, the same year he married Edna Thompson. Some of the members of his first great band were already colleagues, including Sonny Greer, Arthur Whetsol, and Otto Hardwicke. After a shaky start, Ellington and his friends settled in New York in spring 1923, calling themselves the Washingtonians. They hustled some club work before landing a residency at the Hollywood Club. By 1926 Harry Carney, Fred Guy, Joe Nanton, and Bubber Miley were members; the following year the band recorded classics such as "East St Louis Toodle-Oo" and "Black & Tan Fantasy," with "The Mooche" following in 1928. That same year saw the arrival of Johnny Hodges and Cootie Williams and a full year of employment at the Cotton Club, whose radio link gave Ellington wider exposure. In 1930 he enjoyed his first big hit with "Mood Indigo." By the time Ellington left the Cotton Club in 1933 and made his first triumphant European tour, he was already a star.

Ellington prospered through the 1930s, touring across America, making movie shorts and writing hits such as "Solitude" and "Sophisticated Lady" and innovative extended works such as "Diminuendo and Crescendo In Blue." In 1939 composer/arranger Billy Strayhorn came aboard, bringing with him "Take The 'A' Train." Other new recruits included bassist Jimmy Blanton and sax man Ben Webster. Some feel that the opening years of the 1940s were the peak of Duke's creative development. Small masterpieces like "Concerto for Cootie," "Ko-Ko," "Bojangles," "Sepia Panorama," and "Harlem Airshaft" and the first of his suites, *Black, Brown and Beige*, a 50-minute work premiered at Carnegie Hall in early 1943, are prime examples. Ellington kept up annual Carnegie Hall concerts where he would premiere a new major work until the end of the decade. Ellington's was one of very few orchestras not to disband during the difficult 1947-50 period. His innovatory role had also been usurped by bebop. The band was increasingly subsidized by Ellington's songwriting royalties.

Like Miles Davis, Ellington may have been tempted to claim after his 1956 triumph at the Newport Jazz Festival, "I've never been away." *Such Sweet Thunder*, *The Newport Suite*, *The Queen's Suite*, and *The Nutcracker* demonstrate his renewed ambition. He was also part of Ella Fitzgerald's *Song Book* series. The early 1960s saw big-band recordings with Louis Armstrong, Count Basie, and Coleman Hawkins; John Coltrane, Charles Mingus and Max Roach appeared in two small-group sessions. Ellington also collaborated with Frank Sinatra. His own work was uneven, *The Far East Suite* of 1967 being a standout; his *New Orleans Suite* of 1969-70 was the last major success. Ellington also mounted three Sacred Concerts in this period, before succumbing to cancer in 1974.

fact file

BORN 1899

DIED 1974

MUSICAL SELECTION
Black, Brown and Beige
Such Sweet Thunder
The Far East Suite

Duke Ellington, a jazz icon, pictured here with His Famous Orchestra in 1942

SEE ALSO: Miles Davis, Louis Armstrong, Charlie Parker, John Coltrane, Johnny Hodges, Billy Strayhorn, Jimmy Blanton, Ben Webster, Ella Fitzgerald

Don Ellis

fact file

BORN 1934

DIED 1978

MUSICAL SELECTION
How Time Passes
Electric Bath

Trumpeter and band leader Don Ellis was renowned for his challenging approach to jazz composition and arrangement and his acerbic wit

Trumpeter Don Ellis, a Los Angelean with a formidable intellect who arrived in New York in 1961, rapidly became a controversial figure in early 1960s jazz, both for the provocative music he produced, which often contained many ideas taken over from contemporary classical music, and for his trenchant observations on other musicians and what he perceived as their limitations.

Ellis's mother was a church organist and he came to music early, running his own dance bands in his early teens. Exceptionally well trained for a jazz musician of this period (he gained a BM in composition from Boston University in 1956), Ellis had a year with Ray McKinley before his two years in the army in 1957-58, re-emerging to join first Charlie Barnet and then Maynard Ferguson. After his move to New York he played and recorded with George Russell's Sextet before recording *How Time Passes* for Candid, touring in Europe and in 1963 launching the Hindustani Jazz Sextet, a short-lived group combining a number of Ellis's interests, including Eastern music and the use of quarter-tones in jazz. This latter study eventually led him to evolve a new type of trumpet, incorporating a fourth valve, which allowed him to play quarter-tones in the general run of normal improvisation. A 1964 big band also failed to last beyond the year.

After a period in the mid-1960s when he was involved in music education, Ellis had a second stab at running a large band, this time from Los Angeles. Using a large personnel, with augmented brass and percussion sections, Ellis showed intense interest in the use of complex and novel meters (13/8, 32/8 and the relatively "normal" 7/4) and rhythms, including rock beats, the augmentation of acoustic sound by electronic means, and further explorations of harmonic theory deemed exotic at the time in jazz circles. Contrary to expectations, the band was a hit, especially with festival audiences the world over, and its records sold well, especially *Electric Bath* (Columbia, 1967). Ellis was perceived as one of the men of the moment as the 1960s drew to a close, the excitement of his music for a time masking the low emotional quotient which many observers commented upon. He turned to composing for films, winning awards for his soundtrack to *The French Connection* in 1972, while his pace on the road did not slacken in the early 1970s. A heart attack in 1975 gave him pause for thought, a full return to his lapsed career not possible until 1978. Unfortunately, Ellis's heart was not the equal of his music commitments, and a second attack brought about his death at the close of the year.

SEE ALSO: Charles Barnet, Maynard Ferguson, George Russell

Booker Ervin

fact file

BORN 1930

DIED 1970

MUSICAL SELECTION
That's It
The Freedom Book
The Space Book

Texas saxophonist Booker Ervin worked with such jazz greats as Charlie Mingus during his career

Ervin was a modern-day Texas tenor (born in Denison) who was possessed of a remarkably individual tone and approach and played with some of the best talent of his generation, including Charles Mingus. He received vastly less than was his due of economic and professional recognition, however.

Son of a swing trombonist, Booker began his music studies on that instrument, swapping to tenor sax at the age of 20 while serving in the US Air Force in 1950-53. A Berklee Student for two years after returning to civilian life, Ervin first recorded in an R&B setting in the mid-1950s before roaming the United States and finally settling in New York in 1958. Coming to the attention of Charles Mingus, Ervin worked with the bassist in spurts between then and 1963, appearing on a succession of landmark Mingus albums and appearing with him both in the US and overseas: he is featured on the 1960 Mingus small-group date recorded live at Antibes Jazz Festival, alongside Eric Dolphy and Ted Curson. Ervin's direct, heartfelt playing and harmonic sophistication brought him critical acclaim and contracts, initially with Candid (*That's It*, 1960), then with Prestige, who between 1963 and 1969 made a series of small-group classics with him, often featuring the rhythm team of Jaki Byard, Richard Davis, and Alan Dawson. This line-up is featured on *The Freedom Book* (1963) and *The Space Book* (1964). Ervin also made a spectacular head-to-head recording with Dexter Gordon in Germany in 1965.

Despite all this and membership of other bands, such as that of Randy Weston, Ervin failed to make a substantial impact on the public, possibly because his playing was not in the tradition of either Rollins or Coltrane, the twin fountainheads of 1960s tenor style, but he was not a sufficiently charismatic personality to put over his music to a wider public. Thus, up until his death, he remained a minor cult figure, fervently appreciated by his devotees and admired by other musicians, but sadly lacking in work opportunities. He died in 1970 of kidney failure.

SEE ALSO: Charles Mingus, Eric Dolphy, Jaki Byard, Dexter Gordon, Sonny Rollins, John Coltrane

Kevin Eubanks

Guitarist and composer Kevin Eubanks, a consummate jazz player effortlessly combining tradition and innovation

fact file

BORN 1957

MUSICAL SELECTION
Guitarist
Spirit Talk

Eubanks grew up in Philadelphia with music all around him at home, his mother being a composer and a D.Mus. Her favorite music was gospel and baroque, while her brothers (and Eubanks's uncles) were pianist Ray and bassist Tommy Bryant. His older brother, Robin, was to become a successful jazz trombonist. Kevin chose the guitar while young and attended Berklee, running a jazz-rock band at the time while under the influence of John McLaughlin's Mahavishnu adventures. Toward the latter 1970s Eubanks listened further, becoming a Wes Montgomery admirer; he also began traveling, appearing in Europe with Chris Hinze in 1978. By 1980 he had joined Art Blakey, spending two years with the drummer and touring widely, establishing a strong reputation among the drummer's fans.

After leaving Blakey and playing with, among others, Sam Rivers and Mike Gibbs, Eubanks debuted on records as a leader with *Guitarist* (Elektra/Musician), an album presenting him on acoustic and electric guitars. From that time on he was a regular recording artist, also appearing with a string of top players, including Chico Freeman, Dave Holland, and Slide Hampton. A switch to GRP records launched a series of fusion records which sold respectably but were uniformly mundane. A switch of labels to Blue Note at the dawn of the 1990s led to much more meaty fare: with *Spirit Talk* (Blue Note, 1993), Eubanks hit his stride as a mature composer, arranger, and guitarist with a fine, flowing amalgam of written and improvised music. Eubanks continues to perform and record worldwide in a multitude of contexts.

SEE ALSO: John McLaughlin, Wes Montgomery, Art Blakey, Chico Freeman, Dave Holland

Gil Evans

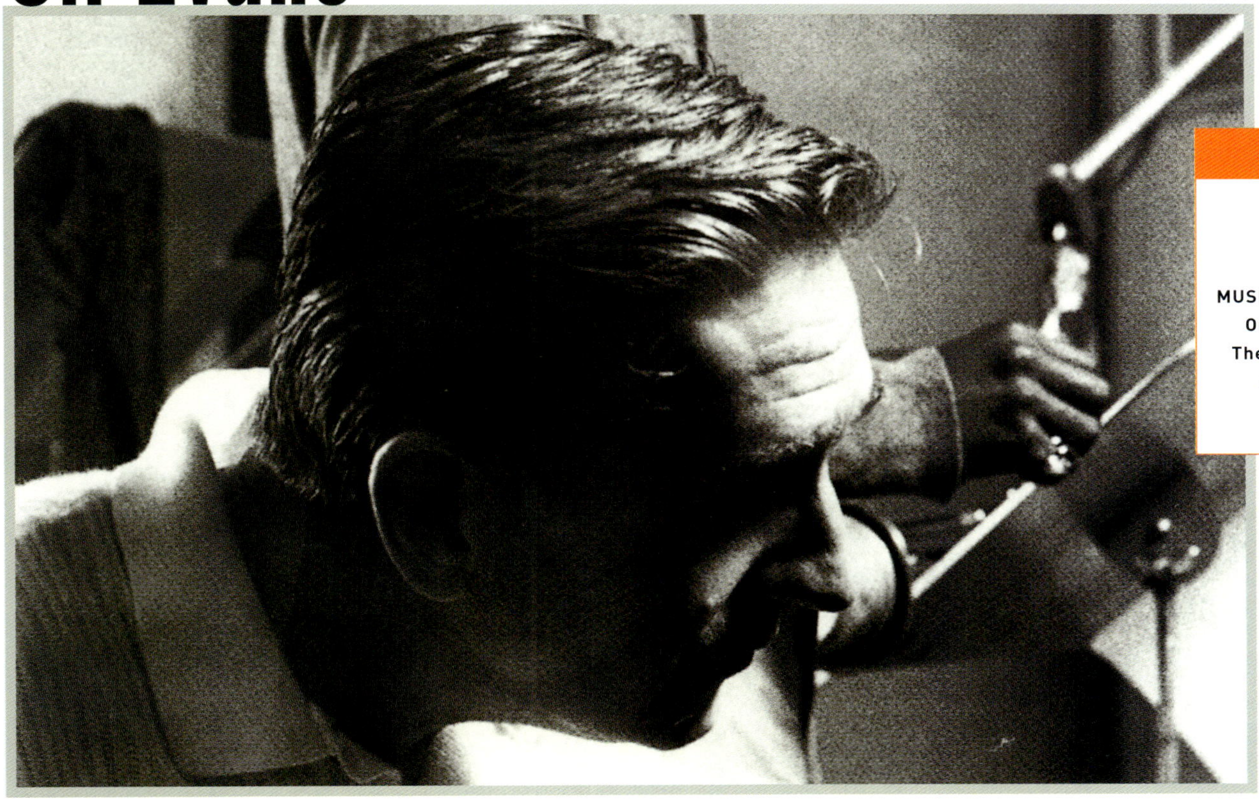

fact file

BORN 1912

DIED 1988

MUSICAL SELECTION
Out of the Cool
The Individualism of Gil Evans

Arranger and composer Gil Evans, pictured here during his famous 1950s collaborations with Miles Davis

Evans has often been described as a type of orchestral Svengali, conjuring quasi-mystical sounds from large jazz ensembles to provide the perfect musical backdrop for soloists such as Miles Davis and singer Helen Merrill. He was certainly a perfect foil for such people, but he also engaged in a restless exploration of the possibilities inherent in his field of orchestral arrangement and composition, later in his career being happy to include a variety of electronic instruments in his unique array of sounds.

Evans was born in Toronto of Australian parents, moving around a lot as a young man and landing eventually in Stockton, California, where as a self-taught musician he led his own band, in 1933-38. The band was taken over then by Skinnay Ellis, and Evans stayed on as arranger until he left for Claude Thornhill's band in 1941. Army service (1943-46) aside, Evans stayed with Thornhill until 1948, absorbing Thornhill's requirements for a "floating," evanescent sound typified by his big hit and theme tune "Snowfall." This encouraged Evans's adventurous mind and brilliant orchestral ear, and the arranger began incorporating unusual instrumental combinations into standard band arrangements, making a name for himself and becoming something of a guru for the younger generation of arranger/composers in the late 1940s such as Gerry Mulligan and John Carisi. These, with Miles Davis and John Lewis, pooled their ideas and launched the short-lived but tremendously vibrant "tuba band" which made the Birth of the Cool album in 1948-50 and helped launch "cool" jazz. Evans dropped out of the jazz spotlight then until the mid-1950s, when Helen Merrill insisted on having him to arrange the music on her album, *Dream of You* (EmArcy, 1956). The beautiful, strange, and lush arrangements of standard songs there led to his work for Miles Davis on *Miles Ahead* (Columbia, 1957) and, later, *Porgy and Bess* (1958) and *Sketches of Spain* (1959). By the time this triptych had been completed Evans was a major jazz personality credited with some of the most profound jazz writing ever. His public work with Davis stuttered to an inconclusive end in 1962 with the Brazilian-influenced *Quiet Nights*, but he produced his best solo efforts in the first years of the 1960s with *Out of the Cool* (Impulse!, 1961) and *The Individualism of Gil Evans* (Verve, 1963). Both these albums reflected in part his fascination with the German composer Kurt Weill. The latter part of the 1960s found him composing and also arranging albums for various people, including Astrud Gilberto.

He turned down the opportunity to arrange Laura Nyro's *New York Tendaberry* in 1968, but had agreed to make an album with Jimi Hendrix just weeks prior to the guitarist's death. Evans began a new phase in his career in 1970 when he appeared regularly at New York's Village Vanguard with his own big band, sporting a personnel which, though constantly changing, was looked upon as one of the great jazz experiences by the players involved. Evans's albums of the 1970s are uneven, the studio dates often dominated by fierce percussion and a newly strident note in his writing, the live dates (many taken from concert tapes) featuring long, rambling solos with a minimal Evans involvement. He toured assiduously when finances permitted, remaining active up to his death in 1988.

SEE ALSO: Miles Davis, Helen Merrill, Gerry Mulligan, John Lewis

Bill Evans

Evans is possibly the most influential of post-bop pianists, his choice of harmonies, his lyricism and his economy of means providing the role model for literally thousands of subsequent pianists. His direct influence on younger men such as Herbie Hancock, Keith Jarrett, and Chick Corea has extended his influence indirectly into every aspect of the contemporary jazz scene, while many of today's players also continue to turn to his copious recorded output for unalloyed inspiration.

Evans was born in Plainfield, New Jersey; he studied piano, violin, and flute from adolescence onward, reaching the point where he could start joining bands for local dances and gigs, meeting brass player Don Elliott at this point. His interest in music was broad from the beginning, embracing many modern classical figures as well as jazz history. Later he studied at Southwestern Louisiana College, gaining a B.Mus there and playing privately with local jazz musicians and with the Herbie Fields Band in 1950. Three years in the army kept him away from the scene, but coming out in 1954 he played for a time with Jerry Wald before deciding to complete his music studies in New York. In 1956 Evans, now sure he was ready, joined Tony Scott's group and debuted as a record leader in September 1956 with *New Jazz Conceptions* (Riverside). After the impact of that album and his live work, Evans quickly became one of the busiest pianists in New York, playing for a succession of leading men including Charles Mingus and George Russell and appearing on various all-star sessions. This attracted the attention of Miles Davis, who persuaded Evans into his band in February 1958. The pianist stayed only until November that year, but his musical thinking and his spare approach to accompaniment made a huge impact on Davis's own music, leading to the classic March 1959 so-called "modal" recording, *Kind of Blue*, for which Evans returned to the band, penning some of the songs as well.

Once away from Davis, Evans freelanced for a while before forming his own trio, comprising bassist Scott LaFaro and drummer Paul Motian. In this time he also appeared on the classic modern jazz album, Oliver Nelson's *Blues and the Abstract Truth*. In the less than two years the trio existed it created a body of music both impressive in its own right and tremendously influential on all other piano trios. Two studio albums and two live albums resulted before LaFaro's death in a car accident in summer 1961. Evans took a year to recover and find the will to resume working in a trio. He changed record labels in 1963, recording prolifically for Verve up to 1970 and winning several Grammys, the first for his multi-tracked solo effort, *Conversations With Myself* (1963). Evans's style, relying on ingenious harmonic substitutions, spare use of the left hand, and elegant melodic variation, changed little after this point, although he presented himself in many different contexts, from symphony orchestra to solo to duets with Jim Hall. His later trios, with a succession of fine bassists and drummers, featured players such as Eddie Gomez, Marc Johnson, Gary Peacock, and Chuck Israels on bass, Jack DeJohnette, Larry Bunker, and Marty Morell on drums. Evans, for many years troubled by a crippling drug habit, managed to live a more balanced life during the 1970s, but the damage to his constitution had already been done. He died in 1980 from heart failure.

fact file

BORN 1929

DIED 1980

MUSICAL SELECTION
New Jazz Conceptions
Conversations With Myself

Bill Evans, the greatest single influence on contemporary jazz piano

SEE ALSO: Herbie Hancock, Keith Jarrett, Chick Corea, Charles Mingus, George Russell, Miles Davis, Scott LaFaro, Paul Motian, Oliver Nelson, Jim Hall

Art Farmer

fact file

BORN 1928

MUSICAL SELECTION
Listen To Art Farmer
Modern Art

Art Farmer blowing his horn in July 1995

Iowa-born Farmer was raised in the jazz-rich town of Phoenix, Arizona, along with his twin brother, bassist Addison Farmer. From a musical family, he studied violin and piano before swapping to the brass family and moving to Los Angeles in 1945 at the age of 18. By this time a trumpeter, Farmer played with the legendary Johnny Otis band and traveled to New York with them, though he returned to LA in 1948, playing with resident LA big bands such as Benny Carter, Wardell Gray, and Lionel Hampton. He went with Hampton on the same European tour in 1953 as Clifford Brown and Quincy Jones, coming back to settle in NYC the same year, where he played with Teddy Charles briefly.

After this Farmer settled into Gigi Gryce's quintet, making it a co-led group until his drafting into the Horace Silver group in 1956. By this time his mature style was formed, his careful melodic statements and beautifully proportioned solos being a trademark as much as his rich, mellow sound. Farmer diversified into flugelhorn around this time, playing it and trumpet when with Gerry Mulligan in 1958, during which time he played the Newport Jazz Festival, made a classic date *What Is There To Say?* (Columbia, 1958) and two film soundtracks, *I Want To Live* and *The Subterraneans*. At the end of the year he formed the Jazztet with Benny Golson, combining his leadership and improvisatory talents with Golson's gifts for composition and arrangement. The Jazztet enjoyed limited success, skirting with the soul-jazz made popular by Horace Silver, Cannonball Adderley, and others, but their main ingredient was updated bop. The group broke up in 1962 and Farmer formed a quartet with Jim Hall which lasted until 1964. Later in the 1960s, with jazz on its knees in the US as rock took over, Farmer moved to Europe, where he swapped between leading his own groups and guesting with various big bands, including the Clarke-Boland Big Band. He has since spent his time between continents, with a re-formation of the Jazztet in 1982 leading to a number of successful albums. Since then Farmer has returned to leading his own bands, splitting his time between Europe and the US, playing his own invention, the flumpet – a unique cross between a flugelhorn and a trumpet.

SEE ALSO: Benny Carter, Wardell Gray, Lionel Hampton, Clifford Brown, Quincy Jones, Horace Silver, Gerry Mulligan

Maynard Ferguson

Canadian-born jazz great Maynard Ferguson, hitting a peak in mid-performance

fact file

BORN 1928

MUSICAL SELECTION
A Message From Newport

Born in Verdun, Canada, in the same year as Art Farmer was born in Iowa, Ferguson was to become the high-note specialist for a string of bands, culminating in his 1950s stint with Stan Kenton and his own rowdy but enjoyable big bands, which he has led on and off ever since.

Ferguson took to music early, studying eventually at the French Conservatoire of Music in Montreal. Before leaving for the US, he led his own young band in Canada between 1943 and 1947; after this he tried New York for a while, where he worked initially with Boyd Raeburn in 1948, but it was not until 1949 that he moved permanently to the US, joining Charlie Barnet that year and revealing his incredible trumpet virtuosity for the first time. This led to his being taken on by Stan Kenton, never a man to ignore the possibilities of high trumpet parts in his writing, where Ferguson became a talking point for audiences and other musicians alike as his hair-raising screaming trumpet leads became a stock part of many Kenton arrangements and compositions. Ferguson left Kenton in 1953, burying himself in LA studio work of all descriptions, including a jam session on EmArcy led nominally by Dinah Washington and including Clifford Brown. Ferguson began to miss the excitement of the big bands; this led to his forming his own after a brief experience leading the Birdland Dream Band in 1956.

As the 1950s gave way to the 1960s Ferguson gradually worked the more excessive lapses of musical taste out of his system and his bands became popular and swinging units, not afraid of displaying awesome technique and formidable power, but also capable of playing charts with panache and taste. During the 1970s he effortlessly adapted to the prevailing tastes, using rock beats where appropriate; in more recent years he has returned to his first love, the style of modified mainstream music which gave him fame to begin with. Now a long-standing bandleader and a consistent draw live, he continues to record and direct his band from the front, as always.

SEE ALSO: Stan Kenton, Boyd Raeburn, Charlie Barnet, Dinah Washington, Clifford Brown

JAZZ SINGER: 1917–1996

Ella Fitzgerald

Fitzgerald, born in Newport News, Virginia, was an orphan as a child, and endured hardships before being discovered in 1934 at Amateur Night in Harlem's Apollo Theater. Within a short time she became the singer with Chick Webb's band, then a fixed asset of the Savoy Ballroom, her sweet, young voice and good intonation setting her apart from most of her "canary" contemporaries. She and Webb enjoyed a major hit in 1938 with the upbeat arrangement of a nursery rhyme, "A-Tisket, A-Tasket," but within a year Webb was dead from tuberculosis and Fitzgerald was installed as director.

This was not a situation built to last: within a year the band had become her orchestra, then two years after that she disbanded and went out with a trio. Continuing on from her time with Webb, she maintained a long association with American Decca through Milt Gabler, making many hits for the label and becoming the number-one female jazz vocalist long before the end of World War II. By this time her characteristic timbre and smoothness of phrasing had become pronounced, as well as her general buoyancy of approach: in the later 1940s she landed major hits with her scat versions of two standards, "Lady Be Good" and "How High The Moon," and was seen by millions of people on stage with the JATP package tours organized by Norman Granz, which by the end of the decade were the biggest live attraction in jazz. In 1948 she married the bassist Ray Brown, though the relationship foundered in 1952. Fitzgerald stuck with Decca until 1956, though the artistic steam had run out of the relationship some years before and Granz was itching to get her on his own label. After protracted negotiations the deal was done and Granz immediately embarked on the series of *Song Books*, each "book" containing the greatest songs by an individual composer, which were kept in motion until the mid-1960s. Composers such as Porter, Kern, Rodgers, Gershwin, Ellington, Arlen, Berlin, and Mercer were all addressed with Ella in front of a big band (in the case of Ellington, it was the Ellington band itself, plus a small group featuring Ben Webster). The project was one of the grandest ever seen in jazz and is still a milestone in jazz history: Ella's consistency of performance is staggering to behold.

Fitzgerald made two classic small-group duet records with Louis Armstrong, plus an orchestral album with him reworking *Porgy and Bess*. She made every conceivable type of jazz record in every conceivable setting, and even made albums with string orchestra backing. Her live albums were every bit as exciting as her studio ones, with *Ella In Berlin* (Verve, 1960) winning many awards on its initial release. By this time Granz and Verve were content to release albums by her without her name on the cover – just her picture. Everybody knew who she was: hers was one of the most famous voices in music history, as were her face and her smile. During the 1960s Fitzgerald continued to perform at her peak, though suffering some personal sadness during the decade: she recorded again with Ellington, both live in Europe and in the studio; she made an album with Basie, and many others with her own groups. Fitzgerald continued to pursue a hectic professional life, loved by all she came into contact with in the music business and the recipient of countless awards, up to the last handful of years of her life, when serious illness confined her to home for long periods. She never sang music in bad taste and never compromised her own musical standards, and the consistent beauty and humanity she endowed even the tritest of lyrics with raises her art to a level inhabited by few singers of any genre or any era.

SEE ALSO: Chick Webb, Ray Brown, Duke Ellington, Ben Webster, Louis Armstrong

fact file

BORN 1917

DIED 1996

MUSICAL SELECTION
Song Books
Ella in Berlin

With the passing of jazz singer, Ella Fitzgerald, the world lost a distinct and very popular jazz voice

George "Pops" Foster

George "Pops" Foster, pictured here in 1934, was given his nickname not for his patronly demeanor but for his "popped" style of bass playing

fact file

BORN 1892

DIED 1969

MUSICAL SELECTION
The Legendary Bechet

Born George Foster on a plantation near McCall, Louisiana, at no great distance north of New Orleans, "Pops" Foster came from a musical family (his older brother Willie was a well-known violin, banjo, and guitar player who later played on the riverboats and with King Oliver, among others) which resettled in New Orleans in 1902. Foster initially played the cello and performed with a family trio including his brother and sister. By 1905 he'd switched to double bass and discovered the "hot" music currently being forged by a number of young bands. By 1908 he had left home and begun playing with various groups, including Kid Ory, King Oliver, Freddie Keppard, and Armand Piron. By the teens he was working the riverboats, stopping for a time in St Louis and playing there with Charlie Creath. After 1918 he joined Fate Marable's riverboat band, staying three years and often doubling on tuba before heading out to California to hook up once more with Kid Ory. For the next few years he traveled a good deal and worked constantly, reaching New York in 1928 and immediately joining the King Oliver band there. Foster moved on to the Luis Russell band in the following year, staying on when Louis Armstrong took the band over in 1935: by this time his strongly rhythmic "slap bass" playing – his nickname came from the way he "popped" the notes to accentuate the bounce and lift of the beat – had made him a well-known and respected figure. However, with the break-up of the old Russell-based Armstrong orchestra in 1940, Foster went through hard times and for a few years worked outside the music business, coming back in only when the traditional jazz revival was well under way.

In the second half of the 1940s Foster played with such leaders as Bechet, Mezz Mezzrow, Art Hodes, and Bob Wilber, being identified with the so-called "moldy fig" element, a most unjust accusation, considering the music he had played with Russell and Armstrong in the 1930s. Foster appeared on Rudi Blesh's *This is Jazz* radio series and also in the famous *Jazz Dance* short film of 1954, made by Roger Tilton. In the mid-1950s he moved to San Francisco, working regularly with Earl Hines at Club Hangover, and in the following decade he became a regular on traditional jazz packages touring Europe. He continued performing up to the time of his death in 1969.

SEE ALSO: King Oliver, Kid Ory, Freddie Keppard, Louis Armstrong, Sidney Bechet, Earl Hines

Bud Freeman

fact file

BORN 1906

DIED 1991

MUSICAL SELECTION
"Crazeology"
"The Eel"

The impeccable Bud Freeman and his saxophone enjoyed popularity both in the native United States and in the UK

Born Lawrence Freeman in Chicago, Bud Freeman took up C-melody sax in 1923 and became part of the so-called Austin High School Gang, a group of like-minded young men who included Frank Teschemacher and Jimmy and Dick McPartland and banded together to produce "hot" music. By 1925 he was playing tenor sax and had turned professional, moving to New York in 1927 to play with Ben Pollack. Freeman at this stage was the only tenor player not in Coleman Hawkins's thrall, his rhythmic but consistently melodic approach providing many later players with an example of how they could develop their own musical identities. After a brief sojourn in Paris in 1928 with Dave Tough, Freeman returned to New York and freelanced assiduously, joining Red Nichols for a time and appearing on many recording sessions, including his own first as a leader, cutting *Crazeology* for Okeh. His reputation growing, Freeman began working in the big bands during the 1930s, holding down chairs in the Ray Noble, Tommy Dorsey, and Benny Goodman orchestras, but by the end of the decade he'd had enough of large aggregations and turned to small group work. He recorded his most famous title, "The Eel," in 1933 with Eddie Condon and again in 1939, using his own group, the Summa Cum Laude orchestra; he also made a string of sides in 1938 for Commodore with a trio featuring Jess Stacy and George Wettling.

During the next two decades Freeman was usually found either with his own small groups or with Condon's bands; playing and recording regularly, he retained a high profile which served to extend his career in the 1960s when he became a perennial tourer, appearing all over the world as a solo act and making many very popular records with pick-up groups. Freeman was a founder member of the World's Greatest Jazzband in 1968, but by the mid-1970s had settled in London for a few years: an Anglophile, he had long been a frequent visitor to Britain and sported a British Gentleman image for most of his professional career. Moving back to Chicago as the decade progressed, Freeman remained active to his death: his music is preserved on recordings spanning every decade of his career.

SEE ALSO: Frank Teschemacher, Red Nichols, Tommy Dorsey, Benny Goodman, Eddie Condon

Chico Freeman

fact file

BORN 1949

MUSICAL SELECTION
Spirit Sensitive

Son of Chicago legend and fellow saxophonist Von Freeman, Chico Freeman

Son of the near-legendary Chicago saxophonist Von (Lavon) Freeman, Chico, born Earl Freeman, was first attracted to trumpet after hearing records by Miles Davis. However, while studying at Northwestern University (1967–72), Freeman gradually became enamored of the saxophone, taking up studies on it during his third year there. Freeman initially found inspiration in the music being made by Chicago's many blues and R&B bands but came to study more advanced ideas with Muhal Richard Abrams, in the process becoming a member of the AACM. Further studies with a range of Chicago musicians resolved into a course of postgraduate composition studies at Governors State University, ending in 1976, at which point his formal education was completed.

The following year Freeman moved to New York and quickly came to the attention of some of the music's top bandleaders. He played with Elvin Jones, the Sam Rivers Big Band, Sun Ra, and Don Pullen, touring Europe with Jones in 1977. Soon after, he began leading different quartets, both live and in the recording studio, his playing causing immediate interest both sides of the Atlantic. The 1978 album *Spirit Sensitive*, one of the few India Navigation titles on CD, is one of his most representative from this time and features regular partners Cecil McBee and John Hicks. Freeman joined forces with his father in the early 1980s and toured with him with a father-and-son-led quintet. Toward the end of the 1980s Freeman became increasingly absorbed in bridging the gap between acoustic jazz and rock and funk beats, many of his albums in recent years looking for a successful fusion of the two. He continues to lead his own group and tours assiduously, playing tenor and soprano sax in a lithe, forward-looking way while not neglecting the music's tradition.

SEE ALSO: Miles Davis, Muhal Richard Abrams, Elvin Jones, Sun Ra, Don Pullen

Bill Frisell

fact file

BORN 1951

MUSICAL SELECTION
Have A Little Faith
In Line

Guitarist Bill Frisell, quite at home with both the avant garde and Americana

Born in Baltimore, guitarist Frisell grew up in Denver, Colorado, studying clarinet and saxophone before swapping to guitar while at North Colorado University (1969–71). Moving on later to Berklee College, Frisell studied composition with Mike Gibbs, emerging in 1977 with a diploma and the Harris Stanton Guitar award. He later took lessons with Jim Hall and Johnny Smith, among others, perfecting the all-round technique he was after. Quickly coming to attention at the opening of the 1980s, Frisell made a string of sideman appearances on the ECM label, notably in the company of Jan Garbarek and Paul Motian, then made his debut album, *In Line* (1982) for the label. Frisell spent the majority of the 1980s exploring ever more exotic musical textures and situations, becoming an integral part of saxophonist/composer John Zorn's home of musical dementia, Naked City, and making albums such as *Strange Meeting* (Antilles, 1987) in an avant power jazz trio, for want of a better phrase, including Ronald Shannon Jackson and Melvin Gibbs. Frisell signed for Elektra Nonesuch soon after this and began producing a string of memorable albums, including *Have a Little Faith* (1993), a record which, while containing Frisell's gutsy and affectionate version of Muddy Waters' "I Can't Be Satisfied," pointed to the direction he is still mostly taking – a new synthesis of Americana, using pieces by Aaron Copland, Nashville, the pop charts, and folk material in stripped-down arrangements and interpretations which are getting ever closer to literalism. Frisell remains breathtakingly in demand as a star session guitarist for a vast range of musicians, one the latest being his appearance along with Pat Metheny on bassist Marc Johnson's *The Sound of Summer Running* (Verve, 1998), a pastiche of 1960s folk rock and country influences.

SEE ALSO: Jim Hall, Jan Garbarek, Paul Motian, John Zorn, Pat Metheny

Curtis Fuller

Trombonist Curtis Fuller, on stage and doing his thing in 1982

fact file

BORN 1934

MUSICAL SELECTION
Bluesette
Soul Trombone

A Detroiter, trombonist Curtis Fuller was the leading disciple of the 1950s J.J. Johnson school of trombone, blossoming later into an accomplished arranger and composer. He started out in high school playing baritone horn before switching to trombone. Once in the army, he played in the same band as Cannonball Adderley and Junior Mance (1953–55), returning to Detroit and a professional career in music on his discharge in 1956. Once there he played with many leaders, most notably Yusef Lateef, and began appearing on records, mainly for Savoy, often in the company of Kenny Burrell. By 1957 he was permanently stationed in New York and making many recording sessions. Six months with Lester Young the following year helped his wider profile, and work in 1959 with Benny Golson led to work in the Jazztet on its formation. Fuller was by now making a series of albums under his own name for Savoy, including *Bluesette* (1959), featuring Golson and bassist Jimmy Garrison.

This led eventually to his being called into Art Blakey's Jazz Messengers in 1961, a group in which his arranging skills thrived. One of his best albums, *Soul Trombone* (Impulse!), came in the same year, using Messengers personnel but with Jimmy Cobb on drums. Fuller stayed with the Messengers until 1965, appearing on many of the band's greatest albums. Later in the 1960s he toured briefly with a Gillespie big band, then settled into a freelance existence. His next major change came with *Crankin'* (Mainstream, 1973), where he attempted to combine acoustic and electric approaches to jazz, but by mid-decade he was in the Basie trombone section, leaving in 1978 to co-lead the quintet Giant Bones with Kai Winding. Since that time Fuller has played regularly as part of the Timeless All-Stars group and continued to be very active in arranging and composing material for a range of musical activities. He also appeared in the reconstituted Jazztet in 1982. Fuller continues to pursue an active career.

SEE ALSO: J.J. Johnson, Cannonball Adderley, Yusef Lateef, Kenny Burrell, Lester Young, Art Blakey

Slim Gaillard

fact file

BORN 1911

DIED 1991

MUSICAL SELECTION
"Laguna"
"Dunkin' Bagels"

Musical wit Slim Gaillard in 1984, still talking, still charming audiences

Gaillard led such a varied and peripatetic life that it was only for relatively short stretches of it that he was involved in the jazz mainstream. However, he made an indelible impression during those periods with his zany vocals, onstage antics and professional musicianship.

Born Bulee Gaillard in Detroit, Slim led a wayward existence as a youth, even claiming to have spent a number of years working on board cargo ships before throwing in his lot with bassist Slam Stewart in 1937 and forming the comic duo Slim and Slam. The pair landed a radio slot on a New York station and quickly became a sensation when Gaillard's patter, which was soon expanded and elaborated into an invented jargon incorporating snatches of many other languages, jive talk and even food recipes, was heard on air decorating their basic, almost singsong tunes. This, along with Slam Stewart's somewhat tiresome technique of humming along with his arco bass solos, translated into a big hit, "Flat Foot Floogie," in 1938, making the duo for a time very hot property. With Stewart drafted, Gaillard relocated to LA in the most fashionable Hollywood nightclubs, foxing and entertaining at turns the film-star clientele. This led to his appearance in the manic comedy *Hellzapoppin'* with Abbott and Costello. After a spell in the army, Gaillard returned to LA and teamed up with bassist Bam Brown, enjoying an Indian summer of success with the film crowd again and recording local hits such as "Laguna" and "Dunkin' Bagels." In addition to appearing riotously on a 1946 JATP concert series, Gaillard that year recorded a session with session musicians including Charlie Parker, Dizzy Gillespie, Dodo Marmarosa, and Jack McVea.

A brush with the law relating to marijuana use in California led to Gaillard talking a distinctly lower profile as the decade closed. Although he continued to appear in clubs dotted around the West Coast and make occasional recordings for Norman Granz, Gaillard dropped largely from sight, appearing internationally only in two of Jack Kerouac's novels, where the writer describes the jazz comic's act in some detail.

Gaillard dropped out of the music business until the early 1980s, when he relocated to London and picked up the threads of an almost extinguished career. Although he had nothing new to add to his previous triumphs, Gaillard was a warm-hearted and engaging performer, eventually landing himself a six-part TV series purporting to recount his life story. Gaillard finally succumbed to cancer, dying in London in 1991.

SEE ALSO: Charlie Parker, Dizzy Gillespie, Dodo Marmarosa

Jan Garbarek

fact file

BORN 1947

MUSICAL SELECTION
Belonging
Officium

Finnish saxophonist and band leader Jan Garbarek, one of Europe's greatest post-war musicians

Norwegian-born Garbarek established himself in the 1970s as one of the most distinctive and influential of the post-Coltrane saxophonists. His granite-hard tone and avoidance of vibrato, on tenor and soprano sax – allied to the often ethereal accompaniment which became a trademark of ECM, the record company he was contracted to – became a European alternative to the American 1970s attempts to rework the familiar old elements of blues, rock, funk, avant, and mainstream music.

Garbarek was inspired by Coltrane broadcasts to play saxophone, teaching himself the rudiments and picking up semiprofessional work while he finished his schooling. Continuing his music interests while studying law at Oslo University, Garbarek eventually felt the pull of music to be overwhelming, dropping out and becoming a professional. In 1965 he came into contact with the Pole Krzyszof Komeda and the visiting American theoretician George Russell. Inspired by the ideas he came into contact with, he began studying Russell's methods intensely, working his way through the Lydian Chromatic Concept of Tonal Organization and incorporating much of the theory into his own approach. He appeared in various Russell bands along with such future European stars as guitarist Terje Rypdal and drummer Jon Christensen, featuring strongly on Russell's major 1969 effort, *Electronic Sonata For Souls Loved By Nature*, and composing certain sections of it as well. His debut album as a leader followed that year, for the Freedom label, then Garbarek spent an instructive year in America soaking up the musical atmosphere. Back in Norway in 1971, he was involved in Russell's *Listen to the Silence* that year and began his long-term association with ECM, one which holds up to the present. Running his own trio with Arild Andersen and Edward Vesala up to the mid-1970s, he also became involved in two outstanding projects: he was a member of the Ralph Towner-led group which recorded the influential album *Solstice* for ECM in 1974, and he became a member of Keith Jarrett's so-called European Quartet, making the classic album *Belonging* and touring extensively worldwide. By the beginning of the 1980s Garbarek was one of the biggest names in modern improvised music: his quartet of that time, co-led with Eberhard Weber, toured to great acclaim in Europe and the US: he also appeared on successful ECM outings by L. Shankar and his own group's pianist, Rainer Brünninghaus.

As the 1980s gave way to the 1990s Garbarek's musical concerns and activities have broadened: he has appeared and recorded with various troupes of percussionists from different musical disciplines around the world, and has also combined his improvisations with medieval and Renaissance plainsong and polyphony sung by the Hilliard Ensemble, as the bestselling album *Officium* (ECM, 1993) showed. At 50 years of age Garbarek shows no sign of slackening the pace of his inventiveness.

SEE ALSO: John Coltrane, George Russell, Keith Jarrett

Erroll Garner

fact file

BORN 1921

DIED 1977

MUSICAL SELECTION
Concert By The Sea

The ever-swingin' Erroll Garner at the keys in 1956

Pittsburgher Garner had a father who was a pianist and his own pianistic talents were recognized from boyhood onward, although he was largely self-taught and never at any stage learned to read music. Garner was appearing on local radio by the age of 10 and at high school was a contemporary of early bop great Dodo Marmarosa. He also knew Billy Strayhorn while in his teens. From 1938–41 he played with the local orchestra run by Leroy Brown, but by 1944 was impatient to broaden his horizons: arriving in New York, he quickly established himself on 52nd Street, becoming a member of the Slam Stewart Trio for a year, then sallying forth as a leader – a position he never relinquished again. Garner chalked up a number of All-Star appearances – on record with Charlie Parker in 1947, or at the 1948 Paris Jazz Festival – but his career was contained within his trios. Early hits, such as "Laura" and "Penthouse Serenade" for various record companies (Garner recorded for over 25 labels during his career) brought Garner quickly before an audience far beyond jazz which appreciated his great romanticism as well as his rhythmic ebullience.

As the 1950s began Garner had completed his pianistic evolution, his romping, driving left-hand figures powering the music along whether accompanied or not, the same hand occasionally delivering shattering offbeat emphases for dramatic effect, while the right hand delivers cleanly executed arabesques and melodic excursions. Garner was also fond of delivering out-of-tempo passages where the lush romanticism of his approach was fully revealed, arpeggio'd chords and elegant flourishes repeated in elaborate detail. All of this came together most memorably in his composition "Misty," first recorded in 1954 and instantly a bestseller; later, with words added, it quickly became a standard in every popular singer's repertoire. Garner recorded it regularly over the years, but his concerts – for he moved up the ladder from nightclubs to concerts during the 1950s – remained exciting events where he would always take enormous risks with his material, often literally starting with no idea what he was going to play, waiting for a familiar melody or harmonic sequence to present itself. This method led to the creation of the most famous of his LPs, *Concert By The Sea*, made in California in 1957 and full of inspired spontaneity. Around the same time he also made a studio album accompanied by strings and voices which was popular but not well liked by jazz critics. In the early 1960s Garner also supplied a number of film soundtracks.

Garner was never part of the jazz mainstream, being such a stylistic maverick, and the bewildering changes of jazz fashion during his career had little or no effect on him or his audience. At the end of his life he was appearing before packed arenas and concert halls and playing in the same style and with the same spirit as he had close to 30 years earlier.

SEE ALSO: Dodo Marmarosa, Billy Strayhorn, Charlie Parker

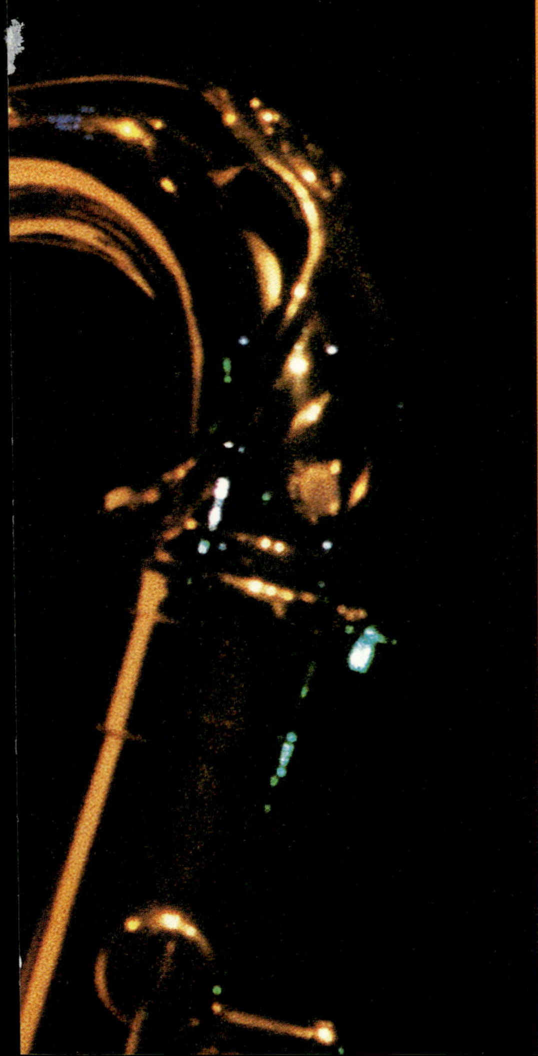

Stan Getz

Born in Philadelphia into a family originally from Russia, Getz moved when young to the Bronx in New York, starting off on the bassoon but switching early on to saxophone. His first professional situation was at 15 with Dick Rogers; the following year he played in Jack Teagarden's band, making his recording debut with them. Quickly recognized as an outstanding talent, Getz played in Stan Kenton's band in 1944–45, then moved on to Benny Goodman, staying a year before freelancing with smaller outfits. In 1947 Getz moved to LA, picking up with Woody Herman as that leader was organizing his Second Herd. Getz became one of the famous Four Brothers sax team of three tenors and one baritone and also scored a major success with his pellucid solo on Ralph Burns's "Early Autumn."

Within a year Getz was out on his own, leading small groups of varying personnel and touring widely. His native melodicism, smooth but full tone, and agile rhythm quickly established him as one of the most popular and respected saxophonists in jazz, and he was identified closely with the emerging "cool" school of jazzmen, though his own perception of himself never fitted that definition. Narcotics problems, leading to arrest in 1954, interrupted his career throughout the 1950s, and for three years (1958–61) he lived in Copenhagen, starting a family and straightening out his life to the extent that he returned to the US that year a reinvigorated musician burning with ambition. His contract with Norman Granz's Verve label had kept his name in front of the public during this period: he also appeared regularly in JATP packages in America and Europe. In 1961 he made the exquisite sax-and-strings album *Focus* (Verve) with Eddie Sauter doing the composition and arrangements and also reunited with a former member of his early 1950s group, Bob Brookmeyer, to make *Fall 1961* (Verve), but he faced a struggle to renew the United State's acquaintanceship with his music. This problem was inadvertently solved by Getz's involvement in a number of recordings of the new Brazilian music being written by Jobim, Gilberto, and others. By late 1962 Getz was selling hundreds of thousands of copies of *Jazz Samba* and *Jazz Samba 2* and had a hit single with "Desafinado." A year later, with the bossa nova craze seemingly dying, he made an album with Jobim and Gilberto which included Gilberto's wife Astrud on one track, "The Girl From Ipanema." By the mid-1960s Getz was a household name worldwide.

Unconcerned by commercial pressures to stick to music fashions, Getz returned to leading straight jazz groups, spending most of the 1960s making outstanding albums with sidemen such as Chick Corea, Gary Burton, Roy Haynes, and Tony Williams. *Sweet Rain* (Verve), from 1967, shows the fully evolved nature of his melodic improvisational style. At the dawn of the 1970s Getz became interested in the new electric instruments being introduced into jazz, using electric piano and guitar at certain times, but by the mid-1970s all such experimentation had ceased. The rest of his career found Getz performing much as he had done earlier in his life: now financially secure, he toured when he chose and recorded for his own production company, hiring accompanists for specific projects. A remarkably consistent and highly motivated performer rarely lacking in inspiration, Getz made few poor records and usually delivered the goods on stage right up to his death, from cancer, in 1991.

fact file

BORN 1927

DIED 1991

MUSICAL SELECTION
Focus
Sweet Rain
At The Shrine
Getz-Gilberto

Stan Getz, pictured here in 1990, was once described by Zoot Sims as "a nice bunch of guys"

SEE ALSO: Jack Teagarden, Stan Kenton, Benny Goodman, Woody Herman, Bob Brookmeyer, Chick Corea, Gary Burton, Roy Haynes, Tony Williams

Jimmy Giuffre

fact file

BORN 1921

MUSICAL SELECTION
Dragonfly
Trio

The man who wrote "Four Brothers," Jimmy Giuffre, seen here in 1989

Clarinetist Giuffre's career has been somewhat hit and miss; at times keenly in tune with public taste to the extent of enjoying minor celebrity, he has also followed his muse into musical areas few wanted to share with him. Giuffre is an accomplished and talented composer and arranger as well as an individualistic clarinetist and saxophonist; today more likely to be found in a campus teaching position rather than out on the road, Giuffre continues to play and record resourceful and challenging music.

Giuffre was born in Dallas and was learning clarinet prior to his 10th birthday, adding tenor sax to his repertoire in his mid-teens. Giuffre is a well-schooled musician, having gained a B.Mus. at North Texas State Teachers College in 1942 and, after army service, an M.Mus. at USC in 1946. By this time settled in LA, Giuffre joined Tommy Dorsey's band briefly in 1947, followed by a stint with Buddy Rich before joining Woody Herman in 1949, where his composition for the famous three-tenor sax line-up of Stan Getz, Zoot Sims, Herbie Steward, and Serge Chaloff, "Four Brothers," became a theme tune for Herman's several Herds subsequent career. Giuffre left Herman in 1950 and freelances in LA, often playing with the Lighthouse All-Stars and also, to make some ready cash, making records with Shorty Rogers and Gerry Mulligan under the name of Boots Brown and His Blockbusters which out-hooted, out-honked and out-screeched such one-note R&B experts as Big Jay McNeely and Willis "Gator" Jackson. Giuffre also played typical West Coast jazz with Rogers up to the middle of the decade before branching out with his own trio, initially comprising Jim Hall on guitar and Ralph Peña on bass (Peña later gave way to trombonist Bob Brookmeyer). The original trio often used a folksy edge in their material, and one Giuffre tune, "The Train and The River," became a minor hit in 1958. Giuffre, involved in a fair amount of so-called "Third Stream" composing and arranging at this time and guesting on a delightful album with the Modern Jazz Quartet, headed off in an unexpected direction between 1960 and 1962, forming a trio with Paul Bley and Steve Swallow which explored highly abstract, often emotionally cold themes and textures: at one point Giuffre would stand in front of abstract paintings and improvise on the themes he noticed there.

The 1960s were a difficult time for Giuffre as the jazz world changed dramatically; by the 1970s he was sharing his time between performing and teaching, often touring Europe between his teaching commitments in New England. In the 1980s he made a series of fine albums for the Italian Soul Note label, only a few of which have reappeared on CD. Some of these, such as *Dragonfly* (1983), show Giuffre's interest in electronic sounds.

SEE ALSO: Tommy Dorsey, Buddy Rich, Woody Herman, Stan Getz, Zoot Sims, Serge Chaloff, Shorty Rogers

Paul Gonsalves

fact file

BORN 1920

DIED 1974

MUSICAL SELECTION
Gettin' Together
Salt 'n' Pepper

Paul Gonsalves, the last tenor star of the incredible Duke Ellington organization, as he appeared in 1960

Bostonian tenor saxophonist Gonsalves was raised on Rhode Island and chose guitar for his earliest musical lessons around 1936; however, he soon switched to tenor, playing in local Boston bands until being inducted into the army in 1942. On discharge in 1946 he returned to Boston for a short period, then joined Count Basie's band, his Webster- and Jacquet-influenced sound and style leavened with touches of bop modernism, making him a star soloist for the band until its demise in 1949. After a period in the Dizzy Gillespie band in 1949–50, prior to its own dispersal, Gonsalves was drafted into the Duke Ellington Orchestra. After a long struggle to gain critical and public recognition in the band, he suddenly hit the headlines with his solo, joining the two sections of "Diminuendo and Crescendo in Blue" at the 1956 Newport Jazz Festival. Ellington's set that night had the audience dancing in the aisles and, his star in the ascendant, he vigorously promoted Gonsalves as a star soloist from that point on. Gonsalves, a diffident man and one with a major drink problem, let the mantle of fame settle uneasily on stage, but continued to deliver the musical goods for Ellington in a variety of musical settings. An assured balladeer, he could contribute sensual solos and melody readings as much as swinging medium-tempo solos, and was a fine ensemble player.

Gonsalves from time to time ventured out from behind the Ducal ranks to make appearances and albums under his own name, including *Gettin' Together* (Riverside, 1960) and *Salt 'n' Pepper* (with Sonny Stitt) (Impulse!, 1963), but his major defining achievements lie within the Ellington arena. He died in 1974, just two months after Ellington.

SEE ALSO: Count Basie, Ben Webster, Illinois Jacquet, Dizzy Gillespie, Duke Ellington

Dizzy Gillespie

John Birks Gillespie, born in Cheraw, South Carolina, became with Charlie Parker the most important innovative figure in the bebop movement of the mid- and late 1940s, revolutionizing jazz trumpet playing, introducing bop harmonic concepts to big-band music, fusing modern jazz with the rhythms of Cuba and other Latin countries, and nurturing many younger players, from Ray Brown, John Lewis, and Milt Jackson to John Coltrane, Miles Davis, and Fats Navarro.

Dizzy's father, who died before his son reached adolescence, was an amateur pianist: Dizzy started out on trombone at 14 but switched to trumpet. He studied theory at Laurinburg Institute in North Carolina in 1932, staying until 1935, when he and his family moved to Philadelphia. Gillespie stayed for just two years, pushing on to New York in 1937 and joining Teddy Hill's band. He made his first recordings for Hill and also toured Europe with the Hill band. From Hill Gillespie progressed to Cab Calloway, where he met Cuban trumpeter Mario Bauzá in the trumpet section, Bauzá inspiring Gillespie's lifelong fascination with Afro-Cuban music. Fired from Calloway in 1941 over a misunderstanding, Gillespie freelanced widely in New York, sitting in on the jam sessions taking place at Minton's in Harlem, where young players were beginning to assemble the harmonic and rhythmic language of what would become bebop. For three years Gillespie appeared in various big bands, making an impact on record with Lucky Millinder in 1942 and being a member of the famous Earl Hines band, which included Billy Eckstine and Charlie Parker. Gillespie spent 1944 on 52nd Street playing with different small groups, late in the year joining Billy Eckstine's new band and gaining much attention. A 1945 small group with Parker foundered after a few recordings, but in 1946 Gillespie formed his own big band. A fully fledged bop unit with contributions from himself, Tadd Dameron, and Gil Fuller among others, this band had an enormous impact on jazz both sides of the Atlantic and Gillespie had become a cult hero.

Gillespie had to disband in 1950, sticking thereafter until the mid-1950s to a small group. In 1956 Gillespie was invited to form a new big band by the US State Department for a tour of Europe and parts of Asia Minor, followed by South America. The tour was warmly received everywhere it went, prompting Gillespie to keep it intact after the end of state aid: it continued until late 1957, appearing memorably at the 1957 Newport Jazz Festival. Gillespie thereafter returned to small groups, most often with his old friend, saxophonist James Moody, beside him, punctuated by occasional commissions allowing him to use a big band for such projects as *Gillespiana* and *The New Continent* by his ex-pianist Lalo Schifrin, *Perceptions* by J.J. Johnson and *A Portrait of Duke Ellington*, arranged by Clare Fischer. In 1965 he also appeared with the Monterey Jazz Orchestra in a program of music arranged by Gil Fuller. By the late 1960s Gillespie was assuming an elder-statesman role, as his leadership of the Jazz Giants touring group of 1971, where he shared the stages of the world with Thelonious Monk, Art Blakey, and Sonny Stitt, showed. In the 1970s he renewed his old recording relationship with Norman Granz, recording prolifically for Granz's Pablo label until Granz sold the label toward the end of the 1980s. A greatly revered and loved figure in the music, as well as being one of the few modern jazzmen known by the man in the street, Gillespie died early in 1993 from pancreatic cancer.

fact file

BORN 1917

DIED 1993

MUSICAL SELECTION
Gillespiana
The New Continent
Perceptions

The truly legendary Dizzy Gillespie, one of the most erudite and accomplished of all jazz musicians, whose influence continues to be felt to this day

SEE ALSO: Charlie Parker, Ray Brown, John Lewis, Milt Jackson, John Coltrane, Miles Davis, Fats Navarro, Roy Eldridge, Cab Calloway, Cozy Cole, "Chu" Berry

Dexter Gordon

fact file

BORN 1923

DIED 1990

MUSICAL SELECTION
One Flight Up
Go!
"The Chase"

A young Dexter Gordon, at his coolest best in 1947, coming to grips with bebop celebrity

Big-toned, powerful tenor player Gordon, born and raised in Los Angeles, came from a middle-class black family, his doctor father including for a time Duke Ellington as a client. Gordon took up music in his early teens, studying theory as well as instrumental technique. Joining the new Lionel Hampton big band in 1940, Gordon became a mainstay of the sax section until leaving in 1943. Having giggled around LA with Lee Young and Jesse Price, he then spent six months in Louis Armstrong's band before jumping into Billy Eckstine's new bop-oriented big band. With Eckstine Gordon got his first opportunity to cut a solo, on "Blowin' The Blues Away" (1945). That same year he moved to New York and jammed with the bop heavyweights like Parker and Gillespie, becoming recognized as the first "bop" tenor, but by early 1948 he was back in LA, working up a highly stimulating informal partnership in the early 1950s with the gifted tenor player Wardell Gray. Drug offenses took Gordon off the scene for virtually the entire 1950s (1952–54; 1956–60). His return in 1960 was greeted with some astonishment that he still had the staying power to be excitingly creative after his incarceration, and his Blue Note Records from this time won high critical praise. In 1962 Gordon visited Europe, first settling in Paris and then making himself at home in Copenhagen, where he lived contentedly, playing constantly and recording prolifically, until 1977. Having made infrequent trips back to the US during the 1970s, Gordon was caught unawares by the fanfare which greeted his 1976 tour: festival appearances, club dates and new recordings (with Columbia and Warner Bros) were given ecstatic welcomes. Gordon decided to come home, running a successful second Stateside career until the middle 1980s, when his health began to fail and he slowed his activity almost to a halt.

However, one last great swansong remained: the lead acting role in Bernard Tavernier's 1986 film, *Round Midnight*. Based on the Parisian experiences of Bud Powell and Lester Young, its portrayal of the hard-drinking, seriously wasted middle-aged saxophonist played by Gordon fitted him to a tee – very little acting was actually required. The film won awards and Gordon ended his life in glory, his body gradually succumbing to an assortment of illnesses associated with his hard-lived existence.

SEE ALSO: Duke Ellington, Lionel Hampton, Louis Armstrong, Billy Eckstine, Charlie Parker, Dizzy Gillespie

Teddy Grace

fact file

BORN 1905

DIED 1992

MUSICAL SELECTION
"Rock It For Me"
"Over The Rainbow"

Singer Teddy Grace enjoyed only a brief jazz career but left an indelible impression on her listeners

Louisiana-born Grace had a purely amateur involvement in music until she was in her early twenties. She was brought up in comfort and surrounded by both white and black cultures, and her natural musicality made her as familiar with the blues as with white popular and folk music. In 1930, while in her mid-teens, she was goaded by a friend to sing in front of the band at a local Louisiana country club. Grace made an immediate impact on both the audience and the band. She had a robust alto voice capable of great expressivity, as her later records attest, and as word got around about her, she had turned professional within a year, singing on local radio and appearing with touring bands such as Al Katz and Tommy Christian. In early 1937 she joined New York-based Mal Hallett, who ran a band capable of both non-jazz and jazz performances, and she cut her first sides in February that year, for Decca, the company for whom all her records would be made. She stayed with Hallett until the fall of that year, by which time she was operating as a solo, recording with a pick-up band and covering a song made famous by Hot Lips Page, "Rock It For Me."

In the next three years Grace made all the records – just over 20 – on which her reputation is based. Recording with groups including Charlie Shavers, Bobby Hackett, Billy Kyle, Buster Bailey, Dave Barbour, Jack Teagarden, and, in 1940 on her last session, with Bud Freeman's Summa Cum Laude Orchestra, Grace showed herself to be the outstanding prewar white female jazz singer. In summer 1939 she joined Bob Crosby as cover for Marion Mann, cutting "Over The Rainbow" at her second session. With the US involvement in World War II, Grace joined the war effort; on her return to civilian life she chose not to return to music: certainly the loss to jazz was greater than the loss to her.

SEE ALSO: Hot Lips Page, Bobby Hackett, Jack Teagarden, Bud Freeman, Bob Crosby

Benny Goodman

Chicago-born Goodman is one of the most famous popular musicians of the century, his clarinet technique married to a single-minded determination for excellence but his career milestones are mostly packed into the first 15 years of his professional life.

From a poor Jewish family, Goodman began clarinet studies at 11; a year or so later he appeared on stage with local bandleader Benny Meroff. He was first noticed by the wider world as a member of the Ben Pollack orchestra, making his debut recordings with them in 1926. His solo style at this stage was a combination of Jimmy Noone, Ted Lewis, and Leon Rappolo. Leaving Pollack in 1929, Goodman became a successful freelancer in New York. By 1934 Goodman wanted his own band: landing a spot on a national NBC radio broadcast, he played New York's hotels and music rooms and waited. Sent out on a tour to the Californian coast, Goodman and his band played in a "hot" smooth-swinging style which left their audiences bewildered until they reached the Palomar Ballroom in Los Angeles. Here the band got an overwhelming response from the young audience, many of whom were familiar with the band from the radio broadcast, which was late-night in New York but mid-evening in California due to the time difference. Within months Goodman was a national craze and the Swing Era was officially launched.

Goodman was dubbed the "King of Swing": his reign lasted almost to the end of the 1930s, long enough at least to score a triumph at Carnegie Hall in early 1938, the first jazz artist to present a complete evening's entertainment in that august setting. Goodman's hankering after the approval of "serious music" performers led to his performing and recording clarinet music by Mozart and commissioning Béla Bartók to write *Contrasts* for clarinet, violin and piano. However, more substantial musical progress was made through the vehicle of Goodman's small groups, inaugurated in 1935 and utilizing during the 1930s a racially mixed personnel (virtually unheard of at that time) of Teddy Wilson, Lionel Hampton, and Gene Krupa. This was expanded during the early 1940s to include the guitar genius Charlie Christian, trumpeter Cootie Williams, and saxophonist Georgie Auld.

By that time Goodman had been overtaken in popularity by such bands as those of Glenn Miller, Artie Shaw, Charlie Barnet, and Tommy Dorsey, although in 1942 he enjoyed a million-seller with "Why Don't You Do Right?" featuring a newcomer called Peggy Lee. After WWII Goodman started his policy of running a big band only for specific periods. By this time he was suffering acute pain from chronic back problems, and this physical handicap did much to dictate the shape of his subsequent career. In 1955 he was the subject of a Hollywood biopic, leading his own band in the making of the soundtrack; later in the decade he made US State Department-sponsored tours of Europe and the Far East: this proved to be the prelude for the much-ballyhooed Goodman visit to Russia in 1962. Goodman worked when it suited him during the 1970s and early 1980s; he combined excitingly with George Benson for a small-group workout on US TV in 1975, but otherwise paced himself carefully. Goodman's unwillingness to incorporate later jazz developments relegated him to the jazz backwaters during his later career, but the exemplary standards he set remain a golden and instructive legacy for those who have followed.

fact file

BORN 1909

DIED 1986

MUSICAL SELECTION
"Why Don't You Do Right?"
"Sing Sing Sing"
"Don't Be That Way"

Benny Goodman on stage and going strong in the 1980s, still sounding as sweet

SEE ALSO: Jimmy Noone, Leon Roppolo, Fletcher Henderson, Teddy Wilson, Lionel Hampton, Gene Krupa, Charlie Christian, George Benson

Stephane Grappelli

fact file

BORN 1908

DIED 1997

MUSICAL SELECTION
Grappelli Story

A latter-day picture of violinist Stephane Grappelli in typically intense playing pose

Grappelli had a long and distinguished career as the pre-eminent European-born jazz violinist, with only Jean-Luc Ponty, from an entirely different and electrically powered generation, to offer him any competition. However, it is for the music he created as a young man with guitarist Django Reinhardt that he is most fondly remembered.

Grappelli was born in Paris and was for the most part self-taught, although he attended the Paris Conservatoire from 1924 to 1928. Picking up professional work in theaters and cinemas, Grappelli had embraced jazz by 1927, although the bands he played in were mostly dance orchestras. By the turn of the decade he had become acquainted with Reinhardt, and, sometime after, their informal jams evolved into the suggestion for a group to be formed playing their own band of jaunty, swinging jazz, the chordal and rhythmic basis being supplied by guitars. Formed in 1934, the Quintette du Hot Club de France quickly became a popular recording and performing unit, its reputation spreading throughout Europe. Although Reinhardt received the lion's share of the plaudits and there were constant tensions between the two front-line men, Grappelli's swinging violin came in for praise and the combo survived until 1939, when Grappelli finally departed. Later that year, with war in the offing, Grappelli settled in London. Playing both as a solo and in different combinations with George Shearing, Grappelli saw out the war in England before returning to France in 1946. The relationship with Reinhardt after this was sporadic, both men needing to run their own groups; after Reinhardt's death in 1954, Grappelli, a hard-working and committed professional, kept touring Europe with his own bands, but with little recognition until the climate of opinion toward jazz violin shifted at the close of the 1960s.

Grappelli was, along with Joe Venuti, the beneficiary of this renewed interest, and toured the world, appearing at the 1969 Newport Jazz Festival and in 1972 joining up with a trio led by guitarist Diz Dizley. From that point on Grappelli was recording assiduously and touring relentlessly with different supporting trios and also making records with famous musicians from other disciplines such as Yehudi Menhuin and André Previn. In the last decade, although in his eighties, Grappelli never slackened his pace or his ability to swing, and became something of a musical institution, loved and respected wherever he played.

SEE ALSO: Django Reinhardt, George Shearing

Milford Graves

fact file

BORN 1941

MUSICAL SELECTION
Percussion Ensemble

The revolutionary drummer Milford Graves, seen here in New York, 1971

Graves was born in Jamaica and became interested in percussion as a boy, teaching himself from an early age and specializing in congas. Having switched to sticks and a more conventional drum setup as well as additional percussion in late teens, he moved to New York in his early twenties, finding work in the percussion sections of bands led by Miriam Makeba and Hugh Masekela. Moving among the young jazz and percussion players in New York, Graves became involved in the burgeoning avant-garde jazz scene, being a founder member of the Jazz Composers' Guild in 1964 and playing in the so-called "October Revolution in Jazz" that year. Appearing and recording with Paul Bley and Giuseppi Logan (also members) as well as, a little later, Albert Ayler, he formed in 1966 a duo with pianist Don Pullen. He and Pullen formed their own record label to promote their activities. By this time Graves, along with Sunny Murray and Rashied Ali, was regarded as the drummer at the cutting edge of the music, dispensing with meter in his playing, concentrating on dense textures of sound and largely abandoning the cymbals as being a non-African element, although, as his 1965 self-titled album for ESP-Disk demonstrated, he was rather partial to gongs.

After moving into music teaching as the decade progressed, Graves moved to Vermont in the early 1970s to teach there at Bennington College. He began touring Europe with his own ensembles and also appeared as part of the Dialog of the Drums trio, the other members being Andrew Cyrille and Rashied Ali. In the 1980s this concept was expanded into Pieces of Time, a percussion quartet made up of Graves, Kenny Clarke, Don Moye, and Andrew Cyrille. Since then Graves has concentrated on private and institutional percussion education, occasionally appearing on record or in concert.

SEE ALSO: Paul Bley, Don Pullen, Kenny Clarke

Wardell Gray

Wardell Gray in action in Los Angeles in 1947 with everything to play for

fact file

BORN 1921

DIED 1955

MUSICAL SELECTION
"Twisted"
"The Chase"
"Blue Gray"

Gray emerged in the 1940s as the tenor saxophonist most likely to lead other bop-generation tenors to the promised land, only to die in murky circumstances in Las Vegas in 1955. Gray was born in Oklahoma City, moving to Detroit with his family as a youngster, where he initially studied clarinet at Cass Technical High, a school closely associated with the postwar blossoming of jazz talent in Detroit. After school Gray joined a succession of local bands, including Jimmy Raschel, his professionalism and polish creating an impression which eventually led to his being hired by Earl Hines late in 1943 after the departure of Billy Eckstine and a number of his younger players to form a new band.

Gray was hired on alto but switched to tenor during the three years he spent with Hines, leaving him finally during a slack period when the band was in LA in summer 1946. Gray took advantage of a bustling modern jazz scene, working with bands led by Benny Carter and Billy Eckstine and playing concerts for promoter Gene Norman, as well as making records (unreleased at the time) for the Sunset label. The following year Gray made a Dial session with Charlie Parker and a popular long-play 78rpm single for Dial, "The Chase," featuring himself and Dexter Gordon in a simulated cutting session: this routine was followed up by concert versions for Gene Norman, some of which have been issued on LP, while other Norman concerts pitched Gray in with people such as Sonny Criss, Vido Musso, and Erroll Garner. Gray, being of the Lester Young school, was the logical tenor choice when Benny Goodman put together a brief experiment in bop-tinged music in 1948. This helped establish Gray on the East Coast, and in 1949 he led a small-group session which saw the recording of his most famous tune and solo, "Twisted" (later set to lyrics by Annie Ross). Gray was part of Count Basie's small groups in 1950–51, but the early 1950s fond him mostly working freelance out of LA. This period is adequately documented on record, but the manner of his death is not. Part of a Benny Carter band playing in Las Vegas in early summer 1955, Gray, who according to pianist Hampton Hawes was the only musician he knew not on heroin, was murdered by unknown assailants. One rumor explaining his death was that he was mistaken by drug dealers for Sonny Stitt, a tall, thin saxophonist like Gray and certainly a user, and they settled a debt the hard way.

SEE ALSO: Earl Hines, Billy Eckstine, Benny Carter, Charlie Parker, Dexter Gordon, Sonny Criss, Erroll Garner

Grant Green

fact file

BORN 1931

DIED 1979

MUSICAL SELECTION
Idle Moments
Grantstand

His Majesty, King Funk, in a relaxed mood – the urbane Grant Green

St Louis-born Green was one of very few modern guitarists to successfully combine the drive and blues feel of Charlie Christian with the smooth phrasing and modified rhythms of Wes Montgomery. Like Christian he was a keen adherent of the idea that guitars could and should be able to phrase like brass instruments. Green began guitar prior to adolescence, playing around locally with different groups as young as 13. From the first, Green was equally drawn to jazz and R&B and his first nationally known employer was Jimmy Forrest in the early 1950s; later he played with Sam Lazar and others, including Harry Edison on the jazz side, before finally making the move to New York in 1960. A few gigs with Lou Donaldson led to the altoist recommending him to Blue Note. Although Green debuted on record in March 1961 as a sideman with drummer Dave Bailey for Jazztime, it was his work on Blue Note that immediately drew attention from critics and public alike. Green recorded prolifically for Blue Note in many different situations, sharing album space with Ike Quebec, Joe Henderson, McCoy Tyner, Elvin Jones, and Big John Patton, among others. Toward the end of the 1960s his career took a dip as he wrestled with drug problems: on his recovery he found little demand for his type of jazz, so he fell back on his R&B experience in putting together club bands and recording groups with a very poppy, blues-based feel and sound.

This dominated his 1970s music, resulting in some lukewarm albums, but the occasional return to stretching out, both live and in the studio, proved his faculties to be undimmed until his final hospitalization in 1978.

SEE ALSO: Charlie Christian, Wes Montgomery, Harry Edison, Lou Donaldson, Ike Quebec, Joe Henderson

Johnny Griffin

The fastest tenor in 1950s jazz, Johnny Griffin

fact file

BORN 1915

MUSICAL SELECTION
The Little Giant

Known among musicians in the 1950s as the fastest tenor on the block, Griffin displayed a post-bop style of playing, laced with ebullience occasionally bordering on aggression and projected through a gigantic tone, and this kept him among the most respected saxophonists in jazz for well over 40 years.

Griffin was born in Chicago and took up sax in adolescence, joining the Lionel Hampton Big Band in 1945 before his 18th birthday. Versed in the ways of R&B as well as jazz, Griffin thrived with Hampton, leaving him in 1947 to join the R&B unit of Joe Morris, and then leaving in 1950 to play with similar bands led by, among others, Arnett Cobb. From 1952–54 he was in the army, returning to Chicago in 1955 and playing professionally there with Thelonious Monk. During 1956 Griffin ran his own quartet in Chicago, but by 1957 he was based in New York, becoming a member of the Jazz Messengers that year. Participating in the famous session where the Jazz Messengers recorded with Monk, Griffin impressed the pianist/composer sufficiently to join Monk's quartet in 1958: his work with Monk is captured accurately on a series of albums for Riverside from that year. By 1960 Griffin had struck up a two-tenors partnership with Eddie "Lockjaw" Davis, their tenor battles in clubs around Harlem becoming legendary and preserved in modified form on a series of virile albums for Prestige and Jazzland.

The group broke up in 1962 when Griffin began to spend more of his time in Holland and France, eventually deciding to stay in 1963. Griffin has remained domiciled in France ever since, recording and playing live with expatriates and local musicians alike and becoming one of the most highly regarded musicians in Europe in the process. Since the late 1970s Griffin has made it a habit to tour the US regularly, keeping his art and his reputation intact on both sides of the Atlantic. Johhny Griffin continues to perform and record regularly in much the same style as he did 30 years ago.

SEE ALSO: Lionel Hampton, Arnett Cobb, Thelonious Monk, Eddie "Lockjaw" Davis

Vince Guaraldi

fact file

BORN 1928

DIED 1976

MUSICAL SELECTION
A Boy Named Charlie Brown

Vince Guaraldi, popular composer of both "Cast Your Fate To The Winds" and A Boy Named Charlie Brown

Guaraldi has never been very popular with jazz critics and pundits. His style was a distillation of the more popular aspects of West Coast players such as Brubeck and Cal Tjader as well as popular groups such as Nat King Cole's and Ahmad Jamal's, and his improvisation, while being neat and spirited, showed little originality. However, Guaraldi was a highly talented composer whose music brought jazz in an undiluted form to a very wide audience otherwise utterly ignorant of its felicities.

Born in San Francisco, Guaraldi started out on piano imitating the great boogie-woogie pianists of his youth, then formed a Cole-inspired piano-bass-drums trio in the late 1940s before going out on the road with Woody Herman for a few months, then joining the Cal Tjader group at the opening of the 1950s. This Tjader work gave Guaraldi a taste for Latin music which was to be important later, but the rest of the 1950s passed with Guaraldi swapping between leading his own trio and doing sideman work for a succession of top West Coast leaders, including Frank Rosolino and Bill Harris. During this time he debuted as a leader on record, making little impact with a style mostly drawn from Cole and Peterson, yet his compositions were beginning to take on an individual cast. By the early 1960s Guaraldi was using bass and drums and leaning more toward Latin music and Ahmad Jamal's style: his 1962 composition and recording, "Cast Your Fate to the Winds," was a massive hit and, combined with Guaraldi's treatment of bossa-nova songs from the soundtrack to *Black Orpheus*, gave the pianist a top selling and Grammy-winning disc. Guaraldi followed this up in the mid-1960s with his compositions for the soundtrack to *A Boy Named Charlie Brown*, a massive seller in the US and popular worldwide. Guaraldi also had a jazz Mass performed in San Francisco in 1965 and continued to work in composition and performance during the 1970s, though his main peak of popularity was never again duplicated.

SEE ALSO: Dave Brubeck, Cal Tjader, Nat King Cole, Ahmad Jamal, Woody Herman, Bill Harris

Bobby Hackett

fact file

BORN 1915

DIED 1976

MUSICAL SELECTION
Coast Concert

Bobby Hackett in-between takes with pianist Joe Bushkin, 1950

Hackett was born in Providence, Rhode Island, and came to music through the ukulele, progressing to the guitar, for a number of years splitting his talents and time between guitar and cornet. One of many players inspired by Bix Beiderbecke, Hackett cultivated a clean-toned melodic style as well as the behind-the-beat phrasing of Louis Armstrong in his melody statements. Hackett joined Pee Wee Russell in a trio in 1933, working the Boston clubs before moving to New York in the mid-1930s and joining up with Joe Marsala. Hackett from time to time led his own groups, but leadership was not his strong point, and he joined up with Glenn Miller in 1941, playing both guitar and cornet for the trombonist leader. By the mid-1940s Hackett had decided to enter the studio bands, playing every type of music for NBC and eventually in the 1950s fronting a stream of Jackie Gleason-inspired commercial sessions for Capitol, where his winning balladry was put out in front of a glutinous string section.

Hackett did not abandon jazz, however, as the band he led in New York with Dick Cary on piano in 1957 and his outstanding work with Jack Teagarden's small group in 1958 demonstrated. Work in the early 1960s on tour with Benny Goodman and Tony Bennett kept him in front of international audiences, while his occasional work and recordings with George Wein's Newport Jazz All-Stars also brought deserved attention. But Hackett most regularly continued beautiful cornet playing to rather undistinguished musical surroundings, and his luminous playing was admired by all, as was his undying benevolence toward the music and the men who played it, whether they were known to him or not.

SEE ALSO: Bix Beiderbecke, Louis Armstrong, Pee Wee Russell, Glenn Miller, Jack Teagarden, Benny Goodman

Charlie Haden

fact file

BORN 1937

MUSICAL SELECTION
Liberation Music Orchestra
Ballad For The Fallen

Bassist Charlie Haden, a man of singular talent and strong personal convictions, as evidenced by his well-known Liberation Music Orchestra

One of the most important bassists in jazz since Jimmy Blanton, Iowa-born Haden first came to prominence on the West Coast in the late 1950s as a member of Ornette Coleman's LA group. Haden's huge, resonant sound and unique phraseology, based on an eloquent simplicity of phrase achievable only by a truly gifted melodist, has driven not just Coleman's band but those of Paul Motian, Keith Jarrett, and countless studio-assembled groups, in addition to Haden's own bands such as the occasional orchestras he has led with Carla Bley and Quartet West.

Haden learned music very early, his family being active in Iowan folk-music circles before he was born. Haden moved to LA in the late 1950s, first appearing with Art Pepper and Paul Bley, then in 1959 splitting away from Bley with Ornette Coleman and others to form Coleman's first Quartet in 1959. This band opened at New York's Five Spot in December of that year and caused a sensation, with Haden's powerful bass playing attracting much admiration. Paired on Coleman's *Free Jazz* with Scott LaFaro, Haden and he created a role for the bass, alone or in duet, simply undreamed of before then: at times on this album Haden makes the bass sound like a deeper-toned Spanish guitar. By late 1962 Haden had decided to break his heroin habit, which he did with the help of the Synanon rehabilitation center. Stints with pianist Denny Zeitlin (during 1964–66), Coleman (again), Archie Shepp, and Keith Jarrett followed as Haden flung himself back into music after 1964. By the end of the decade he was ready to debut on record as leader with the masterpiece, *Liberation Music Orchestra* (Impulse!, 1969), featuring recorded extracts from old Spanish Civil War songs as well as compositions by Coleman and Carla Bley.

During the 1970s Haden kept up a phenomenal work rate on both sides of the Atlantic, playing in Jarrett's American Quartet, recording prolifically with a large range of people including Paul Motian and Alice Coltrane, cutting albums under his name consisting of a number of duets, co-founding New & Old Dreams with Don Cherry, Ed Blackwell and Dewey Redman, and guesting on many projects. In the 1980s came the tours with the Liberation Music Orchestra and the award-winning *Ballad For The Fallen* album (ECM, 1983), again undertaken with Carla Bley. He also performed with Jan Garbarek in mid-decade. Later he formed Quartet West, a group featuring Ernie Watts on saxophone which has continued to the present and recorded regularly, often using Haden's patented device of deploying old recordings amid his group's music. Haden remains one of the busiest musicians in jazz.

SEE ALSO: Jimmy Blanton, Ornette Coleman, Paul Motian, Keith Jarrett, Carla Bley, Art Pepper, Paul Bley

Edmond Hall

Edmond Hall, captured warming up backstage in Rochester, New York, 1956

fact file

BORN 1901

DIED 1967

MUSICAL SELECTION
1937-44

New Orleans clarinetist Hall was the son of a clarinetist, Edward Hall, and started appearing regularly in New Orleans ensembles soon after World War I, including those of Jack Carey, Buddy Petit and Lee Collins. An accomplished stylist able to play in bands beyond the classic New Orleans style, on moving to New York in 1928 he settled into a series of big bands such as those of Claude Hopkins (from 1929 to 1935) and Lucky Millinder, as well as appearing in various small groups and pickup units. Hall's drive, good tone, and versatility made him an in-demand player and by the early 1940s he was playing regularly with Teddy Wilson and Henry "Red" Allen. Turning down the opportunity to replace Barney Bigard in the Duke Ellington Orchestra in 1942, Hall played in small groups of his own around New York and Boston and often appeared with Condon's aggregations, becoming a favorite of the Dixieland crowd in the early 1950s, although his style, like that of that other Condon acolyte, Pee Wee Russell, could never have been construed as straight Dixie or New Orleans. In 1955 he replaced Bigard in the Louis Armstrong All Stars, touring and recording widely with the master and becoming an internationally loved and admired clarinetist. Having left Armstrong in 1958 after deciding that the pace of life on the road was not to his taste, Hall returned to freelancing with Condon and leading small combos of his own in and around New York. A gentle man and greatly respected among his peers, he died of a heart attack at his home in February 1967.

SEE ALSO: Lucky Millinder, Teddy Wilson, "Red" Allen, Duke Ellington, Eddie Condon, Pee Wee Russell, Louis Armstrong

Jim Hall

fact file

BORN 1930

MUSICAL SELECTION
Intermodulation
Telephone

The guitarist's guitarist, Jim Hall, in action in 1993

Hall has for decades been regarded as one of the most knowledgeable and original musicians working in jazz. His bland tone and his entirely sympathetic approach to accompaniment have led to his being taken for granted by most listeners, but musicians, especially other guitarists, hero-worship him for his astonishing chordal knowledge, his unexpected melodic figures, and his uncanny ability to follow the thoughts of his fellow musicians.

Hall is from Buffalo, New York, and began his professional life in Cleveland while studying at the Cleveland Institute of Music. He moved from Cleveland to LA in 1955, joining the Chico Hamilton Quintet the same year and becoming instantly successful among the soft sounds of the cool jazz then predominant on the West Coast. Leaving Hamilton for Jimmy Giuffre in 1956, Hall was part of that group's late-1950s success story, and also began a freelancing career in studios and live, which has been hectic up to the present day. Hall played or recorded with Ben Webster, Lee Konitz, Bill Evans (in duet), John Lewis, and Paul Desmond between 1959 and 1961, when he joined the Sonny Rollins Quartet, which found Rollins pushing the boundaries of his music to new and fresh worlds. Now with a major profile, Hall formed a Quartet in 1963 with Art Farmer, but personal problems pushed him off the circuit between 1964 and 1966. After a stint in a TV band, Hall made a much-acclaimed rematch duet album with Bill Evans, *Intermodulation* (Verve), then began leading his own trio and giving informal lessons. In 1972 he began making regular appearances and recordings with bassist Ron Carter, a sometime partnership which persists up to the present day, and in latter decades he has most often appeared with his own trio or as a solo performer.

SEE ALSO: Chico Hamilton, Jimmy Giuffre, Ben Webster, Lee Konitz, Bill Evans, John Lewis, Paul Desmond

Chico Hamilton

fact file

BORN 1921

MUSICAL SELECTION
Gongs East!

Percussionist Chico Hamilton led a popular quintet in the late 1950s as well as appearing with a multitude of jazz future greats, from Chet Baker to Charles Mingus

For a short while Forestorn "Chico" Hamilton, born and raised in Los Angeles, ran one of the most popular groups in jazz. Learning drums while at school, Hamilton played in a band as a teenager which included many of the West Coast's future stars, including Ernie Royal and Charles Mingus. Picking up with Lionel Hampton in 1940, Hamilton toured with the Hampton band as well as appearing with Lester Young and others prior to service in World War II. Out again in 1946, Hamilton returned to big bands, working with Jimmy Mundy and, briefly, Count Basie, then became a long-term member of singer Lena Horne's backing group, staying with her from 1948–55, when she took her show out on the road. In 1952 Hamilton became a jazz celebrity through his membership of the original "pianoless" Gerry Mulligan Quartet with Chet Baker, in 1955 deciding that his sideman days were over and forming his first Quintet, bringing to it a "chamber-jazz" approach which used musicians such as flautist Paul Horn, guitarist Jim Hall, and cellist Nathan Gershman and scored a number of live and recording successes. The Quintet was in demand, even appearing in Hollywood films such as Burt Lancaster's *The Sweet Smell of Success*. Later editions of the band had Eric Dolphy and Ron Carter (Dolphy was a member of the band which played at the Newport Jazz Festival), while the early 1960s group utilized the instrumental and compositional talents of Charles Lloyd and Gabor Szabo. With the departure of these two talents, Hamilton kept going for a time with Larry Coryell and others, but in the late 1960s turned to composition, writing the soundtrack for Roman Polanksi's *Repulsion* and then moving into advertising jingles.

In subsequent decades Hamilton has continued to run his music business, interspersing it with occasional tours, sometimes conjuring the unique flavor of his most popular small ensembles. He remains a strong figure on the jazz scene.

SEE ALSO: Charles Mingus, Lionel Hampton, Lester Young, Count Basie, Gerry Mulligan, Chet Baker, Jim Hall

Scott Hamilton

fact file

BORN 1954

MUSICAL SELECTION
Race Point

Swing-inspired latter-day tenor sax player Scott Hamilton

Tenor player Hamilton, born in Providence, Rhode Island, was one of the first saxophonists to show that there was life after bop, fusion, and the 1960s. Hamilton began sax lessons in 1970, gradually playing around the New England area and getting up the confidence to attempt New York.

He moved there in 1976 and began playing regularly with surviving swing-era players such as Tiny Grimes, Benny Goodman, and Roy Eldridge, quickly gaining acclaim for his swing-style playing, lush tone and impeccable taste. That same year he teamed up with cornetist Warren Vaché, and in 1977 he debuted for Concord Jazz, the label he still records for. The novelty of having a young white man playing tenor sax like they did prior to 1944 brought Hamilton acres of jazz-world publicity and a sustained demand for live appearances in the US, Europe, and Japan. He also became a constant presence as a sideman on Concord Jazz dates with Vaché and others, including the singer Rosemary Clooney. Hamilton became a fixture in the late 1980s with the Newport Festival All-Stars, the mainstream band par excellence, but as the 1990s have unwound the tenor player's scope and depth have consistently increased. He is now a fully mature, massively assured player who has in recent times made an impressive with-strings album and even managed to pull off a Christmas album (with strings again) that combines natural bonhomie and warmth with his usual impeccable taste. Consistently inventive within his stylistic ambit, Hamilton is one of the contemporary giants of his instrument.

SEE ALSO: Benny Goodman, Roy Eldridge

Lionel Hampton

Born in Louisville, Kentucky, Hampton has proven over eight decades and more to be a true jazz great, full of the spirit and verve of jazz even if not always worrying overly about finesse. Spending a hard youth in various places, by the time he reached Chicago with his family in 1916 he had begun his fascination with the drums and joined the Chicago Defender Newsboys' Band. Encouraged by an uncle in the music business, Hampton pursued his interest in music and began gigging around Chicago with bands such as those led by Curtis Mosby and Paul Howard. With the latter he moved to California in 1928, later joining the Les Hite band during the time it was employed as Louis Armstrong's backing band in LA. During this time he married Gladys, who in time became a business partner as well as the love of his life, and who encouraged him to study music and take up the vibraphone. By 1930 Hampton was proficient enough to take a solo on a Hite/Armstrong record, "Memories of You." By 1932 he was ready to lead his own band, doing so with flair and localized LA success for four years.

In the summer of 1936 the newly famous Benny Goodman caught Hampton's band at an LA venue and persuaded him to join the small group he had recently been featuring with his own big band. Making the Goodman Trio into a Quartet, Hampton stayed with Goodman for four years, in that time cutting many classics with the group and becoming an internationally recognized giant on the vibes. He also led a series of classic small-group swing sessions for Goodman's record label, RCA Victor, featuring the top section men from every major big band in jazz. When it came to forming a big band of his own, Hampton chose personnel judiciously and was never afraid to employ the best: the list of names which went through his band – from Dinah Washington and Illinois Jacquet to Clifford Brown, Charles Mingus, and Dexter Gordon – could make a *Who's Who* of jazz. Hampton's brand of music – loud, brash, often with a huge backbeat and boogie touches – often unsettled critics and observers who viewed his blatant showmanship with distaste, but the vitality of the music and the commitment of the band have always been second to none. Hampton has kept his band together, through many generations of personnel, up to the present day, making it easily the longest-serving band in jazz history, and has toured just about every country in the world at one stage or another. His hits include two different versions of "Flying Home," with a solo apiece from Illinois Jacquet and Arnett Cobb, and Hampton could justly claim to have had a large impact on the development of rhythm and blues in the 1940s and 1950s as well as the continued promotion of young jazz talent. During the 1950s and 1960s Hampton made many small-group recordings which are the equal of his best small-group work of the 1930s, and at one point in the 1970s he ran a record label. Today Hampton remains one of the three greats of the jazz vibes and the last living swing era giant.

fact file

BORN 1909

MUSICAL SELECTION
"Flying Home"

Irrepressible vibist and band leader Lionel Hampton in a classic pose

SEE ALSO: Louis Armstrong, Benny Goodman, Dinah Washington, Illinois Jacquet, Clifford Brown, Charles Mingus, Dexter Gordon, Arnett Cobb

Herbie Hancock

A major presence in acoustic jazz and fusion, keyboardist Herbie Hancock delved into both experimental jazz and popular dance rhythms with enthusiasm

fact file

BORN 1940

MUSICAL SELECTION
Takin' Off
Headhunters

Chicago-born Hancock came from a musical family and was learning piano from seven onward. Adept at classical and popular music, in 1951 he performed at a Chicago Symphony Orchestra young people's event. Graduating from Grinnell College in 1960, Hancock became a regular on the Chicago jazz scene and impressed the visiting Donald Byrd, who invited him to New York as a member of his quintet in December 1960. Hancock's technique soon put him in demand. Recording with Byrd for Blue Note in spring 1962, Hancock was offered his own date and responded with *Takin' Off*, which contained his own composition, "Watermelon Man." Hancock worked freelance in New York after that, playing a season in Eric Dolphy's short-lived 1962–63 quintet, being drafted into the Miles Davis Quintet in May 1963. From then until 1968 Hancock was a Davis mainstay, recording in parallel a string of classic albums for Blue Note. Hancock left Davis in 1968 to pursue his interests in combined acoustic and electronic music. Between 1969 and June 1973 he switched between populist music, studio work with Davis, and electronic explorations with his Sextet, as evidenced on a series of albums culminating in 1972's *Crossings*. In 1973 he disbanded, forming a quartet, swapping record companies, and making a modest retrenchment. The resultant LP, *Headhunters*, supplied fusion's biggest-selling record of all time. By the late 1970s Hancock was making overtly popular records. At the same time he felt the need to renew his acoustic jazz roots, combining with all the old members of the Miles Davis Quintet in a band titled VSOP. During the 1980s Hancock maintained this dual career, More recently Hancock made a duet record with old colleague Wayne Shorter. Hancock has claimed publicly a number of times not to be in the same league as Davis, Parker, Ellington, and Coltrane, but his overall contribution as composer, arranger, group leader, and improviser will not be too far short of them.

SEE ALSO: Donald Byrd, Eric Dolphy, Miles Davis, Freddie Hubbard, Chick Corea, Wynton Marsalis, Wayne Shorter

John Handy

Altoist John Handy possessed a beautiful tone and a vivid musical imagination

Dallas-born altoist Handy came to prominence quite late, not making his national reputation until his stint with Charles Mingus in the late 1950s. By then he had been a professional for a decade, learning clarinet as a teenager and moving to the Oakland, San Francisco, area soon after, where he worked often with blues bands. During the 1950s he studied music and continued working clubs, where after swapping to alto he gradually moved toward jazz. In 1958 he moved to New York, picking up with Mingus, playing in the bassist's working group (often alongside Booker Ervin) and featuring his full and beautiful tone strongly on the 1959 Columbia album, *Ah Um*. That same year he formed his own group and played New York clubs, then toured Europe in 1961 as part of a US State Department deal. By this time he had debuted as a leader on the Roulette label. Returning to San Francisco in 1963, Handy was involved in playing and teaching in the Bay area; he joined Mingus for a residency at the Jazz Workshop in late summer 1964 as well as the Monterey Festival that year, then formed his own group, an important band which signaled some of the changes afoot in jazz in the mid-sixties, made up as it was of sax, violin, guitar, bass, and drums. Handy was the hit of the 1965 Monterey Festival with this group and made a string of bestselling albums on Columbia in the next two years, including the record of the Monterey performance. Visa problems led to the break-up of the quintet, some of the members being Canadians, and Handy re-formed in 1967 with vibist Bobby Hutcherson joining. After one album and a spate of live appearances, this group broke up and Handy tried once more, this time with a trio of violinist Michael White, pianist Mike Nock, and bassist Ron McClure, which, with the addition of a drummer, would later split from him and form the proto-jazz-rock band, Fourth Way.

After this Handy concentrated on both performing and educational work: he was involved in a number of diverse projects in the 1970s, from Indian music to cod-funk records, but by the end of the decade was at least including acoustic jazz in his brief once more with work as part of Mingus Dynasty and Be-Bop & Beyond. Handy continues to live and work on the West Coast.

fact file

BORN 1933

MUSICAL SELECTION
New View!
At Monterey

SEE ALSO: Charles Mingus, Booker Ervin, Bobby Hutcherson

Tom Harrell

Tom Harrell, regarded as one of the outstanding contemporary trumpeting talents, pictured here with his other instrument, the flugelhorn

fact file

BORN 1946

MUSICAL SELECTION
Play of Light
Moon Alley
Labyrinth
The Art of Rhythm

Trumpeter Harrell has fashioned one of the most original lyrical trumpet and flugelhorn styles of the past 20 years, combining an appreciation of Gillespie, Davis, Dorham, and Clifford Brown with other more esoteric influences. His natural improvisational abilities lend themselves to long, elegant lines and a small range of dynamics, but he is a complete technician and able to thrive in most musical situations.

Harrell was born in Urbana, Illinois, but moved with his family to San Francisco in 1951 when still a very young boy. Living just south of San Francisco near Palo Alto, Harrell was playing in local bands while a teenager, appearing at the Jazz Workshop in his twenties. Brought to Stan Kenton's attention, he joined his band in 1969, moving on to Woody Herman in 1970. By 1973 his talents had earned him a place in Horace Silver's group, and he stayed with Silver until 1977, moving to New York in the process. A run of top freelance positions resulted in a regular spot in Lee Konitz's nonet (1979–81), followed by work with George Russell in 1982. In this year he made his debut album as a leader (it was left unreleased), then in 1983 joined the Phil Woods band, staying for six years. In 1984 he finally made an album as leader which got released, *Play of Light* (Palo Alto) and followed it in 1985 with *Moon Alley* (Criss Cross Jazz). By then he was touring regularly through the States and Europe with Woods and creating a stir. His progress was slowed down by the diagnosis of schizophrenia, but on his return to full-time playing he has worked hard on the festival circuit and made a string of first-class albums for RCA Victor, including the award-winning *Labyrinth* (1996) and his latest, *The Art of Rhythm* (RCA Victor).

SEE ALSO: Dizzy Gillespie, Miles Davis, Kenny Dorham, Clifford Brown, Stan Kenton, Woody Herman, Horace Silver

Bill Harris

fact file

BORN 1916

DIED 1973

MUSICAL SELECTION
Bill Harris and Friends

Trombonist Bill Harris in 1949 alongside guitarist Irving Ashby, bassist Joe Comfort, and pianist Nat "King" Cole

As a trombonist, Willard "Bill" Harris was a great individualist capable of driving an entire big band as well as caressing a ballad with the most sensual playing imaginable. Coming from a background which included an appreciation of Vic Dickenson, Harris exploited this most human of brass instruments to the full, especially during his tenure with the Woody Herman Herd, but his less well-known work with his own small groups is also worthy of classic status. Next to J.J. Johnson, Harris is the most influential trombone stylists after World War II.

Born in Philadelphia, Harris (not to be confused with the Nashville-born guitarist) started out on trumpet, also doubling on piano and tenor sax, finally getting around to the trombone in his early 20s. Harris worked with Gene Krupa, Ray McKinley, Buddy Williams, and Bob Chester before joining Benny Goodman in New York in 1943 and appearing briefly with him in the film *Sweet and Low-Down*. In 1944 Harris formed his own group but later that same year joined Woody Herman's First Herd, becoming in the next two years a key component in that band's musical and popular success: his ballad, "Everywhere," became his calling card for decades and profoundly influenced later players such as Roswell Rudd. Harris starred at the Herman band's Carnegie Hall concert in 1946, but when Herman disbanded in 1947 he worked with Charlie Ventura and was part of the famous "Midnight Jazz at Carnegie Hall" JATP concert that year, along with fellow Hermanite Flip Phillips, Illinois Jacquet and Howard McGhee. This proved a prelude to regular JATP tours in the 1950s, after Harris had once more spent two years (1948–50) in Herman's Second Herd and then withdrawn to Florida. After a spell as a disc jockey in Miami, Harris once more had two years with Herman (1956–58) before rejoining another old boss, Benny Goodman, for the clarinetist's 1959 season of touring. In 1957, on the West Coast, Harris recorded a classic small-group album, *Bill Harris and Friends* (Fantasy), featuring Ben Webster and Jimmy Rowles. Returning to Florida, Harris spent the 1960s playing with old colleagues. He died in 1973 of a heart attack.

SEE ALSO: Vic Dickenson, Woody Herman, J. J. Johnson, Gene Krupa, Benny Goodman, Roswell Rudd, Flip Phillips

Eddie Harris

fact file

BORN 1934

DIED 1996

MUSICAL SELECTION
"Freedom Jazz Dance"
"Listen Here"
"Compared To What?"

Popular and gifted saxophonist and band leader Eddie Harris struck gold twice during his career with two best-selling worldwide hits

Chicago saxophonist Harris was an odd combination of restless experimenter and hard-nosed populist. An outstanding technician happy to play electric saxophone and even experiment with trumpet mouthpieces on saxophones and vice versa, Harris often played very basic music indeed, sticking to well-worn funk and soul-jazz ruts, managing in the process to land a number of sizable hits.

Harris had a dose of Baptist music as a child which stayed with him for life, then at high school began learning a number of instruments, vibes and piano included: in fact his first professional engagement, with Chicago saxophonist Gene Ammons, was as a pianist. During army service (1959–61) Harris played in big bands across the US and Europe, gaining valuable experience. On his release, he returned to Chicago and made a debut recording for Vee Jay, a cover version of the theme to the movie *Exodus*, then doing record box office in the US. The single was one of the year's bestsellers and launched Harris's career virtually overnight. Leading his own small groups from then on, Harris became an accomplished composer – his "Freedom Jazz Dance" attracted a Miles Davis cover version – and continued to provide hits. His second million-seller, "Listen Here," resurrected a stalling career in the mid-1960s and propelled him in a soul-jazz direction; after this he and Les McCann combined for the million-selling "Compared To What?," taken from a live recording at Montreux in 1969. After that Harris landed no more million-selling hits, but he continued to be inventive in his approach to his music, using electronics and other methods to add spice to his creativity, and even for a time in the 1980s returning to a bop-based style. However, his real métier was the combination of blues, funk, and sophisticated jazz harmonies, and his innovations in this area are what he will be remembered for by fans of his music.

SEE ALSO: Gene Ammons, Miles Davis, Les McCann

Jimmy Harrison

fact file

BORN 1900

DIED 1931

MUSICAL SELECTION
Fletcher Henderson: A Study in Frustration

Jimmy Harrison, pictured here in 1928, only three years before his untimely death from stomach cancer

Born in Louisville, Kentucky, trombonist Harrison had a short life but managed a considerable impact on later practitioners of the instrument, his bold improvisatory style, big round tone and easy sense of swing giving the lead to the swing generation of players. Harrison moved to Detroit with his family when young and grew to mid-adolescence there. He began playing the trombone at age 15, and within a couple of years was touring with Midwest combos and minstrel bands, playing a rudimentary but effective style. In 1921 Harrison settled into a routine of playing with Charlie Johnson and Sam Wooding in Atlantic City, then moved on to New York City with Fess Williams. Working freelance in New York with a number of bands, including Duke Ellington's, Harrison became a member of Fletcher Henderson's 1926 orchestra, perhaps then the top black band in jazz, appearing at many venues and on many records with this unit: this is the principal source of his recorded legacy. Harrison became close to Coleman Hawkins during his time with Henderson, also becoming a close companion to the other great trombonist of the time, Jack Teagarden: they would often jam together at after-hours clubs. Harrison stayed with Henderson until his death, with occasional forays into other bands, including Charlie Johnson's at Small's Paradise in Manhattan, his friend Benny Carter's Chocolate Dandies (with whom he recorded in 1930), and Chick Webb in the last year of his life. Harrison was discovered to have stomach cancer when it was in an advanced stage, and died soon after the initial diagnosis.

SEE ALSO: Duke Ellington, Fletcher Henderson, Coleman Hawkins, Jack Teagarden, Benny Carter, Chick Webb

Hampton Hawes

The young Hampton Hawes in 1954, a lesser-known but essential jazz sideman and influence

fact file

BORN 1928

DIED 1977

MUSICAL SELECTION
As Long As There Is Music

Los Angelean Hawes taught himself piano at an early age, inspired by the spirituals he heard at his clergyman father's church. As a teenager he began gigging around LA, picking up some highly instructive work in 1944 with Big Jay McNeely. After this Hawes moved quickly into the camp of the younger jazzmen in the area, playing with Dexter Gordon, Sonny Criss, and Wardell Gray and eventually playing informally with Charlie Parker in 1947. By the beginning of the 1950s he was the West Coast's hottest resident bop pianist and playing in Howard McGhee's group, where he renewed his acquaintance with Parker when the altoist came out west. Hawes by this time had formed his mature style, a percussive and driving approach which combined his initial love of gospel with the harmonic sophistication of bop: this was later to become prevalent in jazz through the good offices of Horace Silver, Art Blakey, and others, but Hawes arrived at some similar musical conclusions at an earlier stage than most.

After stints with Shorty Rogers and Howard Rumsey, featuring often with the Lighthouse All Stars, Hawes did his military service in Japan, returning to LA in 1955 and forming a trio with Red Mitchell which recorded regularly and toured widely in the US. On the verge of a major career but already having spent years struggling with a major heroin habit, Hawes was arrested for possession in 1958 and spent five years in jail. Back on the scene in 1963, Hawes gained fitful work until reuniting with Red Mitchell in 1965 and running a trio together for a year before joining up with Jimmy Garrison, then on the rebound from John Coltrane, and touring internationally during 1967–69. This did much to give Hawes a renewed profile in Europe and Japan, but the US remained unconcerned with his music.

Duets in LA with bassists such as Carol Kaye and Mario Suraci, interspersed with more European trips, filled his remaining years: he made an outstanding duet album with Charlie Haden, *As Long As There Is Music* (Artist's House), in 1976, although it was released posthumously. He also wrote a witty but harrowing autobiography, *Raise Up Off Of Me*. An influential and greatly talented player, he remains unknown to the majority of jazz fans.

SEE ALSO: Dexter Gordon, Sonny Criss, Wardell Gray, Charlie Parker, Howard McGhee, Horace Silver, Art Blakey

Coleman Hawkins

fact file

BORN 1904

DIED 1969

MUSICAL SELECTION
"Queer Notions"
"Body and Soul"
"Picasso"

The first giant of the tenor sax, Coleman Hawkins

Jon Hendricks once introduced Coleman Hawkins to a crowd as "the man for whom Adolf Sax invented the horn." Hawkins gave the tenor saxophone its first mature jazz personality, style, and vocabulary.

Hawkins was born in St Joseph, Missouri, and was learning to read music even before books. He started piano at five and moved to C-melody sax at the age of nine. Just prior to his teens Hawkins began playing for money. After high school, he attended Washburn College in Topeka, where he learned the foundations of theory and harmony. He had been playing on weekends in Kansas and Chicago and was offered a job by the touring Mamie Smith and Her Jazz Hounds when she heard him play in Kansas City in 1922. Ending up in New York with Smith, now on tenor sax, he cut his first records with her in 1923 before joining Fletcher Henderson in 1924. He was to stay with Henderson until 1934. Hawkins's prowess, forcefulness and large tone brought him fame; the arrival of Louis Armstrong soon afterwards brought him focus. Using a clipped rhythm (often emphasized by the type of slap-tongue playing Hawkins was soon doing much to dismantle) and his harmonic invention, Hawkins became the dominant tenor stylist. His talent is witnessed in "Queer Notions," recorded in 1933 by the Henderson band.

Hawkins offered his service to the Jack Hylton band, a dance orchestra with jazz associations based in London, and joined them in 1934. touring all over Europe in the next five years, returning to the US only when World War II was imminent. In New York in July 1939 Hawkins formed his own band, recording his immortal "Body and Soul.". By then, both "Chu" Berry and Ben Webster had risen to challenge him and Lester Young was offering an entirely different method to a new generation of players. Hawkins, a man equally at home with Roy Eldridge, Django Reinhardt, and Eddie Condon, played with all the new tenorists, besting most of them and when bop arrived he was one of the first established leaders to welcome the best of the young players into his bands, hiring Thelonious Monk in 1943 and Howard McGhee in 1945. Hitched with the JATP tours from as early as 1946, Hawkins met Lester Young on stage for the first time that year in a tour and had Charlie Parker along for the LA dates. Hawkins returned to Europe after World War II a number of times and in 1948 he recorded his unaccompanied solo, "Picasso," setting another saxophone precedent. During the 1950s Hawkins recorded with Thelonious Monk (with Coltrane in the same band, lead his own groups, made a series of dates with Ben Webster, toured widely. The 1960s started off similarly, Hawk recording sessions with Duke Ellington, Sonny Rollins and Bud Powell (the last in concert in Germany). By this time, he was a hard drinker, and his habits began to catch up with him in the mid- to late 1960s. He died in 1969.

SEE ALSO: John Hendricks, Louis Armstrong, Fletcher Henderson, Bud Freeman, "Chu" Berry, Ben Webster

Roy Haynes

Drummer Roy Haynes, famed for both his dress sense and his music, has been in demand as an outstanding player throughout his career

fact file

BORN 1926

MUSICAL SELECTION
Out of the Afternoon

Haynes, a drummer noted for his immaculate timekeeping and his sartorial sharpness, was born in Roxbury, Massachusetts to parents who had come originally from Barbados. Learning drums prior to adolescence, Haynes began gigging part-time around Boston, working with Sabby Lewis before playing professionally with altoist Pete Brown and trumpeter Frankie Newton in 1944. Like many other later bop drummers, Haynes had limited experience with big bands, two periods in the mid-1940s with Luis Russell accounting for most of it. But by 1945 he was sufficiently well thought of as a youngster in New York to be hired by Lester Young, with whom he stayed for two years. At the end of the 1940s Haynes also enjoyed two years in the Charlie Parker band, leaving Parker in 1952 to freelance, then picking up the drummer's chair with Sarah Vaughan in 1953, a position he retained until 1958. One of the busiest freelancers in the business at the start of the 1950s, he was John Coltrane's first-call drummer when Elvin Jones was indisposed, and also joined the Stan Getz group in the mid-1960s, traveling extensively with the saxophonist. He was also a key part of the Gary Burton group with Larry Coryell. During this decade he often ran his own groups, including the Roy Haynes Hip Ensemble, and in the late 1960s began a musical friendship with Chick Corea which has been documented on record, from time to time, ever since, in the form of Trio Music records. Haynes has played with virtually every important member of the postwar modern-jazz fraternity at some point or another (he even hired Roland Kirk for one of his albums in 1963) and his busy, thrusting style of drumming appeals in virtually every environment it is found within. Haynes developed through Kenny Clarke, Max Roach, and others a style which is original but not widely influential, but to this day he remains a respected and in-demand drummer at the very highest level.

SEE ALSO: Lester Young, Charlie Parker, Sarah Vaughan, John Coltrane, Elvin Jones, Stan Getz, Gary Burton

Joe Henderson

fact file

BORN 1937

MUSICAL SELECTION
Inner Urge
So Near, So Far

Tenor player Joe Henderson, whose career reached a second peak during the 1990s with his switch to Verve Records

Tenor saxophonist Henderson was born in Lima, Ohio, a town just over 100 miles from Detroit. After studying at Kentucky State College he moved to Detroit to study first at the Teal School of Music, latterly flute and double bass at Wayne University (1959). Inducted into the army in 1960, Henderson won friends and allies with his musical ability and traveled through Asia and Europe after winning an army talent show. On discharge in 1962 he settled in New York, meeting Kenny Dorham and Jack McDuff and quickly becoming a member of Dorham's group. This brought Henderson abruptly into the Blue Note Records fold; for the next five years Henderson recorded prolifically for the label, both as leader and as sideman with Dorham, Andrew Hill, Horace Silver, and others. He joined Silver's group in 1964 as replacement for his friend, Junior Cook, ran a band in the late 1960s with Freddie Hubbard, then joined Herbie Hancock during 1969–70, before dabbling briefly with jazz-rock fame in Blood, Sweat & Tears.

In the 1970s Henderson worked mostly in his own groups, also recording with Alice Coltrane, and relocated to the West Coast in mid-decade. A long association with Milestone records, started in 1967 and incorporating a wide range of settings, ended in 1976, with Henderson enduring a relatively low profile for the next ten years, his highly intelligent and original synthesis of Rollins and Coltrane seemingly out of step with jazz fashion of the time. A return to Blue Note and a live recording at the Village Vanguard in 1985 emulating the famous Sonny Rollins trio date of 1957 brought much-needed re-evaluation for Henderson, leading eventually to a high-profile series of tours and concerts worldwide and a switch to Verve, where he has recorded in the 1990s a string of award-winning and best-selling albums, including tributes to both Miles Davis and Billy Strayhorn. Henderson is, next to Rollins, the greatest and most consistently creative living tenor saxophonist, and his sound continues to impress and inspire.

SEE ALSO: Kenny Dorham, Jack McDuff

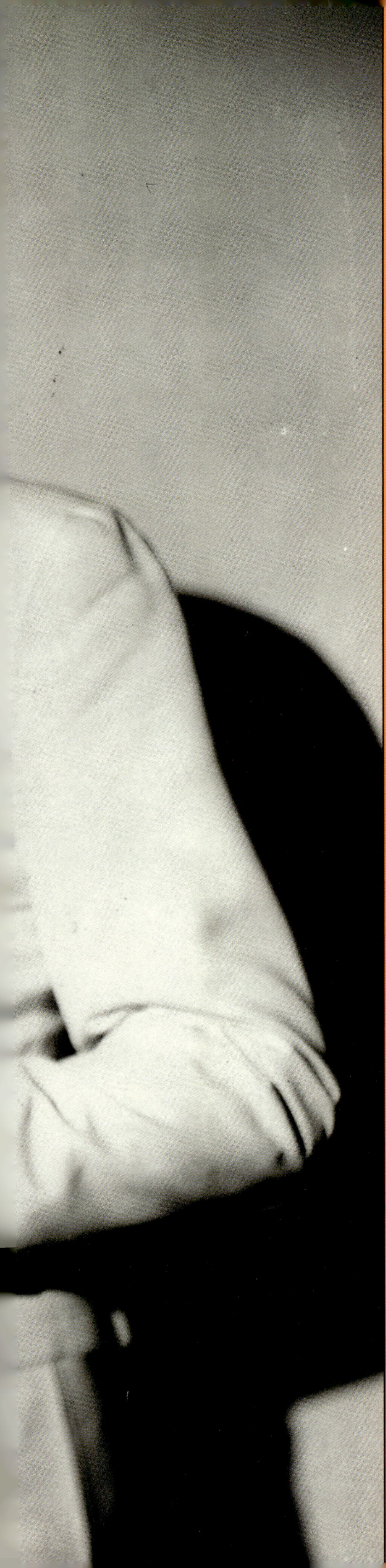

Fletcher Henderson

Henderson is a key figure in the development of big-band jazz and the launch of the swing era. A pianist, composer and arranger, Georgia-born Henderson came from a middle-class family and had a brother, Horace, who also played piano, led bands, and was a gifted arranger. Henderson received a good education, majoring in chemistry and mathematics at Atlanta University, but during a 1920 postgraduate sojourn in New York he worked part-time as a pianist and became known to W.C. Handy, who employed him in his band. In 1922 he took work as house pianist and recording producer at the independent Black Swan records, the following year appearing for other labels as an in-demand accompanist for a huge range of singers, including Bessie Smith and Ethel Waters. Late that year he landed a job at the Club Alabam, and in January 1924 began leading his own band there. Before long he was resident with his band at the Roseland Ballroom and had a wealth of talent employed in its ranks, including Coleman Hawkins, Buster Bailey, and, most importantly, Louis Armstrong. Henderson's was the premier big band in jazz, and not just because of the strong solo characters: he and his staff were evolving a method of arrangement which would in time become incorporated into every jazz big band, whatever style it played. Using the then prevalent two-beat rhythm of early jazz, Henderson concentrated on using each instrumental group – trumpets, trombones, reeds, piano, rhythm – in contrast and counterpoint to each other, thereby automatically providing color, contrast, and secondary interest to each melody and harmonic progression, especially as the idea of riffs (simple repetitive melodic devices) evolved fully.

Henderson's arrangements were models of simplicity and clarity, his methods easily adaptable to the demands of swing rhythm as the more even four-beat feel of the 1930s became the norm. Yet Henderson himself was not the principal beneficiary of his own innovations: by all accounts a diffident man who inspired loyalty but no real discipline in his players, in 1928 he suffered a major car accident, receiving head injuries which left a permanent mark: he left most day-to-day affairs after that to his wife. By the early 1930s Henderson was writing arrangements for many bands, and with the rise of Benny Goodman in 1934–35 he was a prime source for Goodman's superior swing feel.

Yet the inadequacies of Henderson's own leadership can easily be detected when a Henderson band and a Goodman band performance of a song – for example, "King Porter Stomp" or "Honeysuckle Rose" – are compared, the fire and discipline in the Goodman band being in a different class. Henderson maintained a band with varying personnel and success and with regular breaks, up to 1939, when he briefly became Goodman's pianist; after that his own bandleading was occasional, and he was most often employed by stars such as Ethel Waters and Goodman for playing or arranging work. A return of sorts to active leadership in 1950 was curtailed by a stroke, after which Henderson was virtually housebound until his death in December 1952.

fact file

BORN 1897

DIED 1952

MUSICAL SELECTION
"King Porter Stomp"
"Honeysuckle Rose"

The influential arranger and band leader Fletcher Henderson, pictured here in 1930

SEE ALSO: Coleman Hawkins, Louis Armstrong, Benny Goodman

Jon Hendricks

fact file

BORN 1921

MUSICAL SELECTION
Sing a Song of Basie

Singer and lyricist Jon Hendricks, founding member of Lambert, Hendricks & Ross

Born in Newark, Ohio, singer Hendricks has been one of the most creative vocalists in jazz, able to hold his own in the company of musicians of the highest caliber. He is also able to express a wide range of emotions and ideas, including many varieties of humor, an aspect of musical creativity which, even in the informal jazz community, is sometimes at a premium. Hendricks came from a large family (15 children), singing in church with his mother from an early age, moving on to include local parties and banquets from 1929 onward. In 1932 the family moved to Toledo, Ohio, where Hendricks appeared on the radio, occasionally accompanied by a friend of the family by the name of Art Tatum.

After high school Hendricks moved for a time to Detroit, then entered the army, which took up his time between 1942 and 1946, in the European theater of war. After discharge Hendricks returned to Toledo, where he studied law at the local university. Meeting Charlie Parker while playing drums one night, he was gradually dissuaded by the altoist from a law career and by 1952 he was living in New York. After five years of hard times Hendricks teamed up with singer/arranger Dave Lambert to make a number of records, including Hendricks's vocal arrangement of "Four Brothers," backed by Hendricks's vocal version of "Cloudburst." Shortly after, Hendricks and Lambert teamed up with vocalist Annie Ross, between them making the multi-tracked vocalese-cum-three-and-more-part-harmony version of some of Count Basie's greatest hits. *Sing a Song of Basie* (Decca, ABC/Paramount/Impulse!, 1957) was a major success, allowing the trio to go out on the road. Hendricks, as the main lyricist for the group, became much in demand, his witticisms and observations being appreciated by hipsters and more casual listeners alike. By the time of the group's eventual demise in 1964 (by which time Ross had been replaced by Yolande Bavan) Hendricks was a figure of major stature. For the rest of the 1960s he led a high-profile life, living for a time in Europe up to 1973, when he returned to the US. After this he performed regularly as a solo and also with a family ensemble which included his daughter, Michele Hendricks (now pursuing her own singing career), and, on regular occasions, Bobby McFerrin. Hendricks has continued to involve himself in many projects, appearing as a headliner at many festivals and special events.

SEE ALSO: Art Tatum, Charlie Parker, Count Basie, Bobby McFerrin

J.C. Higginbotham

fact file

BORN 1906

DIED 1973

MUSICAL SELECTION
"I'm On My Way From You"

The ever-urbane and popular trombonist J.C. Higginbotham's career took him throughout the United States and to Europe

Trombonist Higginbotham, a native of Atlanta, Georgia, was raised in Cincinnati, starting out at 15 in 1921 with Nel Montgomery in Georgia, then playing with Wes Helvey in 1924–25. After various adventures on the Eastern Seaboard, Higginbotham reached New York in September 1928, where he joined the Luis Russell band. He stayed until 1931, becoming fast friends in particular with Russell's star trumpeter, Henry "Red" Allen. Leaving to play at first with Chick Webb, Higginbotham soon graduated to Fletcher Henderson's top-line band, sharing the spotlight with Hawkins and others until 1933, when he went to Benny Carter and, later, Lucky Millinder. By this time Higginbotham was a major swing stylist, his big, gutsy tone, good-humored approach, and his ability to string together entertaining phrases all much in demand and much imitated. Invited to join Louis Armstrong's band (in fact the Luis Russell band fronted by Armstrong) in 1937, Higginbotham joined up with his old colleagues, staying until 1940, when Armstrong dissolved the entire unit. A blessing in disguise, this led to Higginbotham joining his old friend "Red" Allen for seven years in a small group which played in both New York and Boston.

The 1950s found Higginbotham working under similar circumstances, but with a pronounced drop in enthusiasm, as the mainstream jazz he was best at went through a period of neglect. Working in Boston and Cleveland, only at the end of this decade did he begin to pick up again, visiting Europe and being rejuvenated by the veneration he received there. Thus buoyed, Higginbotham found a new impetus in the 1960s, arrested at last only by serious illness, the onset of which in 1971 led to his permanent retirement in his last two years of life.

SEE ALSO: "Red" Allen, Chick Webb, Fletcher Henderson, Coleman Hawkins, Benny Carter, Lucky Millinder

Woody Herman

Not noted as either a composer or arranger, Herman was still one of jazz's great bandleaders as well as being the leader of one of its greatest bands (not always the same thing). A natural leader of men, a serviceable singer, and a fine lead clarinetist and saxophonist, Herman was always open to new sounds and had an interest in music beyond the narrow confines of big-band jazz, as his mid-1940s commissioning of Igor Stravinsky for a concerto proved.

Herman was born in Milwaukee and from childhood was involved in vaudeville, as both singer and dancer. Starting on sax in 1922, he was out on the road at the age of 17 and attempting (unsuccessfully) to put his own band together by the time he was 20. Between 1934 and 1936 he was a mainstay in the conservative Isham Jones Orchestra; when Jones retired in 1936, Herman took the nucleus of the band as a basis for his own first venture, which was quickly dubbed by publicity agents "the band that plays the blues." This of course was an economy with the truth, for Herman played the hits of the day and old chestnuts like everyone else, but he did concentrate more than most on blues pieces, racking up a major hit in 1939 with "Woodchopper's Ball." This and the oddball "Golden Wedding" gave this early Herman unit its audience, but by 1943–44 Herman was bringing in younger players and changing his repertoire, using both "head" arrangements and pieces by Neal Hefti and Ralph Burns, both then playing in the band, to spearhead a new approach. This unit, given its character by Herman and people like Sonny Berman, Flip Phillips, Bill Harris, Chubby Jackson, Red Norvo, and Dave Tough, created a body of live and recorded work which stands comparison with the best of its time. Known as the First Herd, this band was broken up by Herman in 1946, but the following year he re-formed, calling his outfit the Second Herd and using three tenor saxophonists (Zoot Sims, Stan Getz, and Herbie Steward) and a baritone (Serge Chaloff) for a new reed section sound, codified by the theme song "The Four Brothers," written for Herman by Jimmy Giuffre. This, plus work by Shorty Rogers and the glowing pastorals such as "Early Autumn" from Ralph Burns's pen, earned Herman more plaudits worldwide.

After that Herman went through several new editions of his "Herd," finally calling one 1960s band "His New Herd," always pursuing the same instrumental excellence, good charts, and real jazz-based excitement which had been his calling card since the early 1940s. During this and following decades Herman took note of contemporary developments by bringing in special arrangements of newer material such as "Opus de Funk," "Giant Steps," "Better Get Hit In Your Soul," and "Filthy McNasty," finding this material to be a later combination of the elements which had always been in his music – blues and exciting harmonic and rhythmic exploration. Herman lived to see himself and his band reappraised many times over and awarded countless honors. He also found his reputation for fairness and loyalty to musicians rewarded when, in the last stage of a terminal illness, he was hit by unexpected tax demands and was allowed to rest easy by the generosity of a string of famous people who cared, Frank Sinatra especially.

fact file

BORN 1913

DIED 1987

MUSICAL SELECTION
"Woodchopper's Ball"
"Golden Wedding"
"Apple Honey"

World-famous clarinetist and band leader, Woody Herman

SEE ALSO: Flip Phillips, Bill Harris, Red Norvo, Zoot Sims, Stan Getz, Serge Chaloff, Jimmy Giuffre, Shorty Rogers

Andrew Hill

fact file

BORN 1937

MUSICAL SELECTION
Point of Departure
Judgement

The brilliant pianist and composer Andrew Hill broke away from the influence of bebop during the 1960s to produce music that was influential and strikingly original

Pianist Hill once mischievously claimed to be from Haiti but in fact was born in Chicago. He was attracted to music very early on, singing and dancing on stage as a child. From 1950 he began learning piano, starting with the blues and moving on from there, working initially with R&B bands in Chicago, including that of Paul "Hucklebuck" Williams in 1953. During a jazz apprenticeship in 1950s Chicago Hill jammed with many players and played in the bands of Von Freeman, Johnny Griffin, and others on occasion. After joining Dinah Washington in 1961 as accompanist, he swapped to Roland Kirk's ground-breaking outfit in 1962, settling in New York in late 1963, where he hooked up with saxophonist Joe Henderson and began an association with Blue Note records (often with Henderson involved) which lasted until 1969. During this time he made several albums which have now been granted "classic" status, including 1964's *Point of Departure*, with Henderson, Kenny Dorham, and Eric Dolphy and *Judgement*, with Bobby Hutcherson and Elvin Jones (1963).

Hill evolved to be one of the most challenging and determinedly original pianist-composers of the 1960s, unafraid to ignore both traditional post-bop jazz patterns and the unfettered license of the avant-gardists. By the beginning of the 1970s Hill had begun a music-teaching career at Colgate University and also became involved with the Smithsonian Institute during this decade. European tours and frequent recordings suggested a long career in the spotlight, but personal problems and family illness forced his attention elsewhere until the late 1980s, when he began performing and recording regularly once more, touring Europe regularly, the latest occasion being in 1996 with a trio including Pheeroan AkLaff and Reggie Workman.

SEE ALSO: Johnny Griffin, Dinah Washington, Roland Kirk, Joe Henderson, Kenny Dorham, Eric Dolphy

Earl Hines

fact file

BORN 1903

DIED 1983

MUSICAL SELECTION
"Apex Blues"
"Deep Forest"

Pianist and band leader Earl Hines, surrounded by a bevy of admirers at the Grand Terrace, Chicago, 1939

Pianist Earl Hines – nicknamed "Fatha" – was born in Pittsburgh to a musical family (his father played trumpet in the Eureka Brass Band) and by the age of nine was taking piano lessons from his mother and local teachers. He played his first professional engagement at the age of 15, moving to Chicago when 20 years old, playing with Jimmie Noone at the Apex club and touring with Carroll Dickerson. By 1927 Hines was a major Chicago piano stylist, his well-developed technique and sparkling runs appreciated by none other than Louis Armstrong who, alongside him for a time with Carroll Dickerson, happily used him on a number of classic 1928 Hot Five recordings, the famous "Weather Bird" duet included. Hines's modern-sounding right-hand lines, his very full accompaniment and his rhythmic sophistication all perfectly suited Armstrong's creative muse. Hines also cut the memorable "Apex Blues" with Noone that year.

Hines formed his own big band in the same year, taking a residency at Chicago's Mob-run Grand Terrace which lasted until 1940, when the band broke up. During this long enforced residency Hines hired his fair share of young talent, including Budd Johnson, Valaida Snow, Charlie Allen, Trummy Young, Ray Nance, Omer Simeon, and Horace Henderson, and hired good writers to supply his material. However, it was not until the 1940s, when he was free to tour, that he assembled a band containing Billy Eckstine, Dizzy Gillespie, and Charlie Parker, which became a legendary ensemble for the brief time it existed. Hines disbanded, like many other leaders, in 1947 as the economic climate became forbidding. Initially he intended to open his own club, but was talked into becoming a member of the new Louis Armstrong group, the All-Stars. He was part of this setup until the fall of 1951, when the clash of temperaments between him and Armstrong – both strong leaders – could no longer be sustained. Based on the West Coast, Hines kept in shape by running a band in San Francisco, but was largely forgotten by the wider jazz world until a string of small-group engagements in New York in 1964 led to rave reviews from critics and full houses wherever he appeared. A spate of new records, revealing a Hines mostly unchanged but even more florid and apt to improvise tangentially, let the world know he was back. From then until his death, despite long spells of ill health, Hines toured regularly all over the world and appeared at countless festivals; he also made one of the great albums of Ellington interpretations in 1977 (New World Records), a vintage solo piano outing. At his death Hines was universally regarded as a jazz pianist of the first rank.

SEE ALSO: Jimmy Noone, Louis Armstrong, Budd Johnson, Billy Eckstine, Dizzy Gillespie, Charlie Parker

Johnny Hodges

Altoist Johnny Hodges, long-term Ellington kingpin, seen here playing with the Ellington band at Basin Street, 1956

fact file

BORN 1907

DIED 1970

MUSICAL SELECTION
Back to Back

Alto (and occasional soprano) saxophonist Hodges was one of the most instantly recognizable sounds in jazz during his lifetime, either soaring out of the Ellington reed section, leading it like no other, or taking an impassioned solo while standing rooted to the spot, staring into space and looking as emotional as the average lamppost.

Hodges was born in Cambridge, Massachusetts, and originally learned drums and piano, not swapping to sax until 1920. The self-taught Hodges took some instruction from the maser, Sidney Bechet, while he worked for him, then worked in a number of bands in Boston and New York before, in 1928, landing the position of lead alto with Ellington. Hodges slowly emerged into the limelight in a band which was dominated initially by Ellington's love of his brass sounds as conjured by Bubber Miley and Tricky Sam Nanton, but by the middle of the 1930s Hodges was the nominal leader on many Ellington small-group masterpieces, recording a string of self-penned tunes such as "Jeep's Blues" and "Good Queen Bess." Hodges's two great strengths were as a ballad player and as an interpreter of the blues, his big tone and passionate attack suiting to perfection both forms. Ellington milked these strengths to perfection with an endless series of pieces crafted to suit him. By the time he left the Ellington band in 1951, Hodges was possibly the most famous altoist in jazz. He ran a small band from 1951–55, which combined a typically swinging style with a hefty dose of R&B riffing. Hodges, not a natural leader, had initial success but was relieved to eventually re-join Ellington in 1955. Since that time, however, Hodges continued to record in his own (invariably ex-Ellingtonian) settings under his leadership, a habit which persisted until shortly before his death. He also made two classic small-group dates as co-leader with Ellington in 1959, one of them, *Back to Back* (Verve), being a reinvestigation of some of the oldest blues numbers associated with jazz history, from W.C. Handy onward. Hodges stayed with Ellington until his death in 1970. His 1967 reading of Billy Strayhorn's last composition, "Blood Count," is one of jazz's most moving aural documents.

SEE ALSO: Duke Ellington, Sidney Bechet, Billy Strayhorn

Dave Holland

fact file

BORN 1946

MUSICAL SELECTION
Conference of the Blues

Virtuoso British bassist Dave Holland, who came to international fame in the late 1960s with Miles Davis

Holland is a virtuoso bassist who came to international attention on joining the Miles Davis group in 1968. Since then he has fulfilled the promise his talents then showed. Holland was born in Wolverhampton in the UK and began playing the double bass at the age of 17, later attending the Guildhall School of Music in London from 1964 to 1968. Holland was an enthusiastic participant in the London music scene of the time, both classical and modern jazz, and was heard there by Miles Davis, who noted his talents and in the fall of 1968 rang him from New York to request his presence in his band. Holland joined Davis then, staying with the trumpeter through one of his most turbulent artistic periods when he switched from acoustic to electric music. Holland left late in 1970 to form Circle with Chick Corea and Barry Altschul, with Anthony Braxton soon making it into a quartet. This experimental band made a number of tours and records and some fine music into the bargain, but broke up in 1972. By then Holland had already made one of the classic double-bass albums, with Barre Phillips, *Music From Two Basses* (ECM, 1971). Holland went on to play with Stan Getz and John Abercrombie's Gateway during the mid-1970s, as well as running an occasional group of his own which featured Sam Rivers and, with the addition of Anthony Braxton, recorded *Conference of the Birds* for ECM in 1972. This occasional event became a more fixed idea in the 1980s, Holland forming a band which at various times has included Kenny Wheeler and Steve Coleman. Holland's focus began to switch to teaching toward the end of the 1980s, and he took a position in Canada which allowed him time to teach and to play. He continues to tour with his own bands and record with all-star line-ups, his virtuosity, tone, and taste unimpaired.

SEE ALSO: Miles Davis, Chick Corea, Anthony Braxton, Stan Getz

BH

Billie Holiday

Holiday is regarded by many as "the voice of jazz": her style of singing – heart-on-sleeve and with large helpings of a phraseology developed from listening to melodies paraphrased by jazz greats such as Louis Armstrong – made her an instant icon to music lovers. Her life, full of incident and containing more than its share of sordid and shabby moments, seemed to many the stuff of jazz as well. This makes no allowances for the rich diversity to be found either in jazz or in Holiday's own life, personality, and art. She is bigger than such perceptions.

She was born Eleanora Fagan in Baltimore, the daughter of banjoist Clarence Holiday, but her early life is obscure. Abandoned by her father and left with relatives at an early age by her mother, Billie moved to New York around 1929 and lived with her mother, picking up menial jobs where she could. By 1930 she was singing for change at Harlem clubs, but she was not accorded any real recognition until 1933, when jazz talent scout John Hammond heard her singing in a Harlem club and arranged for her to appear on a series of recordings featuring Benny Goodman. The following year she appeared in the short film *Symphony In Black*, a vehicle for the Ellington band, then in 1935 signed a management deal with Joe Glaser. From that point on Holiday's voice becomes central to the ongoing history of jazz, her sides with Teddy Wilson's assorted small groups for Brunswick being rightly prized as some of the greatest jazz ever recorded. Her singing on tour with the Basie band in 1937 is still recalled as an all-time high (virtually no recording remains from this brief tenure). Her change of style – from the bright-eyed enthusiasm of the up-tempo numbers with Wilson and the dreamily beautiful ballads, with Lester Young, Ben Webster, or "Chu" Berry adding their perfect accompaniments, to the more seriously melancholy repertoire and treatment she took up in the 1940s – shifted both her artistic base and her core listnership, from now on increasingly made up of young white intellectuals.

By the mid-1940s Holiday was deeply involved in drugs, her heroin habit wreaking havoc with her professional life, while her personal and professional existence became hopelessly entwined with a series of disastrous boyfriend/husband/personal managers. In 1946 she was arrested for heroin usage and underwent a cure. The following year she appeared in the seriously skewed Hollywood telling of the story of jazz, *New Orleans*, where, to her chagrin, she got to play a maid. By the end of this decade Holiday was drinking heavily and still not entirely free of drug dependency, her voice no longer the full-ranged, flexible instrument of her youth. Yet she learned to use its now severe limitations to her advantage, the recordings and concerts of her last decade being among the most moving musical documents of the 1950s from any artistic discipline. Holiday appeared in the 1957 CBS TV documentary, *The Sound of Jazz*, singing with Count Basie, Gerry Mulligan, Buck Clayton and a visibly ailing Lester Young, and also gave many concerts and made festival appearances, but time was running out. In her last year she made two albums with string orchestras, the better of the two named *Lady In Satin* (Columbia), and pronounced herself deeply satisfied – she had always wanted to do it, she said. A few months later, and shortly after the death of Lester Young, Holiday died in a New York hospital bed, technically under arrest for heroin possession, a policeman at her bedside to prevent her escape.

fact file

BORN 1915

DIED 1959

MUSICAL SELECTION
Lady In Satin

Lady Day: Billie Holiday preparing for a broadcast in 1945

SEE ALSO: Louis Armstrong, Benny Goodman, Duke Ellington, Teddy Wilson, Count Basie, Lester Young, Ben Webster

Freddie Hubbard

fact file

BORN 1938

MUSICAL SELECTION
The Artistry of Freddie Hubbard

Freddie Hubbard, a trumpeter who had the technical capacity and imagination to develop the Clifford Brown legacy during the 1960s and 1970s

Hubbard was perhaps the first post-Clifford Brown trumpeter to emerge who was not principally indebted to that great formative stylist for his own musical character. Hubbard was born in Indianapolis into a musical family, his sister displaying unusual talents in classical music. Hubbard began serious music studies in high school, switching to trumpet in late teens and picking up work with the Montgomery Brothers band as well as sitting in on occasional visits to Chicago venues. His brilliant technique and willingness to rise to any challenge won him admirers. After moving to New York in 1959, he shared an apartment with Eric Dolphy and worked with a string of top leaders, including Sonny Rollins, Quincy Jones (with whom he toured Europe) and J.J. Johnson. He appeared on Eric Dolphy's first LP as a leader and ended 1960 with a strong contribution to Ornette Coleman's seminal *Free Jazz* album. In 1961 Hubbard joined The Jazz Messengers and also appeared on the classic Oliver Nelson album, *Blues And The Abstract Truth*. He signed with Blue Note and made a steady stream of albums up to 1966, including appearing as sideman on Eric Dolphy's classic *Out To Lunch* album of 1964, although his best album as leader in that decade, *The Artistry of Freddie Hubbar* (1962), was ironically made for Impulse! records. Hubbard's arresting style, powerful technique, and bright musical imagination enabled him to fit in all these contexts brilliantly and made him one of the most in-demand trumpeters in jazz. In 1965 Hubbard went out as a leader, but the following year he joined the new Max Roach group, swapping to Atlantic as a recording artist as well and beginning his long affair with rock and funk on his album, *Backlash*.

At the beginning of the 1970s Hubbard signed with CTI records and began a series of records aimed at the perceived crossover market of the time, his brilliant facility and personal eclecticism making him a natural for the role. His own quintet, with Joe Henderson on tenor, was a popular live group but Hubbard continued to move increasingly into the electric pop and funk areas, landing a number of commercially viable hits but not producing music of any lasting value. By the end of the decade this notoriously fickle market was moving away from him, and he had also rediscovered his jazz roots on the road with the VSOP quintet, making world tours and successful albums with them. Hubbard's rejuvenated jazz career picked up pace in the 1980s and he made some fine double-leader albums with trumpeter Woody Shaw as well as appearing annually at many large jazz festivals in Europe and the US. He has led his own groups for the best part of three decades now, but in the past few years his previously imperious technique has shown signs of wear and some of his astonishing agility has been lost.

SEE ALSO: Clifford Brown, Eric Dolphy, Sonny Rollins, Quincy Jones, J. J. Johnson, Ornette Coleman, Art Blakey

Bobby Hutcherson

Vibist Bobby Hutcherson, a fan of Milt Jackson but a possessor of a highly individual style of his own

fact file

BORN 1941

MUSICAL SELECTION
Happenings

Los Angeles-born and raised in Pasadena, vibist Hutcherson has spent the majority of his life in California, paying the price normally exacted on a fine career for not having made New York a permanent base. He took piano lessons from an early age but was sold on vibes after hearing a Milt Jackson record at the age of 15. Mostly self-taught but with a few lessons from vibist Dave Pike, Hutcherson was gigging around LA with local groups like Curtis Amy's and Charles Lloyd's in the late 1950s, moving to San Francisco to play with the Al Grey–Billy Mitchell group and traveling with them to New York in 1961. Once there he quickly attracted attention for his exciting, fluent playing which, while using Jackson as a starting point, was rare in its freshness and invention. He began playing with a range of different leaders, including Jackie McLean, Grachan Moncur III, and Eric Dolphy, making recordings with all three and in 1965 landing a contract with Blue Note records, for whom he produced a series of forward-looking albums featuring players such as Joe Henderson, Sam Rivers, Andrew Hill, and Joe Chambers. The same year he cemented his avant-garde reputation by playing in the Archie Shepp group for a number of months. In 1968, after a stint with John Handy, he formed a group with tenor player Harold Land, moving back to the West Coast with it and settling there permanently. He continued to record regularly for Blue Note, making a wide variety of albums, being one of the last jazz artists to quit the label as it was gradually wound down by its owners, Liberty, in the mid-1970s. By this time Hutcherson had evolved into a mature stylist with his roots firmly in bop but with a constantly inquiring musical mind. A contract with Columbia in the early 1980s brought out Hutcherson's Latin leanings (a side of him also present on 1970s Blue Note records), while the latter-day albums for Contemporary and Landmark show what a thoroughly accomplished and imaginative player he is in more orthodox jazz contexts. Recent duets and small-group partnerships with McCoy Tyner have once again raised the profile of a West Coast legend who, with Gary Burton, is easily the best of the post-Jackson vibists.

SEE ALSO: Milt Jackson, Charles Lloyd, Jackie McLean, Eric Dolphy, Joe Henderson, Andrew Hill, Archie Shepp

Abdullah Ibrahim

fact file

BORN 1934

MUSICAL SELECTION
No Fear, No Die

Pianist and band leader Abdullah Ibrahim, long-term promoter of South African musical creativity

Abdullah Ibrahim was born Adolf Johannes (Dollar) Brand in Cape Town, South Africa, and took lessons on piano from an early age. Ibrahim was surrounded by music as a child, hearing classical music, spirituals, hymns, local popular music, American R&B, and jazz, especially that of Duke Ellington. After experience with a number of local bands he started his own group, the Jazz Epistles, in 1960, and in the two years of its existence it employed some of the best and brightest on the Cape Town scene, including Hugh Masekela and Kippie Moeketsi. In 1962 Ibrahim came to Europe with his own trio and played a number of engagements; discovered by Duke Ellington in a Zürich club, he recorded for Ellington's then record label, Reprise, and began appearing on the festival circuit, creating a considerable stir. For the rest of the 1960s he remained in circulation in Europe and America, playing mostly with avant-garde musicians but using a style extracted fundamentally from Ellington and Monk. In 1968 he converted to Islam, publicly assuming, in the mid-1970s, the name he still lives under. As the 1970s unwound, Ibrahim began to make regular visits back to South Africa and to adopt progressively larger elements of African jazz practice into his compositional and improvisational output.

By 1977 Ibrahim had settled in New York and was running his own band there, but his musical reputation was progressively more identified with the music of his homeland. By the opening of the 1980s he had struck up a partnership with altoist Carlos Ward which was to bear fruit all through the decade through the various incarnations of the Ekaya band; other members at various times included Ricky Ford and Charles Davis. The simple beauty of this band's music brought Ibrahim great international recognition and made him one of the top draws on the live jazz circuit as the 1980s came to a close. During the 1990s he has continued to celebrate his South African musical and cultural roots, and has also completed outstanding film soundtracks as well as pursuing various solo, duet, and group ventures.

SEE ALSO: Duke Ellington, Thelonious Monk

Milt Jackson

fact file

BORN 1923

MUSICAL SELECTION
Bags & Trane

Milt Jackson, vibes star of both the Modern Jazz Quartet and a variety of his own groups

Jackson is universally acknowledged as the greatest postwar vibes player, a man with effortless expressive facility in the general bop musical language, but with an equally profound wellspring of inspiration to be found in the blues. Jackson began by studying music in his native Detroit at Michigan State University. Accomplished on piano and xylophone as well as vibes, Jackson was also adept in gospel singing. In 1945 he was heard in Detroit by the visiting Dizzy Gillespie, who shortly after hired him to play in his own New York-based quintet, for whom he made many live appearances and important early bop recordings for a number of labels. Leaving Gillespie after some time in the 1946 big band, Jackson freelanced around New York, playing with Tadd Dameron and Thelonious Monk among others, then settling into Woody Herman's band (1949–50) before becoming once more a part of the Gillespie setup in 1950–52. In 1953 Jackson combined with some ex-Gillespie sidemen to form the Milt Jackson Modern Jazz Quartet. After a short amount of experimenting with personnel, this settled down with Jackson, pianist John Lewis, bassist Percy Heath, and drummer Kenny Clarke. The name was also shortened to the Modern Jazz Quartet. From then until 1974 the band persevered, with just the 1955 substitution of Connie Kay for Kenny Clarke, in this time becoming one of the most creative, respected, and popular jazz groups in history.

During this long tenure Jackson kept up a very active solo career, recording prolifically with a string of jazz greats in the 1950s including Ray Charles and John Coltrane, with his own occasional groups in the 1960s featuring players such as Jimmy Heath and Hank Jones, and guesting with Oscar Peterson and Ray Brown. The MJQ re-formed in 1982 as an annual touring group, allowing Jackson to pursue other ventures in the meantime – something he has consistently done, his creative energies nowhere near exhausted in this, his sixth decade of professional music-making.

SEE ALSO: Dizzy Gillespie, Tadd Dameron, Thelonious Monk, Woody Herman, Milt Jackson, John Lewis, Kenny Clarke

Harry James

Harry James leading his own band in New York city, 1942

fact file

BORN 1916

DIED 1983

MUSICAL SELECTION
"Peckin'"

James was born in Albany, Georgia, to circus parents, playing in the circus orchestra led by his father after attending high school in Beaumont, Texas. Winning a trumpet award at age 14, James came up through local Texas bands to join Ben Pollack in 1935, staying with him until his famous move to Benny Goodman's band in December 1936. Leading Goodman's trumpet section for two years, James proved himself one of the great lead trumpeters of jazz as well as an exciting, bold, swaggering soloist, certainly the most entertaining trumpet soloist Goodman engaged as a regular. Many arrangements were fashioned for the James style and sound, with "Peckin" being perhaps the most famous. During this period James also habitually attended jam sessions, espcially in New York, and became involved in some of the immortal Teddy Wilson-Billie Holiday small group recordings of this period.

In late 1938 James left Goodman's orchestra, debuting with his own big band in January 1939. James, a great showman as well as a consummate technician, spread his stylistic ambit broadly from the beginning, recording both driving swing material and more sentimental arrangements, including the kitsch "Carnival of Venice" (1940), a massive hit which was instrumental in establishing him as more than just a jazz bandleader. James's style never evolved past the swing era, but the drama of his playing and his brilliant attack have brought him admirers in every subsequent generation. With his good looks and talent, a string of appearances in Hollywood films came his way between 1943-47, and he continued to lead his band with great enthusiasm, using altoist Willie Smith as straw boss for the band. The economic straits of the late 1940s forced James to scale down, and the shift of Smith, Juan Tizol and Louis Bellson to Duke Ellington in the early 1950s forced James to re-assess the situation as much as changing fashions. As a consequence, the trumpeter ran a small group for a time. By the end of the decade, however, he had Smith back on board and a new big band which he maintained until the end of his career, touring regularly and appearing on every continent, right up to his final battle with cancer in 1983.

SEE ALSO: Benny Goodman, Louis Bellson

Illinois Jacquet

fact file

BORN 1922

MUSICAL SELECTION
The Kid & The Brute

The indefatigable Texas tenor, Illinois Jacquet

Born in Broussard, Louisiana, but moving to Houston in early infancy, Jacquet came from a musical family, his father being a semipro bassist. Making his stage debut at the age of three, Jacquet started out on drums, but by the mid-1930s was proficient on both alto and soprano sax. He joined the Milt Larkin band in 1939, moving on to the Floyd Ray Orchestra in 1940, with whom he traveled to LA in 1941, where he joined the Lionel Hampton band. With Hampton he made a quick transition to one of the hottest tenor players in the country, landing a sizable hit with his solo on the band's version of "Flying Home," a track which served as a virtual blueprint for screaming and honking tenor sax players. Stints with Cab Calloway (1943–44) and Count Basie (1945–46) only increased his popularity and exposure, while the records released from the first JATP concert in 1944 made him a major celebrity. A star of Gjon Mili's famous short film, *Jammin' The Blues* (1944), from 1946 onward he made annual tours with JATP as well as running his own small group, which until the end of the 1940s remained one of the hottest acts in jazz. Another triumph with JATP in 1947, a Carnegie Hall duel with Flip Phillips, once again kept Jacquet's name to the fore. With the slow-down in fiery jazz, the advent of cool and the rise of R&B and rock 'n' roll, Jacquet's role as the firebrand Texas tenor gradually lost its cachet, and though he made superb records (including a double-header with Ben Webster) and played coherent and swinging jazz throughout the 1950s, his star waned.

With the demise of the international JATP tours at the close of the 1960s, Jacquet returned to the US club circuit as a solo act and, from the mid-1960s onward, as a regular partner with organist Milt Buckner. In the 1970s Jacquet finally shook off the "honking tenor" opprobrium which had followed him for many years, his huge, beautiful tone, verve, and swing, as well as his personal amalgam of Hawkins and Young, being recognized for the unique and valuable contribution it undoubtedly is. In the late 1980s Jacquet began running a big band for part of each season, making the rounds of the festivals with it as well as making solo appearances all around the world. An elder statesman in the music, he remains active and energetic today.

SEE ALSO: Lionel Hampton, Cab Calloway, Count Basie, Flip Phillips, Ben Webster, Coleman Hawkins, Lester Young

Ahmad Jamal

fact file

BORN 1930

MUSICAL SELECTION
But Not For Me

Pianist Ahmad Jamal, a seminal influence on 1950s and 1960s jazz

Jamal created his own distinct hybrid of Nat Cole's trio and Erroll Garner's formal design and use of musical drama in the late 1940s, emerging in the 1950s as a popular and highly influential stylist in his own right. His popularity hardly endeared him to the jazz establishment, who have consistently downgraded him ever since, but Jamal's musical integrity has remained intact to the present day.

Born in Pittsburgh, Jamal studied early with the singer and teacher Mary Caldwell Dawson as well as pianist James Miller, moving on to make a professional debut at 11. By the close of the 1940s Jamal was playing with a drummerless combo, the Four Strings; in 1951 he started his own version, led by himself with Ray Crawford on guitar, called the Three Strings. This group debuted for Okeh in 1951 and immediately scored hits with their clever arrangements of material such as "The Surrey With The Fringe On Top" and "Billy Boy" as well as his own "Ahmad's Blues." The trio became a mainstay in New York and Chicago, changing in 1955 to the Ahmad Jamal Trio and shifting to piano-bass-drums, with Israel Crosby and Vernell Fournier. It was this band which cut the classic million-selling *But Not For Me* session live at Chicago's Pershing Lounge in 1958. Jamal was quickly recognized as the most fashionable pianist in jazz, with all sorts of musicians, including long-term fan Miles Davis, learning to take the Jamal approach to arrangements of old standards. The interplay in Jamal's trio, plus his complete technique, use of space, and his immaculate and provocative arrangements of his material, all proved study models for others, including Bill Evans; meanwhile, Jamal's career continued unabated until the close of the 1960s, when he developed a more vigorous, expansive style, experimenting with electric keyboards, then dropped out of music for a period after disillusionment with the business. A return to high-profile performances with a trio reflecting the subtlety and interplay of his great Crosby–Fournier group has placed Jamal back in the front rank of jazz pianists.

SEE ALSO: Nat King Cole, Erroll Garner, Miles Davis, Bill Evans

Joseph Jarman

fact file

BORN 1937

MUSICAL SELECTION
Song For
As If It Were The Seasons

Joseph Jarman, founding AACM member, spent some 30 years with the Art Ensemble of Chicago

Musician, composer, and poet, Jarman was born in Pine Bluff, Arkansas, moving with his family to Chicago while still a small boy. His first instrument being the drums, he played in high school bands in the early 1950s before doing military service from 1955 to 1958. Playing in all sorts of bands on his release, including rock 'n' roll and blues, Jarman found his true musical calling, according to his later claims, when Roscoe Mitchell introduced him to Richard Abrams and his Experimental Band in the early 1960s. As Jarman commented in 1967, "That band was the most important thing that ever happened to me". Jarman played with Abrams and developed his own ideas about contemporary music, becoming an early member of AACM and forming his quartet, made up of himself on reeds, pianist Christopher Gaddy, bassist Charles Clark, and drummer Thurman Barker. Jarman was creating closely controlled compositional structures, interweaving written parts, improvisation, recitation, and elements of theater, his quartet operating as a perfect sounding board for his new approach. His first albums as a leader, *Song For* (1966) and *As If It Were The Seasons* (1967), detailed the development of this approach, also expressed in the unrecorded *A Tribute to the Hard Core* (1965), but a combination of events demanded the different unfolding of Jarman's talents. The birth and development of Roscoe Mitchell's cooperative quartet, the Art Ensemble, with Lester Bowie, Malachi Favors, and Phillip Wilson, as well as the deaths in short sequence of Christopher Gaddy and Charles Clark, prompted a joining of forces, with Jarman becoming a full-time member of the Art Ensemble in 1969.

He has functioned as a member since then, as well as pursuing solo interests from time to time, including duet albums with Anthony Braxton, Don Moye, and Don Pullen and a book of poetry, *Black Case (Return From Exile)* (1977).

SEE ALSO: Roscoe Mitchell, Muhal Richard Abrams, The Art Ensemble of Chicago, Lester Bowie, Anthony Braxton

Keith Jarrett

Born in Allentown, Philadelphia, Jarrett came from a large and musical family, beginning piano studies at the age of three and making his recital debut at seven. After this he progressively took up drums, soprano sax, and vibes. Outside of school hours he was constantly appearing professionally in a number of settings, then moved to Boston in 1962 to spend a year studying at Berklee College before starting up his own trio and playing professionally around the Boston area. In 1965 he moved to New York, at first struggling to make an impression but finally being noticed by Art Blakey at a jam session. In December of that year he joined the Jazz Messengers, gaining peer-group visibility during the months he was with the band before joining the quartet that the tenor player Charles Lloyd was forming in spring 1966. By the end of the summer 1966 Lloyd's quartet had become a jazz sensation; by the following year the band had crossed over to the large new market for more sophisticated music now being created by the progressive tendencies in the rock movement of the day. With Lloyd, Jarrett played festivals all over the world and was a constant visitor to the Fillmore West, where the band built a loyal following. Their record of their appearance at the 1966 Monterey Festival, *Forest Flower* (Atlantic), sold in excess of a million copies. By the time Jarrett left Lloyd in 1969 he was a major piano star. He made a series of trio albums for Neshui Ertegun's Vortex offshoot from Atlantic, including *Life Between The Exit Signs* (1968), with Charlie Haden and Paul Motian. By 1971 the trio had become a quartet with the addition of saxophonist Dewey Redman; meanwhile, Jarrett had spent some time in the highly charged electronic environment of the Miles Davis band and finally opted for acoustic music. In 1971 he made his debut solo piano album, *Facing You* (ECM), continued working with his quartet (later known as the American Quartet after Jarrett formed a similar line-up in Europe with Jan Garbarek on saxophone), and in 1973 began his trailbreaking series of solo piano recitals. Playing often uninterruptedly for an hour or more to rapt audience attention, Jarrett became the first jazz artist to create and sustain a demand for wholly extemporized solo concert performances. He toured the world intensively in the 1970s and early 1980s using this format. In the 1980s Jarrett began to have his own compositions recorded, both by himself and by others; he also embarked upon a reinvestigation of old Broadway standards, naming the trio he used for this, with Gary Peacock and Jack DeJohnette, the Standards Trio. This band continues to reconvene from time to time. Jarrett cut down on his solo recitals, although they continued to occur, concentrating on other projects: in 1991 he recorded one of the first and most effective tributes to the recently deceased Miles Davis (*Bye Bye Blackbird*, ECM) while also becoming involved in the performance and recording of classical repertoire, from Bach to Shostakovich. His latest large project has been the issuing of a six-CD box of four nights at New York's Blue Note club with his trio, allowing the CD audience to hear every musical moment of any significance from those nights and the development of the trio's overall performance. Jarrett remains one of the busiest and most committed of musicians today, while his music will continue to fascinate for years to come.

fact file

BORN 1945

MUSICAL SELECTION
Facing You
Bye Bye Blackbird

Pianist Keith Jarrett, equally at home in solo recital or with his own small groups, known to accompany himself by humming while playing

SEE ALSO: Art Blakey, Charles Lloyd, Herbie Mann, Charlie Haden, Paul Motian, Jack DeJohnette, Miles Davis

Eddie Jefferson

fact file

BORN 1918

DIED 1979

MUSICAL SELECTION
Letter From Home

Singer Eddie Jefferson, seen here in a 1950s publicity portrait, brought jazz singing to new popularity

Jefferson was for a short time one of the more significant vocalist innovators in jazz, helping create the improvised jazz vocal with appropriate words added to tell a story which would be appreciated by the audience. Jefferson, born in Pittsburgh, was as much a dancer-entertainer as a singer: he studied tuba in school but played a number of instruments as well as featuring successfully as a tap dancer: in this capacity he appeared at the 1933 World's Fair in Chicago. He joined Coleman Hawkins in 1939, moving on to all-round singing and dancing in a number of settings, evolving during the 1940s his penchant for a type of vocalese where the so-called scatting (usually copying the instrumental solo of a jazz great from a record) carried its own lyrics. This technique later became hugely popular through the endeavors of King Pleasure and Lambert, Hendricks, and Ross in the late 1950s and early 1960s, but Jefferson only marginally benefited from these later conquests. During the 1950s he worked with James Moody for five years, but after a number of albums on Riverside/Jazzland he dropped out of sight until the late 1960s, when he rejoined Moody, newly out from Dizzy Gillespie's band, and attempted to revive his jazz following. In the 1970s he worked with the groups of both Roy Brooks and Richie Cole, but never reached a point where he could support a solo career. One evening, after an engagement in a Detroit club, he was murdered on the street outside.

SEE ALSO: Coleman Hawkins, Dizzy Gillespie

Budd Johnson

fact file

BORN 1910

DIED 1984

MUSICAL SELECTION
Let's Swing!

The resourceful and persuasive tenor saxophonist Budd Johnson

Johnson, younger brother of trombonist Keg Johnson, was born in Dallas, Texas, and studied music with Booker T. Washington's daughter. Originally a drummer, he was touring with territory bands from 1924 onward, picking up the tenor sax in 1926, moving to Kansas City the following year to work with George E. Lee, later running a combo in Chicago with Teddy Wilson. This band lasted until 1933, when both men joined the Louis Armstrong band for a while, then Johnson moved on to the Earl Hines band at the Grand Terrace in late 1934. He stayed with Hines until 1942, creating his reputation as a soloist in the meantime. Johnson's remarkable fluidity and his ability to use the most up-to-date ideas in music led to his being a consistent advocate of new talent in jazz and a soloist who was remarkably forward-thinking for his day. A swing tenor man with roots in Hawkins, Johnson quickly embraced the ideas of bebop when they were first becoming known in the early 1940s, arranging for younger players to join the ranks of bands such as Earl Hines, Billy Eckstine, Woody Herman and Boyd Raeburn between 1942 and 1945. A fine composer and arranger, Johnson also promoted the new thinking in his own pieces and arranged for Dizzy Gillespie to appear with Coleman Hawkins on a 1944 recording date, the first with bop musicians. Johnson later played in the Gillespie big band, and also played on 52nd Street with Oscar Pettiford and Gillespie.

During the 1950s, with the waning of interest in swing-style musicians, Johnson picked up with an old colleague, Jesse Stone, now heavily involved in rock 'n' roll sessions, and Johnson helped Stone and Al Sears run various backing bands for rock shows. Coming back into jazz at the end of the 1950s, his timeless sound and conception could be heard with Benny Goodman (1956–57), then later with a number of Gil Evans projects, most notably the "Out of the Cool" sessions. Johnson also made valuable contributions in the early 1960s to the Quincy Jones and Count Basie bands while surfacing occasionally at the head of small-group projects. Johnson remained busy through the 1960s and 1970s with many projects, appeared in the famous documentary *The Last of the Blue Devils* and was a founder of the JPJ Quartet with Oliver Jackson as well as working with the New York Jazz Repertory Company, but he was rarely accorded the attention his first-rate talent deserved.

SEE ALSO: Teddy Wilson, Louis Armstrong, Woody Herman, Dizzy Gillespie, Oscar Pettiford, Gil Evans, Count Basie

Bunk Johnson

fact file

BORN 1889

DIED 1949

MUSICAL SELECTION
1944

The man who unwittingly launched a thousand revivalists, Bunk Johnson

William Geary "Bunk" Johnson is one of the most written-about and controversial figures in the history of jazz. Born in New Orleans 10 years after the date he most commonly claimed in later life to have been his birthday, Johnson was a cornet player on the early New Orleans scene, being active in that city from approximately 1910 to 1914, just at the time when "jazz" music was being associated with "jazz" the word. Johnson claimed in later life to have been a member in the 1890s of Buddy Bolden's pioneering band, but his correct birth date heavily contradicts this. What is proven is that he played with the Eagle Band in New Orleans and that young Louis Armstrong was very taken with his playing, which was not as forceful as that of Joe Oliver and Freddie Keppard, but which carried a melody in an entrancing way.

Johnson left New Orleans in 1915, traveling throughout the US in search of work, turning up in the oddest of musical circumstances as times got hard. Virtually retired due to dental problems and a lack of enthusiasm by the mid-1930s, Johnson left music completely and lived in obscurity in New Iberia, where he was rediscovered by young researchers Fred Ramsey and Bill Russell. The enthusiasm of these earnest young men rekindled Johnson's flame and he resumed playing, becoming the man at the vanguard of the New Orleans revival in the early 1940s, his spare style and lean statements being perceived to be jazz at its earliest and most pristine formation. Johnson himself contradicted these impressions, making plain a preference for repertoire until then not associated with classic jazz and frequently cursing his fellow musicians on stage for playing too loud or too amateurishly. Johnson's band with clarinetist George Lewis foundered in 1946 due to such differences, exacerbated by the cornetist's heavy drinking, but by then the revivalist bandwagon was unstoppable, and every Johnson assertion and evasion – that he taught Louis Armstrong, for example, or that he played with all the major pre-records New Orleans stars – went unchallenged until decades after his death. His stated preference for dance music and latter-day popular tunes is not borne out by the music he recorded in his final years apart from a 1947 session in which he was accompanied by more swing-style players, and where he at least sounds less strained. A figure whose historical importance far outweighs his actual musical worth, Johnson to this day remains a rallying point for all that is backward-looking in the traditional jazz music scene.

SEE ALSO: Buddy Bolden, Louis Armstrong, Leo Oliver, Freddie Keppard, George Lewis

J.J. Johnson

fact file

BORN 1924

MUSICAL SELECTION
Proof Positive
Vivian

J.J. Johnson translated bebop into a language trombonists could relay

Indianapolis-born trombonist/composer Johnson virtually reinvented the trombone for the purposes of postwar jazz. A perfectionist in the realm of music and a man utterly dedicated to making the trombone do what he wanted, Johnson evolved a level of technical expertise previously undreamed of in jazz, his smooth delivery of the most complex passages a constant source of amazement to his contemporaries. This alone would not have amounted to a significant career, but Johnson was also the man to bring bebop harmonic and rhythmic practice to the instrument in a way which made meaningful music rather than simply strings of flashy notes.

Johnson began trombone in his early teens, after early lessons on piano and organ, originally finding inspiration in the work of Trummy Young and Jack Teagarden. Working professionally by his late teens, Johnson played in territory bands, meeting Fats Navarro on the way, before playing in Benny Carter's band from 1942 to 1945, living on the West Coast during this time. Recordings of his style in this period - at length on the 1944 JATP concert sides – show him to be evolving his later style but retaining large portions of the effusive swing trombone approach as favored by Trummy Young. After a stint with Basie during 1945–46, Johnson began working in small groups on New York's 52nd Street, revealing his evolved style among the boppers who were now his favored company. Johnson was kept busy in such circles, even touring overseas under US government auspices, but by the early 1950s he was struggling for work and for a time dropped out of the music business. A 1954 idea for a twin-trombone-fronted small group paired Johnson with fellow bopper Kai Winding and proved successful beyond the pair's expectations, the band becoming a top jazz draw all across the US and selling thousands of records worldwide. In this period Johnson's composition, "Lament," appeared on *Miles Ahead*, while "Poem For Brass" was recorded by Gunther Schuller and Dmitri Mitropoulos in 1956 and other works continued to be commissioned, notably for Dizzy Gillespie, who took a central role in the recording of the orchestral *Perceptions* in the early 1960s. Johnson, meanwhile, swapped to leading his own small group, J.J. Johnson Inc., which had a predictably high-quality repertoire and standard of arrangements and kept the trombonist top in all jazz popularity polls. Johnson disbanded in 1960 to concentrate on composing and arranging, writing a series of major works as well as making a string of more commercial material for RCA Victor and becoming a temporary member of Miles Davis's group.

By the mid-1960s Johnson had formed his own group again and was making small-group recordings revealing a new aggression and expansiveness in his approach, as the modal pieces on *Proof Positive* (Impulse!, 1965), demonstrated. Johnson continued to play live but also found increasing success with his composing work, eventually moving in the 1970s to the West Coast and working for the next 15 years in the studios there as a highly respected film and soundtrack composer. Johnson kept his trombone lip in, however, until the mid-1990s, regularly venturing out on the road to keep in touch with the public and making high-quality albums in front of small and large groups. Johnson now concentrates on writing music.

SEE ALSO: Jack Teagarden, Fats Navarro, Benny Carter, Count Basie, Dizzy Gillespie, Miles Davis

James P. Johnson

fact file

BORN 1894

DIED 1955

MUSICAL SELECTION
Yamacraw
Symphony Harlem

Stride pianist and composer James P. Johnson, seen here in 1921, was influenced by elements of ragtime, blues and classical music

Pianist-composer Johnson was born in New Brunswick, New Jersey, learning music from his mother. He moved with his family to New York in 1908, making a regular living at music before the end of the decade. Johnson eagerly took in all the music then thriving in New York, including ragtime, classical, and blues, and was serving up his version of all this to clients at various mid-town New York dives in the years prior to World War I, cutting his first cylinder rolls in 1916. Equally adept at theater music, Johnson traveled after the war to England with the show, *Plantation Days*, then on his return began to establish a reputation as a first-rate composer of show tunes, completing the score for the hit show *Runnin' Wild* in 1923. By this time his driving piano style had matured into the stride left-hand figures for which he and other New York pianists of this time were to become world famous. Johnson, however, was more than just a pianist and songsmith, for during the 1920s and 1930s he consistently completed larger-scale, through-composed works, such as *Yamacraw* and *Symphony Harlem*, many of which were premiered in New York but most of which failed to find an audience: at this time, a black writing serious music simply had no niche to aim for. Undeterred, Johnson continued to compose, writing operatic works as well as, in 1938, completing a symphonic treatment of "St Louis Blues."

For the rest of his career Johnson continued to write ambitious works and to play with a range of groups in and around New York, establishing himself undeniably as a significant figure in the jazz scene; he also stayed involved in revues and musicals, writing the music for 1949's *Sugar Hill*; unfortunately, a stroke in 1951 rendered him incapable of actively pursuing his career any further. He died four years later.

SEE ALSO: Nat King Cole, Curtis Fuller, Dizzy Gillespie

Elvin Jones

fact file

BORN 1927

MUSICAL SELECTION
Heavy Sounds

Elvin Jones, former drummer with the John Coltrane Quartet, in blissful mid-swing

One of three famous jazz brothers, the others being pianist Hank and trumpeter/composer Thad Jones, Elvin became the leading drummer in modern jazz during the 1960s when he was a vital member of the classic John Coltrane Quartet. His polyrhythmic approach to drumming, where the basic pulse is often implied rather than stated while Jones creates a swirl of contrasting rhythm around it, is still at the heart of every modern jazz drummer's conception. To date, no one has improved upon the original.

Jones, born in Pontiac, Michigan, came late to fame. After army service from 1946 to 1949, he began gigging locally, settling in Detroit and playing with a succession of groups, including that of ex-Gillespie tenor player Billy Mitchell, but it was not until he moved to New York in 1955 that any notice was taken of his playing. In the following two years he made considerable progress, playing with Teddy Charles/Charles Mingus and Bud Powell, appearing on various recording sessions (most often for Prestige) and, most notably, being a member of the Sonny Rollins trio which made a classic album live at the Village Vanguard in 1957. This revealed his debt to Art Blakey (the only other jazz drummer of the time to play so hard and with such drive) but also underlined their differences, for Blakey came from bop concepts, whereas Jones was always looking for off-center ways of driving the beat forward. After a series of jobs, including a stint with Donald Byrd, Jones was hired in 1960 by John Coltrane when he formed his first group after leaving Miles Davis. For the next six years Jones matched Coltrane for passion, staying power and inventiveness, creating one of the great jazz partnerships in the process. By the time he left Coltrane, Jones was the recognized master of modern drumming: at the end of the 1960s he even became a minor cult among rock fans, appearing in the "acid western" *Zachariah* in a mock drum battle with British musician Ginger Baker. Always a busy freelancer even when with Coltrane, Jones ran a trio for a few years, later a quintet with Frank Foster and George Coleman together on sax, but appeared consistently in other setups, mostly for the sheer fun of it. In 1979 he was the subject of a documentary, *Elvin Jones: A Different Drummer*. In recent years he has run teaching courses and led the Elvin Jones Jazz Machine, becoming a father figure to a number of younger players. He tours frequently all over the world and records consistently; his most recent group included John Coltrane's youngest son, Ravi, on tenor and soprano sax.

SEE ALSO: Thad Jones, John Coltrane, Charles Mingus, Bud Powell, Sonny Rollins, Art Blakey, Donald Byrd

Jo Jones

Jo Jones seen here behind his kit in 1940 during his long initial stint with the Basie band

fact file

BORN 1911

DIED 1985

MUSICAL SELECTION
Jo Jones Trio

Born Jonathan Jones in Chicago but universally known as Jo, drummer Jones, along with Chick Webb, set the standards by which other drummers were measured during the heyday of the swing era. Jones spent his childhood in Alabama, studying music and, he claimed, becoming proficient on a number of instruments. Later he became a regular on the carnival circuit, earning a living at one stage as a tap-dancer before settling in Omaha for three years, then finally arriving in Kansas City, where he joined Walter Page's Blue Devils in 1933. This led inevitably to Jones joining Count Basie, for whom he worked, with various interruptions, until 1947. During that time he formed what was commonly referred to as the "All-American Rhythm Section" of Basie, Freddie Green, Walter Page, and Jones. This section was capable of the lightest but most intense swing of any band in jazz history, its perfect balance often imitated but never matched at its best. Jones recorded prolifically with Basie during his tenure, so there are hundreds of examples of his superb playing; he also appeared on some of the great Billie Holiday–Teddy Wilson sessions of the 1930s. After an army stint in World War II, Jones (one of the stars of the film short *Jammin' The Blues*), a man of considerable sartorial elegance, started to freelance more often, becoming something of a regular with JATP in 1947, drumming with Illinois Jacquet's band after leaving Basie, and then playing with old friend Lester Young's group at the outset of the 1950s. Jones ran his own trio from the mid-fifties on, the original band featuring a very young Ray Bryant, but during later periods concentrated on freelance jobs. Held in high esteem by everyone involved in jazz, Jones was also an important figure in the evolution of jazz drumming, pushing the subdivision of the common-time bar toward a four-beat rather than a two-beat phrase, allowing a smooth pulse of rhythm to develop. In this he was instrumental in moving emphasis from a two-beat bass-drum pattern to the "rinky-tink" high-hat beat which became fundamental to every drummer's rhythm by the late 1930s. Add to this his penchant for sudden rim shots and other dramatic devices, and his contribution to jazz drumming is immense.

SEE ALSO: Chick Webb, Count Basie, Billie Holiday, Teddy Wilson, Lester Young, Illinois Jacquet

Quincy Jones

fact file

BORN 1933

MUSICAL SELECTION
Golden Boy
Walking In Space

Quincy Jones, the "golden boy" who has made telling contributions to many genres of popular music

Composer/arranger Jones has been one of the most successful jazz musicians in terms of consistently reaching audiences normally associated with music far removed from jazz. Born in Chicago and beginning musical training on piano, Jones moved to Seattle at the age of 10, where he ran his own church vocal quartet. At 14 he started trumpet, receiving lessons from the touring Clark Terry when he was in town; in 1951 he landed a scholarship to what was later called Berklee School of Music, in Boston, later that same year getting noticed by Lionel Hampton who hired him to be both a trumpeter and arranger for his band. Jones stayed a little over two years, traveling overseas, including a famous trip to Europe in 1953 when he led many furtive after-hours escapes to hastily arranged recording sessions and jams against Hampton's wishes. Leaving Hampton after the band's return to the US, Jones became a highly active arranger, composer, and trumpeter around New York, his often innovative, always fresh-sounding charts becoming much in demand: he spent most of 1956 leading Dizzy Gillespie's trumpet section. In 1957 he went to France to work, spending 18 successful months there, during which time he also studied composition. After this he took a big band on tour internationally; this band spent most of the next two years working regularly under Jones's baton, and he also began a long and successful series of albums for the Mercury/EmArcy label, including work with Billy Eckstine and his award-winning *Golden Boy* album of the early 1960s. He worked closely with Ray Charles on instrumental big-band albums for both Atlantic and Impulse!, and also became involved in writing for Count Basie, Sarah Vaughan, Peggy Lee, Frank Sinatra, and many others.

Increasingly involved in film composing, Jones scored some notable hits with the soundtrack music to *In The Heat Of The Night, The Pawnbroker*, and many other films. During the late 1960s and early 1970s Jones continued his film work, but also scored notable hits with A&M records, including the million-selling *Walking In Space* (1969). Jones's career since then has been a litany of successful projects, none more so than his famous production work in the 1980s and 1990s on Michael Jackson's best albums, but most of this activity has fallen outside jazz. In 1991, however, he pulled together and rehearsed the big band which played the famous *Miles Ahead* charts at the Montreux Festival with the original trumpeter, Miles Davis, taking his original lead parts.

SEE ALSO: Lionel Hampton, Dizzy Gillespie, Billy Eckstine, Ray Charles, Count Basie, Sarah Vaughan, Miles Davis

Thad Jones

Trumpeter Thad Jones in 1956, during his tenure with the Count Basie orchestra

fact file

BORN 1923

DIED 1986

MUSICAL SELECTION
Debut

The middle-born of the three Jones brothers – Hank and Elvin are the other two – Thad Jones was born in Pontiac, Michigan, moving to Detroit with his family in his early teens. Soon after, he began learning trumpet, becoming proficient enough by the age of 16 to be playing occasional jobs with brother Hank and with Sonny Stitt. After army service (1943–46) Jones played professionally in a variety of local Midwest bands, most of them with a tangential involvement in jazz, before in 1950 joining Billy Mitchell's quintet along with his younger brother Elvin. Jones's next important move was to join the Charles Mingus Jazz Composer's Workshop, where he played in Mingus's band, recorded as a leader (for the Mingus–Roach label, Debut) and had some of his early compositions recorded by the Workshop for Savoy. Concurrently with some of these developments, Jones joined the Basie band, becoming a key member of its brass section on flugelhorn and cornet, and also contributing arrangements. He stayed with Basie until 1963, branching out from there to play in the Monk Big Band concert at New York's Carnegie Hall in 1964, also playing with Gerry Mulligan and George Russell's sextet. By the mid-1960s Jones was employed as staff arranger for CBS TV, in his spare time running groups to play at clubs around New York.

Jones, most at home in a big-band setting, founded a rehearsal big band with drummer Mel Lewis, which played Monday nights at the Village Vanguard and other venues: over the years this band became a New York institution, playing adventurous music and training younger players with few opportunities otherwise to play in such a setting. The co-led band was a fixture in New York until Jones's decision to move to Denmark in 1978 after an accident to his lip. Lewis continued the band under his own name. Meanwhile, Jones led a hectic professional life in Denmark, setting up his own big band there, Thad Jones Eclipse, and fulfilling many writing commissions.

Jones stayed in Denmark until the death of Count Basie, when he was contracted to take over the Basie band after the leader's death: he did so, returning to the US to fulfill his duties, but shortly before his own death in 1986 he relinquished all his Stateside positions and returned to Denmark.

SEE ALSO: Elvin Jones, Sonny Stitt, Charles Mingus, Thelonious Monk, Gerry Mulligan, George Russell, Count Basie

Freddie Keppard

fact file

BORN 1889

DIED 1933

MUSICAL SELECTION
"Stock Yards Strut"
"Salty Dog"

New Orleans pioneer Freddie Keppard in Chicago, 1919

Keppard was an important figure in early New Orleans jazz, being the acknowledged cornet "king" after Buddy Bolden was taken off the scene in 1906. Keppard was born in New Orleans, the younger of two musician brothers (Louis, one year older, played guitar and tuba), and learned a number of instruments as a boy, becoming a noted cornetist at the dawn of the 1900s with John Brown's band, then leading the Olympia Band from 1906 onward. His forceful and uncluttered style soon became the standard to which others aspired. Like most of the best New Orleans musicians, he left the town, moving in 1914 to Los Angeles, where he joined the touring Original Creole Band and appeared in vaudeville. The band played from coast to coast, finally breaking up in 1918, in the meantime spurning an offer, in 1916, to become the first jazz band to be recorded. Settling in Chicago in 1918, Keppard continued to play loud and strong, but both history and his drinking habits were catching up with him. Although playing in an orchestra with Erskine Tate and Jimmie Noone, Keppard began to lose his breath control and his lip, as can be gleaned from the recordings he belatedly began making in the mid-1920s; additionally, his style was being consigned to history by a younger generation of players, spearheaded by the unique genius of Louis Armstrong. By the time of his death in 1933, Keppard was a legendary figure, his best years long gone and his present not representative of what he had once been well capable of. He remains one of the few trumpeters in the direct stylistic line from Bolden to have recorded, however, so his latter-day efforts are valuable as historical documents, if nothing else.

SEE ALSO: Buddy Bolden, Jimmie Noone, Louis Armstrong

Louis Jordan

Jordan was the first to bring the disparate elements of blues, rhythm, jazz, jump, and jive into a coherent song-based genre which anticipated the advent of rock 'n' roll by a good decade. Putting great emphasis on small-group discipline derived from the late 1930s "jump" style, a shuffle beat, and the supremacy of the vocal line, sax-playing singer Jordan became a major star and a seller of millions of records even while rarely straying from a 12-bar-blues format.

Jordan was born in Brinkley, Arkansas, halfway between Memphis and Little Rock, and learned the saxophone from his father, a musician who was the leader of the Rabbit Foot Minstrels. Jordan became a member of the summer-touring Minstrels as a teenager and later saw time with other touring companies, including that of Ma Rainey and Kaiser Marshall. His travels finally came to an end when he settled in Philadelphia in 1932, joining Charlie Gaines's band. After three years he moved to New York, where in 1936 he joined Chick Webb's Savoy Ballroom Orchestra, becoming a section sax player, and, as the male singer opposite Ella Fitzgerald, he became a well-known figure. Quitting the band in 1938, a year before Webb's premature death, Jordan took a residency in Elk's Rendezvous in Harlem and started a small group which, on its initial Decca sessions in December 1938, was called his Elks Rendezvous Band but by the time of his second sessions in March 1939 had acquired the soon-to-be-famous title the Tympany Five (there were always more than five players and the drummer never played any timpani).

From the first, Jordan had his "jump"-style formula in place, his fiery sax melodies serving as perfect intros for his streetwise, often humorous vocals, usually set to a shuffle beat. His band, a swing-group personnel augmented by an electric guitar, did the simple things extremely well and were all excellent musicians. By November 1941 Jordan had recorded his first million-seller, "I'm Gonna Move To The Outskirts of Town," and for the next 10 years he was a major presence in the national charts, appealing internationally equally to black and white audiences. Other massive hits include "Five Guys Named Mo," "Is You Is Or Is You Ain't My Baby?," "Ain't Nobody Here But Us Chickens," "Caldonia," "Saturday Night Fish Fry," "Let The Good Times Roll," and "Choo Choo Ch'Boogie." During this decade he appeared in a string of Hollywood films and also made countless "soundies" for the jukeboxes equipped with visuals. As the 1950s went on Jordan lost his place in the public eye, forming a big band just as the big-band craze had ended and wearing his formula thin. He moved record labels to Aladdin (and later Mercury and RCA) in an attempt to revive interest, but the more aggressive sounds of rock 'n' roll had killed off interest in R&B. Jordan continued to tour and record but never recaptured his pre-eminence. A period of ill-health in the 1950s made him readdress his priorities. During the 1960s and early 1970s he continued to work worldwide at his own pace, even making a record with Chris Barber's Band in England, but two heart attacks landed blows from which he did not recover, succumbing to the second in February 1975.

fact file

BORN 1908

DIED 1975

MUSICAL SELECTION
"Five Guys Named Mo"
"Is You Is Or Is You Ain't My Baby?"
"Ain't Nobody Here But Us Chickens"

R&B and jazz pioneer Louis Jordan, pictured here in 1951

SEE ALSO: Chick Webb, Ella Fitzgerald

Rahsaan Roland Kirk

fact file

BORN 1936

DIED 1977

MUSICAL SELECTION
Rip, Rig and Panic

Rahsaan Roland Kirk at the famous Newport Jazz Festival, 1962

Multi-instrumentalist Kirk, born in Columbus, Ohio, lost his sight at the age of two, educated at Ohio State School for the Blind. At the age of nine he started playing reed instruments. By 1948 he was in a school band and by 1951 he was freelancing in various Ohio-based bands, both dance and R&B style. In his mid-teens, while playing with Boyd Moore, he had the idea of playing a number of reed instruments simultaneously, and within a short time had added the manzello and stritch (variants on alto and soprano saxophones) to his arsenal. Kirk debuted on record in 1956, playing a modified R&B style, but was barely noticed. In 1960, now settled in Chicago, he came to the notice of Ramsey Lewis, who pressed his record company, Argo, to sign the reed-man. The resultant album aroused considerable controversy in a deeply conservative jazz community . Despite joining the Charles Mingus band for a short while in 1961, Kirk was dismissed as something akin to a circus performer. Kirk's first acceptance as a major figure came from Europeans, who saw him on tour in 1963. A landmark record, *Rip, Rig, and Panic*, with Jaki Byard, Richard Davis, and Elvin Jones, was made for Limelight in 1965, while he enjoyed brief pop fame with radio coverage of a flute track from *I Talk With The Spirits* from the next year, called "Serenade To A Cuckoo." Later that year Kirk swapped to Atlantic, recording joyously overheated versions of "I Say A Little Prayer" and other chart ephemera, later covering Stevie Wonder repertoire and occasionally indulging in singing. By the end of the 1960s there was no stopping Kirk. Ever one for a challenge, he made albums in this period covering much ground, from solo efforts (*Natural Black Inventions: Root Strata*, 1970) to concept records and sprawling, storming live albums with his Vibration Society (*Bright Moments*, 1973). Kirk was a suffered a debilitating stroke in 1975. Indomitable as ever, he taught himself to play sax with just one hand but the music he produced was only a pale reflection. He was silenced by a second stroke in 1977.

SEE ALSO: Ramsey Lewis, Charles Mingus, Jaki Byard, Sonny Rollins, Elvin Jones

Jimmy Knepper

fact file

BORN 1927

MUSICAL SELECTION
Special Relationship

Jimmy Knepper, a trombonist closely associated with early Charles Mingus triumphs

Trombone great Knepper was born in Los Angeles, beginning his musical studies on alto horn at the age of five, then swapping to trombone in 1938. He was tutored privately prior to attending Los Angeles City and State colleges. Starting his professional career with LA big bands in the mid-1940s, he played in a great many settings, including the Roy Porter big band of 1948–49, an important breeding ground for West Coast boppers, Charlie Parker, Art Pepper, Charlie Barnet, and Ray Bauduc. The stylistic range covered here is enormous, showing Knepper's versatility and the broad jazz roots he developed as his style matured. Knepper moved to New York in 1956, meeting up there with Charles Mingus and becoming a key member of the Jazz Workshop at this time. Knepper was ever present during 1957–58 before playing in 1959 with Stan Kenton, and appeared on most of Mingus's masterpieces made in this crucial period, his warm trombone tone and openly lyrical style providing a perfect foil for the more volcanic aspects of Mingus's music. Knepper continued to play for a number of people as the 1960s started, including Gil Evans and Benny Goodman, but also worked on occasion for Mingus up to 1962, when Mingus, in a fury, broke Knepper's jaw and cut his lip during the tense preparations for the New York Town Hall open recording session of late that year. Knepper never worked for Mingus again. But he did remain very active in the music, playing and arranging for the Thad Jones/Mel Lewis band, playing in Broadway shows, and enjoying a long association with Lee Konitz's nonet of the 1970s. In 1979 Knepper became involved in Mingus Dynasty, the band led by drummer Dannie Richmond, contributing his talents to the group until its demise with the death of Richmond. Knepper continues to freelance on both sides of the Atlantic.

SEE ALSO: Charlie Parker, Art Pepper, Charlie Barnet, Charles Mingus, Stan Kenton, Gil Evans, Benny Goodman

Stan Kenton

Wichita-born Kenton has from the first excited controversy and accusations of pretentiousness, but his achievement, in retrospect, is sufficient for him to be perceived as a major figure in the postwar period.

Kenton moved with his family to California when just five, growing up in LA; having written his first arrangement in 1928, in the early 1930s he played in many local bands, picking up experience of arranging and on-stand playing. Prior to starting his own first band he worked in 1938 and 1939 for Vido Musso and Gus Arnheim in LA and San Francisco. His first band of his own played at Balboa Beach and recorded for Decca, often sounding like a more intellectual version of Glenn Miller, the arrangements dominating the soloists, but it was immediately after the switch to Capitol in late 1943 that he experienced his first hit, with "Artistry In Rhythm." This became his theme tune, and he had a string of instrumental hits during the 1940s using the same basic ideas of stabbing brass patterns, legato sax melodies, and bright tempos. Kenton also catered for dancers, as did every band of the period, scoring a number of vocal hits as well, using the talents of Anita O'Day and, most famously in the late 1940s, June Christy. By then Kenton was regularly featuring arrangements by Pete Rugolo and doing less scoring himself, though still overseeing musical operations. By this time, his band had become a major breeding ground for West Coast moderns, a listing of personnel passing through the band by the beginning of the 1950s sounding like a *Who's Who* of the progressive and "cool" jazz fraternity and including Shorty Rogers, Stan Getz, Lee Konitz, Art Pepper, Maynard Ferguson, Bill Russo, Bud Shank, Shelly Manne, and Laurindo Almeida, to name just a handful. In 1950 he launched a new phase of his career with his "Progressive Jazz" orchestra, on tour with his self-named "Innovations In Modern Music" package. Playing a diverse range of music, Kenton was perhaps the first progressive crossover artist. However, it is important not to confuse publicity with musical worth, and during the 1950s and 1960s Kenton continued to expand upon his previous achievements, rarely the first into a field (for a time he was intensely interested in Cuban and Latin rhythms), but a thorough researcher always delivering properly thought-through results. By the end of the 1950s, embattled like every big band by rock 'n' roll's incursions into the popular psyche, Kenton delivered a number of more commercially slanted albums, such as *The Ballad Style of Stan Kenton* (Capitol, 1958), which helped sustain him financially, but his core listenership remained in jazz. In the mid-1960s Kenton, ever-ambitious, launched his Neophonic Orchestra, a gargantuan setup which played music by a range of composers, including Friedrich Gulda and Wagner, and he shortly after made an album of Kenton-style arrangements of Wagner music. For the last decade of his life Kenton looked to posterity, running his band as efficiently as ever, buying back many of his masters from Capitol and releasing them on his own Creative World label. Kenton's love of triple-forte and his never knowingly looking for understatement have tended to obscure his real jazz worth, for among the bombast and hyperbole there is a substantial body of impressive music covering a surprisingly wide range of emotions and outlooks, even humor, as "Blues In Burlesque," with vocals by Shelly Manne, demonstrates.

fact file

BORN 1912

DIED 1979

MUSICAL SELECTION
Kenton At The Tropicana

Controversial band leader Stan Kenton relaxing at Birdland in 1958

SEE ALSO: Glenn Miller, Anita O'Day, June Christy, Shorty Rogers, Stan Getz, Lee Konitz, Art Pepper, Maynard Ferguson

Lee Konitz

fact file

BORN 1927

MUSICAL SELECTION
Subconscious-Lee

Altoist Lee Konitz in full flight during the early 1950s

Chicagoan Konitz first studied clarinet as a boy, then swapped to alto saxophone, an instrument on which he developed a remarkably pure, uninflected tone. In the immediate postwar period Konitz played with a number of Chicago bands as well as continuing his studies, finally joining Claude Thornhill in 1947 and meeting up with the musical circle around Thornhill arranger Gil Evans. This led directly to his deep involvement in the recordings made by the Evans–Miles Davis Nonet in 1948–50; meanwhile he had met in New York the pianist, teacher and theorist Lennie Tristano, a man who helped shape Konitz's musical character but from whom he split in 1951, undertaking a Scandinavian tour which provoked adulation from local musicians and audiences alike, as radio recordings of the tour attest.

The following year Konitz joined Stan Kenton, spending a little over 12 months with the leader, then struck out on his own, leading small groups for the rest of the decade and appearing regularly in Europe. Konitz played in many contexts during this period, including big-band and orchestral settings devised by composers and arrangers including Jimmy Giuffre, and ran groups which occasionally featured old Tristano colleagues such as tenorist Warne Marsh (such a group was recorded live in New York in 1959). However, for most of the early 1960s Konitz was out of the music business, returning in the latter half of the decade to play in avant-garde circles, a position he subsequently abandoned in favor of chordal improvisation. In the 1970s Konitz formed a Nonet with which to explore further avenues initially opened up by the old Davis–Evans group; he also took up further retrospectives by playing and recording with old Tristano colleagues. In the 1980s he made a duet appearance with Gil Evans which was later released on record, and has kept up a very busy recording and performing schedule, becoming a major contemporary figure, especially in Japan. He presently continues with a very active career.

SEE ALSO: Gil Evans, Miles Davis, Lennie Tristano, Jimmy Giuffre

Steve Lacy

fact file

BORN 1934

MUSICAL SELECTION
The Straight Horn of...
School Days

Steve Lacy, the most gifted contemporary soprano sax player in jazz

Lacy was born Steven Lackritz in New York City and was inspired by the example of Sidney Bechet to take up soprano sax. At first a committed Dixielander, he was a well-schooled musician, studying with Cecil Scott, then at the Schillinger School (later renamed Berklee College) and finally at the Manhattan School of Music in 1954. Lacy began playing with Max Kaminsky and other traditional groups as well as the swing-style units of Charlie Shavers and Zutty Singleton, but in 1956 he discovered the music of Cecil Taylor and underwent a complete reorientation of his music, studying and rehearsing with Taylor and appearing at the pianist's Newport Festival debut in 1957. While playing with Taylor Lacy came to the attention of Gil Evans, who used him on a late 1950s session for Prestige; he also played with Mal Waldron and Jimmy Giuffre and took on a comprehensive study of Monk's music, eventually appearing in the pianist's group for a few months in 1960. This proved to be a seminal experience: a few months later, after recording his debut album for Candid (made up of Taylor and Monk compositions), Lacy formed a pianoless quartet with trombonist Roswell Rudd dedicated to playing Monk repertoire exclusively. A record of this band was released decades after its demise, demonstrating its familiarity with Monk's musical architecture.

In the mid-1960s, discouraged with the US jazz scene, Lacy visited Europe with Carla Bley, among others, then formed a group including Enrico Rava which toured South America. A year in New York with this group convinced him of the need for a change, and in 1967 he settled with his Swiss vocalist wife Irene Aebi in Europe, which has been the center of his operations ever since, firstly in Rome, then later in Paris. As the 1970s gave way to the 1980s, Lacy became increasingly ambitious in terms of compositions, grooming groups of different size and instrumentation to play his complex and increasingly lauded music. Today regarded as one of France's greatest cultural assets, Lacy continues to compose and perform across Europe.

SEE ALSO: Sidney Bechet, Cecil Taylor, Gil Evans, Jimmy Giuffre, Thelonious Monk, Roswell Rudd, Carla Bley

Gene Krupa

Chicago-born drummer Krupa has suffered more than most from critical opprobrium, being constantly criticized as a leaden, flashy, and selfish drummer incapable of swinging a big band or of subtly pushing a small group. For the most part all this does is reveal the alarming narrowness of vision possessed by his attackers, for while Krupa was not big on subtlety early in his career, his strongest suit was his drive and enthusiasm, the excitement he thus engendered being felt by every member of any band he drummed for. His latter-day recordings, on the other hand, demonstrate what a subtle and responsive drummer he developed into after the years of swing adulation died away.

Krupa began on drums at an early age and was playing, self-taught, in youthful groups by the early 1920s. He soon realized the need for proper tuition if he was to progress, taking lessons from a number of professionals. By 1927 he was sufficiently improved to make his debut on record with Red MacKenzie and Eddie Condon's Chicagoans, on which he insisted on playing his bass drum – a first for jazz drummers, until then banned from such indulgences due to the primitive nature of the recording equipment at that time. By 1929 he was in New York with MacKenzie, moving on to Red Nichols that year before playing on innumerable dates for a vast range of leaders in an equally vast number of musical styles. He joined Benny Goodman's orchestra in early 1935, becoming a key part of that band's phenomenal rise to stardom and a featured artist on the famous "Sing Sing Sing" recording of 1938. That same year Krupa left Goodman and launched his own big band, a unit short on subtlety and brimming with showmanship and drum solos for its first two years until Krupa eased up a little, allowing others to share the spotlight. These others included Anita O'Day and Roy Eldridge in the early 1940s, but in 1943 Krupa was arrested for drug abuse (marijuana) and suspicion of corrupting a minor – charges later refuted on appeal – and his career went into a temporary nose dive. Re-employed by Goodman, then by Tommy Dorsey, Krupa found his feet again and restarted a big band, running it until 1951. By then he could see the changes in the music business and scaled down to a small group, initially with tenor star Charlie Ventura (the saxophonist often playing on bass sax as well) and later with Eddie Shu. Krupa also became a fixture on the annual JATP tours, both national and international, in the 1950s, and made numerous albums for Norman Granz's record labels. During all this time he also continued to be a student of the drums: in the 1930s he had published a manual on drumming technique and drum maintenance; now in the 1950s he and Cozy Cole ran a school of percussion. Krupa occasionally enjoyed a reunion of the old Goodman Quartet – they recorded a new album together in 1963 – but for the most part restricted the amount of nostalgia in his live performances. Inextricably bound up in the swing era, he never modified his style, but to criticize him for this is as pointless as ticking Max Roach or Art Blakey off for never modernizing their drumming concepts. Judged on his own terms, he was a major drumming figure.

fact file

BORN 1909

DIED 1973

MUSICAL SELECTION
Drum Boogie

Matinee-idol drummer and band leader Gene Krupa, in a classic "magician's" publicity shot

SEE ALSO: Red Mackenzie, Eddie Condon, Red Nichols, Benny Goodman, Anita O'Day, Roy Eldridge, Tommy Dorsey, Cozy Cole, Max Roach, Art Blakey

Tommy Ladnier

fact file

BORN 1900

DIED 1939

MUSICAL SELECTION
"Really The Blues"

Trumpeter Tommy Ladnier (right) at a 1938 Hughes Panassie recording session

Born in Mandeville, Louisiana, trumpeter Ladnier moved to Chicago sometime prior to 1917 and went on to play in a number of riverboat bands, including those of Charlie Creath and Fate Marable, the latter in the early 1920s. Settling back in Chicago after 1924, Ladnier worked with Jimmie Noone but found his most constant employer to be King Oliver, just then recovering from the departure of Louis Armstrong and Lee Collins. Ladnier stayed with Oliver from 1924 to 1925, freelancing on a number of recordings with blues singers and traveling to Europe with Sam Wooding after leaving Oliver in 1925. A spell in New York with Fletcher Henderson was ended by another trip to Europe with Wooding in 1928, swapping to work with Noble Sissle in 1930–31, with whom he played in tours on both sides of the Atlantic. During these years he developed a friendship with Sidney Bechet and he also began drinking heavily. Back in the US from 1932 onward, he teamed up with Bechet to form the New Orleans Feetwarmers, a band which struggled to find an appreciative live audience but which luckily cut a series of classic sides for RCA Victor.

Finding the prevailing musical fashions against them, both men fell out of music for two years, running a tailor shop in Harlem together, but in 1935 Ladnier put together his own small group and began playing around New York and New Jersey. By this time, however, his health was beginning to give out, and although he made some sides with Bechet and his colleague, Mezz Mezzrow, in 1938, Ladnier's best years were already over and he was heading toward an early demise. His bright, authoritative trumpet lead, couched in New Orleans musical language but with a fire and flexibility rare outside of a handful of trumpeters from that city, was a perfect foil for the driving, loquacious Bechet, and their records together are jewels. Ladnier survived only until the summer of 1939, being found by Mezzrow dead in his apartment.

SEE ALSO: Jimmie Noone, King Oliver, Louis Armstrong, Fletcher Henderson, Sidney Bechet

Scott LaFaro

Innovatory bassist Scott LaFaro was talented enough to merit a tribute by Ornette Coleman, "The Alchemy of Scott LaFaro"

fact file

BORN 1936

DIED 1961

MUSICAL SELECTION
Free Jazz
Ornette!

Like Jimmy Blanton before him, Newark-born bassist LaFaro had very little time in which to change the face of jazz bass playing, but accomplished it with graceful ease. LaFaro began in music on the clarinet while at high school in Geneva, New York, where his family had moved, taking up bass in his mid-teens. He originally worked in R&B bands but landed a job in LA with Chet Baker from 1956 to 1957. After a brief sojourn in Chicago in 1957, LaFaro headed out West again, working with Harold Land and Sonny Rollins in San Francisco and with Barney Kessel at the Lighthouse in Hermosa Beach. He appeared with Cal Tjader and recorded with Victor Feldman prior to going out on the road with Benny Goodman in 1959. Coming off the Goodman tour, LaFaro settled in New York and began his own trio as well as freelancing, working with Stan Getz among others. Before the year was out he had joined the new trio of the pianist Bill Evans, quickly developing a rapport with the pianist and drummer Paul Motian which is still one of the most admired in all of jazz. The music they created in the 18 months of the trio's existence remains some of the most influential in the whole canon of jazz piano trios, LaFaro's amazing facility and his ability to weave counter-lines to Evans's, plus his unusual and characteristic rhythmic patterns being a major contributor to this achievement. LaFaro continued to work outside of the Evans group, recording and playing with Ornette Coleman, appearing on the groundbreaking double-quartet album *Free Jazz* (Atlantic, 1960) with Charlie Haden, and subsequently playing a breathtaking (and still generally critically under-appreciated) melodic and rhythmic foil to Coleman on the quartet album, *Ornette!* (Atlantic, 1961). Coleman certainly appreciated him, titling one track "The Alchemy of Scott LaFaro." His immense promise was to remain just that, however, for after leaving his mother's house in summer 1961 to drive to a rehearsal of the Evans trio, he was killed when his car left the road and hit a tree.

SEE ALSO: Jimmy Blanton, Chet Baker, Harold Land, Sonny Rollins, Cal Tjader, Benny Goodman

Oliver Lake

fact file

BORN 1942

MUSICAL SELECTION
Dedicated to Dolphy

Altoist and band leader Oliver Lake's musical education included drums, sax and flute, his career taking him from Chicago to Paris and New York

Saxophonist/composer Lake was born in Marianna, Arkansas, but was raised in St Louis. He started off in music by learning drums as a boy, taking up alto sax in his late teens and later adding the flute to his accomplishments. Lake attended Lincoln University, emerging in 1968 with a BA, and became a public-school teacher, also simultaneously becoming involved in the St Louis-based Black Artists Group (BAG), an organization with similar aims to that of Chicago's AACM. Lake abandoned St Louis in the early 1970s for Paris, where he ran a quintet exploring avant-garde jazz ideas, but in 1976 he settled in New York and became a founding member of the World Saxophone Quartet, a band which subsequently became one of the most popular avant-garde groups in all jazz, touring internationally and making albums right up to the present day, albeit with a number of membership shifts. Lake also took part in the energetic New York loft scene of the mid-1970s, often appearing with guitarist/singer Michael Gregory Jackson. There are records of some of their live duet work.

An ambitious and resourceful composer, Lake has diversified his efforts outside the World Saxophone Quartet, leading a second group, the reggae-influenced Jump Up, in the early 1980s, and writing music for stage productions. In the past 10 years Lake has continued to advance on a number of fronts, one of his most memorable projects being two albums of his outstanding interpretations of the compositions of Eric Dolphy, formidably difficult musical territory for most musicians and one which has until Lake's involvement been studiously avoided.

SEE ALSO: Eric Dolphy

Harold Land

fact file

BORN 1928

MUSICAL SELECTION
Harold In The Land Of Jazz
The Fox

West Coast stalwart tenor Harold Land, whose talent remains under-appreciated to this day

Land, born in Houston, Texas, but an inhabitant of the West Coast since his youth, began teaching himself the tenor saxophone as an adolescent in San Diego. After building up his technique and resources, Land moved to Los Angeles in 1954, almost immediately coming into contact with Clifford Brown and Max Roach and becoming the saxophonist in their popular and influential quintet. Land toured with Brown and Roach for 18 months, making many record dates with the band and leaving a clear impression of his youthful abilities in this fast company. Leaving the quintet in the cause of being fixed in one place rather than being constantly on the road, Land joined the group led by bassist Curtis Counce in 1956, staying for two years before going out on his own. At the close of the 1950s Land, largely unnoticed by those outside of LA, made a series of classic hard-bop albums for the Contemporary label, including *Harold In The Land of Jazz* (1958) and *The Fox* (1959), the latter one of the unjustly neglected masterpieces of the period.

Never entirely comfortable as a leader, Land switched regularly between running his own groups and playing in other people's, but the consistency of his inspiration was sustained throughout the 1960s. In 1968 he formed a band with vibist Bobby Hutcherson and moved back to LA with it to pursue a new West Coast career, but while the music was uniformly first-rate, the career never caught fire. After the band with Hutcherson ended in 1971, Land joined up with an old colleague, trumpeter Blue Mitchell, and they ran a group together for most of the 1970s. Since that time Land has been content to freelance in any number of situations: he appeared at the 1997 Ravinia Jazz Festival as part of an improvising saxophone ensemble directed by veteran Benny Carter, acquitting himself with his usual improvisatory neatness and aplomb. Land, an original with no great stage presence in a time when the qualities admired are just the opposite, has consistently made great music for his entire career, but remains as underrated now as he was 40 years ago.

SEE ALSO: Clifford Brown, Max Roach, Bobby Hutcherson, Benny Carter

Eddie Lang

Guitar virtuoso Eddie Lang, seen here in 1932, died too soon to enjoy the popularity he deserved

fact file

BORN 1902

DIED 1933

MUSICAL SELECTION
A Handful of Riffs

Lang, born Salvatore Massaro in Philadelphia, was the first great guitar virtuoso in jazz, but died too young to benefit to any great degree from his enormous gifts. As a young boy he studied violin for over a decade, meeting up with the great Joe Venuti in high school and playing in the school orchestra with him. By the time Lang and Venuti left school they had already duetted together many times, originally on violins, but with Lang's switch to guitar in the early 1920s the pair continued to develop their musical routines together. Playing in Bert Estlow's band in Atlantic City in 1923, Lang met the Dorsey Brothers, with whom he and Venuti decided to decamp when the Dorseys decided on starting up their own outfit. The following year, Land joined the Mound City Blue Blowers, run by Red MacKenzie, with whom he toured internationally and recorded. After this Lang settled in New York, where he freelanced extensively, performing and recording with a large array of players, from Jean Goldkette to Red Nichols and beyond. By this stage Lang's technique and musical imagination was at its peak, his playing often being the most arresting thing happening on any record on which he appeared. His duets with Venuti, which were mostly recorded between 1926 and 1928, have since become benchmarks in jazz playing for both instruments, the cleanness of their techniques, the swing they generate, and the emotional and intellectual heat they give off being sufficient to communicate themselves to every subsequent generation. Lang appeared all over New York with the top musicians, including Adrian Rollini and Paul Whiteman, and in 1933 he made another set of recordings with Venuti under the name of the Blue Five. He was also employed at different times as Bing Crosby's favorite accompanist. Tragically, he failed to recover from a routine operation in the spring of 1933, dying in the operating theater. His body of work, including his fine guitar solos and duets, remains hugely influential, his flawless technique and musical vision inspiring guitarists still today.

SEE ALSO: Joe Venuti, Red Nichols, Adrian Rollini

Yusef Lateef

fact file

BORN 1921

MUSICAL SELECTION
African-American Epic Suite

Multi-instrumentalist and musicologist Yusef Lateef's career includes performance, teaching and leading his own group

Born William Evans in Chattanooga, Tennessee, saxophonist and multi-reed man Lateef moved to Detroit with his family in childhood, taking up saxophone in 1937 when in senior high school. Part of a thriving jazz community in Detroit, Lateef was recommended to Lucky Millinder by saxophonist Lucky Thompson and he moved to New York in 1946 to take up the position. For the next three years he played with various swing small-group stars, including Roy Eldridge, then in 1949 joined the Dizzy Gillespie band, staying into 1950. Feeling the need to further his musical education, Lateef attended Wayne University back in Detroit. By the mid-1950s he was running his own group in Detroit and had adopted his Muslim name, attracting interest from New York record companies such as Savoy, Charlie Parker Records, and Prestige, all of whom made a number of albums with Lateef. The Chicago-based Argo also released a record of the Lateef group live at Cranbrook. At this time Lateef's interest in other types of music and instruments began to surface on record and at his gigs. Three stints as a sideman – briefly with Charles Mingus in 1960–61 (he relocated to New York in January 1960), then with Olatunji, and lastly with the Cannonball Adderley Sextet (1962–64) – gave him public exposure and the chance to integrate his musical experimentation into a jazz context more convincingly.

During the rest of the decade Lateef alternated between more musical study, teaching and running his own groups. Making a series of albums for the Impulse! label, Lateef brought his personal synthesis of musical cultures to a peak before shifting labels to Atlantic and leaving a legacy there into the 1970s of increasing eclecticism and a more hit-and-miss approach. Lateef also became a renewed advocate of the most simple blues forms. He continues to pursue a career in teaching, playing, and composing: his recent *African-American Epic Suite* for large orchestra and soloists was premiered in the early 1990s and garnered widespread praise.

SEE ALSO: Lucky Millinder, Roy Eldridge, Dizzy Gillespie, Charles Mingus, Cannonball Adderley

George Lewis

fact file

BORN 1900

DIED 1968

MUSICAL SELECTION
Trios & Bands

Clarinetist George Lewis appearing at a 1945 Bunk Johnson engagement alongside guitarist Lawrence Manners and pianist Alton Purnell

New Orleans-born clarinetist Lewis (not to be confused with the much younger Chicago trombonist of the same name) was a self-taught player and never learned to read music. He took up clarinet in his late teens after fooling around on lesser instruments, landing himself a position in the Black Eagle Band in Louisiana before returning to New Orleans and working with Buddy Petit's Black and Tan Band in the early 1920s. Lewis by this stage had formulated his stark, simple, and driving style, using it to good advantage in the band he formed in 1923 with Henry "Red" Allen, which played around New Orleans for a year. Lewis stayed in the New Orleans area, playing with the surviving players of the jazz revolution still based in the Big Easy, including Chris Kelly and Kid Rena (1929). By the early 1930s he was playing with Kid Howard and Dee Dee Pierce, and also belonged for a while in 1932 to the band run by his friend Evan Thomas, whose trumpeter was Bunk Johnson.

After Thomas's murder onstage, to which Lewis was a witness, the clarinetist gradually dropped out of the music scene, his spirit failing and his chosen instrument in temporary popular eclipse. Lewis was one of the major beneficiaries of the Revivalist movement of the early 1940s: "rediscovered" by researcher Williams Russell in 1941 while Russell was on the trail of Bunk Johnson, Lewis was present at the 1942 recording session which brought Johnson back into the limelight. This gave Lewis plenty of attention of his own, and with it plenty of playing prospects. Performing with both Johnson and with "Kid Shots" Madison up to 1946, Lewis had become such a central figure in the revivalist movement that he formed his own group, the George Lewis Ragtime Band, featuring old friends Jim Robinson and Alcide "Slow Drag" Pavageau. With the death of Bunk Johnson in 1949 Lewis became the rallying-point of born-again traditionalists everywhere, and he spent the 1950s touring first the US and then, with the European trad boom in full swing, all through Europe and Great Britain. By the early 1960s he was a favorite in Japan as well, but by then age was catching up with him. He opted for a long-term residency at the recently refurbished Preservation Hall in New Orleans as the leader of the hall's in-house band. Lewis's primitive clarinet playing and his disregard for the niceties of tuning and time were seen as positive assets by his legion of fans, and his influence on traditionalist music persists today.

SEE ALSO: "Red" Allen, Bunk Johnson

John Lewis

Pianist and composer John Lewis of MJQ fame, a study in concentration

fact file

BORN 1920

MUSICAL SELECTION
"Toccata for Trumpet and Orchestra"
No Sun In Venice
Odds Against Tomorrow

Pianist/composer John Lewis was born in Albuquerque, New Mexico; his mother studied singing while John began piano studies at the age of seven. At the University of New Mexico he studied music along with anthropology before being inducted into the army in 1942. During his service career Lewis met Kenny Clarke, who introduced him to the New York scene after army service in late 1945. He quickly joined Dizzy Gillespie's big band, writing compositions and arrangements as well as fulfilling piano duties, taking further music studies at Manhattan School of Music. Lewis had a major work, *Toccata for Trumpet and Orchestra*, performed by the Gillespie orchestra at its 1947 Carnegie Hall Concert. Lewis stayed behind in Europe after the Gillespie orchestra's tour there in 1948, then returned to New York and worked for a number of top small groups, including Charlie Parker and Lester Young, as well as becoming involved in the Miles Davis Nonet, supplying compositions and arrangements which were recorded by Capitol in 1948 and 1950.

During his tenure with Young in 1950–51 he was also completing his music studies, receiving an M.Mus. in 1952. At this time he joined up with vibist Milt Jackson, working with him in the Milt Jackson Quartet. This group underwent a name change in 1954, becoming the Modern Jazz Quartet, and within a short space of time Lewis had taken on the role of musical director for the group. While he rose to worldwide prominence in the MJQ, which continued as a band until breaking up in 1974, Lewis was highly active in many other musical directions during this period. In addition to providing a number of high-quality soundtracks for films (*No Sun In Venice, Odds Against Tomorrow*), Lewis became the head of faculty at the jazz summer schools at Music Inn in Lenox, Massachusetts, in 1957; he also succeeded that year in having recorded a whole album's worth of his orchestral music by the Stuttgart Chamber Orchestra with guest soloists, including baritonist Ronnie Ross, who joined the MJQ as a guest for their next tour of Europe and the US. Lewis during this period and the early 1960s was a champion of the so-called "Third Stream" approach to music, marrying jazz and classical techniques together. He also actively promoted the early career of Ornette Coleman and used young players like Coleman, Scott LaFaro, and Eric Dolphy in the early 1960s in his Third Stream projects.

Lewis, whether preparing projects for the MJQ or being artistic director of a festival or organizing the performance of his own music with other forces, has been both imaginative and disciplined in his work, casting his ideas widely and producing startling results, from jazz suites reflecting European ideals to radical approaches to the blues. He is also one of the most perceptive and sympathetic of piano accompanists, as Milt Jackson could attest. He and the rest of the MJQ have, since the early 1980s, regathered annually for brief tours to satisfy audience demand for the band's music, but Lewis continues to lead an active and creative musical life in many fields.

SEE ALSO: Dizzy Gillespie, Charlie Parker, Lester Young, Miles Davis, Milt Jackson, Ornette Coleman, Scott LaFaro

Meade "Lux" Lewis

fact file

BORN 1905

DIED 1964

MUSICAL SELECTION
"Honky Tonk Train"

Boogie woogie giant Meade "Lux" Lewis, pictured here in 1938 Chicago

Lewis, a Louisville-born boogie pianist, first came across boogie when he heard Jimmy Yancey playing his version of barrelhouse piano in the mid-1920s. Having originally studied violin, Lewis shifted to piano and moved to Chicago in 1927, recording the first version of his later famous "Honky Tonk Train" for Paramount in 1927, although the record failed to appear until 1929. Involved in a cab-driving business in Chicago with Albert Ammons, Lewis dropped out of music altogether for a number of years, being brought back to the ranks of professional pianist by enthusiast John Hammond who, having heard a copy of "Honky Tonk Train," determined that its author should be appreciated by the wider world. He found Lewis washing cars in Chicago in 1935 and brought him back into a studio to re-record his composition – the first of many re-recordings of it. The tune, enthusiastically delivered by its composer, was one of the prime reasons for the boogie-woogie craze which swept America in the late 1930s, a period when great mounds of ersatz boogie was played by people with no natural connection to it whatsoever. Lewis, along with Pete Johnson, appeared on stage at Hammond's "Spirituals to Swing" concert at Carnegie Hall in 1938, helping push his best composition further into popularity and celebrity chic. Lewis, Ammons, and Johnson became the three most celebrated exponents of boogie piano, the blues harmonies and rumbling left hand provoking excitement wherever they were heard: boogie, after being dismissed by people such as Fats Waller as crude and repetitive, became the height of fashion in the early 1940s, with short films even being made for public consumption, some of them starring Lewis.

The boogie craze passed, leaving Lewis with little room to maneuver, his pianistic limitations and his reputation giving him scant opportunity to adapt to new styles. He made a living as a solo in clubs and lounges on both US coasts, but the only innovation he managed in later years was to play boogie on celeste, a rather disturbing and self-defeating exercise. Lewis died in 1964 a somewhat frustrated artist, but his greatest records testify to an almost elemental talent and artistic force, one that will continue to excite and bewitch listeners who come into contact with it.

SEE ALSO: Albert Ammons

Ramsey Lewis

fact file

BORN 1935

MUSICAL SELECTION
The "In" Crowd

Soul survivor and jazz statesman, pianist and composer Ramsey Lewis became a best-seller in jazz in 1965 and an official member of the "In Crowd"

Lewis, a Chicago-born pianist, composer, and leader, has been one of that city's most popular musical exports for the past 40 years. Interested in music from infancy, Lewis took private studies from the age of six, later completing his schooling at Chicago Music College and De Paul University. Lewis's musical background was, by his own admission, a broad one, his earliest memories being of both gospel and classical music, while the blues and jazz came along a little later. This mixture of disciplines has been very much to the fore in his musical output over the decades. In 1956 Lewis formed a trio with bassist Eldee Young and drummer Red Holt, which was publicized as the "Gentlemen of Jazz," and the trio's earliest records on Chicago's Argo label reflect a genteel approach to its musical sources, which suggests the influence of Nat Cole, the Three Strings, and the West Coast school. Later, Lewis changed his angle of approach as hard bop became a jazz mainstay. This shift was perhaps first discernible in his contributions to Argo albums by other players such as Sonny Stitt, Max Roach, and Lem Winchester, but by the early 1960s Lewis was pushing his trio in the jazz-soul direction and proving a very popular live draw as a consequence.

The dam burst with an album recorded live in Washington in 1965, *The "In" Crowd*, where Lewis's unabashed funkiness and crowd-pleasing simplicity spawned a hit LP and hit singles. Within 12 months he was jazz's bestselling artist. Re-examination of those albums today shows that Lewis always supplied in his program a judicious mix of crowd-pleasers and more sophisticated material, all of it consummately played, for Lewis was a first-rate musician, as were his sidemen. By the end of the decade much of the steam had run out of both soul-jazz and Lewis's original market; a swap of labels to Columbia in 1971 led to a subsequent involvement in electronics and a continuing hunt for the soul and funk market. Lewis has continued to be successful, although nothing has approached the impact of his initial 1960s breakthrough. His music has proven highly influential for later musicians looking to plow the same stylistic furrow; in recent years Lewis himself has combined both acoustic and electronic elements in his music, his apposite improvisations within a rock-beat format always of interest. Lewis leads a varied professional life; a household name in Chicago, he is the musical director for jazz at the Ravinia Festival.

SEE ALSO: Nat King Cole, Sonny Stitt, Max Roach

Abbey Lincoln

fact file

BORN 1930

MUSICAL SELECTION
Talking To The Sun

Abbey Lincoln, an outspoken and outstanding vocalist, took her talents to the theater as well as the nightclubs

Chicago-born vocalist Lincoln (original name Anna Marie Wooldridge) came from a large family (12 children, of whom she is the tenth) and always sang. While in high school in Kalamazoo, where her family had moved, she sang at amateur engagements and social functions; later in her teens she toured with dance bands, gaining early experience before relocating to California in 1951, where she began to find work singing in nightclubs. Two years in Hawaii working under the name Gaby Lee rounded out her apprenticeship. Back in Hollywood in 1954 she began building a solid reputation, by 1956 making her debut recording with Benny Carter and adopting the professional name of Abbey Lincoln. Soon signed to Liberty records, Lincoln made her first album in the nightclub style of the times, then made an appearance in the film *The Girl Can't Help It* as a jazzy nightclub chanteuse, among the frenetic rock of Little Richard and Gene Vincent. Switching to Riverside, Lincoln continued to make jazz-based vocal albums typical for the era, singing ballads and standards, but always employing the best jazz talent around. In 1959 she appeared in the stage show, *Jamaica*. Undergoing a radical change of orientation at the dawn of the 1960s, Lincoln teamed up with Oscar Brown Jnr and Max Roach to produce two searing musical indictments of US bigotry, *We Insist!* (Candid) and *Percussion Bitter Sweet* (Impulse!). Lincoln remained a prominent figure in the 1960s and early 1970s, also developing a parallel career in theater and films, but as the 1970s ended and new political winds of conservatism blew across America, Lincoln's Stateside career slowed.

Spending more time on the other side of the Atlantic, Lincoln became a frequent visitor to various countries in Europe and Africa, becoming a cult in France in particular, her big, expressive voice, her articulate lyrics, and her legato method of delivery provoking a major response in her audiences. Lincoln has always remained politically and culturally aware (adopting the African name Aminata Moseka in the 1980s), has continued to sing and act (appearing in Spike Lee films, for example), and has made records for the French arm of Verve records.

SEE ALSO: Benny Carter, Max Roach

Booker Little

fact file

BORN 1938

DIED 1961

MUSICAL SELECTION
Out Front

The brilliant trumpeter and composer Booker Little was the first to extend Clifford Brown's legacy

Memphis-born trumpeter Little was one of the key musicians in the initial transformation of bop into the harmonically and rhythmically more varied forms that were to follow. A musician of impeccable technique and limitless melodic invention, he had a rare capacity in a trumpeter for thinking orchestrally about the music he played and composed, as his few albums under his own name show.

Little came from a very musical family, his sister becoming an opera singer on international stages, and became interested in the trumpet when 10 years old, eventually studying music both at Manassa High School in Memphis and later at Chicago Conservatory (1955–58), from where he emerged with a B.Mus. While still a student in Memphis he had been part of the informal jamming scene there, becoming friendly with tenor saxophonist George Coleman, whom he would meet again in Max Roach's group. In Chicago he played with many of the best jazzmen on the local scene and came to the attention of Sonny Rollins, who recommended him to Roach as a replacement for the departing Kenny Dorham. Little gained quick and widespread recognition as a major find in the general Clifford Brown tradition, recording regularly during his nine months in the Roach quintet and appearing with Roach at the 1958 Newport Jazz Festival. Leaving Roach at the opening of 1959, Little settled in New York and began freelancing widely, appearing with a great number of leaders, including Donald Byrd, Mal Waldron and recording with Max Roach and Abbey Lincoln. He also met Eric Dolphy, discovering a strong musical confluence which led to his appearing on Dolphy's *Far Cry* album in December 1960, John Coltrane's *Africa Brass* sessions, and inviting Dolphy and Roach on to his own last album, *Out Front* (Candid). He and Dolphy then formed a co-led quintet, which enjoyed a two-week residency at the 5 Spot in July 1961. An evening of this residency was later released on a series of albums by Prestige, eventually earning classic status. Soon after this Little succumbed to the ravages of leukemia.

SEE ALSO: Max Roach, Sonny Rollins, Kenny Dorham, Clifford Brown, Donald Byrd, Abbey Lincoln, Eric Dolphy

Charles Lloyd

fact file

BORN 1938

MUSICAL SELECTION
Forest Flower

Poll-winning saxophonist and band leader Charles Lloyd, seen here in Toronto, 1990

Lloyd, a Memphis tenor, flautist, and leader, became one of the great jazz success stories of the 1960s when his Quartet crossed over from modern jazz fans into the minds and hearts of the hippie generation of rock enthusiasts, managing to do this, moreover, while not compromising any of their musical integrity. Since then Lloyd's career has waxed and waned, but in the most recent decade he has once again returned to the jazz limelight with a sequence of outstanding quartets peopled by major talents.

Lloyd came from a middle-class family and was attracted to jazz through bop big bands he heard locally. He managed to acquire his first sax at around the age of 10 and at first was self-taught, later taking lessons with local teachers. Lloyd attended the same high school as his Memphis contemporaries George Coleman, Booker Little, and Frank Strozier. Being a Memphis tenor, Lloyd was inevitably exposed to the blues, R&B and gospel music all around him and played in many of the local bands, including Bobby Bland's. In 1956 he moved to California, studying at USC with the intention of becoming a dentist, but switched to composition in his second year. Having taught music and gigged around LA for a while after university, in 1961 he, along with guitarist Gabor Szabo, joined the bandleader Chico Hamilton as he was recasting his whole group. Lloyd became music director, writing most of the material – indeed, *Forest Flower* received its first, rather limp, recording under the Hamilton group's auspices. A year with Cannonball Adderley in 1964–65 and a debut album on Columbia continued to widen Lloyd's horizons and popular appeal: in 1966 he formed his Quartet, hiring Keith Jarrett, Ron McClure, and Jack DeJohnette. They were the hit of the 1966 Monterey Jazz Festival (the album of their performance, *Forest Flower* (Atlantic), won copious awards on release) and in the next three years they would become the biggest group in modern jazz, selling millions of albums and touring exhaustively worldwide, even to the Soviet Union and the Far East. The combination of Lloyd's adventurous, Coltrane-inflected, but intensely melodic tenor playing and the dynamic group interaction proved irresistible. By the end of the decade Lloyd was exhausted and his group were ready to go in four different directions: a film documentary of Lloyd, *Journey Within*, chronicles the latter period of the band's existence.

Religiously inquisitive, Lloyd became deeply involved in other cultures and other musics during the 1970s and early 1980s, even making a series of flute albums sold under the "new age" banner in counter-cultural shops, next to the incense counter. His profile in jazz dropped away, but in the early 1980s he put together a new quartet featuring the remarkable French pianist Michel Petrucciani, becoming responsible for bringing him to a world audience. Resuming tours and live jazz work, Lloyd reinstated himself in the jazz world, in the 1990s making a series of award-winning albums for ECM with his latest quartet, which includes the Scandinavian pianist Bobo Stenson. Lloyd has now reached a second career peak, playing as well as ever.

SEE ALSO: George Coleman, Booker Little, Chico Hamilton, Cannonball Adderley, Keith Jarrett, Jack DeJohnette

Herbie Mann

fact file

BORN 1930

MUSICAL SELECTION
Live At The Village Gate
Memphis Underground
Peace Piece

The most popular flautist in jazz, Herbie Mann, performing for the camera in the early 1990s

Born Herbert Jay Solomon in Brooklyn, Mann began clarinet lessons at the age of nine, later swapping to saxophone and flute. He entered the army in 1950 and was stationed in Trieste, where he played in the army band for three years, later returning to New York and working with jazz accordianist Mat Mathews in 1953, with whom he stayed for 18 months. After a period touring Europe, Mann became active on the West Coast in 1957 and began appearing annually at Newport Jazz Festival, where he became a decided favorite. He also started a long-term relationship with New York's Village Gate club in 1959. After touring the Americas, Europe, and Africa in 1960 and 1961 with a group at the behest of the US State Department, Mann began seriously incorporating Brazilian and African elements into his music, changing his group accordingly. This in turn led to wider popularity and a massive LP hit, *Live at the Village Gate* (Atlantic, 1962), featuring the hit track, "Comin' Home Baby." By the mid-1960s Mann was easily the best-known flautist in jazz and a figure with widespread crossover appeal worldwide. The 1965 album *Standing Ovation at Newport* (Atlantic) confirmed this position. Later in the 1960s Mann used his position to set up Embryo, a label funded by Atlantic but over which Mann had artistic control. He signed 1960s fusion-type talents such as Miroslav Vitous, Sonny Sharrock, Ron Carter, and Tower of Power. Some of these players were associated with his next major hit, *Memphis Underground* (Atlantic, 1968), where he mixed jazz with the instrumental soul and funk approach of Booker T and King Curtis.

Funk and fusion were the staple of Mann's 1970s bands, reaching a high point with a disco hit, "Hi-jack," in 1975 with his group Family of Mann. Since then Mann has preferred his early 1960s style of music and has also continued to explore the different styles of the world, including Japanese music. He started his own label and production house in 1981, and in the 1990s produced a number of high-quality releases on his own Kokopelli label, often emphasizing his love of Latin American music but, in 1995, issuing *Peace Piece*, an imaginative reworking of compositions by Bill Evans, a musician with whom he made an album, *Nirvana*, in the 1960s.

SEE ALSO: Bill Evans

Shelly Manne

A young Shelly Manne being "sent" by the massed Woody Herman brass, 1949

fact file

BORN 1920

DIED 1984

MUSICAL SELECTION
At The Blackhawk, Vols 1–5
At The Manne Hole, Vols 1–2

Born Sheldon Manne in New York City, Manne came from a family of drummers, his father and two uncles working in the field. He took lessons on drums, then began his professional career in his late teens playing on liners sailing the Atlantic route. By 1940 he was sufficiently well thought of to replace Dave Tough in clarinetist Joe Marsala's band, progressing from there through a series of swing units and making historic dates with Signature records, including a 1943 Coleman Hawkins session, while in the Coast Guard from 1942 to 1945. Between 1946 and 1951 Manne was most regularly part of the Stan Kenton aggregation, though he spent time in 1947 with Charlie Ventura and in 1948–49 ran his own quintet with Bill Harris as well as playing with JATP and drumming for Woody Herman. By the end of his Kenton years Manne was settled in LA and divided his time between jazz pursuits and Hollywood studio demands. Although a remarkably tasteful and swinging drummer who was instrumental in establishing the West Coast version of cool jazz during 1952–55, Manne had a strong sense of humor, as can be heard in his vocals with the Kenton band (1951) and in his catalytic involvement in the rip-roaring Shorty Rogers-led R&B studio band, Boots Brown and His Blockbusters (1951–52). Manne became one of the most in-demand drummers on the West Coast for virtually every musical situation, even aiding Frank Sinatra in his drumming chores on camera in *The Man With The Golden Arm* (1956). After this Manne formed his own quintet, Shelly Manne and His Men, to parallel his copious film soundtrack and TV work. Regulars in the group included Joe Gordon, Richie Kamuca, Russ Freeman, and Conte Candoli, and two series of live albums became classics of West Coast jazz – *At The Blackhawk, Vols 1–5* (Contemporary, 1959) and *At The Manne Hole, Vols 1–2* (Contemporary, 1962). His club, Shelly's Manne Hole in Hollywood, ran successfully from 1960 until 1974, when a lease expiry could not be renegotiated. Manne freelanced actively, appearing memorably with Coleman Hawkins on *2,3,4* (Impulse!, 1962) and striking up a winning partnership with André Previn, with whom he had enjoyed bestseller status in the treatment of the music to *My Fair Lady* in 1956. His questing musical imagination can be confirmed by his presence on Ornette Coleman's second album, *Tomorrow Is The Question* (Contemporary, 1959). Manne ran his club and his groups until the mid-1970s, when he became a founding member of L.A.4, with Ray Brown and Laurindo Almeida. In the late 1970s he once again led his own group, switching his time between that and freelance work until his death in 1984.

SEE ALSO: Coleman Hawkins, Stan Kenton, Bill Harris, Woody Herman, Shorty Rogers, Coleman Hawkins

Wingy Manone

fact file

BORN 1900

DIED 1982

MUSICAL SELECTION
"Isle of Capri"
"Tar Paper Stomp"

The great entertainer: Wingy Manone in full flight

Manone was born Joseph Matthews in New Orleans. As a teenager he was caught between two streetcars in the city, his right arm being so severely damaged that it was amputated in the subsequent hospitalization. Soon after this setback Manone took an interest in the trumpet, teaching himself to operate it one-handed and within a short time gaining employment in riverboat bands. Manone traveled widely thereafter, playing in Chicago and New York, and then in Mobile, Alabama, where he joined the Crescent City Jazzers, moving with them to St Louis. By 1926 Manone was running a band in Biloxi, then made his debut recordings in New York the following year. Between then and 1934 he lived between Chicago and New York, recording regularly with the top musicians in both cities, before forming a permanent New York-based band of his own in 1934. Using the new swing beat and a gift for melody as well as his characterful, often humorous singing, Manone quickly built up a following, registering a major hit in 1935 with his version of "Isle of Capri" (Vocalion), as well as recording the first version of the riff which later became "In The Mood," under Manone called "Tar Paper Stomp." This success buoyed him through to World War II: just prior to America's involvement Manone switched to living on the West Coast, linking up with old jazzer Bing Crosby and appearing regularly on Crosby's radio show. He also appeared in the film *Rhythm on the River* with Crosby in 1940. A celebrity in his own right far beyond the jazz world, Manone wrote his amusing autobiography, *Trumpet on the Wing*, in 1948, and continued to appear on the West Coast, settling into a regular pattern of shows at Las Vegas in the 1950s. He also appeared occasionally at the Newport Jazz Festival at the beginning of the 1960s, but his career was decidedly more low-profile in that and subsequent decades, as his generation of entertainers lost control of TV and radio output and he found less opportunity to expound his musical and comedy theories to spellbound audiences. By the late 1970s Manone was in retirement, living relatively comfortably though in something of an eclipse on the jazz front until his death in 1984. His reputation has taken an upturn in recent years as his uncomplicated, swinging but melodic trumpet style has been reassessed by various commentators.

SEE ALSO: Jelly Roll Morton, Jack Teagarden

Dodo Marmarosa

fact file

BORN 1925

MUSICAL SELECTION
Complete Dial Sessions

Dodo Marmarosa, a leading bop pianist in the 1940s, was classically trained but learned his art from some of the best, including Charlie Parker and Miles Davis

At an early stage in his career, Pittsburgh-born pianist Dodo Marmarosa had good reason to be seen as the first great exponent of bop piano. Yet his public involvement in music was to be relatively brief, his legacy small, and the hopes of his admirers left largely to wither over time. Born Michael Marmarosa into an Italian migrant family, the boy was given piano lessons from an early age and also listened to the family's collection of opera recordings on 78s. A shy and awkward child, Marmarosa was given a taxing training in classical piano, his parents set on his becoming a concert pianist, but as he grew he began slipping off unnoticed to jazz nightclubs in Pittsburgh to soak up the playing of people such as Mary Lou Williams and Art Tatum. Studying at the same school as Erroll Garner, Marmarosa (who even at school was nicknamed "Dodo") struck up a friendship with clarinetist Buddy DeFranco, following him through a number of swing big bands from 1940 to 1944, including those of Charlie Barnet and Gene Krupa. A stint with Artie Shaw in 1945–46 saw Marmarosa make his first recordings with the band before he moved on to Tommy Dorsey. Leaving Dorsey in 1946, Marmarosa based himself in Los Angeles and began mixing with the emerging bop players living there, recording with the visiting Charlie Parker and Miles Davis in March 1946, then later that year with Howard McGhee's Sextet. Marmarosa's advanced harmonic language, his fleet right-hand runs and strongly independent left hand made for a rich and complex style based on the heritage of Art Tatum, as the recordings of this period make clear. A stint in the Boyd Raeburn band in 1947 extended his horizons, but with a recording ban and the general cooling of the bebop scene on the West Coast as the 1940s drew to a close, Marmarosa moved back to Pittsburgh and almost complete obscurity. An album for Argo in 1961 seemed to augur well, as did an appearance on a Gene Ammons date in 1962, but rather than a beginning, this proved a coda to a brilliant but all too quickly blighted career.

SEE ALSO: Mary Lou Williams, Art Tatum, Erroll Garner, Buddy DeFranco, Charlie Barnet, Gene Krupa, Artie Shaw

Branford Marsalis

fact file

BORN 1960

MUSICAL SELECTION
Scenes In The City
The Dark Keys

Branford Marsalis, sax player and progenitor of Buckshot LeFonque, has taken advantage of contemporary production and sounds to bring the street back to jazz

Older brother of Wynton and Delfeayo Marsalis and son of pianist Ellis Marsalis, Branford was born and raised in New Orleans. Formal musical study, of both jazz and classical forms, commenced while he was still a youth and was expanded while he was at Southern University, Louisiana, through lessons with reed man Alvin Batiste. A number of semesters at Berklee College in Boston completed his formal studies, after which, in 1981, he joined up with brother Wynton in Art Blakey's Jazz Messengers before becoming a member of Clark Terry's big band for a major tour that same year. A founder member of Wynton Marsalis's quintet in 1982, Branford gained his first wide exposure in his role as foil to his brother's fast-emerging post-bop brilliance. This in turn led to appearances and recordings with Dizzy Gillespie and Miles Davis as well as some live work with the latter. This and other work, as well as his own debut as a leader (*Scenes In The City*, Columbia 1993), led to a gradual parting of the ways with brother Wynton, who took an especially dim view of Branford's increasing involvement in electric jazz and funk rhythms. A world tour as part of Sting's backing band in 1985 led to a musical break from his trumpeter brother, after which Branford formed his own band and continued to freelance assiduously. Branford's oblique approach to improvising, his passion for pastiche, and his effortless rhythmic manipulations make him a distinctive and often engrossing player, as his trio album, *The Dark Keys* (Columbia, 1996) demonstrates convincingly. Marsalis, like his brother, has given classical and semiclassical recitals, and has made an album of classical favorites, using his soprano saxophone as the melody carrier against a string orchestra. He has also been heavily involved in TV work, running for a time the house band on *The Tonight Show* in New York. Unlike any other Marsalis, however, he has also become deeply involved in urban black music such as hip-hop, scratch, rap, jungle, and other offshoots: this he has explored with signal success on albums by his group Buckshot LeFonque, named after a pseudonym once used by Cannonball Adderley when moonlighting on a recording session in the 1950s. Marsalis continues to produce exciting and diverse music, heading in fundamentally different directions from the rest of his family, although he made an intimate and successful duet album, *Loved Ones* (Columbia), with his father in 1993. He has recently been named as a director of A&R at Columbia Jazz.

SEE ALSO: Wynton Marsalis, Art Blakey, Dizzy Gillespie, Miles Davis, Cannonball Adderley

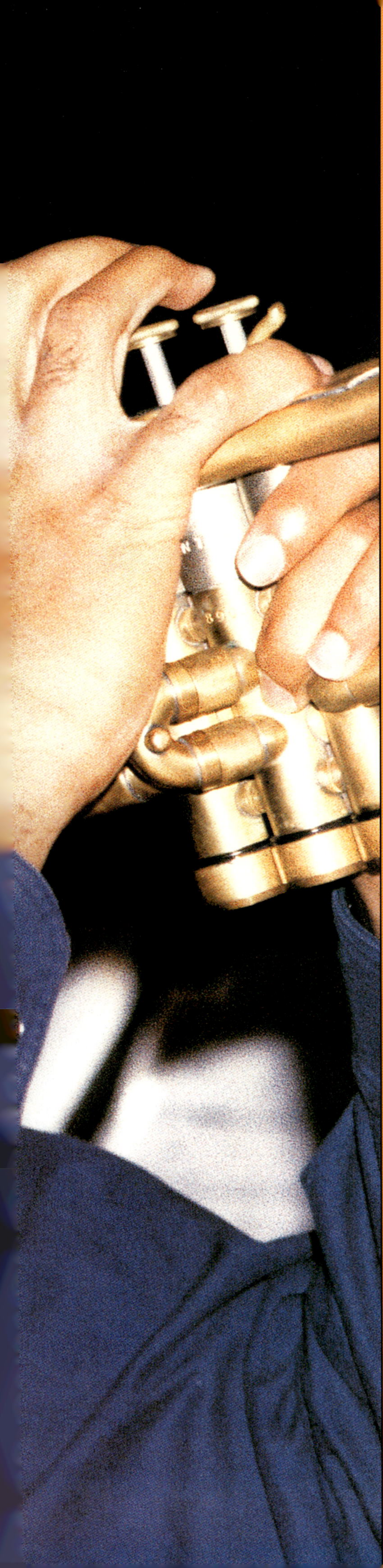

Wynton Marsalis

New Orleans trumpeter, brother of Branford and Delfeayo and son of pianist Ellis Marsalis, Wynton Marsalis has been one of the most consistently creative, outspoken, and influential jazz musicians of the past 15 years. The creator of major jazz pieces and the possessor of an astonishing technique and an imagination to match, Marsalis has often invited debate and controversy through his strongly held views on what constitutes valid jazz expression in a period when multiplicity of inspiration and eclecticism have been the watchwords of the majority of young musicians. By the force of his music and his personality, Marsalis has helped redirect a whole generation of musicians toward self-reliance and responsibility in their dealings with the world, from the way they dress to their timekeeping habits and their deportment on stage, let alone their music.

Marsalis was learning music by his sixth birthday, from both classical and jazz traditions. By the time he was 14 he was performing Haydn's Trumpet Concerto and holding down first trumpet position with the New Orleans Civic Orchestra. In his late teens he attended Tanglewood's Berkshire Music Center, then moved on to Juilliard. While still studying there he joined Art Blakey's Jazz Messengers in 1980, playing coast to coast and traveling overseas with the master drummer. His brilliance was quickly appreciated, as was his sartorial harking back to the pre-avant-garde, Afro-hippie days, and he appeared as guest soloist in a touring Herbie Hancock quartet in 1981, upsetting virtually every trumpeter within hearing distance. That same year he debuted as a recording leader with Columbia, the company with which he still records, using the Hancock quartet as his backing unit and still heavily indebted in style to Miles Davis and Freddie Hubbard. The following year he was leading his own quintet, with brother Branford on saxes, and using a general musical direction not far removed from the acoustic quintet run by Miles Davis in the 1960s. This band, with minor personnel changes, lasted for the 1980s while Marsalis also pursued a successful career as a classical soloist performing and recording trumpet pieces from composers of the eighteenth to the twentieth centuries to great acclaim. During this decade he became renowned for his outspoken criticism of other jazz musicians, including Miles Davis, and for his strongly held convictions about what constituted legitimate jazz history and the music's true legacy, but the quality of his playing continued to disarm most of his critics.

By the dawn of the 1990s Marsalis had reinvestigated jazz history, made a series of concept albums with his group, and then gone on to begin forming a truly original trumpet and composing style drawing on the great brass legacies of the middle and distant jazz past, from Armstrong and Rex Stewart onward, rather than the postwar advances of Davis, Gillespie, and Brown. In his compositions, as revealed on *Citi Movement, In This House, On This Morning* and most recently, his somewhat meretricious jazz opera *Blood On The Fields* (1997), he has drawn heavily on the Ellington, Henderson, and Mingus legacy of extended composition for large and medium-size groups, whether working with his 1990s sextet or with larger forces, to create an identifiable contemporary esthetic. Already one of the largest influences on the music in the past decade or more, Marsalis, still in his thirties, is liable to create an even deeper indelible mark on jazz in the coming decades.

fact file

BORN 1961

MUSICAL SELECTION
Citi Movement
In This House
On This Morning
Blood On The Fields

The most complete trumpeter in jazz today, Wynton Marsalis is both a teacher and traditionalist in the truest sense

SEE ALSO: Branford Marsalis, Art Blakey, Herbie Hancock, Miles Davis, Freddie Hubbard, Duke Ellington, Fletcher Henderson, Charles Mingus

Les McCann

fact file

BORN 1935

MUSICAL SELECTION
Swiss Movement
Invitation To Openness

Keyboardist Les McCann, seen here in the 1970s, enjoyed tremendous success with Eddie Harris with their best-selling "Swiss Movement"

Born in Lexington, Kentucky, pianist/singer McCann was intimately involved with gospel music from his earliest memories, his entire family being involved in church functions including singing in the church choir. Apart from a few lessons, he was mostly self-taught on piano. While he was on navy service he both sang and played the piano and his singing led to an appearance on the Ed Sullivan show in 1956 after he had won a navy talent contest. After discharge, McCann settled in California, leading a trio accompanying Gene McDaniels and quickly becoming noticed for his gospel-drenched jazz playing. Signed by Pacific Records, from 1960 onward, McCann released a number of top-selling trio albums all laced liberally with his special brand of gospel-jazz, not too far removed in style from what many hard boppers were doing in the wake of Horace Silver and Cannonball Adderley. McCann began playing overseas festivals in the early 1960s, confirming his international status. He stayed on the West Coast but traveled extensively, switching in the mid-1960s to the Limelight label and registering hits in the singles chart with songs such as "The Big City," on which his vocals were featured.

He teamed up almost by happenstance at the 1969 Montreux Festival with Eddie Harris, and the two of them stole the festival and also recorded a top-selling album, *Swiss Movement*, which became highly influential in the funk-jazz world. A single from the album, "Compared To What?," charted worldwide. After that McCann attempted to spread his artistic wings further, with long, somewhat rambling affairs such as *Invitation to Openness* (Atlantic, 1971), but as the decade wore on his brand of funk fell from favor and he became less of a headliner in his own right. By the 1980s McCann was splitting his time between a number of projects, including working with Herbie Mann, touring regularly with Eddie Harris's unit, and running his own group. McCann continues to play and record, his style matured into a mix of modern jazz and full-on jazz-soul.

SEE ALSO: Horace Silver, Cannonball Adderley, Eddie Harris, Herbie Mann

Jack McDuff

fact file

BORN 1926

MUSICAL SELECTION
It's About Time
The Honeydripper

Once known as Brother Jack, now universally acknowledged as Cap'n Jack, the master of Hammond B3 funk, Jack McDuff

Organist McDuff, variously using the sobriquets "Brother" and "Captain" at different stages in his career, was one of the organists inspired by Jimmy Smith and the emergence of the tenor and Hammond organ trios in the 1950s to take a particularly down-home funky route to success in the early 1960s. Born in Champaign, Illinois, McDuff started out on double bass in the late 1940s before switching to piano and, after a period running his own groups in Cincinnati, settling in Chicago. Here he played with Eddie Chamblee and Johnny Griffin, among others, before switching finally to organ around 1957 when he hitched up with Willis "Gator" Jackson, a jazz tenor player with a track record of distinction in the "honking tenors" section of the R&B scene, being responsible for "Gator Tail" in 1949 with the Cootie Williams group. McDuff's adroit combination of R&B, groove, and jazz sophistication gave him a different profile from those of the legions of Smith copiers and quickly gave him an appreciative international audience. In 1961 he formed his own group, at various points employing Grant Green, Harold Vick, Red Holloway, George Benson and Leo Wright, and recording for Prestige with tenor stars such as Gene Ammons, Jimmy Forrest, and Roland Kirk. By the mid-1960s McDuff was a major presence in jazz organ terms, his popularity lasting until the end of the decade and the general demise of the Hammond organ as a cutting-edge instrument. Almost two decades in the hinterland of jazz and the vanishing chitlin circuit finally ended in the late 1980s when, like much of 1950s and 1960s jazz, the seductive sounds of the Hammond organ were pedaled by a new generation. McDuff, as one of the survivors, was re-promoted by Muse records when producer/saxophonist Houston Person brought him to the label, leading to a fully fledged second coming. Often in league with his younger organ colleague, Joey DeFrancesco, McDuff played clubs, festivals, and concerts and in the 1990s swapped to Concord Records, where he has been regularly making successful albums, including 1996's *It's About Time*, with DeFrancesco. He also appeared on DeFrancesco's last album for Columbia, along with Illinois Jacquet, Grover Washington and others, entitled *Live At The Five Spot* (1995).

SEE ALSO: Jimmy Smith, Johnny Griffin, Grant Green, George Benson, Gene Ammons, Roland Kirk, Illinois Jacquet

Gary McFarland

Brilliant 1960s arranger and composer Gary McFarland did not take in the jazz scene until he hit university

fact file

BORN 1933

DIED 1971

MUSICAL SELECTION
Big Band Bossa Nova
Point of Departure
Profiles
October Suite

Los Angeles-born arranger, vibist, and composer McFarland moved to Grant's Pass, Oregon, in his mid-teens. He showed no special interest in music until he attended Oregon State University, where he discovered boogie-woogie. By the time he did his army service in the early 1950s McFarland was sufficiently jazz-inclined to begin learning the vibes, but did not begin to read music fluently until the age of 24, in 1957. Taking music courses in the Los Angeles area in 1957–58, McFarland was encouraged to develop a talent for composition and landed a Berklee scholarship for 1959 as well as attending John Lewis's jazz workshops in Lenox, Massachusetts. By 1960 he was based in New York and picking up arranging and composing work for an impressive roster of leaders, including Gerry Mulligan's Concert Big Band and Johnny Hodges. In 1960 he prepared Anita O'Day's *All The Sad Young Men* (Verve), then arranged the music from *How To Succeed in Business Without Really Trying* (Verve, 1961). In 1962–63 he continued to progress, making *Big Band Bossa Nova* with Stan Getz (Verve) and debuting as a leader with a self-titled album featuring Bill Evans as guest soloist (Verve). This album gave a clear picture of McFarland's talents when away from more commercial work, his use of combined instrumental sonorities and his ability to mesh composition with improvisation second only to those of Gil Evans among postwar jazz composer/arrangers. In 1963 McFarland ran a sextet for a short while, making the album *Point of Departure* (Impulse!, 1963) with it, then working as something of a staff arranger for Verve and Impulse!, arranging for artists such as Wes Montgomery and Gabor Szabo.

John Lewis recorded an album of McFarland compositions for Atlantic, *Essence*. In 1966 he made two fine adventurous albums for Impulse!, *Profiles*, and *October Suite*, for strings and woodwind, with pianist Steve Kuhn as soloist. After this, McFarland started his own record label. His commercially oriented music was virtually devoid of interest, while his more deeply felt work showed a remarkably prescient artistic conscience, as shown by his *America The Beautiful: An Account of Its Disappearance* (Skye, 1968). McFarland continued his difficult balancing act between commerce and artistry up to his early death, in 1971, from a heart attack.

SEE ALSO: John Lewis, Gerry Mulligan, Johnny Hodges, Anita O'Day, Stan Getz, Bill Evans, Gil Evans, Wes Montgomery

Bobby McFerrin

The unmistakable voice of Bobby McFerrin has always kept him in the popular eye while his understanding of music earned him professional respect as well

Singer McFerrin, born in New York, came from a musical family, both his parents being opera singers. McFerrin starting piano lessons at the age of six, studying at the preparatory division of Juilliard School, then later at Sacramento State College. After some work as an accompanist, then as a singer-pianist, McFerrin was discovered by singer-lyricist Jon Hendricks, who helped him develop his distinctive improvisational style and involved him in many of the vocal groups Hendricks himself worked with. McFerrin quickly made a big impact, singing in varying situations, including with Wynton Marsalis, George Benson, and Wayne Shorter. By the early 1980s, however, McFerrin, influenced by the impact Keith Jarrett's unaccompanied piano recitals had managed in the 1970s, became increasingly committed to solo vocal recitals. His pioneering work in this direction, combining sensitive rearranging of well-known music and far-ranging improvisatory excursions, exploring a vocabulary of vocal and bodily sounds new to jazz (including hitting his chest rhythmically with his hand), brought McFerrin quick and massive recognition in the jazz world. By the middle of the decade McFerrin was the undisputed new king of jazz vocals, a daring and charismatic figure who was capable of winning Grammy awards.

In the late 1980s McFerrin's career took a quantum leap when he landed a hit single, "Don't Worry Be Happy," made entirely of overdubbed vocals, taken from the similarly constructed *Simple Pleasures* LP (Blue Note, 1988). This track made him something of a superstar in the jazz firmament and a sizable figure in the contemporary music scene, and he became a regular in concert, on TV, and on video. Typically, McFerrin took the opportunity to pause and rethink, resuming his career at the beginning of the 1990s with ventures in a variety of directions, from a trio with Jack DeJohnette and Lyle Mays through vocalese versions of classical music with accompanying orchestra to, more recently, conducting work in Mozart concertos with Chick Corea as soloist. McFerrin has also, with his latest album *Circlesongs* (Sony Classical, 1997), taken a step in a new direction, toward wholly vocal compositions using ensembles which have roots in ethnic rhythmic and melodic repetition and variation. McFerrin's musical career has now extended well beyond its original jazz base, his creativity embracing most musical forms .

fact file

BORN 1950

MUSICAL SELECTION
Simple Pleasures
Circlesongs

SEE ALSO: Jon Hendricks, Wynton Marsalis, George Benson, Wayne Shorter, Keith Jarrett, Jack DeJohnette

Howard McGhee

West Coast-based trumpeter Howard McGhee, pictured here in the late 1940s, has had ups and downs but always worked with the best, including Lionel Hampton and Charlie Parker

fact file

BORN 1918

DIED 1987

MUSICAL SELECTION
Maggie's Back In Town!
Nobody Knows You When You're Down And Out

Trumpeter McGhee was one of the outstanding bop trumpeters in the late 1940s, taking an individual course between the fireworks of Gillespie and the studied melodicism of Miles Davis. Born in Tulsa, Oklahoma, McGhee was originally attracted to clarinet, playing it in his high school band, but was so impressed by hearing Louis Armstrong in the mid-1930s that he took up trumpet. By the end of the decade he was working professionally, joining his first name band, Lionel Hampton, in the fall of 1941, then moving on that same year to Andy Kirk, with whom he debuted on record in 1942. A 12-month interlude with Charlie Barnet saw him rejoin Kirk in 1944, then head out West in Coleman Hawkins's small group of 1944–45. McGhee made a number of outstanding recordings in LA with Hawkins for Capitol, ushering in his sterling high notes, rhythmic assuredness, and general boppish approach, which was a perfect foil to Hawkins's bustling energy. Leaving Hawkins in LA, McGhee started his own group there, running it for two successful years before falling in with a visibly ailing Charlie Parker, with whom he recorded a disastrous session for Dial after which Parker was hospitalized to overcome his drugs dependency. After some appearances with JATP McGhee moved East to New York in 1947, appearing at the "Midnight Jazz at Carnegie Hall" session for Granz's JATP which spawned the three consecutive versions of "Perdido," but, after initial success and popularity, by the end of the decade he began experiencing drug problems of his own which, as the 1950s advanced, slowed his career to a near stop.

Pulling his life together again at the dawning of the 1960s, McGhee launched his own small group and for a time ran a big band, touring and recording frequently and performing at levels matching those of the late 1940s. The album *Maggie's Back In Town!* (Contemporary, 1961) typifies this latter-day approach, as do others, such as *Nobody Knows You When You're Down And Out* (UA, 1960).

McGhee based himself in New York but traveled widely, appearing in many all-star groups as well as running his own ensembles and touring with festival groups. He continued to record and compose, but his last decade was troubled by failing health.

SEE ALSO: Dizzy Gillespie, Miles Davis, Louis Armstrong, Lionel Hampton, Charlie Barnet, Coleman Hawkins

William McKinney

MicKinney's Cotton Pickers, directed by Don Redman (front left), seen here in 1931

fact file

BORN 1894

DIED 1969

MUSICAL SELECTION
The Band Don Redman Built

McKinney's name is inextricably bound up with that of his band, McKinney's Cotton Pickers, one of the premier bands of the 1920s and a considerable musical force during the period when Don Redman was its principal arranger. McKinney was born in Paducah, Kentucky, and didn't settle into a professional career until he had seen action in World War I. Starting as a drummer in circuses, McKinney soon progressed to becoming drummer for the Synco Septet, based in Springfield, Ohio. Advancing to the position of drummer/leader, he oversaw the band's change of name and direction. As the Synco Jazz Band McKinney's outfit became so busy that he gave his drumming position to Cuba Austin and assumed sole leadership of the group in 1923. By 1926 he was the band's manager as well, overseeing a further name change when it became McKinney's Cotton Pickers. By this time based in Detroit at the Greystone Ballroom, the band used trumpeter John Nesbitt as principal arranger on its jazz repertoire, emphasizing a remarkably smooth and powerful rhythm and well-worked section assignments. In 1927 the Cotton Pickers engaged Don Redman as their main arranger, developing an even stronger identity for the band's music alongside their entertaining stage act and comedy routines. Between 1927 and 1931 the Cotton Pickers, catered for by Redman and well drilled by McKinney himself, became one of the top bands in the country and one of the most forward-looking outfits in jazz. The departures of both Nesbitt (1930) and Redman (1931), Nesbitt going to Fletcher Henderson and Redman to form his own outfit, fatally wounded the band: over the next few years almost all the original personnel left and no arranger of commensurate ability was ever hired permanently. The Cotton Pickers, even though they hired Benny Carter and Rex Steward subsequently for short periods, ceased recording in late 1931 and broke up in 1934. McKinney refused to concede defeat, forming another version of the Cotton Pickers that same year and running it until the early 1940s, but fashions had shifted and he was unable to adapt. Returning to Detroit, McKinney gradually faded from the music scene. One report has him working for Ford in Detroit in later years. He never returned to the music business.

SEE ALSO: Don Redman, Benny Carter, Rex Steward

John McLaughlin

Inspirational guitarist and band leader John McLaughlin took some of the earliest steps into the fusion scene in the late 1960s and early 1970s

fact file

BORN 1942

MUSICAL SELECTION
Extrapolation
After The Rain

Yorkshire-born guitarist McLaughlin grew up in a musical family. Attracted to the guitar in his youth he started out being drawn to both the blues and to Django Reinhardt. By the early 1960s he tried his luck in London, coming into contact with both the jazz and R&B scenes. By the later 1960s McLaughlin had embraced free jazz, Eastern philosophy, religion, and music, and loud amplification as well as acoustic music. His first album as a leader, *Extrapolation* (Polydor, 1969), is today seen as an early classic of the nascent fusion genre. That same year McLaughlin moved to New York and joined up with Tony Williams and organist Larry Young in the drummer's LifeTime (later a quartet with the addition of Jack Bruce on bass). This group made *Emergency!* (Polydor, 1970) and McLaughlin was also invited by Miles Davis to become involved in his studio-bound jazz-rock experiments.

McLaughlin left LifeTime toward the end of 1970, forming his own band, Mahavishnu Orchestra, the following year. The band, with ex-Flock violinist Jerry Goodman, keyboardist Jan Hammer and – most crucially – drummer Billy Cobham, soon succeeded where the more disparate LifeTime had failed. The Orchestra split up in 1973, not long after a gig in New York's Central Park. A second unit with the same instrumentation revealed a diminished impact with the same formula. McLaughlin in 1975 formed the band Shakti, combining his familiarity with modern Western music and the classical Eastern forms. In the late 1970s McLaughlin began looking across a wider musical palette, making *Johnny McLaughlin, Electric Guitarist* (Columbia, 1979) which featured various line-ups from his past, then at the dawn of the 1980s going out on tour in an acoustic guitar triumvirate of himself, Paco de Lucia, and Al DiMeola. Now living in Paris, McLaughlin used this as well as duets idea with Larry Coryell as a major outlet for his music; he also appeared on Palle Mikkelborg's *Aura* along with Miles Davis. By the middle of the decade McLaughlin had written a guitar concerto and formed a new version of the old Mahavishnu Orchestra, featuring sax player Bill Evans.

By the end of the decade the guitarist was appearing with a number of different groups, most regularly with a trio. In the 1990s he went back to his roots with a trio, Free Spirits, featuring Joey DeFrancesco and drummer Dennis Chambers, which toured internationally and made a live album in Tokyo (Verve, 1993); a follow-up album, *After The Rain* (Verve, 1995), with Elvin Jones guesting, concentrated on John Coltrane compositions.

During the latter half of the 1990s, McLaughlin has been running a group concentrating on complex but hard-hitting electric music, featuring Matthew Garrison (son of Coltrane bassist Jimmy) on electric bass: this band is featured on 1998's *The Heart of Things* (Verve).

SEE ALSO: Django Reinhardt, Larry Young, Larry Coryell, Miles Davis, Bill Evans, Elvin Jones

Jackie McLean

fact file

BORN 1932

MUSICAL SELECTION
Let Freedom Ring
Hat Trick

Saxophonist Jackie McLean, pictured on stage with Art Blakey in 1956 (including Spanky DeBrest on bass)

New York-born altoist McLean was a Charlie Parker acolyte in his youth, then in the 1960s became one of the few bop players to investigate the greater musical freedoms being opened up by younger players. Born into a musical Harlem family (his father was a professional guitarist), McLean was initially attracted to the records of Lester Young and Dexter Gordon; when he started learning alto in high school he strove to emulate the deeper tenor sound of his heroes. Growing up in the same neighborhood as Sonny Rollins, Kenny Drew, and older players like Bud and Richie Powell, McLean was known and liked on the scene, being nurtured both by Bud Powell (who gave him music lessons) and Charlie Parker, who became a surrogate father to the awe-struck teenager. McLean played with Rollins in the late 1940s and recorded with Miles Davis in 1951. During the last years of Charlie Parker's troubled life he and McLean were often in each other's company, with McLean loaning the older man his alto during the last months of his life. After Parker's death McLean, along with Cannonball Adderley and others, was immediately hyped as a "new Bird" – something neither he nor his colleagues looked for – but by 1956, when he began appearing with Charles Mingus, McLean, though using Parker's musical vocabulary, was attempting to find a different route. A year with the Jazz Messengers in 1957 prepared him for the running of his own quintet before he became involved in playing the music (written by Freddie Redd) for the successful play about drug addiction, *The Connection* (1959–61). While consolidating his career there, McLean began recording the fruits of his long thinking about theme composition, with "Quadrangle" appearing on 1960's *Jackie's Bag* (Blue Note) after being written in 1956, the year "Little Melonae," based around diminished chord progressions, had been composed. McLean later noted that "Quadrangle" had been written free of all chord structures, but he had added "I've Got Rhythm" changes at the recording session for the improvisations so that the soloists didn't become hopelessly lost. Two years later McLean was declaring *Let Freedom Ring* (Blue Note) on a particularly powerful quartet date, following this with two albums, *One Step Beyond* (Blue Note, 1963) and *Destination Out!* (Blue Note, 1963), both featuring trombonist Grachan Moncur III and vibist Bobby Hutcherson.

By the late 1960s, McLean was increasingly disillusioned. He found a solution by the end of the decade in music teaching which has engaged the majority of his time up to the present. He has remained consistently active on tours, spending time in Europe and Japan in particular in the 1970s and 1980s, but his recordings have been sporadic and uneven, including an unusual experiment with electro-funk, *Monuments* (RCA, 1979). Combined efforts with McCoy Tyner and others in the 1990s have seen a return to his boppish best, glimpsed on 1996's *Hat Trick* (Somethin' Else).

SEE ALSO: Charlie Parker, Lester Young, Dexter Gordon, Sonny Rollins, Bud Powell, Cannonball Adderley

Carmen McRae

fact file

BORN 1920

DIED 1994

MUSICAL SELECTION
Blue Moon
Boy Meets Girl
The Great American Songbook
Lady Day

Carmen McRae enjoyed early success as one of her earliest compositions was recorded by Billy Holiday in 1939

New York-born pianist and singer McRae was given private piano lessons when a young girl, her parents wishing a classical music career for her; she began composing tunes in her teenage years. Attracted to jazz, she appeared (like Ella Fitzgerald before her) at the Apollo Theater's amateur night and was noted by Teddy Wilson and his songwriter wife, Irene Kitchings. A song McRae wrote at this point was recorded by McRae's idol, Billie Holiday, in 1939. Her career slow to start, McRae worked as intermission pianist and singer at Minton's Playhouse in Harlem and with Benny Carter and Count Basie briefly before finally making her recording debut with Mercer Ellington's orchestra in 1947. After Ellington's band broke up in 1948, McRae married drummer Kenny Clarke and settled in Chicago. The marriage was brief but she remained in Chicago for some years, finally getting the break she needed and making a series of quality records for a number of labels in 1954–55. A contract with Decca in the latter year led to her making an unbroken string of classic jazz vocal albums, including *Blue Moon* (1956) and *Boy Meets Girl* (1957). McRae's slightly acid tone and remarkable rhythmic flexibility, plus her unique interpretative insights and general musicality, place her in the same league as Sarah Vaughan, Billie Holiday, and Ella Fitzgerald where jazz singing is concerned, even if she never managed their level of popular acclaim. From the late 1950s on McRae ran a trio, beginning with pianist Ray Bryant as her accompanist; she also enjoyed two recording unions with Dave Brubeck in the early 1960s which have proved remarkably enduring.

McRae stuck to her style and repertoire throughout the 1960s and 1970s when most others were being pushed in any number of ways – toward rock, folk, theater, MOR, or film covers – retaining the essence of her approach even when singing Lennon-McCartney. A 1972 live recording of a typical McRae set, *The Great American Songbook* (Atlantic), found her accompanied by a trio led by Jimmy Rowles and in commanding form on songs from Cole Porter, Duke Ellington, Leo Robin and many others. Similarly, a two-disc set, *Live at the Great American Music Hall* (Blue Note, 1976), included supporting efforts from old friend Dizzy Gillespie as well as many songs originally associated with Billie Holiday. This long-term respect for Holiday reached its apotheosis when, in one of a series of late-1980s treatments of music by past greats (including Thelonious Monk), McRae recorded a complete album of songs associated with the great *Lady Day* (Novus). Inactive for most of the early 1990s due to chronic illness, McRae died from heart failure in 1994.

SEE ALSO: Ella Fitzgerald, Teddy Wilson, Billie Holiday, Benny Carter, Count Basie, Kenny Clarke, Sarah Vaughan

Helen Merrill

fact file

BORN 1929

MUSICAL SELECTION
Dream of You
Music Makers

Helen Merrill, pictured in the 1980s, was a key player in the Evans/Davis collaboration of the 1950s

Singer Merrill, born in New York, has had a larger influence on jazz history than is commonly realized. Born Helen Milcetic in New York City, she began singing in an amateur capacity in her mid-teens shortly before the end of World War II, eventually touring with the orchestra of Billy Childs in 1946–47. Towards the end of the decade she fell in with the boppers, hanging out at Nola rehearsal studios, appearing with Charlie Parker, Miles Davis, and Bud Powell among others, but her marriage in 1947 obliged her to slowly withdraw for a period from professional engagements. By 1952, however, she began to pick up the threads of her career again, singing with Earl Hines and then signing a contract with EmArcy in 1954. That year she made a fine jazz album, her burnished tones matched perfectly to the accompaniments of Clifford Brown (arrangements courtesy of Quincy Jones). In 1956 her next album was made, featuring, at her insistence, arrangements by Gil Evans. Showing for the first time the mature Evans style soon evident on his albums with Miles Davis, Evans helped Merrill to create a jazz vocal classic in the album *Dream of You* (EmArcy, 1956). Subsequently, Merrill suggested during the course of a conversation with Miles Davis, who admired the album, that he work again with Evans. *Miles Ahead* was started on not so long afterwards. Merrill continued with her career, leaving EmArcy in 1958 and touring internationally as the 1950s came to a close.

She became a particular favorite in France and Scandinavia before working extensively in Japan from the mid-1960s onward. In Japan, as in France and other European countries, she was regarded as a major jazz vocalist long before she received anything like proper recognition in the US. She took up residence in Japan from 1967 to 1973, then moved to Chicago, taking up Stateside recording once more in 1977 and making an album with John Lewis.

Spending time equally between the US and other countries from the 1980s onward, Merrill made a fine small-group album, *Music Makers* (Owl, 1986), in France with Steve Lacy and Stephane Grappelli, then in 1987 she combined once more with Gil Evans to reinvigorate the charts which they had recorded for EmArcy some 30 years before. Something of a swansong for Evans, this helped re-establish Merrill on the international stage and in the US, and since then she has been very busy both live and in the recording studio offering the jazz public more helpings of her uncompromising, deeply felt artistry.

SEE ALSO: Charlie Parker, Miles Davis, Bud Powell, Earl Hines, Clifford Brown, Quincy Jones, Gil Evans, Miles Davis

Pat Metheny

Guitarist and band leader Pat Metheny, dressed for the occasion, is a popular performer worldwide

fact file

BORN 1954

MUSICAL SELECTION
Secret Story
I Can See Your Place From Here
Missouri Sky

An enormously influential guitarist and composer, Metheny was born in rural Missouri and originally attempted to master the French horn, an instrument he played in early adolescence before swapping to guitar. Emerging quickly from the all-enveloping stylistic embrace of Wes Montgomery, in the late 1960s Metheny not only ended his studentship but, as the 1970s began, assumed teaching duties at schools such as Boston's Berklee College, where he also played with Gary Burton, already on the teaching staff there. Becoming a permanent member of Burton's band in the mid-1970s, Metheny refined his sound and style, blending jazz, rock, and country influences to create a highly sophisticated but intensely melodic approach. This paid dividends when he formed the Pat Metheny Group in 1977 and recorded his eponymous debut album for ECM in 1978 with keyboardist Lyle Mays.

Metheny's music, both on tour and in the studio, created a phenomenal response from audiences worldwide; he and his group became crossover successes with the power to sell albums in quantities usually associated with popular music. Metheny has a naturally wide musical interest and has used this to his advantage, playing and recording with a huge range of musicians, including Sonny Rollins, Ornette Coleman, Paul Bley, Charlie Haden, Eberhard Weber, and Jack DeJohnette. He has written and recorded numerous soundtracks to movies and, after the breakup of the original Pat Metheny Group, has seen to it that his diverse musical interests are well represented in his professional life. A trio with Charlie Haden and Billy Higgins in the early 1980s produced some challenging music, while his formation of a new Group in 1984, allied to a swap in labels to MCA, has meant in-depth worldwide representation of his albums and consistent popularity. Metheny has become legendary in electric jazz circles for his subtle compositional and arranging talents, his use of technology (especially the synth-guitar) blending imperceptibly into the overall musical ambiance he is creating. Metheny has continued in the 1990s to lead a varied and peripatetic musical existence, swapping from one genre to another as his creative muse takes him. In addition to such Group albums as *Secret Story* (MCA, 1992), Metheny has made a double-header with John Scofield, *I Can See Your Place From Here* (Blue Note, 1994), a duet album, *Missouri Sky* (Verve, 1997) with Charlie Haden, and most recently a Midwest-feel record with Marc Johnson and Bill Frisell, *The Sound of Summer Running* (Verve, 1998). Metheny manages to retain that rarest of balances, popular approval allied to unfettered creative inquiry.

SEE ALSO: Wes Montgomery, Gary Burton, Sonny Rollins, Ornette Coleman, Paul Bley, Charlie Haden, Jack DeJohnette

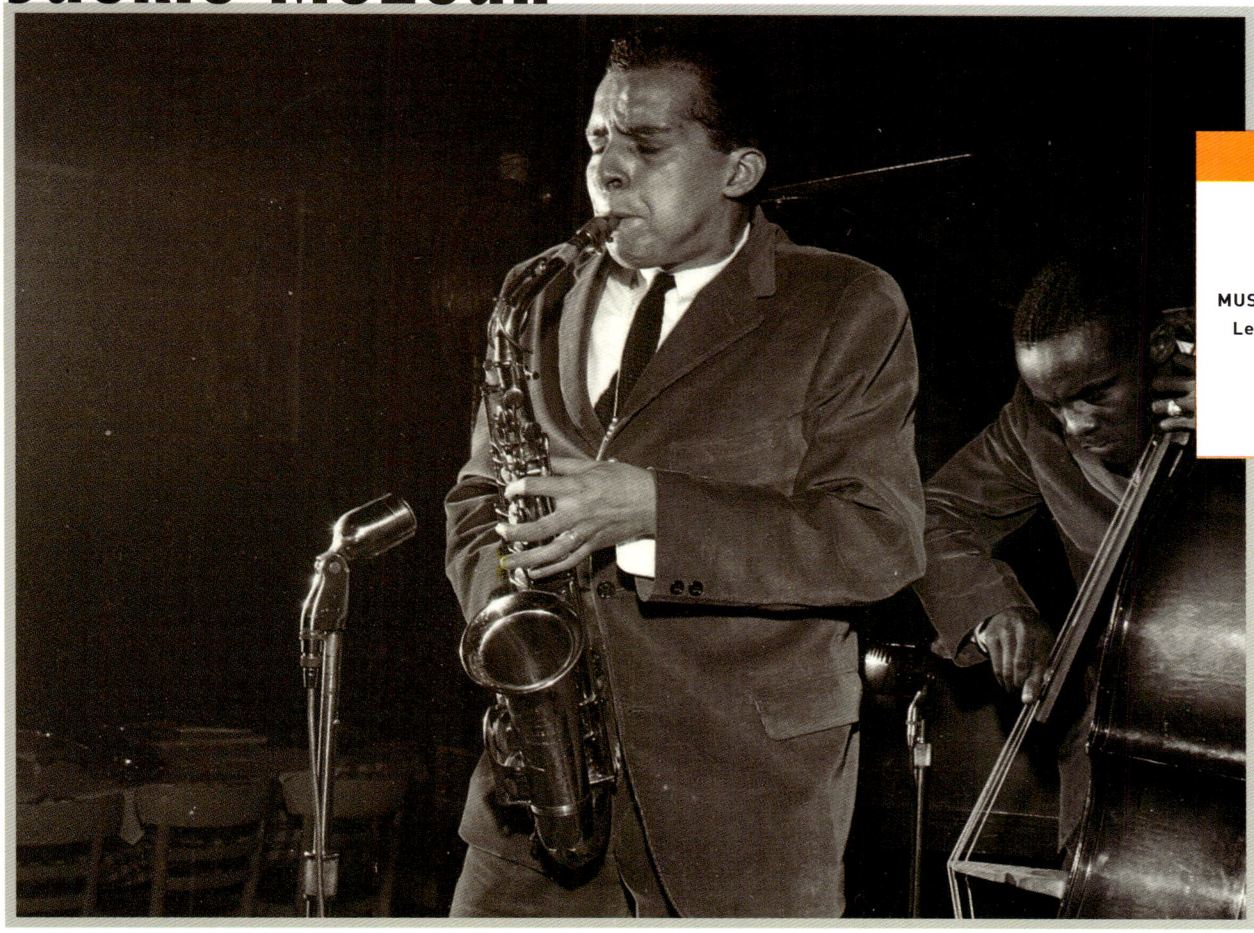

Glenn Miller

The life of swing trombonist and band leader Glenn Miller, pictured here in 1940, was celebrated in the Hollywood film, "The Glenn Miller Story," starring Jimmy Stewart

Iowan-born Glenn Miller is often discreetly dropped from jazz histories and listings. This is somewhat misguided, for, while Miller's band was rarely possessed of first-rate soloists, his band swung as well as most white bands of the time, was a byword for disciplined section work, sported very advanced arrangements for the time and for the most part exuded infectious enthusiasm and joy at its own music-making. The influence of Miller's arrangements, by himself and Gerry Gray in particular, can be traced to some surprising ends, including Woody Herman, Stan Kenton, and Gil Evans.

Miller spent his youth in Fort Morgan, Colorado, taking music lessons there and, in his late teens, playing with Boyd Senter. In 1921–22 he was for a short time a student at Colorado State University. By 1926 he was a member of Ben Pollack's band, as both trombonist and arranger: he went with Pollack to New York in 1928, leaving after Pollack drafted in Jack Teagarden. Miller freelanced in New York, spending time in 1929–30 with Red Nichols and being in demand in New York studios during the Depression. In 1934 he arranged and played trombone for the Dorsey Brothers before joining up in early 1935 with Ray Noble. During his period with Noble he first came across the notion of having an instrument pitched high above four saxophones to create a highly identifiable ensemble sound: he was to use this as his trademark in later years.

Miller left Noble in 1936, running his own band for the first time in 1937 to no great success. Disbanding prior to the year end, he determined that he would try again. This time he had a recording deal with Bluebird, but it was not until 1939, when he landed a key residency at Glen Island Casino and at a venue in Meadowbrook, New Jersey, both of which had lucrative radio link-ups, that he turned the tide of popularity. In 1939 the hits were coming in and by 1940 the classic Miller band was assembled, with players such as Ray Anthony, Tex Benecke, Billy May, Bobby Hackett, Al Klink, and Ray Eberle in place. Between then and Miller's entrance into WWII service, where he ran an Army/Air Force Band and had the rank of major, his was the premier swing band on both sides of the Atlantic.

The Army/Air Force Band operated in the US and the European theater of war (Artie Shaw went to the Pacific). By 1944 the band was based in England. In December of that year the band was due to play a major Paris concert to boost morale: Miller went out a day early to reconnoiter, but his plane was lost, along with all personnel. The band has been kept going, under the leadership of many excellent musicians, including Tex Benecke, Ray Anthony, and Buddy DeFranco.

fact file

BORN 1904

DIED 1944

MUSICAL SELECTION
The Essential Glenn Miller

SEE ALSO: Woody Herman, Stan Kenton, Gil Evans, Ben Pollack, Jack Teagarden, Red Nichols, Ray Noble

Lucky Millinder

fact file

BORN 1900

DIED 1966

MUSICAL SELECTION
1941-42

Lucky Millinder, seen here in 1941 vintage style with (l to r) Billy Bowen and Ernest Purce

Millinder, born in Anniston, Alabama, was not an instrumentalist himself but led a band that was the starting point for many fine musical careers for many of his sidemen. It was also one of the major starting points in the development away from jazz of the rhythm-and-blues sound, combining "jump" jazz, boogie, and blues with big-band swing discipline and inventiveness. Lucius Millinder spent his childhood in Chicago, gaining early experience in South Side cabarets, both dancing and emceeing, prior to going into band leadership in 1930. By 1933 he had already been to Europe on tour, taking his band to the South of France. Returning to New York, Millinder took on the leadership of the Mills Blue Rhythm Band in 1934. A popular leader with his men and a fine judge of musicianship and character as well as being a great frontman, Millinder built up the band's position, over the years taking on first-rate talent such as Harry Edison, "Red" Allen, Charlie Shavers, Buster Bailey, Tab Smith, J.C. Higginbotham, and John Kirby. He also had an outstanding and inventive arranger in Chappie Willett. Millinder left Mills's employ in 1938, fronting the Bill Doggett band until it went bankrupt in 1939. He then formed a band under his own name, bringing in younger talents such as Dizzy Gillespie, Freddie Webster, Sir Charles Thompson, George Duvivier, Sam Taylor, Eddie "Lockjaw" Davis, and Panama Francis, as well as featuring the phenomenal gospel-trained vocalist Rosetta Tharpe (later to become Sister Rosetta).

The band enjoyed solid success through to the mid-1940s, appearing in "soundies" and films, including *Paradise in Harlem* (1939) and *Boarding Room Blues* (1948). By the time of the latter Millinder was ready to come off the road, looking to set up a music-publishing business instead.

By the early 1950s, with the business at the beginning of a major shift, Millinder moved out of music, working in a number of different industries before late in the 1950s becoming a DJ. In later years he very occasionally pulled a big band together for special occasions, but in essence his musical career had ended at the close of the 1940s, his success then at its peak.

SEE ALSO: "Red" Allen, J.C. Higginbotham, Dizzy Gillespie, Eddie "Lockjaw" Davis

Roscoe Mitchell

fact file

BORN 1940

MUSICAL SELECTION
Sound
The Art Ensemble,
1967–8

Multi-instrumentalist and Art Ensemble of Chicago founder Roscoe Mitchell, pictured in Germany, 1979

One of the most active and influential of all AACM musicians, Chicago-born Mitchell began clarinet and saxes while at high school, joining the school band before going into the Army. He played in the Army band in Germany before being discharged and returning to Chicago. Mitchell assembled his own band in 1961, a sextet which included Henry Threadgill and Joseph Jarman. He later played more experimental music with Jack DeJohnette, then joined Richard Abrams's Experimental Band, a melting pot for many of the ideas which would later inform Chicago jazz's avant-garde.

Like Abrams, Mitchell was a founding member of the AACM in 1965. By 1966 Mitchell was running a number of different small groups, made up mostly from a pool of AACM musicians including bassist Malachi Favors, trumpeter Lester Bowie, saxophonist Maurice McIntyre, and drummer Phillip Wilson. In 1966 Mitchell played a number of Chicago concerts and club gigs and made his debut album, *Sound* (Delmark). The following year was spent mostly with Mitchell's band, the Art Ensemble, comprising himself, Lester Bowie, and Malachi Favors, with occasional contributions from Phillip Wilson. Before the year was out Joseph Jarman had become a full-time member; during a 1969 Paris sojourn the group's name was altered to the Chicago Art Ensemble. The gestation of this amazing group is now traceable on the Nessa boxed set, *The Art Ensemble, 1967–8.*

By this time Mitchell's styles had matured; he continued to develop an extraordinary range of projects, including solo recitals, duets, and performances with ensembles. Throughout, his own compositional gifts and his remarkable improvisatory intelligence, demonstrated time and again in the implacable logic of his solos in many contexts, have shown him to be an outstanding musician of his generation. He is also one of the very few musicians shown to be capable of building on aspects of the improvisatory foundations laid down by Eric Dolphy. Mitchell continues to lead a full creative life in Chicago.

SEE ALSO: Henry Threadgill, Joseph Jarman, Jack DeJohnette, Muhal Richard Abrams, Lester Bowie, Eric Dolphy

Charles Mingus

Mingus is one of a handful of jazz-based musician/composers to have successfully evolved a compositional technique that allows an inspirational combination of written and improvised parts. His major works typically last between 10 and 30 minutes, some combined sections reaching the hour. Mingus's music is usually volcanic, habitually chaotic, and often possessed of sharp, sardonic or rollicking humor. He was also a sublime miniaturist. His complete knowledge and use of jazz history allowed him to be the most resourceful composer/leader of his generation.

Mingus was born in Arizona but grew up in Watts, LA. He tried trombone and cello, but moved on to bass in his mid-teens, studying with Red Callender and Hermann Rheinschagen. During this time he played semipro with Buddy Collette and studied composition with Lloyd Reese. In 1939–41 he wrote a number of compositions, including "Half Mast Inhibition" and "What Love," first recorded some 20 years later. Mingus played with Lee Young, Barney Bigard, Louis Armstrong, and Alvino Rey in the early 1940s, then ran his own trio, Strings and Keys, in 1944–45, making his first records before freelancing and then joining Lionel Hampton in 1947–48. With Hampton his "Mingus Fingers" tune was recorded, but after leaving Hampton Mingus moved away from music until his engagement as bassist in the Red Norvo Trio with Tal Farlow, in 1950–51. This took him to New York, joining pianist Billy Taylor's trio and freelancing around the city. In 1952 he and Max Roach set up the record label Debut, which released the famous 1953 concert in Massey Hall, Toronto, which featured Charlie Parker, Dizzy Gillespie, Bud Powell, Mingus, and Roach in a quintet.

In the mid-1950s Debut came to an end, but Mingus had been involved in the Jazz Composers' Workshop for some time and set up his own in 1955. The following decade saw Mingus recording for a string of record companies, exploring a huge range of styles on albums such as *Pithecanthropus Erectus* (1956), *The Clown* (1957), *Tijuana Moods* (1957), *Blues & Roots* (1959), *Mingus Ah Um* (1959), *Pre-Bird* (1960), *Charles Mingus Presents Charles Mingus* (1961), *Oh Yeah* (1961), *Town Hall Concert* (1962), *The Black Saint and the Sinner Lady* (1963), *Mingus Mingus Mingus* (1963), *Mingus at Monterey* (1964), and *My Favorite Quintet* (1965). Mingus worked with musicians able to put up with his demands and interpret his wishes, his musical dialogues with Knepper, Dolphy, Handy, and Kirk particularly noteworthy.

In 1960 Mingus became embroiled in the rebel Newport Jazz Festival. The pace and scale of his life led to Mingus withdrawing from music in the late 1960s. He came back in 1969, hitting his stride again by 1971, the year of his autobiography, *Beneath The Underdog*, was published, and of his first Guggenheim Award. By 1972 his new small group included Don Pullen and George Adams in addition to Dannie Richmond, and he was signed once more to Columbia, who funded the big-band *Let My Children Hear Music* (1972) and a Lincoln Center extravaganza (1972). Combining new works and first recordings of old pieces, including "The Chill of Death," Mingus was once again in the vanguard of his generation; swapping once more to Atlantic, Mingus remained highly active up to his contracting sclerosis in 1977. Confined to a wheelchair, he dictated sessions such as *Cumbia & Jazz Fusion* (1977) and his collaboration with Joni Mitchell, *Mingus*, (1978). He died in Mexico in 1979.

fact file

BORN 1922

DIED 1979

MUSICAL SELECTION
Pithecanthropus Erectus
The Black Saint and the Sinner Lady
Mingus

The highly-influential bassist, composer and band leader Charles Mingus at a 1959 recording session

SEE ALSO: Louis Armstrong, Lionel Hampton, Red Norvo, Max Roach, Thad Jones, Charlie Parker, Dizzy Gillespie, Bud Powell, Jimmy Knepper, Jackie McLean

The Modern Jazz Quartet

fact file

FORMED 1951

MUSICAL SELECTION
Odds Against Tomorrow

The Modern Jazz Quartet, originally featured John Lewis on piano, Milt Jackson on vibes, Ray Brown on bass and Kenny Clarke on drums

The inaugural members of this famous and influential quartet, John Lewis (piano), Milt Jackson (vibes), Ray Brown (bass), and Kenny Clarke (drums), had all been members of the mid-1940s Dizzy Gillespie big band, coming together as a unit for the first time in summer 1951 under the name the Milt Jackson Quartet for a recording session only. The group continued to convene for the occasional session, by 1952 having Percy Heath on bass in place of Brown and having adopted for recording purposes the name by which it is known today. By 1954 sufficient public interest had been shown for the band to become a full-time performing and recording unit; it had already made some of its most famous and characteristic recordings, including the first studio version of John Lewis's classic composition, *Django*. By the end of 1954 the group were already winning awards; the following year they began winning popularity polls as well, even though a final personnel change occurred, with Connie Kay replacing Kenny Clarke on drums.

The MJQ, as it universally became known, managed, like the Dave Brubeck group, to hit an ideal balance between arrangement and improvisation, with the group's musical director and pianist John Lewis providing beautifully judged constructs, both for the group and especially Milt Jackson, to shine within. Lewis's love of European culture and music, allied to his deep belief in restrained and spare expression, gave all the group's members a limitless succession of models, from suites based on 18th century classical forms or Italian *commedia dell'arte* (*Fontessa, The Comedy*) through to soundtracks for films such as *No Sun In Venice* and *Odds Against Tomorrow*. The MJQ also enjoyed making music with guests (they even became a backing group for other artists on a 1957 JATP tour of America), producing in the 1950s outstanding records with Sonny Rollins and Jimmy Giuffre, while in the 1960s and 1970s Laurindo Almeida and Paul Desmond were among the distinguished guests.

The MJQ also made albums with orchestras, usually playing the music of John Lewis, but often interpreting other composers, including Gary McFarland. By the mid-1960s the MJQ was known worldwide by an audience extending far beyond jazz fans, its music loved by those with even the slightest acquaintance with music beyond the pop charts. They were certainly the only jazz group signed by the Beatles' record label, Apple. All the members of the band spent much time on other projects, trying to limit the band's playing together so as to keep it fresh, and this policy undoubtedly worked, given the freshness of their output at this time. But by 1974 all four members felt the need for a complete break. This lasted until 1982, when public demand, especially from Japan, and the express interest of Pablo Records' Norman Granz, persuaded the group to reconvene for a minimum of one tour per year, a policy that holds to this day.

SEE ALSO: John Lewis, Milt Jackson, Ray Brown, Kenny Clarke, Dizzy Gillespie, Sonny Rollins, Jimmy Giuffre

Wes Montgomery

fact file

BORN 1925

DIED 1968

MUSICAL SELECTION
Bags & Wes
The Incredible Jazz Guitar
Full House

Wes Montgomery, the top jazz guitarist of the 1960s and a major influence on the music

Montgomery was the first guitarist to add to and modify the legacy left to guitarists by the pioneer Charlie Christian. Born Lesley Montgomery in Indianapolis, he came from a musical family. After quitting high school early to help earn money for a very poor family, Wes and his brothers all chose instruments to concentrate on, with the self-taught Wes becoming competent in his late teens. He married at the age of 20 and shortly after bought his first electrified semi-acoustic guitar and amplifier. Studying Charlie Christian's records, Montgomery landed his first professional job replaying all Christian's solos. A few weeks' experience gave him a wider range, allowing him to freelance locally. In 1948 he was hired by Lionel Hampton as the band's guitarist. Two years in the band further widened his experience before he went back to Indianapolis. Over the next seven years he worked day jobs and night-time gigs in a variety of groups, making some Pacific Jazz recording dates in 1959 with his brothers' band, The Mastersounds. Yet he remained strictly a local legend. In September 1959 Cannonball Adderley's band played Indianapolis; at an after-hours club he heard Montgomery fronting an organ trio. He persuaded his record company of the time, Riverside, that Montgomery should be signed. Montgomery's first album was recorded and within a year he was winning awards and popularity polls and appearing as a guest on many sessions (including George Shearing, Cannonball Adderley, and a classic with Milt Jackson, *Bags & Wes* (Riverside, 1961)) as well as for a short time that same year joining the John Coltrane group. Montgomery made most of his classic jazz albums in the period 1960–63, including *The Incredible Jazz Guitar* (1960) and the live *Full House* (1962).

By the time Riverside went bankrupt in 1964 and Montgomery switched to Verve, he had assembled a group of his own. He embraced Verve producer Creed Taylor's plans to make him a more broadly successful musician via a variety of accompaniment and repertoire. Montgomery recorded with big bands, occasionally with strings, and used his thumb-plucked single-line and octave style of melodicism to delineate a raft of popular tunes over the next four years. He achieved crossover success matched by few jazzmen of his generation. Live, he remained a committed jazz player. He also made two outstanding jazz dates for Verve, small-group and big-band, with organist Jimmy Smith. By 1968 Montgomery was recording for the new A&M label and making albums with few concessions to jazz sensibilities, but these albums are in many respects superior to the latter-day Verve albums, for the material is often more judiciously chosen and the arrangements are devoid of the crass elements often cluttering such Verve albums as *California Dreaming* (1966) and *Goin' Out of My Head* (1965). Mongomery succumbed to a heart attack in June 1968. His legacy still invests every jazz guitarist playing today.

SEE ALSO: Charlie Christian, Lionel Hampton, Cannonball Adderley, George Shearing, Milt Jackson, John Coltrane

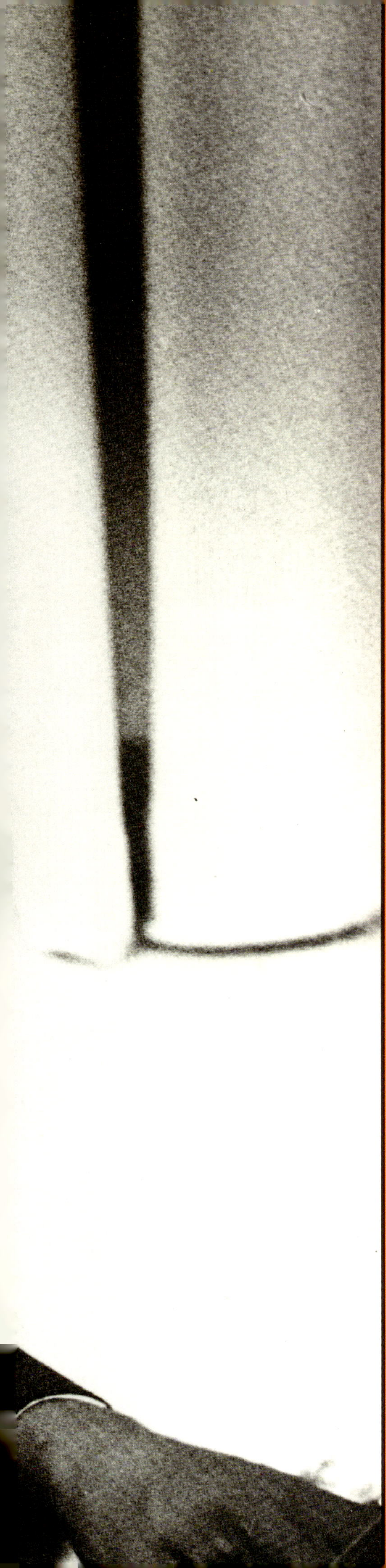

Thelonious Monk

Monk was born in Rocky Mount, North Carolina, but moved in early childhood with his family to New York. Becoming interested in playing music just prior to adolescence, Monk started piano lessons, by the mid-1930s beginning to perform professionally. By the end of the decade he was a regular at Harlem haunts, becoming in the early 1940s the house pianist and a regular at Minton's Playhouse (with straw boss Kenny Clarke) and Kelly's Stables.

On the road with Lucky Millinder in 1942, by 1943 Monk was back with Clarke at Minton's before joining Coleman Hawkins's group, staying with him until 1945 and making his recording debut. Monk became known as one of the leading modernists, along with Dizzy Gillespie, Charlie Christian, and Clarke himself. His ballad, "Round Midnight," was first recorded during a short stint in 1944 with the Cootie Williams band, but Charlie Parker's arrival, plus Monk's reluctance to play second fiddle to anyone led to his being sidelined until the late 1940s, when he began appearing at New York clubs and recording for Blue Note.

At the beginning of the 1950s a trumped-up drugs charge and conviction deprived him of his New York cabaret card. It was not until 1957 that Monk was able to work in his home town again. He endured a lean creative and commercial spell at Prestige in 1952–55, his records selling poorly, his contract finally sold to Riverside. The new label started with a trio album of Duke Ellington compositions. By 1957 Monk was hitting his stride, *Brilliant Corners*, featuring Sonny Rollins and Ernie Henry, *Monk's Music*, with John Coltrane, Coleman Hawkins, and Art Blakey, and *Monk's Music* with John Coltrane added for one track, all displaying his genius. A season at the New York club the Five Spot in 1957 with a quartet featuring Coltrane and Wilbur Ware reached the status of legend before its conclusion. With Coltrane rejoining Miles Davis at the year's close, Monk hired Johnny Griffin and continued to garner fresh praise and controversy. An appearance at the 1958 Newport Jazz Festival with a trio confirmed his rise in jazz stature, while his 1959 showcase at New York's Town Hall with a tentet (arranged by Hall Overton) playing his music, subsequently released on LP by Riverside, continued his progress.

Overseas tours began in 1961, and Monk signed to Columbia the following year. By 1964 Monk was probably as famous a jazzman as any of the postwar generation. A Time magazine cover and a second big-band concert in New York in December 1964 reminded the world of his prominence, but as the 1960s wore on and Monk became a frequent visitor to other countries, including Japan in 1963 and Australia in 1966, his own creative juices were drying up. A member of the Giants of Jazz, with Gillespie, Stitt, Blakey, and Kai Winding, Monk was well below his physical peak, although his last recordings, made in London in 1971, show his musical brain still working at top speed.

Monk withdrew altogether by the middle of the 1970s and lived in seclusion. After, suffering from bouts of illness and depression, he died in early 1982. During his last decade of life, and increasingly since, Monk's compositions were perceived by musicians and critics to be perfect pieces of miniature musical architecture. Songs such as "Round Midnight," "Evidence," "Blue Monk," "Epistrophy," and "Rhythm-a-ning" are ubiquitous in jazz, while even more challenging material such as "Brilliant Corners" and "Gallop's Gallop" are regularly heard.

fact file

BORN 1917

DIED 1982

MUSICAL SELECTION
Brilliant Corners
Monk's Music
It's Monk Time

The eccentric and unique composer and pianist Thelonious Monk, seen here in 1970, was popular enough at his peak to make the cover of Time magazine in 1964

SEE ALSO: Kenny Clarke, Lucky Millinder, Coleman Hawkins, Sonny Rollins, Milt Jackson, Art Blakey, Duke Ellington, John Coltrane, Coleman Hawkins

Lee Morgan

fact file

BORN 1938

DIED 1972

MUSICAL SELECTION
The Sidewinder
The Rumproller
At The Lighthouse

Lee Morgan, trumpeter extraordinaire, pictured here in 1958, earned his chops as a teen, sitting in with stars like Miles Davis, Clifford Brown and Art Blakey

Detroit-born trumpeter Morgan was something of a prodigy. Coming from a musical family, he took private trumpet lessons in early adolescence and by the age of 15 was playing locally on weekends with his own group. Sitting in with visiting players such as Miles Davis, Clifford Brown, and Art Blakey, Morgan began to develop a reputation which led directly to his joining in 1956 Dizzy Gillespie's big band. He was just 18.

Morgan's bright tone, fleet execution and fiery musical personality, all refined through a concept adopted directly from Clifford Brown's, made him an immediate sensation in the jazz world and he appeared on many record dates (initially for Savoy, then for Blue Note) while still with Gillespie before swapping to Art Blakey's Jazz Messengers in 1958. Already known to Blakey (he'd played with the band for a few weeks in 1956), Morgan became one of the drummer's closest professional friends and a vital part of the most popular Messengers band of all, that featuring Morgan, Benny Golson, and Bobby Timmons.

The group toured internationally and enjoyed wide success with its recordings of such classics as "Moanin'" and "Blues March" as well as more sophisticated Golson compositions such as "Whisper Not." Morgan left Blakey in 1961 and moved for a time to Philadelphia, where he played with Jimmy Heath and experienced some drug-related downtimes before returning to New York in 1963. After settling in, Morgan returned to the Blakey band in 1964 to replace his original replacement, Freddie Hubbard, but he unexpectedly landed a major jazz hit simultaneously with his album *The Sidewinder* (Blue Note, 1964), recorded in the last days of 1963 with a group featuring Joe Henderson. The title track was used in mid-1960s America as a backing track for a commercial. Before the end of 1965 Morgan had once more gone out on his own, working freelance and with his own bands, and even recorded a follow-up, *The Rumproller* (Blue Note, 1965), again with Henderson, although it was only a moderate success.

Morgan continued to play his own hard-bop version of modern jazz with complete commitment and also turned up in some surprisingly adventurous settings: a late recorded masterpiece was his set *At The Lighthouse*, with his group featuring Bennie Maupin, recorded in 1970. Morgan by this time was a complete player and individual stylist, fully capable of sustaining a successful career even in the chaotic aftermath of the 1960s, a difficult decade for straight jazzers. However, fate had decreed otherwise – in 1972 Morgan was shot dead at the bar of a club he was working in by a woman with whom he'd had a romantic entanglement.

SEE ALSO: Miles Davis, Clifford Brown, Art Blakey, Dizzy Gillespie, Freddie Hubbard, Joe Henderson, James P. Johnson

Paul Motian

fact file

BORN 1931

MUSICAL SELECTION
Tribute
Psalm

Front-rank drummer and band leader Paul Motian began his musical career on the guitar but later found fairly steady work on the drums

Drummer/bandleader Motian was born in Providence, Rhode Island, taking as his first instrument the guitar. After a stint in the military in 1954, Motian moved to New York and began picking up work as a drummer while studying music at the Manhattan School. Stints with George Wallington and Russell Jacquet led to a steady engagement with clarinetist Tony Scott in 1956–57, then stints with him interspersed with work behind a great number of top performers, including Lennie Tristano and Zoot Sims.

By 1959 he was a leading NYC freelancer, becoming that year the drummer in Bill Evans's first permanent trio, with Scott LaFaro on bass. His intense, discreet, and empathetic drumming was a considerable reason for the trio's unique interplay and sound; by the time this trio reached its peak in 1961 Motian was less concerned with keeping strict time than in fully conversing musically with the other two musicians. The result was some of the most sensitive and colorful small-group drumming of the period. Motian stayed with Evans after LaFaro's death in 1961, forming equally compelling dialogues in the trios featuring bassists Chuck Israels and Gary Peacock. The last year with Evans also saw Motian and Peacock strike up a similar empathy with the more avant-garde Paul Bley, but the mid-1960s was a time of intense freelancing across a range of styles, and Motian once more became part of a recording trio like Bley's – that of Keith Jarrett with Charlie Haden on bass.

With Jarrett and Haden, Motian continued to develop his drumming patterns and style further away from mainstream preoccupations with ride cymbal patterns and snare fills, using a huge range of coloristic means. The connection with Haden strengthened with Motian's involvement in the Liberation Music Orchestra of 1969 and subsequent work with Carla Bley and Michael Mantler's Jazz Composer's Orchestra. He also began appearing on many ECM albums in the early 1970s, some under his own leadership.

Motian was a member of the so-called "American Quartet" of Keith Jarrett, a band which played and recorded consistently through the first half of the 1970s, making a number of classic albums under Jarrett's name. Motian, meanwhile, had begun composing his own material, as his ECM albums, including 1975's *Tribute*, featuring Charlie Haden, Carlos Ward, and Sam Brown, testify. In 1977 Motian began leading his own groups, initially featuring Bill Frisell and Joe Lovano (both present on 1981's *Psalm*, ECM) but later in the 1980s reducing to a trio. In the early 1990s Motian expanded his ambitions again, forming the Electric Bebop Band, a group featuring two saxophonists and two guitarists (Joshua Redman was later replaced by Chris Potter), which produced a unique, rich musical brew and spent much of its time reinvestigating classic compositions by Mingus, Charlie Parker, Gillespie, Monk, and the rest. Motian continues to lead a very active career.

SEE ALSO: Lennie Tristano, Zoot Sims, Bill Evans, Scott LaFaro, Paul Bley, Keith Jarrett, Charlie Haden, Carla Bley

Jelly Roll Morton

For many years there was confusion over Morton's date of birth: 1889 on his death certificate while other commentators pushed for 1885. The precise facts were established by Lawrence Gushee. He also found that Morton, born Ferdinand LaMenthe (the family name was LaMothe and he was baptized Lemott) in New Orleans, took the name Morton from a stepfather (who's name was actually Mouton!) Morton started out on guitar as a boy before switching to piano in early adolescence. He claims to have been playing Storyville bordellos in 1902, though a date closer to the middle of the decade is more realistic; here he met and learned much from pianist Tony Jackson before moving on to other parts of Louisiana and Mississippi. Between 1906 and 1908 he traveled from Florida to California as well as Chicago, St Louis, and Houston, making money as a hustler, pool shark, part-time pimp, and all-round con man as well as learning much from the pianists he encountered, including the legendary "Jack The Bear." In 1909 he worked in a Memphis theater, then joined a vaudeville team eventually making it to New York.

Morton spent time in Chicago, running his own band in 1914–15, then pushed on to LA, where he met Anita Gonzales, later his wife, and more than once made it as far as Mexico.

In 1923 Morton moved to Chicago, attracted by a booming music business there and the chance of recordings and piano rolls. That year he debuted on both recording media, also finding work with the Melrose publishing company and running his sometime band, the Red Hot Peppers.

In 1926 Morton began making the series of 78s for the Victor company, which were to seal his jazz reputation. These were with his studio band, the sometimes septet/octet, the Red Hot Peppers, a band often featuring clarinetist Omer Simeon, trumpeter George Mitchell and trombonist Kid Ory. The style was New Orleans, but very much Morton's own idea of New Orleans: in fact, his arrangements, allied to his humor and compositions, made for a vivid portrayal of the hybrid form of jazz. Pieces like "The Pearls," "King Porter," "Jungle Blues," "Black Bottom Stomp," "Dead Man Blues," "Sidewalk Blues," and many more all testify to his unique abilities. Compared with contemporaneous dance arrangements and tunes in 1926–28, Morton was streets ahead. Unfortunately, he alienated many people who could have helped, including the MCA booking agency.

A move to New York in 1928 presaged his eclipse. Morton wanted no part of the emerging big-band movement. In 1930 his Victor contract was not renewed. Down on his luck he made one Wingy Manone session in 1934 before moving to Washington, DC, once more leaving music for a period.

Working as a pianist in a lowlife Washington club, Morton was approached by folklorist Alan Lomax to make a series of recordings for the Library of Congress in late summer 1938. The resulting records are one of the greatest first-hand archives of New Orleans testimony in existence. In between sessions, however, he was stabbed in a brawl at his club, triggering a round of ill health. A move back to New York in 1938 and radio appearances in the Big Apple led to Morton recording with Sidney Bechet and Albert Nicholas, making a fine session for Bluebird. Morton made further records for General, piano solos, and group recordings, which show him to be in complete command of his abilities. If he had lived, he would undoubtedly have become a focal point for the 1940s revivalists. His deteriorating health was exacerbated by a cross-country winter drive 1940–41, and by the summer of 1941 Morton was dead.

fact file

BORN 1890

DIED 1941

MUSICAL SELECTION
"King Porter"
"Jungle Blues"
"Black Bottom Stomp"

Jelly Roll Morton, pool shark, braggart, fancy man and musical genius, pictured here in New York, 1929

SEE ALSO: Luis Russel, Wingy Manone, Sidney Bechet

David Murray

fact file

BORN 1955

MUSICAL SELECTION
Live At The Manhattan Club

Reedman David Murray, seen here in 1980, is a West Coast player who found success in New York

Murray was born in Berkeley, California, the other side of the bay from San Francisco. From a musical family (his mother played piano in the local church), he began playing piano from an early age, taking up alto sax as a nine-year-old and originally playing R&B with local teenage groups. A student at Pomona College in Los Angeles, Murray met there a number of key jazz personalities, including Arthur Blythe and Stanley Crouch; by the time he left in 1975 he had been shown all jazz styles and, through Arthur Blythe, been taken up by the avant-garde approach of the day. In 1975 Murray moved to New York, quickly making an impact through his re-evaluation of the saxophone tradition and his avoidance – highly unusual for the time – of the standard post-Coltrane approach to the tenor sax. By 1976 he was a force on the scene, forming that year – with Oliver Lake, Julius Hemphill, and Hamiet Bluiett – the World Saxophone Quartet, a group that, with minor personnel changes, continues on a part-time basis up to the present day. By 1977 Murray had also made one of the classic modern free-jazz recordings in *Live at the Manhattan Club* (India Navigation), with Lester Bowie and Phillip Wilson; he also appeared as a sideman with a range of free-jazz groups, including James Blood Ulmer and Sunny Murray (no relation). By the end of the decade Murray was seen as the coming man on saxophone, joining Jack DeJohnette's Special Edition band, touring with the World Saxophone Quartet and beginning what has turned into an unstemmable tide of recordings for an enormous variety of labels: only Sun Ra and John Coltrane have recorded more than Murray, and Murray is still a relatively young man. In more recent years Murray has played and recorded in a bewildering variety of settings, from funk to tenor and organ groups to wild free excursions to spirituals to bop and hard-bop sessions: he has even made his peace with the Coltrane tradition, making successful recordings of key parts of the Coltrane repertoire as well as appearing with McCoy Tyner.

Murray, like Archie Shepp in a previous generation, has taken an idiosyncratic group of influences, from Ayler to Bechet, and molded them into a strikingly original style, ranging across most of the jazz idioms. At turns explosive, funky and caressing, whether he's working with his Quartet, his larger Ensemble, or going solo with a freelance rhythm section, Murray continues to impress as one of the most significant saxophonists to have emerged since the death of Coltrane.

SEE ALSO: Oliver Lake, Lester Bowie, Jack DeJohnette, McCoy Tyner

Fats Navarro

fact file

BORN 1923

DIED 1950

MUSICAL SELECTION
With Tadd Dameron

Fats Navarro in New York, 1948, during which time he was playing with jazz greats including Charlie Parker and Tadd Dameron

Trumpeter Navarro was a key element in the evolution of jazz trumpet, his fiery yet logical and endlessly inventive playing offering a third way between the technical bravura of Gillespie and the more measured, careful approach of Miles Davis. Born in Key West, Florida, Navarro was studying piano at six and by his earliest teenage years had begun his attempts to master the trumpet, at this stage relying on himself for most of his lessons. Gigging locally until the end of his teen years, Navarro broke out of the Florida and Deep South area when he joined the Andy Kirk band in 1943. A year with Kirk gave Navarro quick national recognition among younger musicians, and he was recommended to Billy Eckstine in 1944 by Dizzy Gillespie when the trumpeter was leaving to start his own small group. Navarro stayed 18 months, touring and recording with Eckstine, then settled in New York, where he freelanced with a large number of leaders, including Illinois Jacquet, Coleman Hawkins and Kenny Clarke and even appeared as part of the Eastern leg of the JATP tour in 1947, but by 1948 he was beginning to suffer from the first signs of the tuberculosis, exacerbated by a heroin habit, which would eventually kill him.

Playing with Charlie Parker, Tadd Dameron, and Charlie Parker live and on records in 1948–49 and recording under his own name for Savoy, Navarro was recognized as an uncommon stylist, able to take the rhythmic verve and symmetry of swing and combine it with provocative note-choices and the harmonic sophistication of bop, which his imagination thrived on. He was also possessed of a technique equaled by few at the time. Navarro was perhaps shown to best advantage as part of Tadd Dameron's various groups in the little time he had left to live; his explosive soloing and full, sweet tone combining brilliantly with Dameron's melodic attractiveness and feeling for harmony. Navarro did not live long enough to develop as a composer or arranger, but his trumpeting concepts were taken and developed especially by Clifford Brown into the blueprint for all post-bop trumpet-playing that had a mind to avoid the influence of Miles Davis.

SEE ALSO: Dizzy Gillespie, Miles Davis, Andy Kirk, Billy Eckstine, Illinois Jacquet, Coleman Hawkins, Kenny Clarke

Gerry Mulligan

Baritonist/composer/arranger Mulligan was born in New York City but raised in Philadelphia, starting out on the piano. By 1944 he was writing arrangements for Philadelphia bands before moving to New York in 1946 and joining the Gene Krupa band. Krupa recorded Mulligan's "Disc Jockey Jump" in 1947 before, in 1948, the baritone met up with Gil Evans and working between then and 1950 with a group of musicians involved variously with Claude Thornhill, Elliott Lawrence, and the Miles Davis Nonet of that year. Mulligan's scores for "Godchild," "Jeru," "Venus de Milo," and "Boplicity" were all recorded by the nonet for Capitol, while Thornhill and Lawrence made use of other Mulligan charts.

Mulligan moved to California in 1952 and formed a pianoless quartet with Chet Baker. This was an international success, but a jail sentence took Mulligan off the scene in 1953 and Baker went out on his own. On his return Mulligan started up small and large ensembles and established himself as perhaps the most popular West Coast figure after Brubeck.

A 1954 European tour ended in triumph in Paris, and Mulligan was a star on both sides of the Atlantic as well as the number-one influence on his instrument. Mulligan, an inveterate jammer, appeared at most of the Newport Festivals in the 1950s with his own bands (including the Sextet and the 1958 quartet with Art Farmer) as well as numerous impromptu performances, such as the number with Duke Ellington's band at the 1958 festival. Mulligan remained on cordial terms with many leading figures, making albums, for example, with Thelonious Monk in 1958 and Ben Webster, Johnny Hodges, Paul Desmond, and Stan Getz during the late 1950s. His marriages to Judy Halliday and Sandy Dennis kept him in the media jet set also during this and the following decade.

By 1960 he started up the Concert Jazz Band (1960–63), featuring a number of old Mulligan colleagues, including Zoot Sims. Mulligan also worked successfully on the occasional film soundtrack, including *I Want to Live* (UA, 1961), also during the 1960s and 1970s appearing in cameo roles in various TV series, including *Starsky and Hutch*. He covered a lot of musical ground after the breakup of his big band, forming a successful quartet, making *Two of a Mind* (1964), a second album with Paul Desmond, and trying out a number of projects, some commercial, some esoteric, where his baritone (or, occasionally, clarinet) is the featured soloist. By the end of the 1960s he was ready for a different working environment, joining the Dave Brubeck group after the departure of Paul Desmond, staying with Brubeck from 1968–1972. During the latter 1970s Mulligan spent increasing amounts of time in Europe, and began featuring the soprano sax in his programs. His recordings included big-band projects like *The Age of Steam* (A&M, 1971) and *Walk in the Water* (1973), while a 1974 Carnegie Hall concert saw a reunion with Chet Baker, later released on two LPs. Mulligan picked his work more stringently in the 1980s and early 1990s, touring less frequently, but his regular group of the late 1980s was a fine unit (with Scott Hamilton as a sometime member) and he continued to produce outstanding records, including the small-group *Lonesome Boulevard* (A&M, 1989). He was at the heart of the Dave Grusin-inspired project to re-record the original Miles Davis nonet charts, which resulted in *Re-Birth of the Cool* (GRP, 1992). Mulligan continued to tour and record up to the last year or so before his death, from cancer, in 1996, maintaining his musical standards to the end.

fact file

BORN 1927

DIED 1996

MUSICAL SELECTION
Two of a Mind
The Age of Steam
Lonesome Boulevard
Re-Birth of the Cool

Gerry Mulligan, saxophonist extraordinaire, on stage in July 1982

SEE ALSO: Gene Krupa, Gil Evans, Miles Davis, Chet Baker, Art Farmer, Duke Ellington, Thelonious Monk, Ben Webster, Johnny Hodges, Paul Desmond, Stan Getz

Oliver Nelson

fact file

BORN 1932

DIED 1975

MUSICAL SELECTION
Meet Oliver Nelson
Blues and the Abstract Truth

Respected arranger, composer and saxophonist Oliver Nelson was immersed in music from a very young age and his skill reflects that legacy

St Louis-born Nelson came from an intensely musical family. Oliver started out studying piano at the age of six, then took on the saxophone in 1944. By 1947 he was playing with name bands locally, graduating to the big band of Louis Jordan by 1950. A stint in the Marines (1952–54) kept him out of circulation, but on his return Nelson studied composition and theory (1954–57), spending a year at Lincoln University (1957–58) to round off his musical education. He moved to New York in 1958 playing with a string of top-class swing-based bands, debuting on record as a leader in 1959 with a relatively conventional quintet album, *Meet Oliver Nelson* (Prestige).

Working as a sideman still through this whole period, playing with bands from Eddie "Lockjaw" Davis to Quincy Jones, Nelson began amassing recording credits, among them two small-group albums for Prestige with Eric Dolphy, a major big-band project from late 1961, *Afro-American Sketches*, and a swing-style small-group date with Joe Newman, *Main Stem*. Sandwiched between all this was a record made [illegible] Creed Taylor at the fledgling Impulse! label in February 1961. Called *Blues and the Abstract Truth*, it featured Nelson compositions that have since become oft-covered jazz classics as well as a stellar personnel.

Suddenly his record company, Prestige, could afford big-band dates for him (*Afro-American Sketches*, 1961), and by 1962–63 he was virtually "staff arranger" for Creed Taylor's most ambitious projects at Verve for Jimmy Smith and Wes Montgomery. He also made *Fantabulous* for Argo (1964) and a string of albums for Impulse! after 1964, including the uneven *More Blues and The Abstract Truth* (1964) and *Sound Pieces* (1966). Teaching had become part of his regular work, which also included big-band concerts, small-group gigs, commissions from other leaders, and media work.

By 1967 Nelson relocated to LA. He continued to write works for orchestra, including *The Kennedy Dream* (Impulse!, 1967) as well as *The Spirit of 67* (Impulse!), featuring Pee Wee Russell, and *L.A. All-Star Big Band* (1968). Nelson followed Impulse! producer Bob Thiele to his independent label Flying Dutchman, but most of his later work is anodyne: *Black, Brown and Beautiful* (1969) and *In London* (1971) both show evidence of a musical sensibility derailed by overconcentration on commercial projects, while his arrangements for *Monk's Blues* (Columbia, 1969) make Monk's angular music sound bland. Nelson kept up a punishing routine during the 1970s, and succumbed to a heart attack in October 1975.

SEE ALSO: Louis Jordan, Eddie "Lockjaw" Davis, Quincy Jones, Eric Dolphy, Bill Evans, Freddie Hubbard

Herbie Nichols

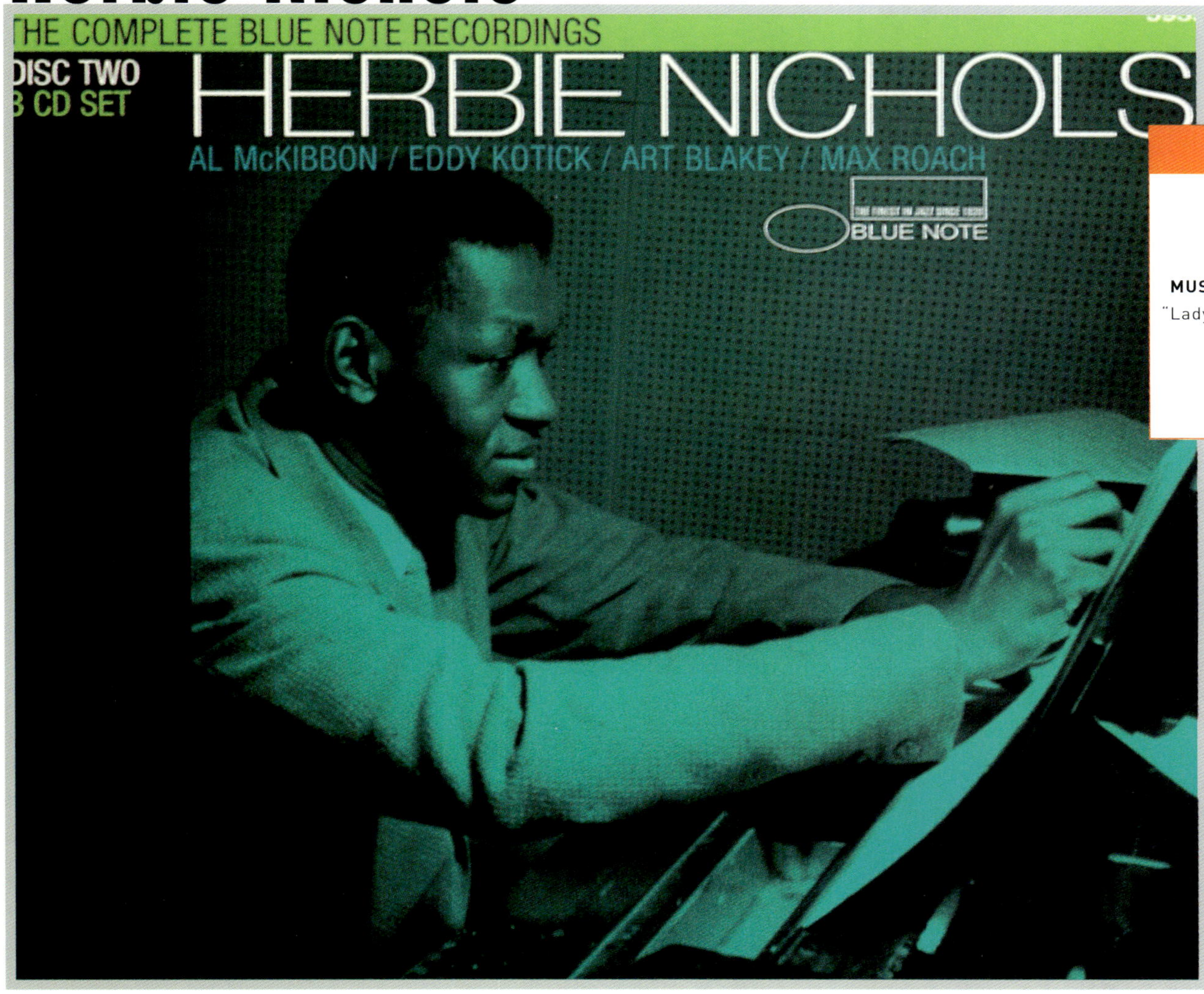

fact file

BORN 1919

DIED 1963

MUSICAL SELECTION
"Lady Sings The Blues"

Herbie Nichols, a neglected giant of the jazz world, suffered endless frustration and relative obscurity during his career, but always retained his musical integrity

New York-born Nichols came from a musical family, his uncle, Walter Nichols, having been a trumpeter with the Paramount Stompers. He took up piano, studying from the age of nine onwards and completing a course at the City College of New York in 1935. His first professional job was in 1937 with the Royal Baron orchestra; between then and his 1941 induction into the Army Nichols played and recorded with a large array of swing small groups including people such as Illinois Jacquet, Joe Thomas, and Arnett Cobb. He also played informally in the late 1930s at Monroe's Uptown House, the rival to Minton's Playhouse in terms of being a place for young musicians to hang out and try their new ideas on for size. Friendly with Thelonious Monk, Nichols however was never accepted by the hipsters and was not an assertive enough personality to force his way in: he continued to play in groups away from the fulcrum of the emerging music, his own style evolving into a unique blend of past and future and his compositions, like those of Monk at this early stage, almost universally discounted or misunderstood.

After World War II Nichols worked infrequently, invariably in groups totally unsympathetic to his own personal musical philosophy, and generated a little extra income through the occasional written essay on music and musicians. Working in cabaret clubs, Dixieland units, R&B bands, or not at all, Nichols had to wait until 1955, when Alfred Lion of Blue Note records heard his work and recorded 17 of his tunes in a trio with Al McKibbon and Art Blakey.

The records sold very poorly, and although Lion conducted another trio session for Blue Note later the same year, he did not persist with Nichols as he was later to do with other poor-selling artists he believed in such as Hank Mobley and Andrew Hill. Nichols receded into an obscurity relieved only by a 1957 trio session for Bethlehem. He collaborated with Billie Holiday to write the haunting "Lady Sings The Blues," but this remained his only brush with celebrity, despite his being employed in the late 1950s as an accompanist for singers in a Greenwich Village bar. Nichols suffered from ill health exacerbated by poverty and frustration (for a detailed glimpse of this, there is A.B. Spellman's heartbreaking interview with Nichols as published in *Four Lives In The Be-Bop Business*, 1964), and while he had a small band of believers, including trombonist Roswell Rudd, most musicians ignored him and his compositions. He died in late 1963 from leukemia.

SEE ALSO: Illinois Jacquet, Arnett Cobb, Thelonious Monk, Art Blakey, Andrew Hill, Billie Holiday, Roswell Rudd

Red Nichols

fact file

BORN 1905

DIED 1965

MUSICAL SELECTION
Rhythm of the Day

One of the most popular pre-swing, small-group leaders in jazz, Red Nichols is often criticized for pandering to public tastes, but his music stands on its own

Trumpeter Nichols's years of fame were relatively concentrated affairs – his first peak was reached in the late 1920s when he was making waves with his group the Five Pennies; the second came after the notoriety gained in the aftermath of the 1959 Hollywood biopic *The Five Pennies*, a film that was to Red Nichols's career what Sal Mineo was to jazz drumming. Nevertheless, Nichols was a hard-working musician and leader whose long career was mostly conducted against the grain of jazz fashions, but which had created a worthy body of music by its end.

Nichols was born in the town of Ogden, Utah, into a musical family: his father was the music professor at the local college and gave Nichols a secure musical training, by having him play in his band at the age of 12. Discovering the early jazz in his teens, Nichols took a liking to the Wolverines, the ODJB, and, in particular, Bix Beiderbecke's unique constructions. By 1923, against his father's wishes, Nichols was living in New York and starting out on a career in jazz; a fleet and accurate player, he soon amassed a great deal of work across a wide range of activities, including Broadway pit bands and Paul Whiteman's orchestra. By 1926 he had begun organizing studio bands which made records for many labels under just as many names, but which had a contract with Brunswick to release music under the name the Five Pennies. Musicians regularly included include Miff Mole (a constant companion in Nichols's bands), Adrian Rollini, Jimmy Dorsey, Eddie Lang, Joe Venuti, and Pee Wee Russell. Towards the end of the decade younger players like Benny Goodman and Glenn Miller were also regular sidemen. This band made some of the most disciplined, advanced, and influential records of the entire period, from the standpoint of both improvisation and arrangements.

Nichols began assembling a band of his own to take out on the live circuit, quitting Whiteman and starting out in 1930. He quickly built it up to be a top big band of the early part of the decade, concentrating on the style and repertoire that had made him famous in the first place and landing lucrative radio slots, often supporting singers and comics of the caliber of Ruth Etting and Bob Hope. As his style of music fell gradually from fashion so Nichols's career slowed down, but he continued to work his own small group around the Los Angeles area, with a break during World War II to work in a munitions factory to aid the war effort.

Nichols took advantage of the rekindled interest in his music occasioned by Hollywood at the end of the 1950s, signing a contract with Capitol records and leading disciplined recording sessions with old friends re-creating the sound and style of his late 1920s bands. He died of a heart attack in 1965. Nichols remains a figure of some controversy in jazz, his trumpet playing and musical style occasionally derided for their lack of depth and obvious concessions to the public taste of the day, but then such accusations have always been leveled at successful jazzmen. Nichols's jazz sense, his competence and his influence on his peers are all indisputable, as is his right to a place in the jazz pantheon.

SEE ALSO: ODJB, Bix Beiderbecke, Adrian Rollini, Jimmy Dorsey, Eddie Lang, Joe Venuti, Pee Wee Russell

Jimmy Noone

The latter-day Noone: Jimmy Noone appearing with his trio in Cedar Rapids, Michigan, 1942

fact file

BORN 1895

DIED 1944

MUSICAL SELECTION
"Sweet Lorraine"
"Apex Blues"

Born in the New Orleans environs, clarinetist Noone started on guitar as a young boy, picking up on clarinet prior to his tenth birthday and eventually moving to New Orleans proper and studying with Lorenzio Tio Jnr and, briefly, Sidney Bechet. By the early teens he was a regular on the New Orleans scene, eventually replacing Bechet in the Freddie Keppard band in 1913 before, in 1916, co-leading the Young Olympia Band with Buddy Petit. Further jobs with Kid Ory and others presaged his eventual move to Chicago in 1918, initially leaving New Orleans for a group led by Keppard but finally playing with King Oliver after the Keppard band broke up. Noone, with his advanced technique, liquid style, and secure intonation, was quickly acknowledged in Chicago as a leading player, joining Doc Cook's Dreamland Orchestra in 1920 and debuting on disc in 1923, for Gennett.

In 1927 Noone moved to the Apex Club, where he joined forces with Earl Hines to run Jimmie Noone's Apex Club Orchestra. Noone's recordings with this band are the foundation of his contemporary and posthumous reputation, his performances of songs like "Sweet Lorraine" and "Apex Blues" quickly becoming much-imitated classics; there were few clarinetists in the next generation who were entirely devoid of Noone's influence and, like Art Tatum, he even drew praise from classical composers and instrumentalists.

Noone spent most of his career in Chicago, venturing to New York once or twice during the 1930s, but work became rather scarce in the aftermath of the Depression and with the onset of swing. Like many other New Orleans stars, he experienced a career boost at the opening of the 1940s with the New Orleans revivalist movement getting under way. Moving to the West Coast, Noone played with a number of traditionalist stars, including Kid Ory. He was playing in the Ory band, which was just enjoying the first fruits of being broadcast on Orson Welles's radio show, when he died from heart failure in Los Angeles in April 1944. His influence lived on in the playing of musicians such as Benny Goodman (a major Noone fan), Barney Bigard, and Joe Marsala, to mention the bare minimum; his recordings have also constantly been in print since their release, his distinctive New Orleans tinge and impeccable technique making for an unbeatable combination in his chosen genre.

SEE ALSO: Sidney Bechet, Freddie Keppard, Kid Ory, King Oliver, Earl Hines, Art Tatum, Benny Goodman, Joe Marsala

Red Norvo

Xylophonist Red Norvo, seen here in 1938, had a varied career that brought him into contact with popular vaudeville and radio, as well as greats like Woody Herman and Benny Goodman

fact file

BORN 1908

MUSICAL SELECTION
Just A Mood

Norvo, born Kenneth Norville in Beardstown, Illinois, started off on piano in 1916, turning to marimba in the early 1920s and leaving Beardstown for Chicago in 1925, where he led a seven-piece marimba band. Various types of work, including vaudeville and tap dancing, saw him through to the end of the 1920s, by which time he had swapped to the xylophone; after a spell as a staff musician for Victor Young's radio orchestra, Norvo joined the Paul Whiteman organization around 1930 in Chicago. He and the band's vocalist, Mildred Bailey, fell in love, marrying before the band returned to New York that same year. Norvo stuck with Whiteman until 1934, when he formed his own band, using Eddie Suater as his arranger. This band was reorganized in 1936 as an accompanying vehicle for the vocals of Mildred Bailey. The band saw out the 1930s and remained consistently popular, both live and on recordings, featuring a restrained type of swing perfectly blending with Bailey's supple vocals. By the end of the decade, however, the marriage with Bailey was close to ending (they finally divorced in 1943 after some years apart) and Norvo was ready for new professional challenges. He retained his group intact until 1943, but hired younger musicians like Eddie Bert, Ralph Burns, and Shorty Rogers; he also switched to vibraphone in an effort to update his sound. By late 1944 he was ready for a change, joining Benny Goodman for a while in 1945, although he had organized one of the first swing-to-bop sessions for Dial, with Charlie Parker and Dizzy Gillespie in attendance, that same year. He spent a year with Woody Herman's First Herd as featured soloist and group leader of the Woodchoppers, Herman's small group within his big band. Norvo appeared at Herman's Carnegie Hall concert in 1946. He settled in LA in the late 1940s with his second wife, Shorty Rogers's sister Eve, forming a trio with Tal Farlow and Charles Mingus (later Jimmy Raney and Red Mitchell); he became caught up in the emerging West Coast "cool scene," running a quintet By 1958 Norvo was ready to rejoin Goodman, touring with the clarinetist. Performances with Goodman from this time were released by Columbia; others have appeared on the Music Masters series of Yale University issues of Goodman's private tapes. Ill health made Norvo semi-active in the 1960s, but a revival of health and fortune gave him international popularity again in the 1970s before he decided, in the 1980s, to enter retirement.

SEE ALSO: Mildred Bailey, Shorty Rogers, Benny Goodman, Charlie Parker, Dizzy Gillespie, Woody Herman

Anita O'Day

Singer Anita O'Day, lipstick at the ready, was immortalized in the film, "Jazz on a Summer's Day," the documentary of the Newport Jazz Festival, 1958

Born Anita Mae Colton in Kansas City, Missouri, O'Day took her professional name when working in dance marathons in the late 1930s before switching to singing, initially with Chicago groups, finally joining Max Miller's band and playing the Three Deuces in 1939. Noticed by Gene Krupa, she joined the drummer's band in early 1941, enjoying a major hit with him, "Let Me Off Uptown" (Columbia), a vehicle for both her and trumpet star Roy Eldridge. O'Day stayed with Krupa until late 1943, when she dropped out for a while, resurfacing with Stan Kenton's orchestra in 1944. Again she enjoyed a hit with a new leader, this time "And Her Tears Flowed Like Wine." O'Day by this time was a nationally recognized jazz singer, able to scat and rephrase melodies as only the best in her field could. After swapping back to Krupa for a year (1945–46), she finally went out as a solo act, running a variety of trios but always singing her repertoire from a jazz viewpoint. During the late 1940s and all through the 1950s O'Day was plagued with problems relating to her heroin addiction, and it was only her 1958 appearance at the Newport Jazz Festival (part of which was preserved in *Jazz on a Summer's Day*, the film of that year's festival) that brought her back in front of her audience. That same year she appeared with the Chico Hamilton Quintet in *The Sweet Smell of Success*, starring Burt Lancaster, and her career once more blossomed. However, it was not until some years later that she finally shook off her heroin dependency (as documented in her forthright and occasionally harrowing autobiography) and was able to tour and record regularly. By the early 1960s she was touring constantly overseas, including Japan, and had amassed a quantity of high-quality albums for the Verve label using her patented jazz vocal style, in both small-group and big-band settings.

By the end of the 1960s O'Day was a popular concert artist in Europe and Japan, her swing-based vocal style, liberally laced with blues and bop tinges and with more than a hint of Billie Holiday at slow tempos, proving irresistible to the Japanese in particular. She set up her own record label in the early 1970s and continued to pursue an active career all around the world until the early 1990s, when she began to pace herself more carefully to conserve her voice and energies. She remains a respected figure in the jazz world.

fact file

BORN 1919

MUSICAL SELECTION
Pick Yourself Up

SEE ALSO: Gene Krupa, Roy Eldridge, Stan Kenton

Original Dixieland Jazz Band

The Original Dixieland Jazz Band (ODJB) in 1917, including (l to r) Eddie Edwards (tb); Nick LaRocca (c); Tony Sbarbaro (d); Larry Shields (cl)

fact file

FORMED 1916

DISBANDED 1925

MUSICAL SELECTION
"Livery Stable Blues"
"Tiger Rag"

The first jazz band to record (in 1917, for Victor), New Orleans-derived Original Dixieland Jazz (or Jass) Band (ODJB for short) was made up of five young white players, all born in New Orleans: leader and trumpeter Nick LaRocca, clarinetist Larry Shields, trombonist Eddie Edwards, pianist Henry Ragas (later replaced by J. Russel Robinson), and drummer Tony Sbarbaro. In a town as acutely conscious of class and race structures as New Orleans, LaRocca and his musicians were brought up in the community of white musicians playing ragtime and syncopated brass music, but listened intently to what the Creoles and darker-hued blacks were creating in their sections of town, and while LaRocca always claimed to have been the originator of most of what he played, it is clear that he and his colleagues dipped into the creative streams running through all the musical output in the Big Easy at this formative time.

The band came together as a unit in Chicago in 1916, a few years after the formation of key units such as Kid Ory's first band or Freddie Keppard's group, applying the same principles to the standard repertoire of the day as did their Creole counterparts. Being one of the first on the scene in Chicago, the ODJB made an immediate impression at Chicago's Booster Club, followed in early 1917 by a residency at Reisenweber's Restaurant in New York. This job gave rise to great interest from New York's café society and led directly to their becoming the first jazz band to make phonograph recordings, for Victor, in February of the same year. These records, ranging from the bucolic slapstick of "Livery Stable Blues" and "Tiger Rag" to the acceptable face of early jazz in "Bluin' The Blues" and "Fidgety Feet," made an immediate and wide impact, the band even garnering an enthusiastic audience in European capitals, as its combination of ragtime, march, and hokum provoked widespread enthusiasm as well as no little amount of disquiet from the custodians of culture. The ODJB's worldwide success led to successful tours of Europe, including trips to England in 1919. Its ensemble discipline and rhythmic drive, allied to the brazenly crowd-pleasing antics, made it a hard act to top at the time and made its records voraciously digested and, in turn, imitated by every band of like-minded souls that followed. The ODJB had to replace Henry Ragas after his death in 1919, and also brought in Benny Krueger on saxophone in 1920, but the basic thrust of the music remained the same until the band's demise in 1925, when LaRocca quit and returned to New Orleans. A decade later the same musicians made a determined attempt to revive the name and the music with live gigs and recordings for Victor, but their time had passed, swing was in the air, and the Trad Revival was still a half-decade away. Still, what the band had achieved is incontrovertible, and their place in jazz history is without question.

SEE ALSO: Sidney Bechet, "Kid" Ory, Buddy Bolden, Freddie Keppard, Louis Armstrong, Johnny Dodds

Joe "King" Oliver

fact file

BORN 1885

DIED 1938

MUSICAL SELECTION
"Snake Rag"
"Dipper Mouth Blues"

Joe "King" Oliver's greatest band, pictured here in 1923, featured (l to r) Warren "Baby" Dodds; Honore Dutrey; the man himself; Louis Armstrong; Bill Johnson; Johnny Dodds; and Lil Armstrong

Oliver, a Savannah-born New Orleans cornet man, was a pivotal figure in the evolution of classic trumpet styles. Starting off in the marching bands of New Orleans, as did Bolden and Keppard, Oliver matured into a player with a complete concept of what he wanted his music to sound like (as heard on the classic Creole Band recordings of 1923) and the means to carry this out. A clear step on the path between the rough brass band style of Bolden and the sophisticated freedom of Armstrong, his own playing used regular rhythmic phrasing and the device of small variations and inflections for its effects, as opposed to the wholesale recasting of rhythm and melody introduced by Armstrong in the mid-1920s.

Born and raised on a plantation, Oliver left home as a boy and moved to New Orleans, initially taking up trombone before swapping to cornet. He began playing in bands around 1907, still little more than a novice though already in his twenties, but by 1912 he was sufficiently advanced to join the Olympia Band led by A.J. Piron. In 1915 he formed his first band, briefly using Sidney Bechet on clarinet, but by 1917 he was a fixture in Kid Ory's band, among others. Ory appointed him "King," raising his status (and therefore his saleability) and placing him in line with Buddy Bolden and Freddie Keppard.

Oliver was not King in New Orleans for long: by the following year he had relocated in Chicago, initially working with a number of bands but eventually assuming the leadership of a group based in the Royal Garden Café. Oliver's strong lead lines and his outstanding ability with a variety of cupped mutes and other effects formed the basis of his fame, but by 1922 he decided he needed an added attraction. This he supplied in the person of Louis Armstrong, who became second trumpet to Oliver in the older man's Creole Jazz Band, now based at the Lincoln Gardens. This group, with the additional bonus of Johnny and "Baby" Dodds and Lil Hardin on piano, soon became a sensation in Chicago and became the first black group to make a series of recordings. Before long, Kid Ory and Barney Bigard were to feature with Oliver's band, and although Armstrong left in 1924 (convinced by Lil, now his wife, that Oliver was holding out on his money), Oliver retained his pre-eminent position in Chicago-based classic New Orleans jazz, continuing to record regularly and running a group called the Savannah Syncopators.

With Armstrong gone, his perfect foil was removed, and as the 1920s proceeded he began to suffer from ill health, the worst aspect of which was the pyorrhea which badly affected his gums. By 1928 he was in New York looking to dominate the new center of jazz, but a series of bad moves and ill luck (he turned down a residency at the Cotton Club which was afterwards awarded to Duke Ellington), combined with the waning of interest in his style of music, led to his gradual eclipse. After 1931 Oliver made no more records. He eventually removed himself back to Savannah, were he lived completely cut off from his former musical life, doing menial jobs as his health allowed. A variety of ailments brought about his demise in April 1938.

SEE ALSO: Kid Ory, Freddie Keppard

Edward "Kid" Ory

fact file

BORN 1886

DIED 1973

MUSICAL SELECTION
"Ory's Creole Trombone"
Song of the Wanderer

A latter-day shot of the inimitable "Kid" Ory, a jazz performer when the genre of music was still being defined

Edward "Kid" Ory was in the thick of things at the birth of jazz as an identifiable music with a name of its own. Born in La Place, Louisiana, trombonist Ory began his musical career in his home town as a banjoist, organizing a local quintet made up of stringed instruments. Having bought a trombone and picked up the rudiments of music, Ory eventually traveled to New Orleans at the opening of the 1910s, quickly setting up his first band and assiduously drumming up work for it. A highly motivated and organized man, by the end of 1911 he was one of the leading bandleaders in the city and was hiring talent like his friend, cornetist Buddy Petit, later seeing both "King" Oliver and Louis Armstrong move through his ranks on their way to Chicago and wider fame. Ory, a Creole, also had other outstanding Creole musicians such as Sidney Bechet and Johnny Dodds in his bands at various times, while he also had a helping hand in the formulation of some of the classic New Orleans repertoire, including converting "Tiger Rag" from an old quadrille into a suitable vehicle for New Orleans-style collective playing, his own so-called "tailgate" trombone style adding a distinctive element to the mix.

In 1919, apparently in search of a less humid, healthier climate, Ory took himself off to California, where he quickly became a leading light in Los Angeles's nascent jazz scene, leading an aggregation which worked under a number of different names before making what are commonly claimed as the first ever recordings by a black jazz band, *Ory's Creole Trombone*, in 1922. Ory's West Coast career continued to flourish, but in 1924 he was offered a position with "King" Oliver's Chicago band which was too tempting to refuse. He joined Oliver the following year, staying with the trumpeter for three years while working and recording with a host of others, including the classic Louis Armstrong Hot Fives and Hot Sevens and Ma Rainey.

Ory was unquestionably the most in-demand New Orleans trombonist of the period, but in 1929 he returned to Los Angeles, seeking better health and a more peaceful existence, retiring from music in the early 1930s and running a chicken farm with his brother. Gradually tempted out of retirement during the early 1940s by the New Orleans revival of that time, Ory became a fixture on Orson Welles's radio show from 1944 onward, bringing his characteristic energy and motivation to his new career. Still based on the West Coast, Ory and his bands became figureheads in the trad boom of the 1940s and 1950s, even appearing with Louis Armstrong and Billie Holiday, among others, in the Hollywood feature film, *New Orleans*. As well as setting up his own LA club, On The Levee, in 1954, Ory and his band toured and recorded extensively up to the 1960s, when he felt the need to retire, which he did in 1966, removing himself to Hawaii and living on his royalties until his death in 1973.

SEE ALSO: "King" Oliver, Louis Armstrong, Sidney Bechet, Johnny Dodds, Billie Holiday

Greg Osby

fact file

BORN 1960

MUSICAL SELECTION
Man Talk for Moderns
3-D Lifestyles
Black Talk
Art Forum
Further Ado

Controversial and brilliant contemporary altoist Greg Osby is still a relatively new face on the jazz scene

Saxophonist/composer Osby came from a musical St Louis family, learning the saxophone while still at school, then moving on to jazz studies at Howard University, in Washington, DC, at the age of 18. After three years at Howard, in 1980 Osby elected to complete his studies at Boston's famous Berklee College, where he concentrated on composing and arranging. By 1983 Osby had moved to New York and quickly began working with top-line leaders, including Ron Carter and Dizzy Gillespie, as well as mixing with the younger players who, in short time, would be propagating M-Base music live and on records.

By 1985 Osby had come to the attention of Jack DeJohnette and had been inducted into Special Edition. This exposure led to more intensive work across a wide range of players and leaders and also indirectly brought him, via Bobby Hutcherson, to recording with Andrew Hill on the pianist's two latter-day albums for Blue Note in 1989–90. By then Osby had been part of DeJohnette's band for half a decade and had recorded with various line-ups, including eventually the groups which, in 1991, made *Earth Walk* for Blue Note. He had also begun recording widely with M-Base musicians in the late 1980s, including an album under his own leadership, which showed him fully conversant with the modern idioms of black urban living as well as more traditional jazz structures and rhythmic patterns.

A contract with Blue Note, started in 1990, is still in force today, the resultant albums demonstrating Osby's wide artistic remit: on albums such as *Man Talk for Moderns* (1990) and *3-D Lifestyles* (1992) he mixes a whole potpourri of styles, while *Black Talk* (1995) delves into urban rap and electronic rhythmic patterns, his liquid alto sound (not unlike Steve Coleman's, in fact) at times seeming in stark contrast to what goes on around it. In 1997 with Osby toured internationally with a young acoustic quartet and released *Art Forum*, featuring imaginative compositions and arrangements as well as his elliptical improvisational style at its best. Although Osby claimed this to be a one-off, it demonstrates that his is a creative vision with a wide ambit and one of the most potent modes of musical delivery in modern jazz. *Further Ado* (Blue Note, 1998), continues in this direction.

SEE ALSO: Ron Carter, Dizzy Gillespie, Jack DeJohnette, Bobby Hutcherson, Andrew Hill

Oran "Hot Lips" Page

"Hot Lips" Page caught in the act, 1941, while he was a hot ticket on New York's 52nd street

fact file

BORN 1908

DIED 1954

MUSICAL SELECTION
"I Ain't Got Nobody"
"Feeling High and Happy"

Born in Dallas, trumpeter Page had taken up his chosen instrument by the age of 12, joining a brass band soon after where he met the future tenor star, Budd Johnson. By the mid-1920s Page was a touring professional, appearing in bands on the TOBA circuit with many star performers, including Ma Rainey and Ida Cox. By 1927 Page had settled in Kansas City, where he became a member of Walter Page's Blue Devils, leaving Page in 1931 to join the Bennie Moten band, the bassist's great rivals. "Hot Lips" stayed with the Moten band until the leader's death in 1935, then elected to remain with the re-formed band under the leadership of Count Basie, who had secured the band a residency at KC's Reno Club. Enticed away from Basie by Joe Glaser, manager of Louis Armstrong and a man with a keen eye for talent, "Hot Lips" moved to New York under a long management contract and appeared up and down 52nd Street to great success between 1936 and 1941, his pleasing personality, spectacular trumpet playing, and winning vocals all combining to make him consistently in demand. However, Glaser was careful not to promote Page to Armstrong's detriment, leaving the younger man in something of a career hole. Page recorded consistently for RCA Victor, combining his easy, blues-inflected vocals with a high-riding trumpet style out front of swing arrangements in a style emulating that of Armstrong, although Page had his own improvisatory approach, but by 1941 he was feeling the need to take a new direction.

To this effect he joined Artie Shaw's band in 1941, staying a number of months and making some excellent sides, including "Blues In The Night," but the momentum dropped from this when Shaw disbanded in 1942. Page went back to leading his own groups, at one stage having a young Pearl Bailey in his band as well as such later stars as Earl Bostic and Don Byas; but the advent of bop, the lack of a big hit, and the cooling of the public to big bands left him continually falling short of that big breakthrough he'd hoped for back in 1936 on leaving Basie. Page appeared at the 1949 Paris Jazz Festival and remained a consistently popular club act, recording right through to the end of his life in 1954 as well as assiduously appearing in his favorite milieu, the jam session, but wider fame eluded him right to the end.

SEE ALSO: Budd Johnson, Count Basie, Louis Armstrong, Artie Shaw

Joe Pass

fact file

BORN 1929

DIED 1994

MUSICAL SELECTION
The Sounds of Synanon
I Remember Charlie

Guitar virtuoso Joe Pass, born Joseph Passalaqua, recorded prolifically during his career and remained always in demand

Born in New Jersey, the guitarist was named Joseph Passalaqua and studied guitar locally at the close of the 1930s, working in local bands while still at high school. By 1947, using his professional name, he had graduated to Charlie Barnet, but by the time of his military service he'd also graduated to hard drugs, spending most of the 1950s alternating between freelance work around the West Coast and time in institutions. Realizing that things had to change, Pass booked himself into the Synanon Foundation in 1961, emerging from there in 1962 clean of drugs and with a new purpose to his career. He first attracted attention during a TV program made about Synanon during the time he was an inmate, followed by some superb playing on a Pacific Jazz album, *The Sounds of Synanon*, on which he was featured.

On his return to professional music, Pass became an in-demand guitarist, his masterful combination of advanced harmonic progressions, the legacy of Charlie Christian, and a sure commercial sense guaranteeing his success. He received greater public acclaim after his signing to the Pablo label in 1973. For Granz's latter-day label Pass made an unconscionable amount of records, as leader and as sideman, also becoming a regular musical companion for Oscar Peterson in particular, both on stage and in the studio.

During the 1980s Pass emerged from the role of star accompanist in Granz's stable of performers to be a guitar star in his own right, recording and performing in virtually every setting imaginable, from solo to any combination of small groups to Latin-fusion to updated bop. Pass continued to impress his audiences and other guitarists with his comprehensive chordal knowledge and facility, retaining a very sizable and loyal audience up to his death in 1994. His live performances were guaranteed to draw crowds world-wide.

SEE ALSO: Charlie Christian, Charlie Barnet

Charlie Parker

Kansas City-born altoist Parker was the single most important creative impetus behind the postwar reinvigoration of jazz most commonly known as "bop." By all accounts a creative genius, Parker gave the impression of being the ultimate romantic notion of such a figure, tossing off astounding improvisations while living the most dissolute lifestyle imaginable. Parker was an only child and doted on by his mother. He began playing alto sax at the age of 11, within two years playing baritone sax in the high school band, but he dropped out of school at 14 and began looking for musical employment in Kansas City, catching Lester Young, Buster Smith, Herschel Evans, and others, in the clubs and bars of KC. After initial derision from the older jazz community, Parker worked steadily with a string of leaders, Smith included, and honed his techniques; he also picked up a heroin habit before the end of the decade. At the start of the 1940s Parker joined the band of Jay McShann, a group modeled closely on the Basie style and for whom Parker had briefly worked in 1938, before spending a year on his own in New York and Chicago. Despite his increasingly willful and unreliable behavior, the altoist became one of the stars of this traveling band. He cut his first sides with McShann in 1941, taking a solo on "Hootie's Blues" which alerted discerning musicians across the United States to his potential.

Parker, by now also known as "Yardbird," "Bird," or "Chan," left McShann in 1942 and settled in New York, working with a variety of big bands, including those of Noble Sissle and Earl Hines (where he played with his new friend Dizzy Gillespie for a couple of months) and also took part in the continuing jam sessions uptown at Monroe's and Minton's. In 1944 he joined the newly formed Billy Eckstine band, but by 1945 he and Gillespie were both leading bands on 52nd Street, sometimes together, sometimes separately. Parker recorded his first session as a leader in November 1945: this Savoy Records date included future classics such as "Billie's Bounce," "Now's The Time," and "Ko-Ko."

On the West Coast in 1946–47 he made a string of classic recordings for the Dial label and a number of appearances on the early JATP concert stages in LA, but also had a complete breakdown which landed him in Camarillo State Hospital for six months. Back in New York later in 1947, he led a quintet featuring Max Roach, Duke Jordan, and Tommy Potter, broadcasting regularly from the Royal Roost in the late 1940s with a succession of men in the trumpet role, including Miles Davis, Kenny Dorham and Red Rodney. Fats Navarro also appeared on occasion.

By 1949 a European tour which took him through Scandinavia and to the Paris Jazz Festival that year, where he met Sidney Bechet. Parker's innovations and style had by now become ubiquitous among younger jazz players; his playing style influenced not just players of his own instrument, but all jazz musicians of his generation, creating endless Parker clones in the late 1940s and 1950s.

In the 1950s Parker attempted to make regular tours and recordings with a string section, but many of the arrangements he used were pedestrian. Parker's chaotic lifestyle and lack of discipline was often to blame.

As the 1950s moved on Parker suffered marriage failures, domestic tragedies (one of his daughters died), and further arrests for narcotics usage. His creative wellsprings became increasingly narrowly focused. Parker died of liver complications in the apartment of his friend, Baroness Nica de Koenigswater, in March 1955.

fact file

BORN 1920

DIED 1955

MUSICAL SELECTION
"Billie's Bounce"
"Now's The Time"
"Ko-Ko"

Charlie Parker during his first trip to Los Angeles, pictured here in December 1946, before his imminent breakdown

SEE ALSO: Lester Young, Earl Hines, Dizzy Gillespie, Billy Eckstine, Ray Noble, Max Roach, Miles Davis, Kenny Dorham, Fats Navarro, Sidney Bechet, Benny Carter

Jaco Pastorius

The young and gifted Jaco Pastorius was considered the world's foremost electric bassist before his untimely death in 1987

fact file

BORN 1951

DIED 1987

MUSICAL SELECTION
Word of Mouth
Invitation

Bassist/composer Pastorius was born in Norristown, Pennsylvania, but grew up in Fort Lauderdale, Florida, having moved there with his family when he was seven years old. His first musical love was the drums (his father played), but by the age of 13 he had switched his attentions to the bass as well as becoming competent on piano and guitar. A fan of R&B and pop music, during his teens he would sit in with local musicians and bands whenever possible, also completing some arrangement work for a Fort Lauderdale big band. Continuing to base himself in Florida, in his late teens he began working professionally on bass, playing in virtually every musical genre available to him as well as jamming with visiting jazz musicians of every hue and style.

This finally led to his discovery by the outside world, including Paul Bley, Pat Metheny, and others, and a New York record session in 1975 under his own name featuring members of Weather Report. The following year Pastorius joined Zawinul and Shorter's band, also that year appearing on a Metheny album. From that time on Pastorius, a charismatic figure on stage and an electrifying player on record, was grabbing music press headlines worldwide. Concentrating on fretless electric bass, Pastorius ushered in a completely fresh approach to it, giving remarkable melodic and rhythmic freedom through the cogency of his long, sinuous phrasing and use of sustain. His sound was heard on many records led by others, including Joni Mitchell's 1977 masterpiece, *Hejira*. Pastorius contributed substantially to Weather Report's repertoire as well as its sound, staying with the band until 1982, by which time he had been involved in his own band, Word of Mouth, for two years, producing *Word of Mouth* for Warner Bros and appearing at festivals with his own big band, for which he composed and arranged. His activities remained at a high pitch for the rest of his life, but Pastorius also ran into troubled waters during his later career when he mixed his naturally up-front character with drugs: it has been suggested that his reaction to a dangerous street encounter led to his untimely slaying, in Fort Lauderdale, in 1994.

SEE ALSO: Paul Bley, Pat Metheny, Weather Report

Big John Patton

fact file

BORN 1935

MUSICAL SELECTION
Soul Connection
Blue Planet Man
Minor Swing

Organic soul with a large dash of class, Big John Patton's popularity has traveled as far as Japan

Organist Patton, often considered little more than a Jimmy Smith bandwagon jumper, is a considerably more sophisticated and intelligent musician, as his long and varied career attests. Born in Kansas City, Patton grew up in a musical environment, his mother teaching him keyboard basics and his cousin showing him blues licks on the piano, which subsequently became his first professional instrument. After under-age listening in KC clubs to visiting jazz stars, Patton moved to Washington, DC, where his brother was at university, eventually landing an audition with R&B singer Lloyd Price. After joining Price in 1954 he stayed in the band for five years, being introduced to the Hammond Organ during that period. Bringing his appreciation of such pianists as Wynton Kelly and Hampton Hawes to his organ playing, Patton moved to New York in 1959 and soon began working with Ben Dixon and Grant Green. This in turn led to his tenure in Lou Donaldson's working band (1962–64) and his introduction to the Blue Note stable of recording musicians. Between 1962 and 1969 Patton made 11 albums as a leader for Blue Note, with two more being issued many years later. These records show the breadth of his musicality – unsurprising for a musician who was as at ease with Sun Ra and his sidemen as with Stanley Turrentine, George Braith, Bobby Hutcherson, and James "Blood" Ulmer.

By the late 1960s Patton was leading a trio featuring saxophonist Harold Alexander which combined elements of funk and jazz freedom in a uniquely interesting way. Indeed, at this time only Larry Young was being as adventurous, albeit in a very different direction. But the 1970s took music in a direction that no longer included Hammond Organs and Patton, by then based in New Jersey, found regular work hard to come by. An isolated album in 1983, *Soul Connection*, for Alvin Queen's Nilva label, found him in the company of Grachan Moncur III and Melvin Sparks and sustaining his previous high musical levels, but only in the 1990s, with its rekindled interest in organ jazz, has Patton been able to make a determined comeback, touring Japan in particular and making albums such as *Blue Planet Man* (Paddle Wheel, 1993) and *Minor Swing* (DIW, 1995) with avant-garde funk man John Zorn on razor sax.

SEE ALSO: Hampton Hawes, Grant Green, Lou Donaldson, Sun Ra, Stanley Turrentine, John Zorn

Duke Pearson

Pianist, composer and Blue Note A&R man, Duke Pearson was never limited in the scope of his talents

fact file

BORN 1932

DIED 1980

MUSICAL SELECTION
Wahoo
Idle Moments

Born in Atlanta, Georgia, pianist/composer/arranger Pearson was given piano lessons by his mother from the age of five onwards, initially choosing in adolescence to study trumpet and other brass instruments. Sticking with the trumpet, Pearson played in high school and Army (1953–54) bands until, on his return to civilian life, he developed dental problems which curtailed his brass career. Switching back to piano, Pearson (now using the nickname "Duke" conferred by a relative who admired Duke Ellington) ran his own small groups and freelanced around Atlanta until moving to New York in 1959. Quickly recognized for his pianistic and compositional talents, Pearson joined Donald Byrd's band that October, appearing on Byrd's *Fuego* (Blue Note), recorded in the same month. Pearson's unusual compositional skills were appreciated by Byrd and others, including Cannonball Adderley: both leaders recorded Pearson's "Jeanine" in 1960, while Byrd incorporated many Pearson pieces into his band's book. Briefly in The Jazztet in 1960, Pearson moved between employers in the early 1960s, including singers Nancy Wilson and Dakota Staton, traveling extensively with both. He also began recording at Blue Note as a leader, his 1964 effort, *Wahoo*, being something of a minor classic and featuring Donald Byrd with Joe Henderson. Pearson, whose lyrical and gracefully structured compositions enjoyed considerable airplay in this period, was also the *éminence grise* behind Grant Green's greatest record, 1963's *Idle Moments* (Blue Note). Recognized by Alfred Lion as a man with unusually wide talents, from 1963 onwards Pearson began working as a producer and A&R man for Blue Note. After Lion's departure and the sale of the label to Liberty in 1967, Pearson became central to the label's output, also occasionally making albums under his own name, both with small groups and with his big band (1967–70), an occasional group which during its existence challenged the Thad Jones–Mel Lewis band for New York supremacy.

At the dawn of the 1970s Pearson began teaching at Clark College, leaving Blue Note and once more taking up accompanist duties with top-line singers such as Carmen McRae and Joe Williams. He also revived his big band for specific tours and concerts, but by the end of the decade he had been diagnosed as suffering from multiple sclerosis, from which he died in August 1980. Pearson remains greatly underappreciated in critical circles some 20 years after his death.

SEE ALSO: Donald Byrd, Cannonball Adderley, Joe Henderson, Grant Green, Thad Jones, Mel Lewis, Carmen McRae

Art Pepper

fact file

BORN 1925

DIED 1982

MUSICAL SELECTION
Meets The Rhythm Section

The ravaged features of a life lived straight: Art Pepper during his 1970s comeback

Altoist Pepper was born in Gerdena, California, studying clarinet and alto privately from the age of nine onwards. By 1943, when still 17, Pepper began freelancing around Los Angeles's Central Avenue, at that time the busiest West Coast club spot, gaining work with Gus Arnheim and Benny Carter, among others. From 1944 to 1946 he was in the Army, returning to LA in summer 1946 and joining Stan Kenton in the fall of 1947 (he had briefly been in Kenton's band prior to his Army draft). Pepper stayed with Kenton, with occasional absences, until 1952, becoming internationally established as a soloist in this time and developing a style which balanced Charlie Parker's influence with more esoteric elements.

Leaving Kenton in early 1952, Pepper started his own group and began recording as a leader, but his addiction to heroin now began to affect his life in a major way; he was off the scene, either through drugs or incarceration, between 1953 and 1956, achieving little of value live or on record until late 1956, when he formed a quintet with West-Coaster Jack Montrose, made various dates for Aladdin and, in 1957–58, started a series of outstanding albums for Contemporary, including the much-praised classic *Meets The Rhythm Section* (1957), in which he played with the Miles Davis rhythm section of the day. Pepper concentrated his career on Los Angeles and Las Vegas between then and 1961, when once again he was jailed for drug usage. Virtually the entire 1960s were spent either behind bars or scuffling for money to buy drugs. His jazz profile evaporated in this period. After a major health scare in 1969 Pepper realized the pattern could not continue: he entered Synanon Foundation's rehabilitation program, first as an inmate (1969–71), later as an out-patient.

Pepper slowly managed to effect a return to music and to performing, beginning as a saxophone demonstrator in 1973, then joining Don Ellis's band (1975) and, that same year, cutting his first new record as a leader in 15 years. These activities, plus a general and widespread media interest in his life and his return, led to Pepper becoming a very much in-demand performer at festivals, clubs, and concerts in the late 1970s. He signed a deal with Galaxy Records and recorded prolifically in his final years, both live and in the studio. His new, occasionally fractured, overtly emotional approach appealed to an even wider audience than before, spurred on by the harrowing, street-smart revelations to be found in Pepper's autobiography, *Straight Life* (1979). Pepper, an ailing man, spent his last few years as a major jazz celebrity, his every move made in the glare of music media interest.

SEE ALSO: Benny Carter, Stan Kenton, Miles Davis, Don Ellis

Oscar Peterson

fact file

BORN 1925

MUSICAL SELECTION
Night Train
West Side Story

Montreal-born Oscar Peterson on stage with bassist Scott Edwards in July 1989

Montreal-born Peterson began piano lessons at the age of six, studying classical technique. By the age of 14 he was winning talent contests and appearing on Montreal radio shows. Around 1944 Peterson began playing with the Johnny Holmes Orchestra, staying with Holmes until the late 1940s, playing in an updated swing style which included elements from Garner, Cole, and Wilson. Persuaded by Norman Granz to join the annual JATP package in 1949, Peterson, on his NYC debut that year with his own trio, immediately impressed both audiences and fellow musicians alike. The pianist formed his own trio (modeled on Nat Cole lines), with bassist Ray Brown and guitarist Irving Ashby, quickly becoming a popular attraction in his own right, a JATP mainstay, and an almost constant presence in the studio for Granz between 1950 and 1959. During this time Peterson made scores of records under his own name for Granz as well as appearing as studio accompanist for virtually every major star Granz had under contract, including Lester Young, Ella Fitzgerald, Coleman Hawkins, Louis Armstrong, Ben Webster, and Billie Holiday.

Although in the trio Ashby was replaced by, in order, Barney Kessel and Herb Ellis, the basic approach and instrumentation remained intact until 1959, when Ellis left and Peterson elected to replace him with a drummer, Ed Thigpen. This ushered in a period many regard as Peterson's best and most characteristic, between 1959 and 1965, when his trio hit a deep groove together and his playing was at its most ebullient. By this time Peterson's style was inimitable, his technical facility the greatest since Tatum's, his swing and blues roots apparent on every session, his harmonic sophistication evident to any musician who cared to investigate his very personal approach to the chord changes of the standard repertoire. Unadventurous in his repertoire choice, perhaps, Peterson nevertheless was a more than competent songsmith himself, as many of his records attest.

During the 1970s and 1980s the pianist was closely involved in the music recorded by Granz for his Pablo label, continuing his habit of recording with a wide array of other jazz stars. A particularly fruitful set of alliances were set up with, in turn, Count Basie, Dizzy Gillespie, and Joe Pass, the latter working in Peterson's group for a while as well. Although Ray Brown left in 1965 and Peterson has used many bassists and drummers since, the basic instrumentation has remained constant up to the present day, as has the pianist's artistic conception. A series of health scares, including a stroke in the early 1990s, for a while threatened both Peterson's life and his continuing musical involvement, but he is working regularly again, recording for Telarc Jazz, in a somewhat distilled, condensed style, as emotionally committed as ever.

SEE ALSO: Lester Young, Ella Fitzgerald, Coleman Hawkins, Louis Armstrong, Ben Webster, Billie Holiday, Count Basie

Michel Petrucciani

fact file

BORN 1962

MUSICAL SELECTION
Plays Duke

The award-winning little giant of the jazz piano, Michel Petrucciani became a popular fixture on the live circuit from the moment he took the stage

Pianist Petrucciani was born in Orange, France; coming from a musical family, he began studying classical piano at the age of six and played with his father and brother, both musicians, in a family band. Petrucciani was born with a bone condition, osteogenesis imperfecta, which prevents normal growth patterns and has resulted in his being of significantly reduced adult height. This has had little or no impact on his professional career, as his abundant talents were recognized very early on: he gave a solo recital at 13 and was sitting-in with visiting overseas jazz musicians by his mid-teens. In 1979 he moved to Paris, where he quickly made his first album, still just 17 years old. After that, career advancement came very quickly indeed: in 1980 he had already wowed New York and toured Europe in duet with Lee Konitz; two years later, after a trip to California, he joined a renascent Charles Lloyd in his new quartet. Festivals, tours and recordings followed in quick succession, with Petrucciani the point of convergence for much of the resultant media attention, his fleet improvisations and ebullient expressionism a perfect counterweight to Lloyd's lyricism.

By 1994 Petrucciani had been out on his own for a while, playing solo concerts, duets, and small-group gigs with a range of top people, including Wayne Shorter, Jim Hall, and John Abercrombie. Winning many awards in different countries around the world, Petrucciani led his own group between 1989 and 1992 and in more recent times has continued to appear as a solo player or in different combinations, especially duets, of which his appearances with organist Eddy Louiss were some of the more unusual. Petrucciani is currently one of the contemporary keyboard masters, his every career move creating something of interest for fans and observers alike.

SEE ALSO: Lee Konitz, Wayne Shorter, Jim Hall

Oscar Pettiford

Jazz cellist and bassist par excellence, Oscar Pettiford's sudden death in 1960 robbed the jazz world of a significant and influential figure

fact file

BORN 1922

DIED 1960

MUSICAL SELECTION
"Bohemia After Dark"

bassist and cellist Pettiford was born in Okmulgee, an Indian reservation in Oklahoma, from black and Native American parents, his father being a vet and amateur musician, his mother a music teacher and pianist. Part of a large brood (there were 10 children), Oscar became a member of the family band started up by his father, Doc Pettiford, when he opted out of the vet's life; he started out learning piano, swapping to bass at the age of 14 and touring with the family three years later, in 1940. In 1942 his obvious prowess was recognized by his joining the Charlie Barnet band, touring with Barnet into 1943, after which he stopped in New York and joined Roy Eldridge's small group. At ease playing with Eldridge and other swing giants, including Coleman Hawkins and Ben Webster, he quickly sought out the younger players frequenting Minton's and Monroe's uptown, falling in with bop radicals such as Gillespie and Monk. Pettiford was quickly appraised as the logical replacement for the recently deceased Jimmy Blanton. His beat and intonation were the equal of Blanton's, and his interest in playing both modern and classic swing style marked him out as something else again.

Pettiford continued swapping leaders (and for a time running his own big band) until joining Blanton's last employer, Duke Ellington, in 1945, staying with the bandleader until 1948. By this time he was universally recognized as the greatest living jazz bassist; within a few years he would also prove his credentials as a composer, his piece "Bohemia After Dark" becoming something of a standard in the 1950s and early 1960s. Pettiford spent the 1950s either running his own groups (some big, some small) or playing and recording in first-rate combos with the likes of Charlie Shavers, Stan Getz, Thelonious Monk, and Art Blakey.

During the 1950s Pettiford began publicly appearing with the cello, an instrument rarely ventured by jazz musicians owing to the higher risks of bad intonation and smaller tone endemic to the instrument's small size. Pettiford had a complete mastery of the pizzicato cello, using it from time to time in many jazz contexts. His professional life continued to be somewhat erratic, due in part to a mercurial character and an inability to mask his contempt for what he perceived as indifferent playing by others, but also in part to alcohol. In 1958 he moved to Europe, basing himself in Copenhagen, and played with many of the expatriate greats then on the continent, including Bud Powell. He died from a sudden and short illness in the autumn of 1960. His bass playing raised standards immeasurably in the two decades of his public activity and many of the techniques still in jazz use today originated with him.

SEE ALSO: Charlie Barnet, Roy Eldridge, Coleman Hawkins, Ben Webster, Dizzy Gillespie, Thelonious Monk

Joe "Flip" Phillips

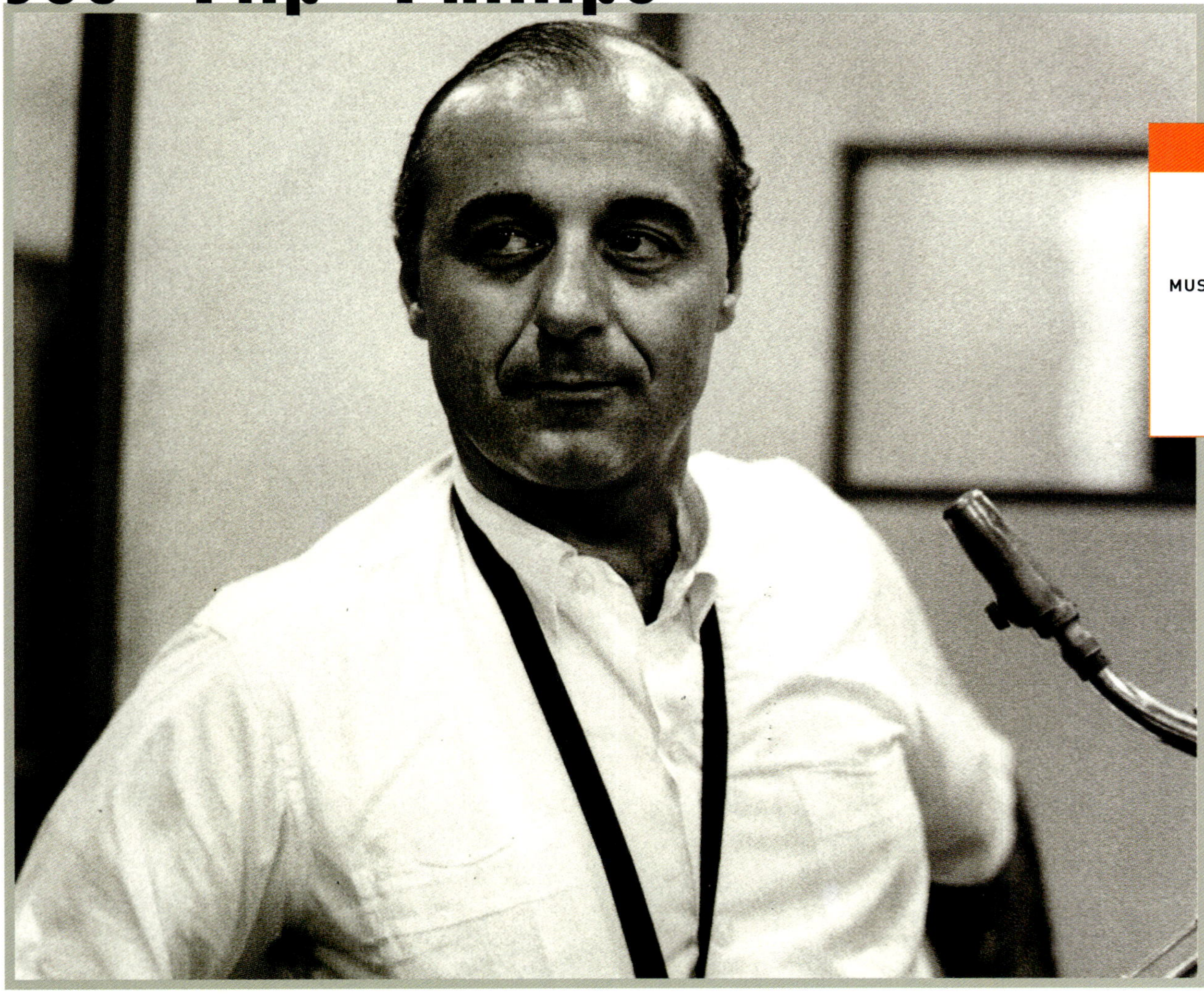

fact file

BORN 1915

MUSICAL SELECTION
Flip Wails

Rabble-rouser and caressing balladeer, Joe "Flip" Phillips, pictured here in the 1950s

Brooklyn-born saxophonist Phillips was in turns one of the most versatile and most exciting tenor players of the immediate postwar era. But to say that this adequately sums up a career that continues to this day is to do him an injustice. Born Joseph Phillipelli, he studied clarinet while young, learning theory as well from a relative before proceeding to work playing clarinet in a local restaurant (1934–39). A jazz fan from youth, Phillips got noticed in this capacity and became a member of Frankie Newton's band (1940–41) at Kelly's Stable, still playing clarinet, finally moving to tenor while working with Larry Bennett in 1942–43. Phillips quickly broke into the big league after joining Woody Herman's First Herd in 1944, replacing Vido Musso.

Phillips's wide emotional and technical range, burning up the high-tempo flag-wavers and dropping to an intimate, almost murmured whisper on the ballads, made him a crowd favorite and a star soloist on records. His ability to contribute to "head" arrangements also made him a valuable member of the Herman troupe. Phillips's own style was not highly original, being drawn in equal measure from "Chu" Berry, Ben Webster, and Lester Young, but he constructed a unique musical persona from this amalgam. That it was also uniquely popular was proven after the disbanding of the First Herd in 1946, when he joined up with JATP in 1947, appearing on the Midnight Jazz At Carnegie Hall concert with Bill Harris, Howard McGhee, and Illionis Jacquet which led to the "Perdido-Mordido-Endido" rave-ups.

After this Phillips rarely missed a JATP tour between then and JATP's eventual demise in 1960, taking his fiery sophistication to every corner of the earth, including Japan and Australia, at one time becoming something of an unofficial tour "minder" for Lester Young. Phillips moved to Florida during the late 1950s, working locally when he chose to, though he joined an international Benny Goodman tour in 1959 and appeared on many of the Goodman recordings of that time. Phillips then stayed well clear of the limelight until a 1972 Herman reunion. Encouraged by the interest in his playing, he gradually took up full-time playing again, working and recording for a number of labels, Concord Jazz included. He still lives and plays in Florida, still records for Concord, and tours when he sees fit: in summer 1997 he was an on-form and blazing part of Benny Carter's Saxophone Summit tour of the US.

SEE ALSO: Woody Herman, Howard McGhee, Illinois Jacquet, Lester Young, Benny Goodman

Bud Powell

Pianist Earl "Bud" Powell, born in New York into a family of musicians, was one of the most brilliant and significant pianists in the history of jazz. No pianist starting out in the music after 1947 was left untouched by what Powell brought to it, with every single development up to the 1960s presaged by one or another aspect of his style. Taught piano and theory from an early age, Powell left school at 15 and began appearing with a variety of bands, including that of trumpeter Valaida Snow. He also became a habitué of Minton's at the beginning of the 1940s, as the first experiments in bop were taking place, observing and learning from what he saw and heard.

Still a teenager when he joined Cootie Williams's band in 1943, Powell debuted on disc there, revealing a nascent bop style as well as incredible technical facility. Sharp, competitive, and completely focused on music, Powell left Williams in 1944 and gravitated to the emerging 52nd Street bop scene, working with all the bop principals, including Parker and Gillespie. Involved in an incident in which he received a brutal beating from members of the NYC Police Department, Powell in some of his friends' opinions was never the same person again, suffering recurring headaches and eventual mental breakdowns and hospitalizations, the first occurring that same year.

By the end of the decade, however, he had made a string of sensational recordings, of his own and others' material such as "Un Poco Loco," "Dance of the Infidels," and "Off Minor," in trio and small-group settings. These 78s revealed a melodic, rhythmic, and harmonic imagination and a technical facility the equal of Parker's, plus an emotional intensity which, at its fiercest, was almost frightening. He did not invent the musical language of bop, but he was utterly at ease with it like few others.

Powell's last indisputably great recordings, including his mesmerizing solo performances for Norman Granz such as "Parisian Thoroughfare" and "Oblivion" were made in the first three years of the 1950s: between 1951 and 1953 he underwent various institutional "remedies," including the first dose of ECT, a practice which was to continue through much of the 1950s, on the advice of his doctors. He was also routinely under sedation. This, allied to an increasingly heavy drinking pattern, made it a small miracle that any of his 1950s work is listenable. As it is, much of it is very greatly more than merely listenable, as evidenced by the many Birdland broadcasts from 1951 to 1953 now on CD and the famous 1953 Massey Hall concert with Parker, Gillespie, and Mingus, although by 1954 his extreme facility had withered. In its place came increasing harmonic astringency, a strengthening of musical ties with Thelonious Monk's music and methods, and at times a heightening of emotional tensions which make some performances verge on the unbearable.

Powell suffered greatly from the death of his younger brother, Richie, who died in the same crash in which Clifford Brown lost his life; he and his wife, Buttercup, moved to Paris in 1958, forming a trio called the Three Bosses with Kenny Clarke and Pierre Michelot the following year, finding a measure of emotional stability through his regular music-making.

In 1965 he returned to New York. After a halting comeback Powell dropped out of sight. Eventually found living on the streets, he was diagnosed as suffering from advanced tuberculosis, among other things. He died in hospital close to a year later.

fact file

BORN 1924

DIED 1966

MUSICAL SELECTION
"Un Poco Loco"
"Dance of the Infidels"
"Off Minor"

Bud Powell, seen here looking slightly concerned at the clash between wall and curtain patterns, was a stunning influence on virtually every jazz pianist who came after

SEE ALSO: Charlie Parker, Dizzy Gillespie, Charles Mingus, Thelonious Monk, Kenny Clarke

Don Pullen

fact file

BORN 1941

DIED 1995

MUSICAL SELECTION
New Beginnings

The young jazz pianist Don Pullen readies for action, earning international notoriety with Charles Mingus in the 1970s

Born in Roanoke, Virginia, pianist Pullen came from a musical family and had his first significant musical experiences in church, where gospel took a hold on him. Like many others, however, Pullen also felt the pull of rhythm and blues, eventually playing piano in various local R&B groups before, in his late teens, discovering jazz. Initially overwhelmed by Art Tatum's recordings, Pullen in the early 1960s then discovered the new ground being broken by Eric Dolphy and others. His move to Chicago around 1963–64 brought him directly into contact with avant-garde jazz in the figure of Muhal Richard Abrams, who helped him find a musical direction of his own. In New York by mid-1964, Pullen came into contact with musician and organizer Giuseppi Logan, into whose group he moved. While playing with Logan he recorded as a sideman for ESP-Disk twice and also met Logan's drummer, Milford Graves. After both men left Logan in the mid-1960s they formed a powerful avant-garde duo and started up their own record label, SRP (Self Reliance Program). Two albums, both recorded live, were eventually released in 1966 and 1967. Meanwhile, work was scarce, leaving Pullen needing to play in soul and rhythm-and-blues groups run by singers such as Arthur Prysock, Ruth Brown, and Big Maybelle to make ends meet. Into the 1970s he also ran his own soul-funk band, playing organ and employing suitable sidemen, including the late Tina Brooks on saxophone. By 1973 he had come to the attention of Charles Mingus, then just in the process of restarting his stalled career: Pullen became a fixture in Mingus's 1970s small groups and it was this tenure that gave him an international following.

By the mid-1970s he was making solo albums for Sackville and enjoying a generally high profile, mixing all his favorite genres into one tumultuous improvisational style and having the intellectual continuity to pull the audiences with him. After Mingus's death Pullen teamed up with a Mingus colleague, tenorist George Adams, and they ran a quartet together until 1988. By this time Pullen, still expanding his musical horizons and absorbing musical influences from both Africa and South America, had become something of a father figure to younger generations of musicians, helping and encouraging players from saxophonist Jane Bunnett to singer Kip Hanrahan and recording with stars such as David Murray, Archie Shepp, and John Scofield. Pullen had been running his own multinational group for a number of years when he succumbed to cancer in 1995.

SEE ALSO: Art Tatum, Muhal Richard Abrams, Milford Graves, Charles Mingus, Archie Shepp, John Scofield

Ike Quebec

fact file

BORN 1918

DIED 1963

MUSICAL SELECTION
It Might As Well Be Spring
Soul Samba

The 1940s tenor giant Ike Quebec stands out, taking the lead with the Cab Calloway band in New York city in 1945

Tenor saxophonist Quebec was born in Newark, New Jersey, deciding on a show-business career when he was a teenager and working initially as a dancer. Plying his trade in Harlem in the 1930s, Quebec inevitably came into contact with musicians and, on the advice of his wife and members of the Jabbo Smith band, eventually decided to learn piano. By 1940 he was competent enough to join the Barons of Rhythm, staying with them two years, but in the meantime he had decided that the tenor sax was to be his instrument of choice, and learned it privately. Initially playing down at Minton's Playhouse with Kenny Clarke, Thelonious Monk, and others, he eventually worked professionally with Frankie Newton, Ella Fitzgerald, and Roy Eldridge, his own sound and approach inspired by "Chu" Berry and Coleman Hawkins perfectly fitting into that context. By 1944 he was gigging and recording with Sammy Price and "Hot Lips" Page before joining Cab Calloway's band. This employment would last, in one form or another, into the 1950s. He also began recording for Blue Note as a session leader in 1944: this would last just two years, but Quebec would renew the relationship much later.

Quebec attempted to launch himself as a leader in 1949–50, but found the economic and music-fashion climate against him, returning to Calloway a number of times before, around 1952, dropping out of music altogether. He worked in various capacities, including that of a chauffeur, and found himself struggling with a heroin habit and doing time on Riker's Island. Quebec came back to Blue Note in 1959, working with the label in an A&R capacity (bringing Dexter Gordon to Blue Note) as well as recording a number of 45rpm singles. These led to full albums such as *It Might As Well Be Spring* and *Soul Samba* as well as guest spots on albums by Jimmy Smith and Sonny Clark. His gruff and wholehearted tenor playing seemed about to reach a new generation of fans, but lung cancer claimed him in January 1963.

SEE ALSO: Kenny Clarke, Thelonious Monk, Ella Fitzgerald, Roy Eldridge, "Chu" Berry, Coleman Hawkins, "Hot Lips" Page

Boyd Raeburn

Progressive 1940s band leader Boyd Raeburn fostered an avant-garde image to rival bands like Kenton's and Eckstine's

fact file

BORN 1913

DIED 1966

MUSICAL SELECTION
"Boyd Meets Stravinsky"
"Dalvator Sally"
"March of The Boyds"

Raeburn was born on a ranch near Faith, South Dakota, and spent his childhood in nearby Platte, where he studied music privately, learning theory and saxophone. Raeburn attended the University of Chicago, where he led a campus band in the early 1930s and eventually oversaw a band involved in the Chicago World's Fair of 1933. The music played by these outfits seems to have been entirely removed from jazz, but by the late 1930s Raeburn was leading a swing-type commercial band. This sustained his largely uninteresting pre-1944 career but in this year Raeburn reorganized, bringing in new blood to the playing and arranging staff, with himself and Ed Finckel initially responsible for arrangements and original compositions, and instrumentalists such as Dizzy Gillespie, Sonny Berman, and Al Cohn on hand for solos and section work. The sounds the new Raeburn band made were suddenly the most modern on the block, even seeing off Eckstine and Kenton, and when arranger/composer George Handy came on board this avant-garde image was reinforced with titles such as "Boyd Meets Stravinsky," "Dalvator Sally," and "March of The Boyds" all exhibiting extreme tendencies.

Raeburn took his band to California in 1945, where other fine young players joined, including Dodo Marmarosa and Johnny Mandel, but his idea of balancing public taste with the intellectual demands of his music was to use vocalist Ginny Powell as a prop on which to hang outrageous arrangements of ballads like "Over The Rainbow." Despite near-unanimous support from critics and the admiration of other musicians, Raeburn's brave efforts were unraveling by 1947. He tried again in 1948, but by the turn of the decade had given up on advanced music, reverting to commercial fare and eventually quitting the business altogether. His marriage to Ginny Powell ended with her death in 1959, while he himself lived away from music until his own demise in 1966.

SEE ALSO: Dizzy Gillespie, Billy Eckstine, Stan Kenton, Dodo Marmarosa

Don Redman

Arranger and composer Don Redman filling in a few details backstage at Connie's Inn, 1936

Composer/arranger Redman, born in Piedmont, West Virginia, was a key participant in the development of the classic big-band jazz sound and style of the 1920s and 1930s. Redman came from a musical family playing trumpet, joining his father's band at the age of six, eventually becoming competent on most instrument families. By his teens he was interested in harmony, composition, and theory, studying privately before enrolling at Boston and Detroit Conservatories.

Redman began a professional music career with Billy Paige's Broadway Syncopators in 1922, then met up with the Fletcher Henderson band in New York, becoming a charter member of the band when it was formed in 1923. Redman played and wrote arrangements, and as Henderson moved up the New York band pecking order (being given an almighty push by the arrival of Louis Armstrong in 1924), Redman gave Henderson a decidedly strong jazz basis.

His work with Henderson continued to evolve, but in 1927 he became music director for McKinney's Cotton Pickers. In four years, Redman revolutionized their playing style, imposed proper section discipline, and encouraged their natural soloistic flair. The Cotton Pickers were the first to record Redman's "Gee Baby, Ain't I Good To You?"

For most of the 1930s Redman led his own band (1931–39) and recorded a number of classics, including "Chant of the Weed," but fading public interest led to his disbanding in 1940 and settling into a freelance existence. Redman for the most part was content with a behind-the-scenes role; joining Pearl Bailey's team in 1951, he was her staff arranger through the 1950s. Redman spent his last years on music projects all over New York, making new recordings of many of his most celebrated older tunes. He spent most of his time composing extended works, most of which have yet to be heard in public. Until they are, his proper place in jazz history cannot be established.

fact file

BORN 1900

DIED 1964

MUSICAL SELECTION
"Gee Baby, Ain't I Good To You?"

SEE ALSO: Fletcher Henderson, Benny Goodman, Coleman Hawkins, McKinney's Cotton Pickers

Joshua Redman

fact file

BORN 1969

MUSICAL SELECTION
Joshua Redman
Wish
Spirit of the Moment – Live at the Village Vanguard

The most talked-about new saxophonist on the contemporary scene, Joshua Redman's talent suggests a long and fruitful career ahead

Son of Fort Worth sax player and Ornette Coleman associate Dewey Redman, Joshua has a mother equally involved in the arts, but from a different perspective, being a trained dancer. Born in Berkeley, California, and growing up in an environment saturated in arts and music, Redman developed his tastes at an early stage, choosing the tenor sax as his instrument and combining his early musical experiments with a thorough education which culminated in a first at Harvard. He turned down an opportunity to study law at Yale and chose the more precarious life of a professional musician. Still in his early twenties, Redman began gigging with various bands and, in 1991, won the Thelonious Monk Competition. The resultant publicity and plaudits gave him something of a jet-propelled start to his music career: a year later he was signed to Warner Bros, making his debut self-titled album as a leader the following year. The next, *Wish*, in the company of Pat Metheny, Charlie Haden and Billy Higgins, revealed a player with as much respect for jazz tradition as his father and a superlative technician with an unusually warm tone and intelligent improvisational approach. In the meantime Redman showed his pluralistic approach to music by playing and recording with a bewildering array of young and old leaders, from Elvin Jones and Paul Motian to Joe Lovano and Melvin Rhyne. Redman has already been on a number of world tours, both as leader and as sideman.

His own records during the 1990s have shown a steady gaining of confidence and broadening of inspiration, his ambitious two-CD set, *Spirit of the Moment – Live at the Village Vanguard* (1995) using his working quartet to demonstrate that here was a player who had a constant and constantly rewarding flow of improvisational ideas. Redman's latest effort, *Freedom In The Groove*, shows him attempting – not always successfully – to incorporate other musical genres into his instrumental repertoire. Redman was perhaps the first tenor player in the Sonny Rollins tradition of free-association soloing for long stretches to exhibit the creative resources to consistently deliver the goods. He shows every sign of being capable of delivering major musical statements for an entire career.

SEE ALSO: Thelonious Monk, Pat Metheny, Charlie Haden, Elvin Jones, Paul Motian, Joe Lovano

Django Reinhardt

fact file

BORN 1910

DIED 1953

MUSICAL SELECTION
"Nuages"
"Swing '42"

The master of the guitar, Django Reinhardt, pictured here in the early 1950s, remains a constant influence on jazz guitarists to this day

Guitarist Reinhardt has often been described as the first European jazz player of genius and the first from the Old World to show the Americans new applications for their own improvisatory invention. Such statements tend to limit Reinhardt as much as laud him. Django was born to a gypsy family in a caravan sited near Charleroi in Belgium. All his family were involved in entertainment of one sort or another. Django's first instrument was violin, but he swapped to banjo and then guitar, beginning his professional career just prior to his teens in 1922. The defining point of his life was in 1928, when a fire in his caravan badly burned his left hand, leaving just two fingers functioning. Reinhardt evolved a fretboard technique which allowed him a dexterity and approach previously unheard in improvised jazz guitar circles, Eddie Lang's influence notwithstanding. An introduction to singer Jean Sablon and André Ekyan led to his appearing regularly in Paris cafés and restaurants, building his reputation to the point where, when he formed a quintet in 1934 with violinist Stephane Grappelli, the Hot Club of France gave its approval for its name to be appended. Their collective sound, driven by the rhythm guitars of Reinhardt's companions and by Grappelli's equally spirited attack, gave the band a tremendous rhythmic kick and brought in an unexpected flavor of gypsy rhythm and timbre. When Reinhardt originals and other more riff-based pieces were attempted, the Hot Club were defining their new genre as they went along. His devilish sense of humor added spice to the mix.

By the time the Quintet broke up in the build-up to Hitler's invasion of France, both Reinhardt and Grappelli were internationally famous. With the war, Grappelli spent his time in London while Reinhardt stayed put in continental Europe. After the war, Reinhardt and Grappelli largely preferred to remain friends rather than colleagues. Django started another quintet, but also took up composition and embarked on a tour of America, at Duke Ellington's behest, appearing (on amplified guitar) with Ellington in the US late in 1946. Reinhardt remained at heart a gypsy, preferring to live in his caravan and affecting a quixotic attitude to public engagements of all sorts. He also enjoyed fishing. Running his own career and developing his playing style through the use of amplification, Reinhardt continued to make intensely satisfying music although his latter-day colleagues were occasionally not up to his high standards. The great virtuoso was stopped by a stroke in May 1953.

SEE ALSO: Stephane Grappelli, Duke Ellington

Emily Remler

fact file

BORN 1957

DIED 1990

MUSICAL SELECTION
Firefly
East To West
This Is Me

Emily Remler, 1980s guitar heroine, was inspired by Jimi Hendrix to pick up her first guitar, but her playing followed a rather different path

Guitarist Remler was born in New York but grew up in Englewood Cliffs, New Jersey, taking up guitar as a 10-year-old after being inspired by the rock-guitar playing of Jimi Hendrix and his contemporaries. Attracted to jazz in her teens, she studied at Berklee College, where she became entranced by the guitar jazz of Charlie Christian, Wes Montgomery, and George Benson. She graduated in 1976, still just 18, then took off to New Orleans, playing a wide range of professional jobs, including the occasional R&B gig – virtually unavoidable in New Orleans, where R&B is as natural for most musicians as breathing. Her reputation spread quickly. By 1979 she was back in New York, her natural Montgomery-inspired swing and her melodic facility impressing all who heard her. Pushed forward by Herb Ellis and Charlie Byrd, by 1980 Remler had signed with Concord and in 1981 she made her debut album, *Firefly*, featuring Hank Jones, as well as appearing at the Concord, Kool, and Berlin Jazz Festivals. Remler contributed many of her own songs to her sessions, helping to establish her own flavor in her music.

Remler's career took off at an astonishing pace in the 1980s: she was leading her own quartet (featuring James Williams) by 1982 and touring widely. Her embracing of the earlier tradition of modern guitar mainstream playing was instrumental in rehabilitating techniques developed by Montgomery, Burrell, and others. Although she showed an interest in a wide cross-section of music, she could play with forceful drive and a freely inventive imagination, whether her band had old heads or young faces in it (her later quartet had Eddie Gomez on bass, Bob Moses on drums). Her last Concord album, from 1988, was a Wes Montgomery tribute, *East To West*; her last album before her untimely death was *This Is Me* (Justice, 1990), a record made up entirely of her own compositions and employing a vast array of backing groups and musicians – a showcase album for her range of talents. Less freely expressive than her early work, it hints at an expanded musical ambition that was thwarted by a fatal heart attack, brought on by drugs misuse, in a Sydney hotel in 1990.

SEE ALSO: Charlie Christian, Wes Montgomery, George Benson, Kenny Burrell

Buddy Rich

fact file

BORN 1917

DIED 1987

MUSICAL SELECTION
Lester Young Trio
The Monster

Notorious jazz drummer Buddy Rich in full swing, July 1982

Brooklyn-born Rich grew from being the infant prodigy "Traps, the Boy Wonder" into arguably the fastest, most technically assured, most hard-swinging and ferociously competitive jazz drummer of his generation. By the time he was six, Rich had been appearing in his parents' vaudeville act for four years, had appeared on Broadway, and had toured Australia as a single. Before his 12th birthday he was leading his own band. He switched into jazz after joining clarinetist Joe Marsala's group in 1938, playing the long-standing Hickory House engagement with the band until swapping to Bunny Berigan's band in 1939. Here he found the demands of big-band drumming very much to his taste, becoming a powerhouse behind the bands of Berigan, Artie Shaw, Tommy Dorsey, Benny Carter, and Tommy Dorsey (again) between 1939 and 1946. Between Carter and Dorsey he found time to fight for Uncle Sam; he also appeared on various small-group sessions – two with Nat Cole in the mid-1940s of particular interest, the *Anatomy of a Jam Session* date with Charlie Shavers, and the *Lester Young Trio* album, which provided some of Young's greatest work.

Rich made his first appearance as part of the JATP bandwagon in 1946, appearing at an LA concert with Buck Clayton, Coleman Hawkins, Lester Young, Willie Smith, and Charlie Parker; in subsequent years he was a tour fixture, often during the 1950s in the role of drum-battle contestant, either with Gene Krupa or, more rarely, Louie Bellson. These quasi-musical wrestling matches brought him enormous notoriety and fame in equal measure, but he still spent the 1950s mostly as a big-band drummer, splitting his time between Harry James (twice) and Tommy Dorsey.

The early part of the decade saw him in Charlie Ventura's Big Four. By the end of the 1950s he was trying a small group again, running his own quintet and singing publicly. A move back to Harry James followed in 1961, preparing Rich for a latter-day flowering, starting in 1966, when he launched his own big band, a unit he kept going until his health gave out in 1987. This band bucked every trend going and stuck to swinging as well as cheesy arrangements of ephemeral hit-parade material, but Rich's own massive stage presence, his frighteningly authoritative behavior toward his players, and his ability to spot and successfully exploit native talent (for example, sax player Steve Marcus, who became a talented arranger under Rich's watchful eye) kept his standards up and his band's popularity bubbling.

Rich remained a larger-than-life personality, at home on television, on stage and in films, consumingly competitive to the last, stuck in his post-swing conception but fully deserving the title given one of his Verve albums, *The Monster*. He died in 1987 of heart failure, after several previous heart attacks as well as bypass operations.

SEE ALSO: Bunny Berigan, Tommy Dorsey, Benny Carter, Nat King Cole, Lester Young, Coleman Hawkins, Willie Smith

Max Roach

Drummer Max Roach was born in New Land, North Carolina, but moved to New York in infancy; his family was musical, his mother a gospel singer. He himself enjoyed his first musical experiences as a drummer with gospel groups before playing secular music with contemporaries and progressing as a teenager to Manhattan School of Music, where he graduated in 1942. He quickly moved to sitting in uptown at Minton's and Monroe's, meeting the prime movers in the nascent bop revolution and being influenced by the ideas of Kenny Clarke in particular. Roach joined Coleman Hawkins in 1943 and made his debut on records with the tenor sax master before appearing on 52nd Street and in the recording studios with Dizzy Gillespie and Charlie Parker in epoch-making sessions between 1945 and 1946. Though he was still barely in his twenties Roach was the most in-demand and influential drummer of the classic bop period. Roach played with top groups all through the 1940s, becoming Parker's regular drummer in the late 1940s and also working with Stan Getz and, briefly, JATP as well as being involved in some of the Miles Davis nonet recordings.

In the 1950s Roach set up Debut Records with Charles Mingus, played at the famous Massey Hall concert of 1953 with Parker, Gillespie, Powell, and Mingus, then in 1954 established the co-led group with Clifford Brown that defined the entire hard-bop movement. Touring widely with Brown Roach maintained his profile as the number-one postwar drummer.

Even after the devastation of Brown's and pianist Richie Powell's deaths in a 1956 car crash, Roach summoned the strength to form a new small group, which rose to a new peak in 1958 with the advent of trumpeter Booker Little and saxophonist George Coleman, both of whom appear on a number of albums Roach made between the 1958 Newport Jazz Festival and his next major project (again with Mingus), the rebel Newport Jazz Festival of 1960. By then involved with Nat Hentoff's Candid label, Roach and Mingus both made recordings of some of the unlikely cross-generation combinations which made that festival a success. This technique was also applied to the *Freedom Now!* album of 1960 (Candid), which featured music by Roach and lyrics by Oscar Brown, Jr protesting the racist history of America and its music. Among the guests on this record was Coleman Hawkins, while Abbey Lincoln, soon to become Roach's wife (the couple divorced in 1970), was the featured vocalist.

Roach continued to make ambitious records, such as *Percussion Bitter Sweet* (Impulse!, 1962) and take militant stances on issues he cared about, but he also turned happily to such projects as the great trio album with Duke Ellington and Charles Mingus, *Money Jungle* (UA, 1962). He ran an excellent quintet for most of the 1960s featuring such talents as Freddie Hubbard, Cecil Bridgewater, and Cedar Walton, but by the early 1970s his pursuits and researches had spurred him to form M'Boom, a percussion ensemble of varying size and personnel performing works written for percussion. He also appeared during the 1970s and 1980s in a series of talked-about concert duets with key figures such as Dizzy Gillespie, Archie Shepp, Cecil Taylor, Anthony Braxton, and Abdullah Ibrahim. During the 1990s Roach has continued to compose and play for a variety of ensembles, including M'Boom, symphony orchestras and his regular quintet, as well as giving virtual drumming clinics from the stage every time he plays, his musicianship and dexterity remaining unimpaired.

fact file

BORN 1924

MUSICAL SELECTION
Percussion Bitter Sweet
Money Jungle

Drummer and band leader Max Roach, seen here in 1991,hard at work on his kit

SEE ALSO: Kenny Clarke, Coleman Hawkins, Dizzy Gillespie, Charlie Parker, Stan Getz, Miles Davis, Charles Mingus

Shorty Rogers

California dreamin': trumpeter Shorty Rogers stretches out

fact file

BORN 1924

DIED 1994

MUSICAL SELECTION
Shorty Stops
The Shorty Rogers Express

Born Milton Rajonsky in Great Barrington, Massachusetts, Rogers studied trumpet as a teenager at the High School of Music and Arts in New York, later polishing up his music theory and arranging skills at Los Angeles Conservatory. After this, he went out on the road in 1942 with Will Bradley before swapping to Red Norvo, with whom he stayed until his army induction in 1943. On his return to civilian life in late 1945, Rogers joined the Woody Herman Herd, playing and arranging ("Keen and Peachy"), staying on and off until the end of the 1940s, and interspersing these stints with times in the bands of Charlie Barnet and Charlie Stone. Now firmly based in the LA area, Rogers joined Stan Kenton in 1950 just as he launched his Innovations Orchestra. Chart work for Kenton included "Jolly Rogers" and "Art Pepper." After 18 months with Kenton in which he consistently wrote challenging and forward-looking charts Rogers decided to work with the pool of West Coast musicians now looking for alternative means of musical employment; he became a regular at Howard Rumsey's Lighthouse All-Stars sessions. A man with a decidedly well-developed sense of humor, he also was straw boss for the R&B inferno of Boots Brown and His Blockbusters, featuring Jimmy Giuffre and Gerry Mulligan, among others. For the rest of the 1950s Rogers maintained a very high profile on the West Coast, running his own groups and working relentlessly in the LA studios, getting increasingly involved in film music work while making memorable records for both Atlantic and RCA Victor under the working name of Shorty Rogers and His Giants. These albums mixed the adventurous with the bland in turns. By the dawn of the 1960s the jazz scene had moved on from West Coast cool and Rogers was so busy writing and arranging music for TV and films that he voluntarily withdrew from the jazz scene for the best part of two decades. During the 1980s he slowly made a jazz re-entry, working with pick-up bands on tours through the US and Europe or playing with old comrades from the West Coast days of the 1950s. By the 1990s this inclination had hardened into a properly constituted latter-day Lighthouse All-Stars band, of which he was nominal leader and which featured line-ups typical of the original Rumsey groups of 40 years earlier. Now in slowly deteriorating health, Rogers withdrew from playing in 1994, dying later in the same year.

SEE ALSO: Red Norvo, Woody Herman, Charlie Barnet, Stan Kenton, Jimmy Giuffre

Adrian Rollini

fact file

BORN 1904

DIED 1956

MUSICAL SELECTION
"At The Jazz Band Ball"

The multi-talented leader Adrian Rollini, seen here in the 1930s, was something of a child prodigy, playing Chopin at the age of four

Adrian and his brother Arthur were both prominent musicians in the jazz scene of the 1920s and early 1930s (Arthur played in the Goodman band for a time). Adrian was the older of the two, there being eight years between them, and his musical abilities were recognized in early childhood, he being allowed to play Chopin to a Waldorf Astoria audience in 1909, when he was still just four. Both boys were born in New York, with Adrian choosing at first the piano and xylophone, and leading his first band when just 14. He joined the California Ramblers in 1922 at the age of 18, soon afterwards taking up the bass saxophone and within a short while becoming a considerable musical force on the instrument, as the many recordings of him playing it demonstrate.

Rollini was one of a small number of early white players to influence musicians in the black bands of the time, his facility and tone on the instrument being the envy of both Coleman Hawkins and Harry Carney. During this period Rollini freelanced widely, recording with, among others, Bix Beiderbecke and Frankie Trumbauer. After five years with the Ramblers Rollini responded to an ad for musicians needed in London by Fred Elizalde, then running a band at the Savoy Hotel. Rollini came to London in 1927 and stayed almost two years, astounding patrons and fellow musicians alike with his dexterity on a range of instruments, including his "hot fountain pen," an ebonite variant of the penny whistle, except that it was fitted with a reed and mouthpiece. He also played the "goofus," a wind-driven instrument with a sound similar to the upper part of an accordion. One of his groups was dubbed "The Goofus Five." Perhaps Rollini was the Roland Kirk of his day. Whatever the case, his novelties were always musically played.

Rollini returned to New York in 1929, picking up where he left off, making hundreds of records, appearing in a variety of New York bands and eventually taking out a lease on some premises in middle Manhattan which he made into a club named Adrian's Tap Room. From there he ran his musical operations, leading his own small group during the 1930s, a decade in which he gradually swapped back from bass saxophone to the new xylophone derivative, the electrically amplified vibraphone. By the middle of the decade Rollini was leavening his jazz with a more "sweet" approach, running a trio which proved successful with the public, but he continued to occasionally venture into the recording studio with talents such as Bobby Hackett and Bunny Berigan to make jazz once again, maintaining his previous high standards. With the total victory of big-band swing, Rollini spent much of the 1940s in long hotel residencies in New York and Chicago, plus the occasional tour. As the 1950s dawned he decided to relocate to Miami, where he became the proprietor of a hotel and installed his own small group in its lounge, also freelancing in other upmarket Miami hotels of the day. He was living there up to his death, under mysterious circumstances, in May 1956.

SEE ALSO: Coleman Hawkins, Bix Beiderbecke, Frankie Trumbauer, Bunny Berigan

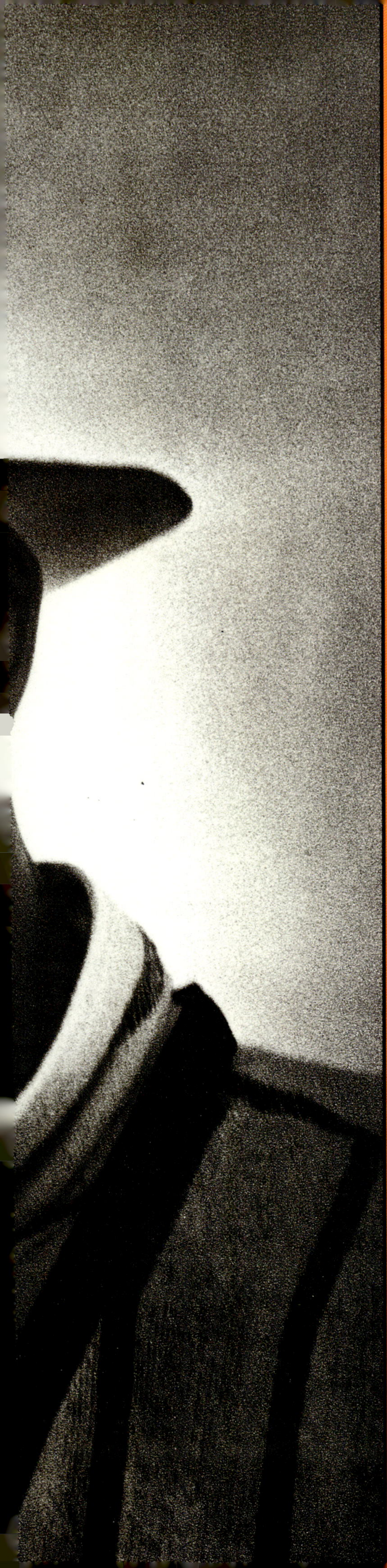

Sonny Rollins

Theodore "Sonny" Rollins was born into a musical Manhattan family and tried the piano when a pre-adolescent, but showed no real interest until high school, when he began learning alto sax. By 1947 he had finished his education and had swapped to tenor sax, playing with young contemporaries such as Jackie McLean and Kenny Drew. Through them he began meeting some of the leading lights in bop. By 1948 he was recording with Bud Powell and J.J. Johnson; by the following year he was recording under his own name and had started an association with Miles Davis which would last until the mid-1950s.

Rollins recorded frequently during this early stage, mostly for the Prestige label, and played in the bands of Art Blakey, Miles Davis, Fats Navarro, Bud Powell and recorded with many of these, plus the Modern Jazz Quartet, Thelonious Monk, and (on a Miles Davis session) Charlie Parker. Rollins's bustling approach and big tone made him a popular sideman as well as an influential stylist; by 1954 he had also introduced three compositions – "Doxy," "Airegin," and "Oleo" – which quickly became standard hard bop repertoire.

Basing himself in Chicago in 1955, he withdrew from public to rehearse and to shake off a heroin habit; on his return in December 1955 he joined the Clifford Brown–Max Roach Quintet and began making a stream of records which were to make him the most talked-about saxophonist since the advent of Charlie Parker. *Worktime, Saxophone Colossus* and *Tour de Force*, all for Prestige, showed his improvising prowess at an early peak, setting standards for others to aim at. Leaving Roach in 1957, Rollins ran his own bands for two years and recorded prolifically for a number of labels with a variety of personnel, though his two most famous late 1950s dates featured trios: the *Village Vanguard* sessions from 1957 featured Wilbur Ware and Elvin Jones, the *Freedom Suite* from 1958 Oscar Pettiford and Max Roach.

Rollins, however, remained unsatisfied with his professional lot, retiring from performance for the two years between August 1959 and November 1961. When he emerged with a new record contract (with RCA) and a new quartet (with Jim Hall on guitar) he also found that jazz had moved on apace. In Rollins's downtime, practicing on Williamsburg Bridge at night, both Ornette Coleman and John Coltrane had taken the cutting edge of music to new areas. Rollins was in danger of becoming last decade's fashion; he replaced Hall with Coleman's trumpeter Don Cherry in 1963, briefly investigating the type of ensemble favored by Coleman (drummer Billy Higgins was also ex-Coleman), but his own playing changed little.

Rollins remained at or near the top of his form, in concert and on record, through to 1968, evolving a rhythmic, tonal, and timbral freedom and flexibility which has to be heard to be believed, but in that year he once again withdrew from public performance. This hiatus lasted until 1971, when Rollins returned with a more relaxed, less willful approach to his playing and the bands he used. This led to much criticism from people accustomed to Rollins always advancing, rather than consolidating, but while his records have been largely – though not all – disappointing or conservative, his live appearances have usually been anything but that. His playing has been a seeming torrent of ideas, the sum total of an evening listening to him often being an overwhelming musical experience. Rollins remains one of the last remaining improvisational colossi in jazz, the single most imposing living figure in the jazz world today.

fact file

BORN 1930

MUSICAL SELECTION
Worktime
Saxophone Colossus
Freedom Suite

Tenor saxophonist colossus Sonny Rollins was and is, along with Charlie Parker, a singular influence on jazz

SEE ALSO: Oscar Pettiford, Elvin Jones, Jim Hall, Don Cherry

Wallace Roney

fact file

BORN 1960

MUSICAL SELECTION
Re-Birth of The Cool
Misterios

Young trumpet virtuoso Wallace Roney was surrounded by jazz from his youth via his policeman father's enthusiasm for the genre

Roney and his sax-playing younger brother, Antoine, came from a jazz-loving Philadelphia policeman's family, both boys growing up to the sounds of modern jazz morning, noon, and night. Wallace began private lessons on the trumpet as he moved into adolescence, keeping up trumpet studies as he attended high school and Howard University. This was all finished off with a course at Berklee, after which Roney joined Art Blakey's Jazz Messengers in 1981. Roney's debt to Miles Davis's trumpet style has often been remarked upon since his initial exposure to the public, but there are several other influences, including those of Clifford Brown, Booker Little, and Woody Shaw. All of these were put to good use during his tenure with Blakey, followed by stints with drummer Cindy Blackman and then, towards the end of the 1980s and into the 1990s, with Tony Williams.

During the present decade Roney has spread his talents far and wide, playing in very many different bands, for different leaders and in differing styles. In 1991 he was invited by Quincy Jones to front the Montreux Festival Band's re-creation of the Miles Davis/Gil Evans *Miles Ahead* charts, playing the lead parts when a visibly frail Davis was unable to: his reward from Miles was the great trumpeter's own monogrammed trumpet. Since then Roney has played with Davis tribute bands led by Williams, Wayne Shorter, and Herbie Hancock and has appeared also on the *Re-Birth of The Cool* album project undertaken by Gerry Mulligan for GRP; he has also continued to tour and record with his own quintet, with brother Antoine on sax and Carlos McKinney on piano. He also made a superb trumpet-and-strings album, *Misterios*, for Warner Bros in 1994. Roney remains a safe bet for future honors in the jazz-trumpet world.

SEE ALSO: Art Blakey, Quincy Jones, Miles Davis, Gil Evans, Wayne Shorter, Herbie Hancock, Gerry Mulligan

Leon Roppolo

fact file

BORN 1902

DIED 1943

MUSICAL SELECTION
Livery Stable Blues
Milenberg Joys

New Orleans clarinetist Leon Roppolo paid his jazz dues, as did many a New Orleans musician, on the nearby riverboats

Roppolo (often misspelled Rappolo) was born in Lutcher, Louisiana, and received his first music lessons from his part-time musician father, who got him started on the clarinet. Young Leon also gave himself a reasonable command of the guitar, an instrument to which he occasionally turned in later life. Roppolo played early gigs around Lake Pontchartrain, joining up with George Brunis (the two families were friendly) before moving into New Orleans and playing with Eddie Shields, brother of ODJB clarinetist Larry Shields, from about 1917 onwards. Roppolo then spent the next four years gaining experience in a welter of engagements throughout the New Orleans and surrounding areas, finally playing the riverboats and traveling up to Chicago with Brunis to join the Friar's Inn Society Orchestra in 1921. This band, a driving unit in the typically no-frills New Orleans style of the time, was quickly renamed the New Orleans Rhythm Kings, a band that was to prove highly influential through its appearances in Chicago, as well as its successful recordings. Roppolo, a charismatic stage presence and a man capable of projecting the clarinet sound through any New Orleans ensemble, became its most famous name. Moving on to New York in 1923, Roppolo played with a number of bands, including Ben Pollack's, but by the mid-twenties his heavy drinking and liberal use of "muggles," or marijuana, was making him unreliable. Leaving New York in 1925, Roppolo made it to St Paul before being taken seriously ill; wending his way back to New Orleans, Roppolo rejoined the New Orleans Rhythm Kings there, making a handful of sides for Okeh that same year. However, before the year was out, Roppolo had suffered a complete mental breakdown and was committed to a Louisiana mental home. He spent the remaining years of his life there.

SEE ALSO: ODJB

Roswell Rudd

fact file

BORN 1935

MUSICAL SELECTION
Everywhere
Numatik Swing Band

Trombonist Roswell Rudd, conferring with old friend and colleague Steve Lacy

Trombonist Rudd was born into a musically inclined family in Sharon, Connecticut, and took to studying the French horn in 1946 while a young boy. During his school years at Hotchkiss Rudd taught himself trombone, initially favoring a traditional-jazz style of playing; when he began his studies at Yale, where he completed a music degree during 1954–58, he became a member of Eli's Chosen Six, a Dixie outfit not above appearing on the backs of trucks to advertise their music. After finishing his studies Rudd continued to play within the trad milieu, appearing with such stalwarts as Edmond Hall, Eddie Condon, and Wild Bill Davison, but in 1960 in New York he came across pianist Herbie Nichols, then playing in Dixie outfits to keep body and soul together but a pianist possessed of real genius and a thoroughly modern outlook on jazz. Through Nichols Rudd became aware of his own capacities more fully, meeting up with soprano saxophonist Steve Lacy and working with him in a pianoless group dedicated solely to playing the music of another pianist and composing great, Thelonious Monk. In 1961 Rudd also appeared on a recording session organized by avant-garde pianist Cecil Taylor.

By the time Rudd was ready to form his own group, in 1964 he joined forces with three thoroughly avant-garde musicians, altoist John Tchicai, bassist Lewis Worrell and drummer Milford Graves. The New York Art Quartet, as it was called, was a revelatory outfit, intensely contrapuntal and often working outside normal chord structures and metric rhythm, but eschewing the expressionistic clichés then doing the New York rounds. The group was short-lived, and Rudd freelanced for a while before joining Archie Shepp's group between 1966 and 1967, but the trombonist, probably the single most gifted exponent of the instrument to emerge in the 1960s, found it nearly impossible to sustain his own groups, the late-1960s Primordial Quartet with Lee Konitz and vibist Karl Berger being an exception.

An isolated album for Impulse! in 1967, *Everywhere*, stands as one of his most ambitious and complete musical statements, featuring a front line of two reeds and one brass instrument. Rudd also worked frequently with Charlie Haden, appearing on the bassist's Liberation Music Orchestra album of 1969. A musicologist and teacher, Rudd moved progressively further into teaching, in the 1970s lecturing and researching at the University of Maine on ancient music and sporadically making albums recording his own compositions. In 1973 he made *Numatik Swing Band* for the Jazz Composer's Orchestra label and around the same time reconvened the New York Art Quartet, with Louis Moholo substituting for Milford Graves, for an album on the French Musidisc company. Rudd continues to play, record, and teach, while his intensely warm, expressive, and welcoming playing and compositions remain a little-known but rewarding part of the history of jazz since 1960, and his researches and educational duties still take prime everyday place. He has done much in the past three decades to bring some proper measure of appreciation to the musical legacy of his old colleague Herbie Nichols.

SEE ALSO: Eddie Condon, Herbie Nichols, Thelonious Monk, Cecil Taylor, Milford Graves, Lee Konitz, Archie Shepp

Jimmy Rushing

fact file

BORN 1903

DIED 1972

MUSICAL SELECTION
The You And Me That Used To Be

Mister Five-By-Five, "little" Jimmy Rushing, seen here in full performing excellence in 1940

The career of Jimmy Rushing demonstrates the close links between classic and swing jazz and the contemporary blues forms. Rushing joined Count Basie's band as it was gradually forging a national reputation. He was the band's star male vocalist, singing undiluted blues phrases and melodies across shouting brass and swinging reeds, allied to the smoothest swing rhythm section in the business.

Rushing was born into a musical family in Oklahoma City, Oklahoma, and learned violin and piano as a boy. Enjoying an unusually thorough musical education, Rushing studied theory at Douglas High School as well as singing in the local church and amateur opera group. His teenage years proved decisive, however, as he was influenced by an uncle who played piano in a whorehouse nearby, with his exotic music and even more exotic lifestyle. It was from him that Rushing learned the blues. He hit the West Coast in 1921, making his professional debut there as a pianist and even singing with Jelly Roll Morton accompanying, but returned to Oklahoma in 1926 and worked in his father's café. However, he went back on the road, eventually joining Kansas City group Walter Page's Blue Devils, an influential band featuring many players who would later be in Count Basie's band, including Basie himself.

A spell with Bennie Moten evolved into membership of the Count Basie band when Basie took over after Moten's death in 1935, and Rushing was from the first an important part of Basie's initial success, as can be seen from the number of sides his vocals are featured on between 1936 and the breakup of the band in 1950. It was during this long partnership that Rushing's repertoire was decided for keeps, with songs such as "Evenin'," "Sent For You Yesterday," "Good Morning Blues," "Going To Chicago," and many others quickly attaining the status of classics, to be imitated by generations of blues shouters.

Rushing's career after Basie remained very much based on the swing genre, as his 1955 recordings for Vanguard and his 1957 reunion with Basie at that year's Newport Jazz Festival testify. A contract with Columbia attempted to vary this formula, putting him in both big-band and small-group formats and dealing with standards such as "Russian Lullaby and "My Melancholy Baby," but in concert Rushing stuck with his normal fare. Rushing continued a successful career all over the world until 1971, when the effects of cancer took a deep hold. *The You And Me That Used To Be*, made for RCA in spring 1971, found him singing songs from the 1930s, one of his greatest recorded performances. He died just over a year later.

SEE ALSO: Count Basie, Jelly Roll Morton, Walter Page

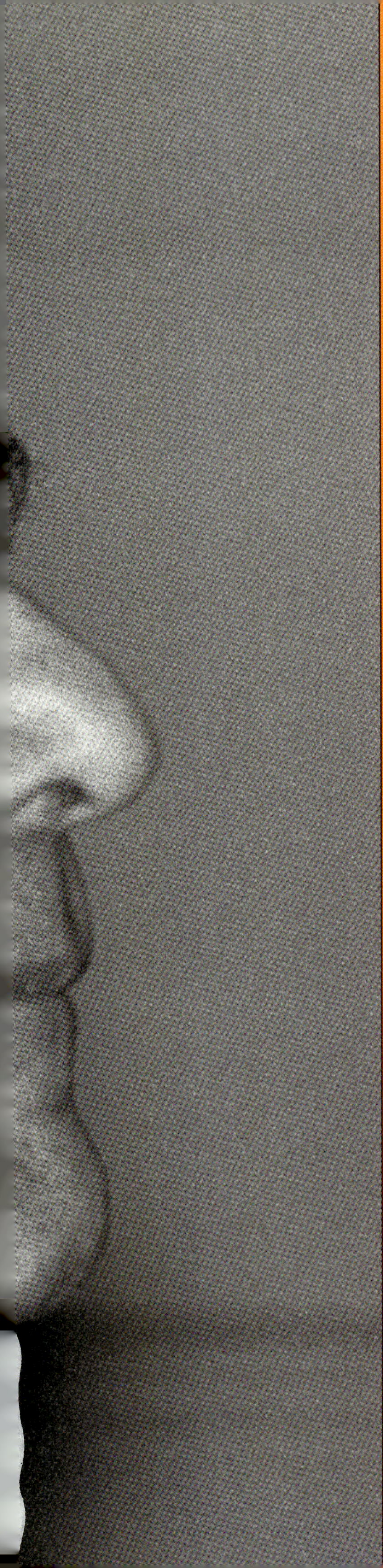

JAZZ COMPOSER: B. 1923

George Russell

Composer/theorist/pianist Russell was born in Cincinnati, Ohio, coming from a family with a strong musical tradition (his father was Professor of Music at Oberlin University). Russell became aware of jazz when he heard Fate Marable's riverboat band in his boyhood, choosing drums as his first instrument, but soon adopted Benny Goodman's band as something to aspire to, especially Jimmy Mundy's arrangements. Russell landed a scholarship to Wilberforce University in 1938, where he met future arranger Ernie Wilkins, but before he could advance his career beyond college, in 1942 he contracted tuberculosis. His stay at the sanitarium was a blessing in disguise for his career, for while he was there he learned the basics of arranging.

On recovering, he joined Benny Carter's band in Chicago around 1943. Hearing some of the early ideas emanating from the bebop pioneers, Russell moved on to New York, where he met Charlie Parker and others and began working on advanced harmony ideas, but his health once again gave way, this time necessitating a 16-month sanitarium stay. Once again Russell used the time advantageously, between 1946 and 1947 forming the basic outline of his original ideas for harmonic organization, later collated and published in 1953 as the Lydian Concept of Tonal Organization.

Russell put some of this system into compositions played during 1947 by Dizzy Gillespie's big band, "Cubana Be" and "Cubana Bop." Russell also contributed ideas to the group around Gil Evans that later produced music for the Miles Davis Nonet of 1948. After composing "A Bird in Igor's Yard" in that same year (recorded by Buddy DeFranco) and "Ezz-thetic", Russell stayed away from jazz engagements in order to properly formulate and expound his music theories. He returned to the scene in the mid-1950s, his ideas slowly gaining credence. This work gave his own music a striking individuality, but further into the mainstream it had a major impact on Miles Davis, Gil Evans, Bill Evans and others. Russell briefly became associated with the so-called Third Stream Movement of the mid- to late 1950s, being a man much concerned with striking a meaningful balance between composition, arrangement, and improvisation. The George Russell Smalltet made recordings (some featuring Bill Evans) which summarized the strengths and weaknesses of his approach. In his early 1960s recordings, the musicians Russell used – Sheila Jordan, Eric Dolphy, Don Ellis, and others – carried such expressive power in their playing as to charge Russell's structures and lines with electrifying vitality. Records such as *Stratusphunk* (Riverside, 1960), *The Outer View* (Riverside, 1962) and *Ezz-thetics* (Riverside, 1961) delivered Russell's theories and he was accorded a position at the forefront of jazz activities. In Europe his ideas and music gained credence; this led to his taking up residence in Scandinavia in 1965, where he stayed, until the close of the decade. In that time he premiered a major work, *Electronic Sonata For Souls Loved By Nature*, which was recorded and released in the US on Flying Dutchman.

Russell returned to the US at the dawn of the 1970s. Since then he has been employed mostly in educational roles, which allow him to compose as he wishes, to tour regularly with bands of his own choosing, and to pace his life according to his health. In the early 1980s he led the Living Time Orchestra, which toured widely and made a string of records, including *The African Game* (Blue Note, 1983). He has also continued his Lydian theories, which he claims to be a life work.

fact file

BORN 1923

MUSICAL SELECTION
Stratusphunk
The Outer View
Ezz-thetics

Master jazz theorist, pianist and composer, George Russell took advantage of the hiatus forced by his ill-health to learn the basics of arranging and sketch outlines for his Lydian Concept of Tonal Organization

SEE ALSO: Benny Goodman, Benny Carter, Charlie Parker, Dizzy Gillespie, Gil Evans, Buddy DeFranco, Bill Evans, Eric Dolphy, Don Ellis, Jan Garbarek

Pee Wee Russell

Pee Wee Russell, letting fly at Nick's, in New York city in 1939

fact file

BORN 1906

DIED 1969

MUSICAL SELECTION
The Spirit of '67

Clarinetist Charles Ellsworth Russell, one of the most individual of players in a highly individualistic musical discipline, was born in Maple Wood, Missouri, but lived in St Louis in early infancy, later in boyhood moving with his family to Muskogee, Oklahoma. He began playing semi-professionally in his teens around the Midwest, later moving with his family back to St Louis and enrolling at the University of Missouri in 1922, although he studied the art of playing on riverboats more than campus courses. Russell was already a popular and spirited player, moving around large areas of the country with different bands, from California, Mexico, and Arizona to Texas and Arkansas and making his recording debut in 1924 with Herbert Berger, whom he had met in Mexico.

The deciding shift in career came with Russell's working with Frankie Trumbauer's band in St Louis in 1925, where he met Bix Beiderbecke for the first time. Russell repeated the experience, teaming up with the two men in a Jean Goldkette band in Indiana, then, as word spread of his abilities, he moved to New York where, in 1927, he joined the top-earning recording jazz band of the day, Red Nichols's Five Pennies. This exposure, plus copious amounts of freelance work with many New York leaders and recording sessions, gave Russell a central position in white jazz making in the New York of the late 1920s and early 1930s, his distorted tone, angular, broken phrasing, and wholly idiosyncratic approach to melody combine to create an instantly recognizable style. As legendary a drinker as was Eddie Condon, Russell fitted the image of the hard-drinking, free-wheeling jazzer to perfection. This image was hardly modified during his two years (1935–37) with Louis Prima on both seaboards and fully confirmed by his long residencies, after returning to New York as a single, at Nick's Bar and with the pool of musicians surrounding Eddie Condon.

Russell made some of his best recordings during the late 1930s and early 1940s with various line-ups revolving around the Condon gang, Wild Bill Davison, and Bud Freeman, plus, later in the 1940s, Muggsy Spanier and Miff Mole. Russell was certainly at ease in these surroundings but never sounded of a piece with the ensembles he played with by choice, his irregular, halting, and often highly dramatic, tortured playing at odds with the usually straight-ahead, happy-go-lucky approach of his colleagues.

Intriguingly, in the 1960s Russell took up abstract painting and, stimulated by the musical changes around him and his work with George Wein's Newport All-Stars, began looking into other musical possibilities, appearing at the 1963 Newport Festival as a guest of Thelonious Monk, recording tunes by Monk and Ornette Coleman and, in 1967, making an album with Oliver Nelson's big-band charts, *The Spirit of '67* (Impulse!), where Nelson and Johnny Mandel rub shoulders as composers with Eubie Blake and Harry Saville. Russell continued to hang out with his old pals in the flesh, his last gig being that of the Inauguration Ball for Richard Nixon in January 1969, with George Wein's All Stars. He died of a liver illness just one month later.

SEE ALSO: Frankie Trumbauer, Bix Beiderbecke, Red Nichols, Eddie Condon, Muggsy Spanier, Thelonious Monk

Pharoah Sanders

fact file

BORN 1940

MUSICAL SELECTION
Pharoah
Tauhid
Karma

All the way from Little Rock, Arkansas, tenor legend Pharoah Sanders is a force to be reckoned with on the contemporary scene

Born Farrell Sanders in Little Rock, Arkansas, saxophonist Sanders learned the piano as a boy with his grandfather, then at high school he started sax and flute lessons, beginning semiprofessional work with R&B bands, where he began to develop his own distinctive tone. Relocating to Oakland, in the San Francisco Bay area, in 1959 and living with relatives, Sanders sat in assiduously all over the Bay area, playing with and learning from a wide range of players, from Ed Kelly and Sonny Simmons to Monk Montgomery and Smiley Winters, his hard sound and urgency often at odds with the hard-bop West Coast sounds many of his contemporaries were accustomed to. By 1962 Sanders felt at odds with Oakland and headed east to New York, at first subsisting on menial work until finding a way into the musical scene, sitting in with Sun Ra and other leaders and moving progressively further toward the out-and-out avant-garde camp. By 1963 he had his own quartet, playing in a style not far removed from that of John Coltrane of the same period, but with considerably less harmonic and rhythmic sophistication; by 1964 he was adopting overblowing and harmonics techniques being pioneered by Albert Ayler, using them to create his own style and committing it to record with his first album, *Pharoah* (ESP-Disk), where on two 25-minute tracks he played in two different styles, one being his Coltrane-inspired modal approach, the other his coruscating, demonic shrieking and honking. This tremendously influential record offered an alternative approach to "free" sax playing from the ideas of Albert Ayler and set the tone for avant-garde music worldwide for the rest of the decade.

During 1965 Sanders began to get invitations to play with John Coltrane's group; before the end of this year he was recording with Coltrane, his work on *Meditations* (Impulse!) marking another important stage in the implementation of revolutionary sax techniques. Sanders toured with Coltrane until his mentor's death in 1967 (also recording and playing occasionally with Don Cherry), then formed his own band and continued to record for Coltrane's last record company, Impulse!, until 1972. Here he experienced considerable success through his deployment of exotic instrumental sounds, drones, and the singing of Leon Thomas, who employed a slow yodeling which proved catchy for concert and record audiences. Sanders gradually lost musical impetus as the 1970s drew on, his music becoming formulaic, but in the 1980s he reinvented himself through turning to the legacy of his youth, reinterpreting Coltrane's compositions, and investigating African High-Life music and other ethnic strains. Although still capable of the occasional blast from hell on his sax, Sanders emerged a more complete musician capable of caressing a ballad or playing the blues. Although no longer anywhere near the pace of the music, Sanders remains a fully committed and creative player and a great favorite on the worldwide festival circuit.

SEE ALSO: Sun Ra, John Coltrane, Don Cherry

John Scofield

fact file

BORN 1951

MUSICAL SELECTION
Still Warm
Flat Out

The artful contemporary electric guitarist, John Scofield, was influenced by all styles of music, including blues and soul

The electric guitarist Scofield was born in Dayton, Ohio, but raised in Wilton, Connecticut. While at high school he became involved in playing guitar in a variety of popular styles, all with deep blues roots, and was an avid listener to the likes of B.B. and Albert King, Ike Turner, and others. He was also a considerable soul music fan; by the time he reached Berklee College in 1970 to study jazz his particular bias was well developed. Scofield stayed at Berklee until late 1973, freelancing around Boston during that time. In November 1974 he landed a place in the group that accompanied Gerry Mulligan and Chet Baker at their Carnegie Hall reunion concert; this led to his joining the Billy Cobham–George Duke group as a replacement for John Abercrombie. Scofield stayed for two years, performing widely and recording regularly. During the rest of the 1970s the guitarist widened his circle of employers, including Charles Mingus, Jay McShann, Ron Carter, Lee Konitz, and Gary Burton, also staying a while in the Dave Liebman group. He ran his own group between other engagements during 1977–78, a quartet featuring pianist Richie Bierach which made a live recording in Europe for Enja.

Scofield began to make heavier waves in the new decade, recording for Arista Novus with a trio featuring Steve Swallow and Adam Nussbaum in which his angular, snaking lines and refreshing approach to guitar sonics and harmony were well evident. All this activity prompted Miles Davis to pull Scofield into his new band in 1982 alongside Mike Stern. The two toured and recorded with Davis until Stern's 1983 departure, after which Scofield took a more central role in the Davis group's musical development. His contribution to Miles can be most readily appreciated on *Star People* (1982) and *Decoy* (1983), where his lean, cutting tone, blues-drenched phraseology and forceful modern harmonic conception spurs the music past fusion cliché into real creativity, both compositional and improvisational. Leaving Davis in 1984, Scofield was rapidly reassessed as a major contemporary guitar stylist, perhaps the most important since the arrival of John McLaughlin, and his albums *Still Warm* (1985) and *Flat Out* (1988), both for Gramavision, confirmed that notion.

Since then Scofield has continued to grow in stature, moving through a quiet, introspective phase in the early 1990s with his quartet featuring Joe Lovano and Charlie Haden, then more lately branching out into updated 1960s-style organ-and-guitar jazz-funk, done as only Scofield's unique imagination could do it, as well as acoustic guitar efforts backed by varying ensembles. John Scofield remains a major presence on the contemporary jazz scene.

SEE ALSO: Gerry Mulligan, Chet Baker, Charles Mingus, Ron Carter, Lee Konitz, Gary Burton, Miles Davis, Mike Stern

Woody Shaw

fact file

BORN 1944

DIED 1989

MUSICAL SELECTION
The Moontrane
Cassandra Night

The oft-neglected trumpet great Woody Shaw's career suffered under the finicky tastes of the jazz mainstream

Trumpeter Shaw was born in Laurinburg, North Carolina, but grew up in Newark, New Jersey. From a musical family (his father sang in a gospel group) Shaw was first attracted to the bugle but moved on to the trumpet when he was 11 years old. Shaw began to take formal lessons and was quickly attracted to the technically demanding styles of Dizzy Gillespie, Bunny Berigan, and, later, Freddie Hubbard. He began to be noticed in early 1963 while with Willie Bobo's band (alongside newcomer Chick Corea). The same year he made his recording debut as part of the summer sessions organized by Eric Dolphy for his album, *Conversations*, later working with Dolphy when the multi-reed man could find work for his own quintet. Shaw came to Europe in 1964, working with many US expatriates before returning to New York and joining Horace Silver's band with Joe Henderson. Shaw's bright sound and explosive soloing, as well as his disciplined section work, won him many admirers and he began appearing on many record dates, mostly for the Blue Note label. An occasional member of the late-1960s Max Roach group, Shaw also worked outside jazz along Broadway and in other theater pits, finally forming a group with Joe Henderson which played good music but performed infrequently. In 1972 Shaw relocated to San Francisco, hooking up with Bobby Hutcherson for a period, and later he played with Art Blakey, among others, but by mid-decade he was determined to lead his own groups. His 1974 album, *The Moontrane* (Muse), gave him a boost, its unclichéd and diverse musical models and structures releasing Shaw and his group to respond with high-level creativity. From that time on he was no longer perceived as an imitator but as an original stylist in his own right.

Shaw co-led a band for most of the rest of the decade with drummer Louis Hayes, by the opening of the 1980s being sole leader of a band that saw some distinguished players come through its ranks, including Larry Willis, Mulgrew Miller, and Steve Turre. Recording for a while for Columbia, Shaw enjoyed little or no commercial success, his combination of modality and post-bop mainstream not hitting the spot with jazz listeners of the period, and the trumpeter returned to the Muse label. Shaw continued to lead his own bands in the 1980s, but health problems, exacerbated by drug usage, meant a somewhat erratic career path, ranging from brilliant double-header albums with Freddie Hubbard in mid-decade to difficulties holding his groups together for any length of time. Shaw was the victim of an appalling accident in early 1989, falling under a New York subway train and dying some time later of his injuries.

SEE ALSO: Dizzy Gillespie, Bunny Berigan, Freddie Hubbard, Chick Corea, Eric Dolphy, Horace Silver, Joe Henderson

Artie Shaw

Born Arthur Arshawsky in New York City, young Artie moved with his family to New Haven, Connecticut, in 1916, attending school there and, in his teens, taking up the saxophone. By 1925 he was appearing with Johnny Cavallaro's band, moving on by 1926 to Cleveland, Ohio, where he spent three years in various musical capacities, including clarinet playing with a number of bands, non-jazz outfits among them. He also discovered twentieth-century classical music, which made a great impact on him.

Shaw arrived in New York late in 1929 and immediately plunged into steady freelance session work, his outstanding tone and technique on all his reed instruments gaining him universal respect. One of his most memorable early 1930s sessions was with Teddy Wilson and Billie Holiday, where his clarinet work perfectly complements Holiday's vocals. By 1935 Shaw's musical ambitions were revealing themselves: he appeared at a concert in the Imperial Theater with a string quartet playing one of his own works. Creating quite an impact, he was given the opportunity to form a swing band with a string section, but the music was ahead of its public; by early 1937 he had disbanded and re-formed with a conventional swing-band line-up. Shaw's adventurous nature continued to declare itself even here, for he hired Billie Holiday as the band's vocalist. Only one number was recorded by her with the band before the racism of a still-segregated America made her position untenable. Still, Shaw was soon to taste success; a July 1938 recording tagged onto the end of a session, "Begin The Beguine," turned into a million-seller for the leader and within months he was the hottest musical act in America, rivaling even Benny Goodman.

A brilliant and original clarinetist and, some feel, an even more complete player than the formidable Goodman, Shaw rode the wave for a year, but by the close of 1939 he was finding success hard to take, abandoning his band and career and flying to Mexico for an extended break. This would set a pattern for Shaw: during the 1940s he would continue to organize successful bands (some with large string sections) and have massive hits ("Frenesi" and "Star Dust," for example); he would also continue to produce first-rate jazz, both with his big band ("Traffic Jam," "Serenade to a Savage") and his Gramercy Five small group. But, though close to being a matinée idol and appearing in films, let alone marrying more than one Hollywood star, Shaw would feel the need to escape from the constrictions of fame. Experiencing the downside of leading a band in a war zone in World War II (he was in the Pacific arena and saw much hardship and suffering), Shaw picked his opportunities sparingly in the postwar years, performing classical-music programs, running a small group, occasionally taking a large band out on the road, and recording a large range of music on into the 1950s.

But his heart was rarely completely committed to such a course, as his 1953 autobiography, *The Trouble With Cinderella*, was at pains to point out. Within two years of its publication Shaw had withdrawn completely from jazz and, for many years, all public musical appearances. In more recent decades he has occasionally appeared, mostly in an all-classical context, leading ensembles and occasionally taking the soloist's role. He continues to write all manner of articles, stories, and sketches and is occasionally interviewed on television, still exhibiting the restless intelligence and brilliance that has marked his entire career.

fact file

BORN 1910

MUSICAL SELECTION
"Begin The Beguine"
"Fremesi"
"Star Dust"

Premier clarinetist and band leader Artie Shaw in 1939, just as fame was striking for the first time

SEE ALSO: Teddy Wilson, Billie Holiday, Benny Goodman

George Shearing

fact file

BORN 1919

MUSICAL SELECTION
"Conception"
"Lullaby of Birdland"

An early shot of pianist and band leader George Shearing

Pianist/leader Shearing was born in London; being blind at birth, Shearing found music very early in life, beginning his piano training when a three-year-old. Mostly self-taught, he received formal lessons while a student at the Linden Lodge School for the Blind (1931–35). Hearing jazz as played by Teddy Wilson, Art Tatum, and Fats Waller on records, Shearing quickly absorbed what he heard and, by the late 1930s, was unquestionably the most able and complete jazz pianist in Britain. Winning awards and public favor all through the war years, Shearing visited the US in 1947 and arranged (with the help of expatriate Leonard Feather) to become a naturalized US citizen by the end of that year. Shearing, up until then still a swing stylist, was greatly impressed by the new bop sounds in New York and became an adept at the style, making forward-looking recordings for a number of companies in the late 1940s, Savoy included. Some of his compositions from this time and the early 1950s have become jazz standards, including "Conception" and "Lullaby of Birdland." In 1949 Shearing hit on a sound – combining the block-chord approach of Milt Buckner and others with unison and octave passages involving piano, guitar, and vibes – which proved immensely popular with audiences all over the world. Sufficiently exotic to be intriguing, but sufficiently restrained to be unthreatening, it served to propel Shearing to the top of the money-earners in jazz all the way through the 1950s. Shearing's innate musicality kept the formula fresh until its second decade, and he also branched out into some non-jazz playing with symphony orchestras, but by the 1960s, when he often combined his quintet with banked strings and anonymous orchestral arrangements, the formula had become stale, although still hugely lucrative.

During the 1980s Shearing dropped the quintet and began appearing with a trio or as a solo, often in tandem with his old friend, the singer Mel Tormé. Records made for Concord at this time reveal still superb technique and subtle harmonic thinking. More recently, Shearing has been appearing with different small groups, including a re-formed old-style quintet, and recording prolifically for the Telarc Jazz label.

SEE ALSO: Teddy Wilson, Art Tatum, Fats Navarro

Wayne Shorter

fact file

BORN 1933

MUSICAL SELECTION
The All-Seeing Eye
Juju
Super Nova
Phantom Navigator

The young night dreamer, Wayne Shorter, in an early 1960s publicity still

Saxophonist/composer Shorter has been a major jazz artist for over three decades, making telling – and occasionally crucial – contributions to the music while being a member of bands such as those of Art Blakey and Miles Davis and, later on, Weather Report, co-led with keyboardist Joe Zawinul. Yet he remains often uncomfortable with the leader's role taking an oblique approach to his own music, preferring to be the *deus ex machina* rather than the figurehead.

Shorter was born in Newark, New Jersey, coming from a family with an interest in music and took up the clarinet in mid-teens before changing to tenor sax while still at high school. At the age of 18 he began music studies at New York University, staying four years and emerging a graduate in 1956. Army service followed, during which Shorter filled in briefly in the Horace Silver Quintet, whose resident saxophonist had gone walkabout. Out of the Army in 1958, Shorter moved to New York, soon playing for a season with Maynard Ferguson's big band; by 1959 he was playing with Art Blakey's Messengers, replacing the departed Benny Golson. During his five-year tour of duty with Blakey Shorter came to maturity as a composer and developed his tenor playing to the point where he could respond with as much passion and fire as Blakey could put out on drums – no mean achievement in itself. In late 1964 Shorter was finally enticed away by Miles Davis, a long-term fan who had originally been tipped off about Shorter by John Coltrane prior to the great tenor man's own departure from the Davis fold, some four years earlier.

Shorter's period with Davis (1964–70) was also a time in which he made consistently stimulating albums for Blue Note under his own name, featuring his own work and a very varied set of line-ups. During this time he traveled from mild avant-gardism on *The All-Seeing Eye* and *Juju* to the electronic jazz-rock experimentalism of *Super Nova*, the last being an album featuring his soprano sax, which was soon to largely supplant his tenor playing. His work with Davis was crucial in the older man's developing drive away from older jazz forms and toward new types of harmonic, rhythmic and sonic hybrids. It was Shorter's oblique, challenging, often almost diffident compositions which gave this Davis group the key to open the doors of its multiple musical personalities. By the time Shorter left Miles *Bitches Brew*, *Super Nova* and Tony Williams's LifeTime had sketched the future. The band he formed with an old friend, Joe Zawinul, was to provide a vital map in tracing the music's path into an electronic future. That band was Weather Report (q.v.).

Shorter's work outside Weather Report in the 1970s and 1980s was low-key, though such albums as *Phantom Navigator* and *Native Dancer* contained many subtle harmonic devices, often allied to Latin rhythms. Shorter continues to be involved in various editions of VSOP and continuing to write his own compositions. Shorter remains a massive contemporary jazz figure.

SEE ALSO: Art Blakey, Miles Davis, Weather Report, Joe Zawinul, John Coltrane, Herbie Hancock

Archie Shepp

Saxophonist/composer/writer Shepp was born in Fort Lauderdale, Florida, but grew up in Philadelphia. Interested in both music and literature from childhood, Shepp learned piano and saxophone while a teenager and often appeared in R&B bands around Philadelphia while pursuing his higher education. Shepp gained a degree in dramatic literature from Goddard College in 1959, then moved to New York. By 1960 he was playing and rehearsing with Cecil Taylor, appearing with the pianist in a production of the play *The Connection.* He was on Taylor's records for Candid and Impulse!, revealing a strangely retrograde tenor-sax approach which combined elements of Ben Webster, "Lockjaw" Davis, and R&B players with advanced, almost primitivistic rhythmic and harmonic thinking.

Shepp co-led a quartet with trumpeter/composer Bill Dixon (they recorded for Savoy in 1962), then co-led the New York Contemporary Five with Don Cherry and John Tchicai. By 1964 Shepp had become an articulate and outspoken advocate of musicians' and blacks' rights in contemporary America and elsewhere. He also became an associate of John Coltrane, appearing with him repeatedly in 1965 after Coltrane had landed him a contract with his own record label, Impulse!. Shepp's work as a leader for Impulse! between 1964 and 1972 remains the body of music on which his reputation is largely based.

As early as 1966 it was evident that, as an avant-gardist, Shepp was a traditionalist, happy to use previous jazz forms from which to fashion his own rough-and-tumble, highly idiosyncratic (and occasionally prolix) performances. Shepp, like Coltrane at this time, thought nothing of improvising at white heat for over 30 minutes at a stretch; he was also happy to let rip with raucous collective improvisations featuring himself with players such as Roswell Rudd, Grachan Moncur III and drummer Beaver Harris. Equally, Shepp could caress an Ellington ballad or recite his own poetry, or at the close of the decade begin to experiment with R&B, funk, and African elements.

All these later ideas were developed further in the 1970s, with the funk side of things reaching a climax in 1974's *Attica Blues* LP, which featured vocals and funk beats as well as arrangements from Cal Massey (as had some earlier Shepp albums). Shepp was also a major presence at the 1969 Pan-African Music Festival in Paris, as the records subsequently released from radio broadcasts attest.

With the end of the Impulse! contract largely came the end of Shepp's more ambitious recording and compositional programs, although his next company, Freedom/Arista, managed a big-band album, *There's A Trumpet In My Soul.* After that, Shepp spent the 1970s and 1980s largely in stylistic retrenchment and teaching, his duet albums with pianist Horace Parlan retracing as far back as nineteenth-century spirituals. He also pursued a parallel career in the theater, succeeding in having at least one play produced in the 1970s. In the 1980s Shepp considerably toned down his more raucous musical elements, also taking up the soprano saxophone assiduously (he had used it briefly in 1969–70). His music was becoming more traditional and predictable. He became caught up in the 1980s and 1990s penchant for retrospection, making a number of small-group records dedicated to past greats such as Bechet and Coltrane. Shepp continues to play worldwide, but his most characteristic contributions to jazz were made some two or more decades ago.

fact file

BORN 1937

MUSICAL SELECTION
Attica Blues
There's A Trumpet In My Soul

The latter-day iconoclast, Archie Shepp, pictured here in Los Angeles in the early 1990s

SEE ALSO: Cecil Taylor, Ben Webster, Eddie "Lockjaw" Davis, Don Cherry, John Coltrane, Roswell Rudd, Sidney Bechet, John Coltrane

Horace Silver

fact file

BORN 1928

MUSICAL SELECTION
Tokyo Blues
Song For My Father

Pianist and band leader Horace Silver in a mid-1950s study of concentration

Pianist/composer Silver was born in Norwalk, Connecticut, and early on was infected with an enthusiasm for music by his father, who played his Cape Verdean music which reflected his own Portuguese descent. Silver took up saxophone when a teenager, but switched to piano within a short time through the influence of his peers and the boogie records he was discovering. This, added to the bop he heard in the guise of Powell and Monk, was to remain at the base of the pianist's mature style. Silver was a Stan Getz discovery: the tenor player heard him in a local Connecticut bar and was sufficiently impressed that he hired Silver along with his bassist and drummer. The pianist managed a year with the mercurial Getz, then settled in New York City, where in 1952–53 he accompanied a long list of top names, including Coleman Hawkins and Lester Young. Toward the end of that period, through the good offices of Lou Donaldson, Silver began recording in a trio with Art Blakey for Blue Note records, his distinctive combination of blues and bop already detectable.

The breakthrough to the big league came with a live Birdland recording in 1954 for the same label featuring Clifford Brown, Lou Donaldson, and Art Blakey. This success led to a cooperative band fronted by himself and Blakey, the Jazz Messengers, featuring Kenny Dorham and Hank Mobley. A split occurred in 1956 whereby Silver took the band with him, Blakey took the name. From that point onwards Silver led his own quintet, playing his own work, right through until the 1970s. In that time he was instrumental in carving out the musical credentials for the hard-bop, sanctified jazz approach which proved so popular then and has undergone such a revival in the 1990s. Talent such as Blue Mitchell, Junior Cook, Joe Henderson, Donald Byrd, Woody Shaw, Art Farmer, both Brecker brothers, and many others moved through the band while such classics as *Tokyo Blues*, *Song For My Father*, *Blowin' The Blues Away*, and *The Cape Verdean Blues* were being created and were DJ favorites. The title track to the album *Song For My Father* eventually had lyrics set to it and was recorded by Steely Dan, while just about every hard-bop group around played "The Preacher," "Doodlin'," and "Opus de Funk" during this time. All through this Silver stayed with Blue Note records, finally parting company with the label in 1981, when he set up his own label. By the 1990s Silver had decided once more that he was better off running the music while others ran the record company, and in recent years he has made fine albums for both Columbia and the revived Impulse! label, still using his patented hard-bop musical formulas.

SEE ALSO: Stan Getz, Coleman Hawkins, Lester Young, Lou Donaldson, Art Blakey, Clifford Brown, Kenny Dorham

Zoot Sims

fact file

BORN 1925

DIED 1985

MUSICAL SELECTION
"Four Brothers"
"Poverty Train"

Zoot Sims, for many the essence of swingin' saxophone, achieved additional popularity through television appearances on The Steve Allen Show

Saxophonist Sims was born in Inglewood, California, into a family of vaudeville artists. He began learning clarinet in boyhood, swapping to saxophone in early adolescence. By 15 Sims was working as a professional musician with touring outfits; by 18 he was working in sax sections in name bands. At 19, in 1944, Sims had sat in Benny Goodman's sax section. That year he started Army service, coming out in 1946 and going back to Goodman, but before long he had joined trombonist Bill Harris in a small group working at Café Society Uptown in New York, his naturally swinging tenor work and light tone suiting Harris's essentially swing style. Through Harris, Sims came to the attention of Woody Herman when he re-formed his band in 1947, creating the Second Herd. At the core of this new band was the three-tenor sax section featuring Sims with Stan Getz, Herbie Steward and baritonist Serge Chaloff. This section was immortalized in Jimmy Giuffre's "Four Brothers," not much more than a glorified riff but one which was subtly arranged to bring out the best sonorities in the four instruments. From that time on Sims was a recognized name who could pull work with any of the top bands in the marketplace right through the 1950s and 1960s. Sims was also a popular sideman in small groups, being featured in Gerry Mulligan's mid-1950s Sextet and, in the late 1950s, striking up a rewarding partnership with saxophonist and arranger Al Cohn. Sims's inventive combination of Lester Young and more robust swing models gave him a free flow of melodic ideas allied to a considerable rhythmic kick; his approach rarely varied during his long and successful career, whatever fast company he might find himself in, and this at times included albums as a soloist in front of string sections and a featured spot on a Laura Nyro song, "Poverty Train," where his obbligato fits perfectly her blues-drenched melody and lyrics. Sims remained in demand as sideman and leader up to his death, from cancer, in 1984.

SEE ALSO: Benny Goodman, Woody Herman, Stan Getz, Serge Chaloff, Jimmy Giuffre, Gerry Mulligan

JAZZ SINGER: B. 1933

Nina Simone

Simone was born Eunice Waymon in Tryon, North Carolina into a large family (eight children) which was introduced to music by the parents, both of whom played music. Simone was making a start on the piano at age four and was singing gospel at the local church not long after that, modeling herself at the time on Marian Anderson. She was trained as a pianist to play all types of music, the classics included, but took a natural liking to jazz and blues in her teens. After leaving school at 17, she moved to Philadelphia and taught piano, then she enrolled at Juilliard School, studying music for two years. After this Simone started out on a career in Pittsburgh which combined her often impressionistic, romantic piano playing with her strong alto voice and a raw emotive edge. This led to a quick record in 1957 for the Bethlehem label and a hit with her intense version of "I Loves You, Porgy."

Simone signed with Columbia Pictures' recording offshoot, Colpix Records, making diverse and satisfying albums which showed her range of material and her utter dedication to expressing whatever lay within her during the time of performance. Colpix albums such as *At Town Hall* (1959) and *At Newport* (1960) gave her audience a considerable taste of her interpretative abilities as well as her imaginative piano accompaniment. By the time of her Carnegie Hall debut in 1963, Simone was drawing on ever-wider sources for her material: her change to the Philips label in the mid-1960s found her recording French songs, protest songs, classical arrangements, and cheesy nightclub ephemera as well as folk-song leftovers and straightforward jazz. For the first time, as well, Kurt Weill crept into her repertoire. Such a disparate lot of working material would have been the end of most singers, but Simone was consistently able to turn dross into gold and to pull all these elements together into an intense and meaningful overall experience, both live and on record. In the later 1960s she went even further, recording Bee Gees and Bob Dylan songs, but her blues roots were never far behind. Simone had a quiet time of it in the 1970s and early 1980s, but a revival of an old 1957 recording of hers, "My Baby Just Cares For Me" (tied to a TV commercial) gave her a number-one hit in the UK and revived her career in Europe. Simone continues to tour internationally and has long gone past the point of being a legendary performer. Although she has never been simply a jazz performer, such strong elements of jazz and blues have been so evident in her music from the start that her audience inevitably see that as her proper image.

fact file

BORN 1933

MUSICAL SELECTION
At Town Hall
At Newport

Nina Simone, a stoic jazz figure to this day, pictured here "live" in the mid-1960s

SEE ALSO: Ella Fitzgerald, Sarah Vaughan

Jimmy Smith

fact file

BORN 1925

MUSICAL SELECTION
Hobo Flats
The Cat
Walk On The Wild Side

Getting his mojo working: Jimmy Smith, Hammond demigod and inventor of the modern jazz organ style

Organist Smith, was born into a musical family in Norristown, Pennsylvania. Smith was something of a prodigy, winning a talent contest at the age of nine. After the Navy he polished his musical education in his early twenties with stints at Hamilton School of Music in 1948, studying string bass, moving to Ornstein School in 1949–50, where piano was his major. By the dawn of the 1950s during his tenure with a quasi-R&B outfit, Don Gardner and His Sonotones, Smith moved to the Hammond organ. In late 1955 he formed his own organ trio and began applying his modernist musical thinking to the instrument.

Smith signed for Blue Note and immediately made an impact. Smith could combine the organ's new-found funkiness with a high level of technical execution. Over the next seven years Smith became a major jazz star, making many trio albums for Blue Note and appearing at all the top clubs and festivals. He was also an incorrigible jammer, welcoming artists on stage and in the studio – people appearing on his albums included Ike Quebec, Lou Donaldson, Stanley Turrentine, Lee Morgan, Jackie McLean, Tina Brooks, and Blue Mitchell, to name a few. But by the early 1960s Smith was looking for wider conquests: these came to be delivered by his new contract with Creed Taylor at Verve records, in late 1962. Albums such as *Hobo Flats, The Cat, Walk On The Wild Side*, and *Peter And The Wolf* gave Smith an audience far beyond the normal jazz one. Smith also continued to turn out first-rate small-group albums such as *Blue Bash, Organ Grinder Swing*, and, in 1969, *The Boss* (featuring George Benson), while his two records with Wes Montgomery were widely hailed as classics of the genre. By the early 1970s Smith was due a rest and the public were moving on from their long infatuation with the Hammond B3 organ. Smith started his own club and took life easy for much of the decade, returning to touring only as the 1980s began. Since then he has maintained his high musical standards but broken little new musical ground.

SEE ALSO: Ike Quebec, Lou Donaldson, Lee Morgan, Jackie McLean, Oliver Nelson, Wes Montgomery, George Benson

Stuff Smith

fact file

BORN 1909

DIED 1967

MUSICAL SELECTION
"I'se A-Muggin'"

Happy music and a happy man: violinist Stuff Smith, pictured here in 1944

Hezekiah Leroy "Stuff" Smith is one of a tiny handful of violinists who have evolved an entirely apposite and authentic jazz style for the violin. While he did not possess the technique of either Joe Venuti or Stephane Grappelli, his playing was hard-swinging, full of passion and made no concessions to conventional notions about how a violin should properly sound.

Smith was born in Portsmouth, Ohio, but raised in Cleveland, learning the basics of the violin from his bandleader father. When Stuff reached an adequate level of proficiency he joined the family band, then in 1926 joined Alphonso Trent's aggregation in Dallas. Smith stayed with Trent for three years, taking time out to play (unhappily, it seems) briefly with Jelly Roll Morton. Returning to Trent for one last season, in 1930 Smith then married and moved to Buffalo, New York, setting up his own band and playing locally until around 1935, when he joined up with Jonah Jones and Cozy Cole and landed a residency at the Onyx Club in 52nd Street. Their hard-swinging little unit became a major clubland attraction. A 1936 single, "I'se A-Muggin'," was a considerable hit in 1936, confirming his popular stature. Smith continued to lead a trio in the 1940s but the changing jazz fashions meant a lower profile for him. During the 1950s he was brought into the recording studios by Norman Granz on a number of occasions, most notably with Dizzy Gillespie in 1956, and these remain possibly his most outstanding recorded statements. Smith became part of the touring circuit during the late 1950s and early 1960s, becoming something of a favorite in Europe. He settled in Copenhagen in 1965 and traveled extensively through Europe, dying while in Munich fulfilling an engagement in 1967.

SEE ALSO: Joe Venuti, Stephane Grapelli, Jelly Roll Morton, Jonah Jones, Cozy Cole, Dizzy Gillespie

Willie Smith

fact file

BORN 1910

DIED 1967

MUSICAL SELECTION
Midnight Session

One of the greatest section leaders ever, Willie Smith, seen here during the mid-1940s

Altoist Smith was one of the great pre-war section leaders and a first-rate swing-style soloist who has rarely been accorded the recognition due to him. He was born in Charleston, South Carolina, and started learning clarinet as a 10-year-old; by the time he was 12 he was appearing at concerts accompanied by his pianist sister. Smith studied at Case Technical College as a teenager, later moving on to Fisk University in Nashville. While there he was noticed by Jimmie Lunceford, who gladly took him on board his new band in 1929 after Smith had finished his chemistry studies. Smith had a long run as leader of Lunceford's saxophone section, staying until 1942 and emerging as a player possessed of a beautiful big tone and beautifully balanced improvisatory phrasing: only Johnny Hodges was his superior in this period in the roles they both fulfilled for their different employers. Smith swapped to Charlie Spivak's band in 1942 as the Lunceford band began to undergo major shifts in musical policy and personnel, but the altoist was soon inducted into the military for the war effort, staying until late in 1944, when he emerged to join Harry James's top-flight band. With James he was given an enlarged role, his lead alto as glorious as ever but his solo space larger than with any other leader he'd been with. Smith also appeared in 1946 at some of the early JATP concerts in Los Angeles.

Smith stayed with James until 1951, when Duke Ellington, reeling from the defection of Johnny Hodges and a small but key section of his band, staged what became known in the music business as "the great James robbery," taking Smith and a number of other skilled personnel from James's band to bolster a desperate situation. Smith, who knew and admired both Hodges and Ellington, blended into the band effortlessly and was featured additionally on a number of Ellington's small-group sessions made in the same period. He also appeared in 1953 on Nat King Cole's highly rated *Midnight Session* album, marking the singer/pianist's return to a small-group jazz format – one of the last times he was to surround himself with top jazz players on record. Smith eventually returned to Harry James in 1954, as Hodges decided to return to the Ellington fold in the same year; both altoists settled in for long stays, Hodges until his death in 1970, Smith until 1963. After that, Smith – by now a long-time resident of California and unwilling to travel – took to the Hollywood studios and enjoyed a lucrative musical trade, with the occasional return to live playing for special projects, until his death, in March 1967, from cancer.

Smith tended to be in the shadow of Hodges and Benny Carter for long stretches of his career, but his music, taken on its own terms, exhibits uniform quality and a high degree of sustained inspiration as well as unstinting professionalism. A model musician, though one who struggled for a number of his Lunceford years with alcohol dependency, Smith was a major swing jazz force and a big influence on altoists of all descriptions, but especially in the R&B arena (Earl Bostic and Tab Smith, for example), in the postwar period.

SEE ALSO: Jimmie Lunceford, Harry James, Duke Ellington, Nat King Cole, Benny Carter

Willie "The Lion" Smith

fact file

BORN 1897

DIED 1973

MUSICAL SELECTION
"Crazy Blues"

Stride piano giant and colourful story-teller Willie "The Lion" Smith

Smith was born with the considerable name of William Henry Berthol Bonaparte Bertholoff, coming from a mixed-race marriage, black and Jewish, but with his father dying when Willie was just four, and his mother's subsequent marriage, the young Bertholoff later took on his stepfather's surname. Smith was born in Goshen, New York, but grew up in Newark, New Jersey, learning piano from his mother, who was a church player. Smith's main musical education was, by his own account, somewhat haphazard, but he was a quick learner and by 1914 he'd made his professional debut. Smith was soon plunged into the hectic and informal music world of Harlem, learning the emergent ragtime strain peculiar to the Eastern Seaboard, which, combined with elements of the gospel piano style and the urge to improvise on dance forms, would soon evolve into what would later be termed "stride." He also learned the essential style accessories for the stride pianist, from his hat and cane (often accompanied by the biggest cigar available) to the braggadocio speech styles and flamboyant keyboard techniques, all of which would also be developed into a personal identifying trait by pianists such as Luckey Roberts, James P. Johnson, and Fats Waller, and which were very evident in the attitude evinced by New Orleans keyboard man Jelly Roll Morton, whom Smith often saw playing in New York prior to World War I.

In late 1916 Smith volunteered for active service in WWI, after a training period being shipped off to the Western Front in summer 1917. Trained in artillery, he proved highly capable and was promoted to the rank of sergeant; he also claimed to have picked up his nickname, "The Lion," there, bestowed on him by an officer inspecting the front, who was told of his expertise with large-bore artillery and his unusual stamina. Smith made sure the nickname stuck. Having left the military in 1919, Smith returned to his old ways in Harlem, fast becoming one of the standouts in the emergent stride school, striking up friendships during the 1920s with the likes of Fats Waller and, especially, Duke Ellington. Smith began appearing on records (he was the accompanist to Mamie Smith on her trend-setting "Crazy Blues" of 1920) and ran his own small group at Harlem's Leroy's as well as, later one, the Onyx Club, Pod's, and, finally, Jerry's.

Smith was a legend among fellow professionals but largely unknown to the general public until he began recording a series of piano solos for Decca in 1935. The striking individualism of these brought him a ready audience on both sides of the Atlantic, which he began to exploit after World War II through regular tours, even reaching North Africa in 1949–50. After that Smith was a regular part of the jazz and entertainment scene, his compelling character and stylized mode of dress making him instantly recognizable. During the 1960s he began to feel the need to document his life and the music he had grown up with: in 1965 he produced (with George Hoefer) his autobiography, *Music On My Mind*, while for RCA in 1969 he recorded *The Memoirs of Willie "The Lion" Smith*, a two-disc LP set of his talking and playing. Smith died in 1973 an honored and fêted man in the US and Europe.

SEE ALSO: James P. Johnson, Jelly Roll Morton, Duke Ellington

Eddie South

The superlatively gifted violinist Eddie South in the early 1940s studied, performed and recorded throughout Europe during his early career

fact file

BORN 1904

DIED 1962

MUSICAL SELECTION
"Old Man Harlem"
"Black Gypsy"

Born in Louisiana, Missouri, but moving to Chicago in boyhood, violinist Eddie South showed extraordinary musical ability at a very young age, taking up violin and beginning formal music studies at the age of 10 with various private teachers. South later attended Chicago Music College and studied with Darnell Howard and with Charlie Elgar, whose band he later joined. In 1924 South joined Jimmy Wade's Syncopators, also spending part of the 1920s with other bands, including that of Erskine Tate. In 1928 South took his own group to Europe, recording in Paris and meeting up with Hungarian gypsy musicians, with whom he played and whose music he appreciated. South also took the opportunity of this tour to take further courses of study in Paris and Budapest.

South, by now a virtuoso on his instrument without parallel in the jazz of the time and a player easily well enough qualified for a career in classical music, found no openings for him into concert music. He also found that his choice of instrument had made it virtually impossible for him to gain adequate public recognition for his skills in the jazz world. Back in the USA in 1931 he formed a fine but short-lived big band, then reconvened a small group with which he played in Chicago and frequently toured the US. Apart from a second European stint in 1937–38, South stuck for the next two decades to playing in clubs with his own group, his unparalleled virtuosity making him a constant draw. He played and recorded with many stars of the period (including Reinhardt and Grappelli in 1937).

South's professionalism and polish made him distinct but his more complete musicianship rarely seemed as valued by the public of the time. By the mid-1940s South was working with the studio band of the radio station WMGM in New York and much of the rest of his musical career was spent outside of what could strictly be called jazz. He appeared on TV shows in the 1950s as well as Chicago radio stations, but by the end of the decade he was in failing health, experiencing a major heart attack in 1960. Able to play only very infrequently, South performed his last work at Chicago's Hotel Du Sable. He died of heart failure in 1962.

SEE ALSO: Django Reinhardt, Stephane Grappelli

Muggsy Spanier

An atmospheric shot of the great classic jazz trumpeter Muggsy Spanier, creator of "The Big 16"

Born Francis Joseph Spanier in Chicago, cornetist/trumpeter Muggsy began playing his preferred instrument in 1919 when just 13, taking his first professional job just two years later, in 1921, with Elmer Schoebel. From the beginning a big fan of men such as Armstrong, Ladnier, and Oliver, Spanier soon became noted for his strong lead playing and spirited improvisations. In 1929 he joined the Ted Lewis band, appearing and recording with him in the US and Europe and also appearing in two films, *Is Everybody Happy?* (1929) and *Here Comes The Band* (1935). Spanier was well on the way to alcoholism by the time he joined Ben Pollack's band in 1936, pursuing his by then old-fashioned style with Pollack's unit for two years until a collapse of health, brought on by his alcohol abuse, impelled him to recuperate in a New Orleans infirmary.

On his release in 1938 he formed the Muggsy Spanier band. Enjoying the best health he'd had for years, Spanier took his band into the RCA studios in 1939 for a series of 16 sides (now known as "The Big 16"), which not only turned out to be his best recorded work but a key event in the turning of the tide in attitudes towards classic jazz styles. Straightforward, hard-driving, with beautifully balanced ensembles and a fine discipline maintained throughout the group, the music from Spanier's men served as a model for countless less talented imitators. On the club circuit, Spanier's group was somewhat ahead of the times; lack of work compelled him to rejoin Ted Lewis in 1940, then he tried co-leading a studio group with Sidney Bechet, the Big Four, before becoming part of Bob Crosby's outfit in late 1940. A 1941 attempt at his own big band was an artistic success but a commercial flop and Spanier was back with Ted Lewis by 1944, planning his next venture. From this time on he worked mostly in the Dixieland small-group format, sometimes as leader, sometimes as featured soloist, often with trombonist Miff Mole. In the mid-1950s he moved to San Francisco, becoming a regular at Club Hangover and playing with Earl Hines (1957–58). Spanier toured Europe with his own band in 1960; he led his own group up to 1964, when heart problems compelled him to retire. He died early in 1967.

fact file

BORN 1906

DIED 1967

MUSICAL SELECTION
"That Da Da Strain"
"Riverboat Shuffle"

SEE ALSO: Ben Pollack, Sidney Bechet, Bob Crosby, Earl Hines

Mike Stern

fact file

BORN 1954

MUSICAL SELECTION
Standards

Accomplished contemporary guitarist Mike Stern began in the blues and rock world of guitar, shifting to jazz at Berklee College where he was taught by, among others, Pat Metheny

Boston-born guitarist Stern was first attracted to rock and blues, growing up with the music of B.B. King, the Beatles, Eric Clapton, and Jimi Hendrix. As his later teens arrived Stern picked up an interest in jazz; by the time he began attending Berklee College in the early 1970s he was ready to expand his listening and playing scope into various jazz forms. This outward urge was encouraged by teachers he had at Berklee such as Mick Goodrick and Pat Metheny. Metheny, impressed by his breadth and proficiency, suggested him as a replacement in the 1976 line-up of Blood, Sweat, & Tears, a band past their commercial peak but still generating a lot of musical interest in the fusion market. Stern's successful move into a professional career with BS&T gave him a national profile and induced Billy Cobham to bring him into his own band in 1978. Once there, he came to the attention of the still convalescing Miles Davis.

When Davis relaunched his public career he soon called upon Stern to add electric muscle to his group. Stern recorded and toured with Davis extensively until 1983, his hard-driven guitar alarming some observers, thrilling others. After leaving Davis Stern worked freelance, appearing with Jaco Pastorius's big-band project as well as running his own groups. He signed with Atlantic Records, his albums becoming a yardstick by which to judge the development of electric and electronic jazz and improvisation throughout the latter 1980s and early 1990s.

Stern continues to record albums reflecting his wide range of musical interests, all cast in his own hard-driven, fleet and resourceful style, his sidemen including many of the people he worked with during his years with Cobham and Davis, such as Al Foster and the Brecker Brothers. Stern continues to tour and record with his own group.

SEE ALSO: Pat Metheny, Miles Davis, Jaco Pastorius

Rex Stewart

fact file

BORN 1907

DIED 1967

MUSICAL SELECTION
"Boy Meets Horn"
"Subtle Slough"

Trumpeter Rex Stewart, an outstanding stylist with many bands and a star with Ellington

Cornetist/trumpeter Stewart, originally from Philadelphia, was raised in Washington, DC, moving there as a seven-year-old; involved in music from his youth, Stewart studied with local brass experts, finally debuting, in 1921, in a musical comedy in Philadelphia. That same year he moved to New York, where he played with various groups (including Elmer Snowden's) before joining Fletcher Henderson in 1926, replacing Louis Armstrong. Stewart never forgot the inadequacy he felt at trying to fill his idol's musical shoes: he lasted just a couple of months before jumping over to the Wilberforce College band run by Fletcher's brother, Horace. Stewart, a forceful player with a huge tone and an outsize ability to swing a note, assiduously developed the half-valving techniques then being explored in New York and other centers by a number of trumpeters, slowly developing a complete range of fascinating, almost speechlike effects to complement his bristling conventional technique. This new musical persona was brought forcefully to bear when Stewart returned to Fletcher Henderson's band in 1928, then extended further with McKinney's Cotton Pickers in 1932. By 1934 he was with Luis Russell.

But Stewart's full musical personality was only revealed by the genius of Duke Ellington. Stewart joined Ellington's band in December 1934, making an immediate impact on a band which already had sitting in its brass section Cootie Williams and Arthur Whetsol. Stewart stayed with Ellington until near the close of World War II, perfecting his incredible half-valving vocabulary as well as his brilliant upper-register work and his unusual gifts for carrying a melody with the minimum of embellishment. He enjoyed personal stardom after his "hit" with Ellington, "Boy Meets Horn," also enjoying a long run as nominal leader of a whole series of brilliant small-group sides conducted by Ellington, including the memorable "Menelik (The Lion of Judah)," "Poor Bubber," and "Subtle Slough" of 1941, the last-named later to be re-cast by Ellington as "Just Squeeze Me."

Stewart left Ellington in 1945 to run his own small groups and freelance, often as a single, touring the world between 1947 and 1951 and even making it to Australia, recording an album with Graeme Bell's band there. During the 1950s Stewart broadened his professional work pattern, taking on jobs such as deejaying as well as studio musician, appearing in 1957 in a Fletcher Henderson Band Reunion as well as a double-header LP with Cootie Williams and Coleman Hawkins, *The Big Challenge*. Two years later he was re-creating the swing era again with Dicky Wells on *Chatter Jazz*. He also appeared in the famous US TV series *The Sound of Jazz*. By the 1960s Stewart had cultivated another artistic discipline, becoming an amusing and insightful essayist about jazz musicians of the 1920s and 1930s, most of them published by *Down Beat* magazine. These essays were later collated into the book *Jazz Masters of the Thirties* (1969). Stewart died in 1967 of a cerebral hemorrhage.

SEE ALSO: Fletcher Henderson, Louis Armstrong, McKinney's Cotton Pickers, Duke Ellington, Fletcher Henderson

Sonny Stitt

Capable of burning at the drop of a hat: Sonny Stitt, tenor and alto master

fact file

BORN 1924

DIED 1982

MUSICAL SELECTION
Stitt Plays Bird
Last Sessions

Stitt, equally capable on tenor or alto sax, was born in Boston, Massachusetts, into a musical family, his father being a college music professor, his brother later a concert pianist. Stitt himself started out on piano as a seven-year-old before moving to clarinet, then finally alto in teenage years. Although he heard Charlie Parker in person and on Jay McShann records at the opening of the 1940s, Stitt always insisted that his style, closely paralleling that of Parker's in harmonic and rhythmic aspects, was evolved independently of Parker. Whatever the truth of this, Stitt joined up with Tiny Bradshaw in 1943, meeting many young players on his travels and eventually joining the Billy Eckstine band in 1945, where he was immediately welcomed by the young beboppers in the ranks.

The following year, Stitt joined Dizzy Gillespie's big band and sextet, also freelancing extensively on record, making tracks with the Bebop Boys and Kenny Clarke, among others. Stitt then became another victim of the decade's curse among young players, heroin, and was largely inactive until 1949, when he reappeared with a co-led septet alongside Gene Ammons. This ended in 1952, when Stitt went out as leader of his own quartets, also occasionally appearing as a solo with whatever local rhythm section was available.

During the 1950s Stitt maintained his career, making many records as a leader and also freelancing assiduously with many companies and many other leaders. He appeared as part of the JATP packages of 1957–59, traveling to Europe with Granz in 1958–59 as well as appearing in the film of the 1958 Newport Jazz Festival, swapping at will between alto and tenor as the occasion took him. Stitt's style by this time had largely been formed and remained unaltered in its basics for the rest of his career, although he adopted the ill-fated Varitone (an electric octave divider developed specifically for brass instruments) in the late 1960s for a few years. Stitt occasionally enjoyed reunions with old friends such as Ammons, Benny Green, Zoot Sims, Ira Coleman, and others, and made some surprisingly felicitous records with organists in the 1950s and 1960s, but during the latter decade he became massively overrecorded, especially by Cadet Records, some of these sessions virtually devoid of interest shown by their leader. Stitt returned to form in the 1970s, especially as part of the 1971–72 package Giants of Jazz with Gillespie, Monk, and Blakey. He continued to appear at all the festivals, giving 100 percent to the end, recording fine late albums for Muse records up to within weeks of his death, in 1982, from cancer.

SEE ALSO: Charlie Parker, Billy Eckstine, Dizzy Gillespie, Kenny Clarke, Gene Ammons, Zoot Sims, Dizzy Gillespie

Billy Strayhorn

fact file

BORN 1915

DIED 1967

MUSICAL SELECTION
The Perfume Suite
Such Sweet Thunder
Suite Thursday

The man Duke Ellington called "Swee'pea" and to whom Ellington's album And His Mother Called Him Bill was dedicated, arranger and composer Billy Strayhorn

Strayhorn, born in Dayton, Ohio, moved to Pittsburgh after a short time in Hillsboro, North Carolina, gaining private music tuition and training as a pianist as well as learning theory, composition and arrangement. In late 1938, just turned 24, he met Duke Ellington in the hope that he might be useful as a lyricist to the bandleader. After playing Ellington "Lush Life" (a song the bandleader never recorded commercially with his orchestra), Strayhorn three months later recorded "Something To Live For" with Ellington, soon after becoming a permanent addition to his staff following a short stint with Mercer Ellington's band. From that time on Strayhorn's career was intimately linked with the great bandleader's: in the early 1940s he contributed a stream of brilliant compositions to the band's book, including its theme tune, "Take the "A" Train," "Johnny Come Lately," Chelsea Bridge," and "Day Dream." He helped Ellington with his major concert projects, writing a good half of 1944's *The Perfume Suite* and arranging many other works.

Strayhorn rarely appeared in public with the band, more likely to take the maestro's role on small-group "Ellllingtonian" sessions for labels the band had no contract with. His albums as a leader are very rare indeed and few of them can match the verve and dynamic range brought to his music by the Ellington band in full cry. Strayhorn's contributions to Ellington's music are notoriously difficult to spot, he being a master of pastiche as well as a distinctive voice when he wanted to be. His work on the late 1950s projects such as *Such Sweet Thunder* (1957), *Suite Thursday* (1959), and *The Nutcracker Suite* (1959) all show an amazing ear for nuance and texture as well as a genuinely individual bent for melody. Ironically, one of Strayhorn's most distinctive and telling collections is on Ellington's tribute album to him, *And His Mother Called Him Bill* (RCA), recorded after his death, from cancer, in 1967. On it, among other highlights, is the heartfelt Johnny Hodges reading of his last completed composition, "Blood Count."

SEE ALSO: Duke Ellington, Johnny Hodges

Sun Ra

The self-dubbed Sun Ra spent many years obfuscating his early history, but it would seem that he was born in Birmingham, Alabama, and that his given names at birth are likely to have been Herman Blount or Herman Lee. He claimed to have had private music tuition in Washington, DC, in the 1920s and to have later learned much from John "Fess" Whatley, a man whose band he joined in the early 1930s. By 1934 he was based in Chicago, occasionally leading a band at the Savoy Ballroom, usually under the name Sonny Blount. In the late 1940s he worked with Fletcher Henderson, playing piano and contributing the occasional arrangement. By the end of the 1940s Blount was running his own trio, appearing as support to visiting jazzmen such as Coleman Hawkins. The trio slowly expanded to a rehearsal band of dedicated musicians willing to work on Ra's progressive ideas.

As the 1950s progressed, the name Sun Ra was adopted and he named his rehearsal band the Myth-Science Arkestra, claiming a raft of esoteric texts and personal philosophies as the rationale for the name and the self-proclaimed mysticism. By 1956 Ra was recording his band's performance of his material, making a virtue of necessity, and releasing the results on his own label, Saturn. Many of the original covers were hand-painted. Ra and his band appeared in the privately financed film *The Cry of Jazz* (1959). Ra contributed the soundtrack. The music he was creating at this time was akin to that of Gillespie, Carisi, Tadd Dameron, Kenton, George Russell, and other more eccentric progressive-jazz composers of the 1940s; the band's occasional lumbering amateurism and self-conscious portentousness being a distinguishing trait which eventually became for many of its listeners part of its attraction. A couple of albums by Ra appeared on other labels, including Savoy and Delmark. By 1961 Ra decided to relocate in New York. A number of his long-term sidemen, such as John Gilmore, Marshall Allen, and Pat Patrick, went with him.

By 1964 he was among the leading avant-gardists in New York and thus extending a considerable influence throughout the music world. His two albums for ESP-Disk, *The Heliocentric Worlds of Sun Ra Vol. 1 & 2* (1964–65), were instrumental in getting people to hear what all the sudden deluge of newsprint was about. He became involved in the ill-fated Jazz Composers' Guild of 1964, while some of his musicians appeared with other members on record (Marshall Allen with Paul Bley, for example). Ra had always believed in the power of spectacle; his stage show at New York's club Slugs, where he was resident throughout the 1960s on a Monday night, became legendary. In the early 1970s, his band members' garb rivaled Funkadelic and Gary Glitter for their outsize pseudo-scientific glad rags and stage antics, and the crowds loved it.

Ra appeared on the festival and concert circuit worldwide in the next two decades. In the early 1970s he also arranged for Impulse! to reissue about a dozen of his old Saturn albums. This made him financially solvent and allowed his band to work full-time. For the rest of his career Ra dabbled in many different musical areas, including amateur electronics. By the mid 1980s Ra was beginning to feel the effects of failing health. Although his performances and recordings maintained their previous standards, they were becoming less frequent. He died in 1993.

fact file

BORN 1914

DIED 1993

MUSICAL SELECTION
The Heliocentric Worlds of Sun Ra, Vol. 1 & 2

Next stop: Jupiter – the ever-challenging and eccentric Sun Ra in rare earthly guise

SEE ALSO: Fletcher Henderson, Coleman Hawkins

John Surman

fact file

BORN 1944

MUSICAL SELECTION
Such Winters of Memory
Brass Projects

One of Europe's finest, multi-instrumentalist John Surman has never enjoyed great success in the US, preferring to remain based in Europe

Multi-instrumentalist Surman was born in Tavistock, Devon, discovering jazz while at school and taking up the saxophone. He participated in jazz workshops organized by Mike Westbrook in the 1958–62 period, graduating eventually to formal studies at the London College of Music in 1962. Rounding off this educational stage with a year at the London University Institute of Education, Surman played in Westbrook's band all through this period and up to 1968, by which time both his and Westbrook's reputations were becoming international. During the rest of the 1960s Surman worked with a great many players, including Mike Gibbs, John McLaughlin (a notable contribution to his album *Extrapolation*), Dave Holland, and John Tchicai, to whose album *Afrodisiaca* (1969) he contributed an amusing virtuoso bass-clarinet performance.

In 1969 he formed a group with Stu Martin and Barre Phillips called the Trio. This unit toured the UK and Europe to unanimous acclaim, its acoustic music being greeted with astonishment for its adventurousness and its accomplishments. The band made a couple of albums, both recently reissued on CD, before disbanding in 1972. By the following year Surman had combined with saxophonists Alan Skidmore and Mike Osborne to form SOS. By this time Surman was regularly incorporating synthesized sound into his work, and this helped develop a range of contexts for the playing of the three saxophonists. Surman kept up a similarly intense level of creativity during the 1970s with a variety of partners, including the Carolyn Carlson Danec Company (1974–79), Stan Tracey (1978) and a re-formed Trio with Albert Mangelsdorff added on trombone (the group was dubbed Mumps). Surman, by now a musician of major stature with a completely evolved improvisatory style of his own, joined up with bassist Miroslav Vitous, playing with him between 1979 and 1982, thus establishing a relationship with Manfred Eicher's ECM label, for whom Vitous was recording. That relationship remains unbroken, leading to an immensely distinguished line of recording projects.

Surman has traveled widely with his music, has regularly collaborated with a varied range of musicians, including Karin Krog and Brass Project leader John Warren, and has made a number of solo performing albums and appearances, but he remains based in Europe, thus robbing him of the large Stateside audience his brilliance undoubtedly deserves. He continues to evolve and create new musical entities today.

SEE ALSO: John McGlaughlin

Art Tatum

fact file

BORN 1910

DIED 1956

MUSICAL SELECTION
"Tiger Rag"

Jazz pianist extraordinaire Art Tatum was a virtual lion of the recorded and live jazz world, as revealed by the prodigious recordings available

For many years regarded as a nonpareil jazz pianist in terms of technique and harmonic imagination, more than four decades after his death Tatum still has few if any peers in these areas. Born in Toledo, Ohio, and from birth suffering from blindness in one eye and severe limitations in the other, Tatum was drawn to music from boyhood, taking up both violin and piano. By the time he was 13 the violin had been jettisoned in favor of piano, with Tatum receiving some formal training while at Toledo School of Music. He mastered the Braille method of reading music as well as using powerful glasses to read ordinary manuscripts, but the majority of his learning was done after leaving school. During the 1920s he learned from records, piano rolls and other means, perfecting the most effortless stride technique ever heard as well as embarking on his lifetime fascination with ever more sophisticated chord substitutions and elaborate rearrangement of popular tunes, overlaid by a richly baroque right-hand technique and a uniquely flexible approach to metric time. Tatum was already known by word of mouth before his arrival in New York in 1932, but his debut there as accompanist to Adelaide Hall, followed by an engagement as a solo at the Onyx club and his first recordings (including the legendary "Tiger Rag" at what was commonly acknowledged by other pianists to be an "impossible" tempo) caused astonishment.

Tatum was quickly and widely acknowledged as so far ahead of the pack (including his original idol, Fats Waller) as to be in a league of his own. By the mid-1930s he was internationally known as a true phenomenon on his instrument, his later piano-guitar-bass trio with Tiny Grimes a model for hundreds of other piano trios to follow in its level of musical interplay.

Tatum's fame breached parochial jazz borders, bringing musicians such as Horowitz and Toscanini to Harlem clubs after Carnegie Hall performances to witness his genius. His innovations, often skirted by pianists overawed by his technique, were most successfully incorporated by sax players, from Coleman Hawkins onward, who were able to transfer Tatum's quicksilver harmonic thinking to their melody instruments.

Tatum's popularity took a tumble in the late 1940s as jazz fashions changed and other, more startling and energetic styles came to the fore. However, in the 1950s he signed to Norman Granz's label and began in 1953 on a project to record one of the most substantial aural legacies in jazz history. All this music, taped over the next three years, is available on CD on the Pablo label: the solo performances alone take up seven CDs, while the group performances range from a trio session with bass and drums to separate dates with Roy Eldridge, Ben Webster, Benny Carter, Lionel Hampton, Buddy DeFranco, and Harry Edison. Tatum was often criticized for being an overwhelming accompanist: here he shows that, with players of commensurate stature, he complements busily but always appositely. With the solo performances, he so thoroughly rethought the standards he played that they became vessels for his own musical messages. Tatum died in 1956.

SEE ALSO: Coleman Hawkins, Roy Eldridge, Ben Webster, Benny Carter, Lionel Hampton, Buddy DeFranco

Cecil Taylor

Pianist/composer Taylor has proved to be one of the most dedicated and uncompromising of the avant-garde musicians who came to the fore in the late 1950s and early 1960s. Born in New York, he grew up on Long Island, where his dancer/musician mother started him off on lessons at the age of six. Taylor progressed to the New York College of Music, moving on in 1952 to the New England Conservatory, where he fell under the influence of Dave Brubeck's music, along with the more frequently quoted influences, Ellington and Powell, while studying theory and piano technique. After an apprenticeship with various small groups run by swing-era stars, Taylor started up his own quartet featuring saxophonist Steve Lacy. This group was the first to play jazz at the Five Spot, a New York bar which in 1956 was just starting to experiment with a music policy. It also recorded an album for the tiny Transition label.

In summer 1957 Taylor's group played a set at the Newport Jazz Festival, but the pianist turned down an offer from Norman Granz (who recorded almost the entire festival that year) to sign him to a long-term record contract. He went instead to United Artists, making at turns awkward and fascinating records there with a range of players, including John Coltrane on one date, while landing virtually no live work at all. Indeed, drummer Sunny Murray recalls that his first meeting with Taylor at the end of the 1950s was in a club where he occasionally sat in with the resident band. All the musicians walked off the stage when Taylor entered, determined that the "weirdo" pianist could not sit in.

During the 1960s as his music became progressively more abstract, prolix, and overtly emotionally overcharged it was easier to identify him as one of the burgeoning New York avant-garde. Taylor worked in musical engagements equally sparsely this decade, but managed a string of classic records. In 1960 he had extended sessions for the Candid label, some featuring Archie Shepp; in 1961 Gil Evans invited him to fill one side of an album called *Into The Hot* (Impulse!); in 1962–63 he made his first trip to Europe and was recorded at the Café Montmartre in Copenhagen; in 1964–66 he recorded two classic dates for Blue Note, *Unit Structures* and *Conquistador!*, both featuring medium-size ensembles. After this, apart from a galvanic performance with the Jazz Composers' Orchestra in 1968, Taylor for many years was only recorded live, solo, or with his Cecil Taylor Unit of the day. This led to a rather distorted view of his musical accomplishments and scope.

During the 1970s, Taylor began working in music education, a career that has subsequently developed into a separate and rewarding vocation. His various positions over the subsequent two decades allowed him to retain his fierce commitment to his own individual style of playing: during the 1970s his performances became legendary, audiences came out bathed in sweat, as did the pianist.

In the late 1970s and early 1980s Taylor played a few more formally structured concerts, including duets with Mary Lou Williams and with Max Roach; he also became widely acknowledged as a formidable musical theorist, a capable writer and an unflinching spokesman for his people and his art. All this combined to elevate his standing during the 1980s and 1990s to that of a musical icon. Taylor still appeals to a small audience, his music's intensity and dimensions daunting to all but the dedicated listener, but the rewards can be well worth the effort.

fact file

BORN 1933

MUSICAL SELECTION
Into The Hot
Unit Structures
Conquistador

Avant-garde by any standard, pianist Cecil Taylor was sometimes rejected by fellow jazz artists early on, and only recognized as a jazz icon later in his career

SEE ALSO: Dave Brubeck, Duke Ellington, Bud Powell, John Coltrane, Archie Shepp, Gil Evans, Mary Lou Williams, Max Roach

Jack Teagarden

fact file

BORN 1905

DIED 1964

MUSICAL SELECTION
Big T's Dixieland Band
Gotham Jazz Scene

Jack Teagarden created an improvisory vocabulary for the trombone which was unparallelled, bringing the instrument on a par with the rest of the brass

Trombonist/leader Teagarden, born in Vernon, Texas, is universally acknowledged as the man who created the first viable improvisatory language for the trombone: prior to him trombonists, from Kid Ory to Miff Mole, had largely played in their short solo passages largely what they played in ensembles, only louder, resorting to smears, whoops, and rasping noises to fill up the space. Like Louis Armstrong before him on trumpet, Teagarden created a style of playing which allowed the trombone to retain its own character yet compete with the other front-line instruments for solo honors.

Teagarden was an early starter on trombone, beginning at 10 years after some early lessons on piano from his mother. Teagarden progressed quickly, playing in bands in his mid-teens and joining legendary pianist Peck Kelley's band in 1921. He played with Kelley and other bands for the next three years before moving on to Kansas City, where he led his own unit for a while. In 1927 he decided to head for New York City, immediately finding work with a number of bands, including Wingy Manone's, and debuting in the recording studio on both trombone and vocals within months of his arrival. By 1928 Teagarden had joined Ben Pollack's band and became a prominently featured personality. Staying with Pollack for five years, Teagarden had a massive impact on all jazz trombonists and jazz-influenced singers, his casual ease of delivery masking a consummate musicality.

He freelanced extensively during his time with Pollack, recording with Eddie Condon, Red Nichols, and others, but in 1933 a substantial raise in pay and the chance of a higher profile led him to sign a five-year contract with Paul Whiteman. The radio, live, and recording exposure which came as a natural part of being in Whiteman's band gave Teagarden a substantial personal following and led him to believe that he could succeed at the helm of his own band. Given the opportunity to do this from 1939 onward, he started brightly enough and made good recordings, but his lack of business sense, his heavy drinking habits, and the absence of a clear goal led to bankruptcy in 1946.

Teagarden joined Louis Armstrong in 1947 as the trumpeter formed his All-Stars, but within a short while he became bored. The trombonist stayed until 1951, by which time his hankering after leading his own groups again, plus his love affair with the bottle, had come to seriously undermine his desire to stay full-time with Armstrong or any other leader. For the rest of his career he led or co-led small units, often appearing live with Bobby Hackett. He also collaborated with Hackett on some memorable LPs for the Capitol label during the 1950s, including *Big T's Dixieland Band* and *Gotham Jazz Scene*. Teagarden spent his last years touring worldwide, but his heavy drinking finally killed him, bringing on a stroke in a New Orleans hotel in the first month of 1964.

SEE ALSO: Kid Ory, Louis Armstrong, Wingy Manone, Ben Pollack, Eddie Condon, Red Nichols, Bobby Hackett

Frank Teschemacher

fact file

BORN 1906

DIED 1932

MUSICAL SELECTION
"Nobody's Sweetheart"

Despite a short life and consequently short career, clarinetist and pianist Frank Teschemacher was a powerful presence on the Chicago scene

Kansas City-born clarinetist and saxophonist Teschemacher grew up in Chicago, starting on piano and other instruments while quite young. A student at Austin High School, young Frank met up with the musicians there who later became identified with the "Austin High School Gang," including Eddie Condon, Bud Freeman, and Jimmy McPartland. He progressed to playing with these musicians between 1922 and 1925 under a variety of band names and leaders. By 1926 his superior instrumental technique, fluent improvisation, and professionalism gave him positions in various dance bands in Chicago; by 1928 he had moved on to New York, where he played and recorded with Red Nichols and Ben Pollack before returning to Chicago at the end of the year.

Teschemacher continued to play in Chicago, running his own bands and playing with most of the top Chicago musicians. His clarinet technique was credited by many in that period as being superior to any other's, including that of the young Benny Goodman, and there is evidence that he had an impact on both Goodman and Pee Wee Russell.

Teschemacher's recordings do little justice to this high contemporary opinion, finding him more often than not stiff and overanxious, apparently unable to overcome his nerves. He had little time to sort this problem out, however, as he was to die young, in a car crash on the way to a band rehearsal. He nevertheless had a large impact on all Chicago white jazz for the next decade or so and still represents a strong influence.

SEE ALSO: Eddie Condon, Bud Freeman, Red Nichols, Ben Pollack, Benny Goodman, Pee Wee Russell

Henry Threadgill

fact file

BORN 1944

MUSICAL SELECTION
You Know The Number
Carry The Day

Chicago multi-instrumentalist and composer Henry Threadgill

Multi-reed player/composer Threadgill was born in Chicago and was attracted to music early on, starting out on drums. By high school he was learning baritone sax and clarinet and by the early 1960s he was good enough to be playing with Chicago explorers such as Joseph Jarman and Muhal Richard Abrams, playing extensively in the Experimental Band in 1962–64. In at the beginning of the AACM, Threadgill was very active within that organization from early on as well as touring the US with gospel singer Jo Jo Morris. In 1967 he started his military stint, returning to Chicago and taking up with a blues band as well as pursuing his former links with the AACM and Abrams in particular. By the opening of the 1970s Threadgill had become a highly distinctive player, competent on a very wide range of instruments beyond the reed and woodwind family, after a period studying at the American Conservatory of Music emerging with a B.Mus.

In 1971 Threadgill formed the trio Reflection with drummer Steve McCall and bassist Fred Hopkins. After some initial experimental playing together, the band dissolved, but it re-formed in 1975 as Air. This group, with its profound grasp of composition, collective play, music history, and showmanship, became one of the supreme latter-day products of the AACM approach to music-making. Air became a much-appreciated avant-garde act which was always welcome at festivals and concerts anywhere in the world. In 1982 drummer McCall left, to be replaced by Pheeroan AkLaff (later on he was similarly replaced by Andrew Cyrille while the group became New Air).

By this time Threadgill was working with a large number of different musicians outside Air and also living in New York, where projects with David Murray and Roscoe Mitchell gave him fresh impetus to pursue new courses. This first manifested itself in his mid-1980s Sextet, which recorded a series of brilliant albums for RCA Novus in the latter half of the decade, playing Threadgill's increasingly abstract but always witty and well-focused compositions with brilliant precision. During the 1990s Threadgill has continued to develop, forming, Very Very Circus, which records for Columbia, bringing increasingly diverse musical stimuli, especially aspects of world music and musical comedy, into his already rich melting pot. Threadgill possesses a brilliant creative mind and is one of the premier composers and reedmen in jazz today, his level of creativity undiminished over more than two decades as a leader, however wayward his muse occasionally seems to the larger public.

SEE ALSO: Joseph Jarman, Muhal Richard Abrams, Roscoe Mitchell

Bobby Timmons

fact file

BORN 1935

DIED 1974

MUSICAL SELECTION
This Here Is Bobby Timmons

Pianist Bobby Timmons, composer of the international favorite "Moanin'" made popular by Art Blakey and The Jazz Messengers

A Philadelphian, born into a churchgoing family (his grandfather, who raised him, was a minister), pianist/composer Timmons began piano and organ studies at the age of six, learning initially from an uncle who held a master's degree in music. As an adolescent he attended Philadelphia Music Academy as a scholarship student, then at around the age of 17 began a serious interest in playing jazz. After two years playing semipro locally in Philadelphia, Timmons moved to New York in 1954, joining the Kenny Dorham band in 1955, with whom he claims he played his first professional gig. Timmons appeared on the Blue Note Dorham classic *At The Café Bohemia* (1956). Stints with Chet Baker (he is featured on *Chet Baker and Crew*, Pacific Jazz 1956) and Sonny Stitt followed, after which Timmons spent eight months (1957–58) in the big band of Maynard Ferguson. Up to this point Timmons had not contributed any compositions to the bands in which he played.

This changed with his induction into the Art Blakey group in summer 1958. On his first album for Blakey he offered the band "Moanin'," a song that has subsequently become a jazz-funk anthem, with words set to its melody, big-band arrangements, and any number of treatments. A Messengers tour of France in winter 1958 spread the appreciation of his talents so that, by the time he joined Cannonball Adderley in the fall of 1959, he was a coming talent. His fame grew exponentially during his year with Adderley, his compositions "This Here" and "Dat Dere" proving equally massive jazz hits for his new group.

Adderley saw to it that Timmons signed with his own label, Riverside, to make albums as a leader, the first being *This Here Is Bobby Timmons* (January 1961). These mostly trio dates reveal a much more complete stylist than his populist tunes and playing with Baker and Adderley would suggest, his assertion that Wynton Kelly was his favorite pianist suddenly evident in his playing. Timmons returned to Blakey in 1960, staying around a year and contributing "So Tired" to the Messengers' book. This title was in some ways prophetic, for by this time Timmons was already struggling with the alcoholism that would eventually lead to his premature death, from cirrhosis of the liver, over a decade later. In that intervening time Timmons would lead his own trios and record regularly, but he was unable to sustain the knack of supplying regular catchy compositional updates on his earlier hits. A musician with wide stylistic horizons, he was trapped by his own early success.

SEE ALSO: Kenny Dorham, Chet Baker, Sonny Stitt, Maynard Ferguson, Art Blakey, Cannonball Adderley

Cal Tjader

fact file

BORN 1925

DIED 1982

MUSICAL SELECTION
La Onda va bien

Cal Tjader cut his percussive teeth with greats Dave Brubeck and George Shearing before venturing out on his own in the 1950s

Callen Radcliffe Tjader Jnr, drummer and vibes player, was born in St Louis and came from a family with a long history in music and the stage, his mother being a pianist and his Swedish father being a vaudeville entertainer. The family moved west while he was at school, settling in the San Francisco area, and Tjader went on to study music and education at San Francisco University. After completing his studies Tjader joined up with Dave Brubeck, first in his Octet of 1948, then his Trio of the following year, playing drums in both groups. Toward the end of his stay with Brubeck Tjader began featuring his vibes playing and an extended array of percussion. This propelled him to form his own group in 1951, but an offer in 1953 from George Shearing saw him take over the vibes role in the pianist's highly successful quintet, helping introduce new Latin tinges to Shearing's arrangements.

By 1954 Tjader felt ready to form a permanent group of his own, based in San Francisco, and one which leaned heavily in the direction of Latin American and Cuban music. During the 1950s he experienced a steady rise in popularity and continued to expand his Latin base, employing percussionists such as Willie Bobo and Mongo Santamaria, as well as pianist Vinve Guaraldi. Tjader continued on occasions to play straight jazz, making a fine album with guest Stan Getz at San Francisco's Blackhawk in 1958, but he was no great improviser, his real talents lying in the direction of arrangement and pastiche.

During the 1960s Tjader moved record labels to Verve, where producer Creed Taylor provided him with the means to score heavy commercial success with his Latinate musical brew, either in a small-group or big-band setting, especially after his major chart success in mid-decade with "Soul Sauce," a reworking of an old Dizzy Gillespie composition. During the rest of the 1960s and early 1970s much of what Tjader recorded and played live bore little relationship to jazz, but it was usually marked by good taste and skillful arrangements. An album from 1979, *La onda va bien*, won a Grammy Award that year with music heavily sourced from roots quite distant from jazz. Tjader continued successfully in music until his death, from a heart attack, in 1982.

SEE ALSO: Dave Brubeck, George Shearing, Vince Guaraldi, Stan Getz, Dizzy Gillespie

Ralph Towner

Acoustic guitar giant Ralph Towner (l.) was raised learning piano and trumpet before switching over to his greatest love

fact file

BORN 1940

MUSICAL SELECTION
Solstice
Lost and Found
Ana

Guitarist/composer Towner was born in Chehalis, Washington. Coming from a musical family, he first studied piano and his father's instrument, the trumpet, while very young. Committed to music from an early age, Towner was playing with local groups, in a variety of genres, in his early teens. He progressed to the University of Oregon, where he studied theory and composition (1958–63), receiving a BA at the end of his course. After this he studied classical guitar at the Vienna Academy of Music under Karl Scheit (1963–64), returning in 1967–68 to complete his tuition.

During the latter half of the 1960s, in addition to his continuing studies, Towner was appearing as a performer in both classical music and jazz, on piano and guitar, with other artists, including Jimmy Garrison and Paul Winter, before appearing on Weather Report's *I Sing The Body Electric* in 1971, performing a 12-string guitar solo, which became influential at the time. That same year Towner, along with other members of the Paul Winter group, broke away and formed the band Oregon, which became a key harbinger of much of the musical cross-pollinations of the next two decades between many cultures. Towner's full range of skills, including composing and his expertise with synthesizers, were all deployed alongside the talents of the other members, Glen Moore, Paul McCandless, and Collin Walcott. The group continued together until Walcott's death in a car crash in 1982, although all members pursued other activities as well. Towner toured with Gary Burton's group in 1974–75 and also began a recording career as a solo star with the label ECM. With ECM he recorded one the definitive ECM-sound albums, *Solstice*, with Jan Garbarek and Eberhard Weber, in 1974. This relationship between artist and company has persevered up to the present day, providing the listener with a very wide range of self-penned music, from solo recitals to group improvisations to multilayered compositions where all the parts are executed by Towner himself. He has played with the re-formed Oregon in the past decade as well as a series of performances and recordings with guitarist John Abercrombie. His two most recent records, *Lost and Found* (1996) and *Ana* (1997), found him, respectively, in quartet and solo guitar contexts.

SEE ALSO: Weather Report, Gary Burton, Jan Garbarek, Eberhard Weber

Lennie Tristano

To know his music is to (possibly) love his music: Lennie Tristano applied a strict discipline to his musical ethos, influencing virtually every musician with whom he came into contact

fact file

BORN 1919

DIED 1978

MUSICAL SELECTION
Lennie Tristano

Pianist/composer/teacher Tristano has always occupied an uneasy place in the history of postwar jazz, his asceticism and his penchant for playing only music that wholly conforms to his own rigorous esthetic a considerable stumbling block to listeners who do not come to his music fully equipped with a working knowledge of what he is trying to achieve. Yet his influence has been deeply felt, largely through other musicians, some of them his own pupils such as Warne Marsh and Lee Konitz, others simply players who have been fascinated by one aspect or other of his ideas. Pianist Bill Evans, for example, falls into this second category.

Tristano, born in Chicago, suffered from poor eyesight from birth and was completely blind before reaching adolescence. He came from a musical family, his mother being an amateur classical pianist and singer. His own musical education started at the age of nine, when he began attending a school for the blind and was formally trained on the piano, and in music theory, and became competent on a number of wind instruments (he led a Dixieland group on clarinet for a while). Tristano moved on from this school in 1938 to the American Conservatory in Chicago, emerging in 1943 with a B.Mus. Immediately after graduating he set himself up as a private teacher, a career which would run parallel with his live work for the rest of his life. By 1946 Tristano had relocated in New York and formed a trio. He began attracting attention with his progressive ideas on harmony and his ready appreciation of what the young beboppers were attempting to do, but after initial contact with Parker and Gillespie, Tristano veered off in his own direction.

He worked with a small coterie of like-minded musicians, many of whom were also his students; by 1948 these included saxophonists Warne Marsh and Lee Konitz. Tristano had an exploratory mind but very firm ideas about how music should be performed. Regarding explicit displays of emotion as distracting, he insisted on the most uninflected execution of melody and rhythm possible, feeling that the music's own beauty and excellence will shine through. Thus he attempted (for Capitol records) spontaneous improvisations and performances based on no given tonal center toward the end of the 1940s, but these works come across as abstractions rather than artifacts with a life of their own.

Tristano's explorations were avidly studied by many of his contemporaries and his champions declared him a misunderstood musical great, but very little of his own music has the ability to reach out to an uncommitted listener in the way that Parker, Monk, and Powell of his generation so unequivocally did. Tristano recorded sparingly, his two albums for Atlantic in the 1950s being the most readily available legacy. On the first of these, *Lennie Tristano* (1955), the pianist records his lament for the recently deceased Charlie Parker, "Requiem." Tristano continued to work up to his death, in Chicago, in 1978.

SEE ALSO: Lee Konitz, Bill Evans, Charlie Parker, Dizzy Gillespie

Frankie Trumbauer

Frankie Trumbauer, a pre-swing era powerhouse matched only by Bix Beiderbecke for his influence on saxophone playing

Saxophonist Trumbauer, born in Carbondale, Illinois, was undoubtedly the leading white saxophonist of the 1920s and probably one of the most important stylists of the pre-swing era, influencing not just other saxophonists, but trumpeters and trombonists well into the following decade. Trumbauer moved to St Louis early in life, spending most of his childhood there. Coming from a musical family, he studied a wide range of instruments in his boyhood and teens, from violin to piano to saxophone. By 1917 he was leading his own local band, playing mainly the C-melody saxophone for which he would later become famous (the C-melody is a legitimate member of the saxophone family, pitched between alto and tenor, but it has rarely found favor in jazz circles since the 1920s). He saw service during World War I, with the Navy, eventually settling after his discharge in Chicago and playing with the Benson Orchestra and Ray Miller. Around the middle of the 1920s Trumbauer struck up a fast friendship with cornetist Bix Beiderbecke, the two of them from then on throughout the rest of the 1920s appearing on many recording sessions together, usually under Trumbauer's name but from time to time using Beiderbecke's. Trumbauer also ran a small group out of St Louis with Bix on cornet between 1925 and 1926. Both joined the Jean Goldkette band that year, later progressing via Adrian Rollini's group to Paul Whiteman's band, Trumbauer joining in 1927, Bix shortly after. During their time with Whiteman Trumbauer, Beiderbecke, and their pals made such timeless jazz sides as "Singin' The Blues," "At The Jazz Band Ball," and "Since My Best Girl Turned Me Down." Although all these sides are justly famous for Beiderbecke's contributions, those of Trumbauer were, at the time, equally telling, for he was a brilliant technician and one of the first saxophonists in jazz to employ a clear, round tone, good intonation, and an approach to melody and phrasing that allowed the notes to properly "sing."

This good musicianship also applied to his work with Whiteman, with whom he stayed until 1934, running a series of recording bands on the side which included many of the most talented white jazz players of the time. By the mid-1930s Trumbauer was involved in a group with Jack and Charlie Teagarden (The Three Ts), then co-led a group with trumpeter Manny Klein, but his style and tone was becoming increasingly passé, his inability to adapt to the new rhythmic emphasis and timbral and pitch distortions leading to a popular eclipse. By the end of his World War II service Trumbauer was no longer a full-time musician, though he kept his hand in, playing with old friends and colleagues up to his death. It is a long-known fact that Trumbauer was a primary influence on Lester Young and thus all reed players influenced in turn by Young, but his influence extended beyond them to pianists (Earl Hines was an admirer) and brass players, all of whom found his characteristic approach to melody paraphrasing an art worth studying.

fact file

BORN 1900

DIED 1956

MUSICAL SELECTION

"Singin' The Blues"
"At The Jazz Band Ball"

SEE ALSO: Bix Beiderbecke, Adrian Rollini, Jack Teagarden, Lester Young, Earl Hines

"Big" Joe Turner

fact file

BORN 1911

DIED 1985

MUSICAL SELECTION
The Boss of The Blues
"Shake, Rattle and Roll"

Rattlin' them pots and pans, blues great "Big" Joe Turner brought a new voice to the jazz scene

Blues shouter "Big" Joe Turner was a man who, during the course of a long career, managed to combine jazz, swing, boogie, jump jazz, rhythm and blues, and, finally, prototype rock 'n' roll through an identifiable style which was both unique and widely influential (his prototype rock and roll was widely imitated by young white bands, including Bill Haley). Yet he was probably at his best in the styles he started out with, either singing with Kansas City-style swing bands or with the type of boogie-woogie provided by his long-term partner, pianist Pete Johnson.

Turner, born in Kansas City, learned to love music through his involvement with the church. As he grew to adolescence he began singing on street corners to earn some money, finally graduating at the age of 14 to the level of cook in Kansas City's then wide-open club scene. The town was, even in the age of prohibition, notorious for its lax moral and commercial attitudes, especially in clubland, and young Turner soon graduated to being a barman and occasional entertainer, gaining the epithet "the singing barman." This led to occasional work with the top KC bands, including Bennie Moten and, later, Count Basie, as well as a linking up with boogie pianist Pete Johnson. The duo were invited by John Hammond to appear at the 1938 Spirituals To Swing Carnegie Hall concert and was one of the major hits of the show, Turner's exhortations to "roll 'em, Pete!" becoming a catchphrase. This appearance was one of the major factors in the subsequent boogie-woogie craze, which eventually went worldwide. Turner and Johnson became resident performers at New York's Café Society and international stars after beginning their recording career in 1938.

With the shift in taste at the outset of the 1940s toward jump music and rhythm and blues, Turner moved into the R&B genre with ease, his big baritone and bluesy wail suiting the music perfectly. More standard parts of his repertoire were forged in that decade, including "Corinna, Corinna" and "Careless Love." As the 1950s dawned Turner continued to evolve his style, combining boogie shuffles with R&B electricity to pave the way for rock 'n' roll. His 1954 hit "Shake, Rattle, and Roll" was neither the first nor the last of such numbers, but had the most profound effect on what was to follow.

An astute man and now well into middle age, Turner stayed with the proto-rock-'n'-roll style until sales fell off, then went back to his first love, teaming up again with Pete Johnson and others, spending the 1960s and 1970s traveling the world in various revivalist Kansas City troupes and combinations. In 1956 he made one of the great classic recordings of the genre, accompanied by Joe Newman and Lawrence and Pete Brown, *The Boss of The Blues* (Atlantic). He latterly appeared in the famed KC filmed documentary, *Last of the Blue Devils*, in 1974. During his last decade he toured widely, making many records for Norman Granz's Pablo label with a large selection of his old KC and swing-time colleagues. Long regarded as an elder statesman of popular music, he died in 1985 of a heart attack.

SEE ALSO: Count Basie, Pete Johnson, John Hammond

Stanley Turrentine

fact file

BORN 1934

MUSICAL SELECTION
Sugar

Stan Turrentine's family was thick with musicians, his own style sitting prettily between jazz, funk and R&B

Saxophonist Turrentine has long been a major figure on the soul-jazz scene, his big tone and easeful style winning many fans during the early 1960s, while his updating of his music and image in subsequent decades has meant that his audience has not simply grown older, but renewed itself in each generation.

Born into a musical Pittsburgh family which included his brother, trumpeter Tommy Turrentine (later to partner him in the Max Roach Quintet), father Thomas (who played sax with Al Cooper's Savoy Sultans), and younger brother Marvin, a drummer, Stanley began on sax at 13, his father being his first tutor. By 1951 he was ready for his first professional job, working with blues man Lowell Fulson, whose band at that time also featured a young Ray Charles on piano and vocals. Moving on in 1953 (after a second period of study) to Tadd Dameron, he then met up with brother Tommy in Earl Bostic's band in 1954. A stint in the Army, late 1956 to 1959, was not lost to music, as he played in the Marine band. On his discharge he joined Max Roach in March 1959, replacing George Coleman, touring Europe, and then leaving in summer 1960 to run his own band.

From the start of his recording career Turrentine alternated between pianists and organists as his ideal accompanists, hiring organist Shirley Scott in the early 1960s and eventually marrying her: they appear together on a great many records during the 1960s, on Prestige, Blue Note, and Impulse!. Turrentine also appeared on a number of Jimmy Smith albums during this period. Turrentine signed to producer Creed Taylor's CTI label in the early 1970s, creating a number of bestselling albums with large musical forces which are best termed "crossover," the most well-known being *Sugar* (1970), and as the 1970s progressed he continued to have success at a number of different labels while maintaining a steady live schedule, often playing earthier and more jazz-inflected music in the flesh than on record.

Turrentine has maintained a remarkable general popularity for a nonvocalist – his was the tenor used to supplement Will Downing's voice in his international hit version of John Coltrane's "A Love Supreme" at the tail end of the 1980s – and he continues to maintain a steady career for himself, as always nestling between jazz and funk or R&B, as he works into his seventh decade with an unflagging commitment to the music.

SEE ALSO: Max Roach, Ray Charles, Tadd Dameron, John Coltrane

McCoy Tyner

Pianist and band leader McCoy Tyner, the most influential piano stylist after Bill Evans

fact file

BORN 1938

MUSICAL SELECTION
The Real McCoy
Time For Tyner
Manhattan Moods

Philadelphia-born pianist/composer Tyner was interested in music from early youth, his mother being a pianist in church, and he studied a wide selection of repertoire as an adolescent pianist before choosing a jazz path in his teenage years. Influenced early on by Monk and Bud Powell, Tyner studied with private tutors, learning theory in addition to technique and further educating himself at Granoff School of Music and at Music City.

By his late teens he had met and begun playing with Philadelphia trumpeter and composer Cal Massey, whose long-term friendship with John Coltrane led to the saxophonist hearing Tyner play on a number of occasions in the 1950s. In 1959, when Coltrane played a week as a solo in the city, both Tyner and Massey supplied musical support. It was agreed at that time that Tyner would join any permanent group Coltrane might form. Coltrane was taking his time, so in the meantime Tyner took up an offer to join the Jazztet, staying into 1960, when he joined what became the classic Coltrane Quartet. While with Coltrane, Tyner became a world-famous pianist and an influential stylist, detectable in younger players from Chick Corea to Joe Bonner and beyond. He is second only to Bill Evans for the influence he has wielded among modern pianists. After leaving Coltrane in late 1965 Tyner formed his own trio and freelanced widely. He also signed a deal with Blue Note, making increasingly ambitious records as the decade wound to an end. In addition to perfectly arranged small-group sessions such as *The Real McCoy* (1967) and *Time For Tyner* (1968), the pianist went on in 1970 to explore a more African-influenced sound. Records like *Extensions* and *Asanti*, both cut in 1970, were not released until 1972 and 1974 respectively, long after Tyner had changed labels to Milestone.

Tyner developed his playing considerably during the 1970s, becoming a much more powerful and dynamic performer, showing that a professed admiration for Art Tatum had percolated down into his dazzling right-hand runs while his unceremonious pounding of the keyboard recalled Powell and, at times, Cecil Taylor, though Tyner always retained a tonal framework for his compositions and improvisations. His star continued to rise in the 1970s and 1980s, with albums such as *Supertrios* and *4x4* (Milestone) garnering awards and much praise, pairing him as they did with the elite of jazz rhythm sections of the time, including Tony Williams and Jack DeJohnette. Tyner's own working groups were a major training ground for many younger players, with saxophonists Sonny Fortune and Azar Lawrence both coming to prominence through him.

During the 1980s and 1990s Tyner has been a constant presence. He has run a steady trio and has often worked with vibraphonist Bobby Hutcherson: they made a duet album together, *Manhattan Moods* (Blue Note) in 1993 and in 1997 toured widely in a co-led quartet. Tyner continues to play commanding and committed piano, compose, and record his own influential and resourceful music.

SEE ALSO: Thelonious Monk, Bud Powell, John Coltrane, Jack DeJohnette, Elvin Jones, Pharoah Sanders

Joe Venuti

fact file

BORN 1903

DIED 1978

MUSICAL SELECTION
"Stringing The Blues"
"Raggin' The Scale"

Violinist and natural charmer Joe Venuti found himself playing alongside such popular performers as Bing Crosby and Jackie Gleason during his career

Born aboard an immigrant ship en route from Italy and raised in Philadelphia, violinist Venuti took up his preferred instrument when a boy and quickly showed a marked aptitude for it. He met and befriended guitarist Eddie Lang in boyhood, the two of them forming a musical partnership which would survive until the guitarist's untimely death in 1933. In 1924 Venuti was working for the Jean Goldkette organization; the following year he moved to New York, where he and Lang began associating and recording with the hot players in the city, including Red Nichols (for whom all the best players recorded at this time) and Benny Goodman.

In 1926 the first of their classic violin-and-guitar duets were made, setting a precedent which would continue for the next three years, producing not only the first artistically mature violin-and-guitar music in jazz, but some of the greatest such duets in the jazz repertoire. In a parallel development, the Lang–Venuti "Blue Four," featuring at different times stars such as Adrian Rollini and the Dorsey Brothers, made a series of intimate small-group records which would presage the efforts of Goodman, Shaw, and others 10 or more years later.

Venuti and Lang were both virtuosos, bringing a workable jazz vocabulary to their instruments, and with Venuti it was an approach which would serve him well long after Lang's death. As a solo leader, Venuti maintained his previous high levels of musicianship and continued to tour widely, making it to Europe in the mid-1930s and for a time running his own big band, but the advent of swing, followed by bop in the 1940s, relegated him to a minor role in these decades, his stylistic constraints and lack of a wider public appeal leaving him at the mercy of jazz fashion. After World War II, in which he served, Venuti drifted out of the jazz picture; although he appeared on radio with jazz fan Bing Crosby in the early 1950s and in 1956 appeared on Jackie Gleason's popular TV show, Venuti was finding it hard to sustain his career. Alcoholism complicated the picture, and by the 1960s Venuti was reduced to playing Las Vegas lounges.

A guest appearance at Dick Gibson's Jazz Party in 1967, in which his natural ebullience charmed the guests and stole the show, put Venuti back on the jazz map, leading to invitations to appear at the following Newport Jazz Festival and resume recording. He also appeared in Europe on package tours for the first time in decades. Venuti's late renaissance lasted up to his death, his professional fortunes restored and his pulling power guaranteed. He kept his very active schedule up until his death, from cancer, in 1978.

SEE ALSO: Eddie Lang, Red Nichols, Benny Goodman, Adrian Rollini, Benny Goodman, Artie Shaw

Sarah Vaughan

Singer Vaughan was born in Newark, New Jersey, into a religiously observant family who attended church regularly. As a young girl she sang in Newark's Mount Zion Baptist Church, later becoming an organist there after starting piano lessons in her adolescence. By late 1942 she was confident enough to try an amateur night at the Apollo in Harlem, winning that particular contest. Recommended by Billy Eckstine to his then employer, Earl Hines, she joined the Hines band in spring 1943 as vocalist and second pianist. Vaughan followed Eckstine when he left to form his own big band in 1944, then debuted on record as a vocalist leader on the last day of that year. Quickly gaining a following for her impeccable musicianship and her uncanny ability to embroider her own versions of common repertoire, Vaughan left Eckstine in 1945 and, apart from a spell with John Kerby, led her own combos. A major contract with Musicraft led to her making many records, in a large number of settings, many of them of a decidedly modern cast. Hailed by many as the first bop vocalist, Vaughan also showed a convincing way with a ballad, but her career took most of the rest of the 1940s to really gather enough momentum for her to become a top nightclub act.

A change of record label to Columbia in 1949 led to a concerted effort to make her appeal to an audience beyond jazz in the manner of Ella Fitzgerald and Lena Horne, but her own musical instincts rarely allowed her to treat her material in such a way as to make it appeal to the widest possible market, massed strings or none. By 1954 she was in need of a career shift, receiving it when she switched to Mercury/EmArcy records. Here, she recorded with mostly jazz settings, including sessions with Clifford Brown and Gil Evans, a group extracted from Count Basie's band and Cannonball Adderley on the EmArcy label, while her Mercury releases gave her more commercial, often very lush backings such as featured on many of the popular vocal albums of the day. This, plus a determined push to get her established on radio and television, probably brought her career to a popular peak at the end of the decade, when she switched to Roulette records. Still sticking to a small-combo jazz format live, Vaughan was an established entertainment-business name into the 1960s, when she decided to take something of a career break.

Returning in 1971 to active performance, Vaughan once again worked with a small group, continuing to develop her vocal style in extraordinary and virtuosic ways: her improvisatory interpretative abilities, her way with a phrase, were unmatched, her rich voice the perfect vehicle for her explorations. She began working and recording with Norman Granz's Pablo label in the 1970s and 1980s, continuing to explore every type of repertoire, including Brazilian and other Latin-derived sources, but her core repertoire and jazz approach remained her most used and most requested in the years up to her death.

fact file

BORN 1924

DIED 1990

MUSICAL SELECTION
With Clifford Brown
Sassy Swings The Tivoli
Crazy and MIxed up

The divine Sarah Vaughan, looking her best in a latter-day "live" appearance

SEE ALSO: Billy Eckstine, Earl Hines, Ella Fitzgerald, Clifford Brown, Gil Evans, Count Basie, Cannonball Adderley

Mal Waldron

fact file

BORN 1926

MUSICAL SELECTION
The Quest
Sweet Love, Bitter

Mal Waldron worked closely with Charles Mingus during the 1950s as part of the latter's Jazz Workshop

Pianist/composer Waldron has led a long creative career distinguished by spells when he has been at the center of significant creative workshops, those of Charles Mingus and Eric Dolphy included. Waldron was born in New York City and began classical piano in his youth, planning a career in that area. Beginning to play jazz on the saxophone, he then began composition studies at Queens College, where he later emerged with a BA in music. On his graduation Waldron dropped professional use of the saxophone, sticking to piano and landing work between 1949 and 1953 with such saxophonists as Big Nick Nicholas and Ike Quebec, recording with Quebec in 1950.

By 1954 Waldron had linked up with Charles Mingus, now based in New York, becoming part of his Jazz Workshop group and appearing with him at successive Newport Jazz Festivals in 1955 and 1956. Waldron's distinctively spare left-hand chord formations and unfussy comping was ideal for Mingus at this time, who was looking for players prepared to step outside the normal bebop formulations. Waldron appeared on a number of Mingus's records from 1955 to 1957, including *At The Café Bohemia* (Debut, 1955) and the famous *Pithecanthropus Erectus* (Atlantic, 1956); at the same time he was also running his own small groups and regularly recording for the Prestige label as something of a house composer/arranger/pianist. Appearing as a sideman with Jackie McLean, Gene Ammons, Ray Draper, Donald Byrd, and others, he also led a series of sessions using his own compositions, including an early Coltrane reading of his ballad, "Soul Eyes." Waldron kept up an impressive pace in the Prestige studios until 1958. Apart from co-leading a short-lived group with Gigi Gryce, in April 1957 Waldron became Billie Holiday's accompanist, touring the US and Europe with her and writing "Left Alone" for her, a song now classed as a jazz standard. Waldron stayed with Holiday until her death in 1959, then began playing with Abbey Lincoln and, in 1960, leading his own groups as well as working regularly in the studios.

In summer 1961 he recorded his classic *The Quest* (Prestige/New Jazz), featuring his own resourceful compositions along with Eric Dolphy and Booker Ervin, then he held down the piano seat in the Eric Dolphy–Booker Little Quintet which played a two-week engagement at the Five Spot in late summer 1961, one evening's worth of which was later released by Prestige/New Jazz.

As the 1960s progressed Waldron began picking up work on film scores, his music for *The Cool World* being played by the Dizzy Gillespie group, while a later score, *Sweet Love, Bitter* (1965) was recorded for Impulse! by Waldron himself and a hand-chosen group. By the late 1960s Waldron was a particular favorite of European audiences, touring there regularly before deciding to settle in Munich in 1967. Waldron has continued to make Europe his base, touring the US and Japan frequently and making many records with visiting US musicians as well as other expatriates, including Archie Shepp and Steve Lacy. Waldron continues to be an intelligent and resourceful composer and pianist, his music always offering more than reruns of familiar post-bop patterns.

SEE ALSO: Charles Mingus, Eric Dolphy, Ike Quebec, Jackie McLean, Gene Ammons, Donald Byrd, Billie Holiday

Dinah Washington

fact file

BORN 1924

DIED 1963

MUSICAL SELECTION
Dinah Jams
Jazz On A Summer's Day

Dinah Washington found fame as a vocalist in both jazz and R&B styles, having a profound influence on other singers even after her death

Dinah Washington (a name given her by her first employer, Lionel Hampton) was one of the few R&B stars of the 1940s who managed to increase her popularity in a number of musical genres, jazz included, to the point that, on her death in 1963, she was an international star in both the pop and jazz worlds. Her vocal style changed very little over the 20 years of her career, with blues at its very core, but her tremendous musical gifts and her fondness for sophisticated musical surroundings made her at ease in any musical setting. Her influence on other female singers was immense, her phrasing and emotionalism being imitated by scores of would-be crossover jazz, blues, and R&B artists, but few had the quality of voice or sheer musicality Washington effortlessly displayed.

Born in Tuscaloosa, Alabama, she moved to Chicago with her family when an infant. By her 11th birthday young Ruth Jones was appearing at St Luke's Baptist Church, both singing and playing the piano, and in 1938 she won an amateur talent contest at the Regal Theater by singing the blues. Her big break came when Lionel Hampton heard her singing while working as the washroom attendant at the Regal Hotel in 1943. He hired her on the spot and gave her the stage name that stuck with her for good. Her two years with Hampton gave her a wide following and she picked up a contract with Apollo Records immediately on leaving Hampton in late 1945.

Her sessions for Apollo set the tone for many of her later records, concentrating on the slower blues but kept company by modern jazzmen of high quality. Joining the young Mercury label in 1948, she settled into a relationship which lasted until 1962, when she joined Roulette Records. Her years at Mercury put her in a vast array of musical situations, backed by trios, jump bands, big bands, orchestras, and more. She also presided over jam sessions with contemporary players such as Clifford Brown, Max Roach, Maynard Ferguson, and others (*Dinah Jams*, 1954) as well as dates with string orchestras. Her hits often crossed over to white audiences, the biggest perhaps coming with "What A Diff'rence a Day Makes" (1959) along with her duets with Brook Benton, but her blues roots were never far away: in the late 1950s she made a complete album of tributes to Bessie Smith, albeit in her own fashion. Her performance of Smith's "Back Water Blues" at the 1958 Newport Jazz Festival in the company of Terry Gibbs and Max Roach was a career highlight, while some of her set from that festival appears in the classic film *Jazz On A Summer's Day*.

Explosive in temperament but a charismatic stage character, Washington led an increasingly hectic and chaotic professional and private life. She was obsessed with her ever-fluctuating weight, and in 1963 she went on a crash diet which weakened her constitution to the point where she died of an overdose of diet pills mixed with alcohol. She was just 39.

SEE ALSO: Lionel Hampton, Clifford Brown, Max Roach, Maynard Ferguson

Fats Waller

Thomas "Fats" Waller was not only one of the greatest stride pianists in jazz and an inspired small-group leader, but was also a world-class tunesmith, an equable and occasionally moving singer, and one of the most charismatic personalities to emerge in the music-entertainment business between the wars.

Waller was born in New York City into a Baptist lay preacher's family; the young Fats played organ at his father's services and was given a thorough training at the keyboard by private teachers. By his mid-teens Fats was working as a professional in the local Harlem theaters. Waller's mother died in 1920 and he moved in with family friends; through them he met James P. Johnson, who gave him a gilt-edged introduction into the world of Harlem stride piano. During the 1920s he began recording for Okeh as an accompanist to blues singers such as Sara Martin and Alberta Hunter; he also played in theaters all over Harlem, accompanying most of the great acts appearing in New York cabaret at the time, including Bessie Smith.

Waller benefited from association with Okeh's Clarence Williams, having some of his early compositions such as "Squeeze Me" published in 1923. By the late 1920s Waller had begun regularly appearing on local radio as a pianist and singer and had also met up with lyricist Andy Razaf. Together they began writing for various New York theater shows, including *Keep Shufflin'* (1928) and *Hot Chocolates* (1929). Songs such as "Honeysuckle Rose," "Ain't Misbehavin'," and "Black and Blue" made their debut in such productions before the end of the decade. During this time Waller began his association with the Victor record company, one which would survive until his death; some of his earliest sides for Victor were with Fats Waller's Buddies. He would record a varied program of music for Victor in the next few years, including solo piano pieces and duets such as "Handful of Keys" and "Smashing Thirds."

Waller began traveling widely in the early 1930s as well as assiduously making radio broadcasts, while playing in a number of different bands. He reached Europe for the first time in 1932, but the most significant musical development was the formation in 1934 of Fats Waller and his Rhythm, a band of varying size (but usually a sextet) most regularly featuring trumpeter Herman Autry, saxophonist Gene Sedric, and guitarist Al Casey. This band became his primary musical vehicle and he made literally hundreds of records for RCA Victor with them. These ranged from the low satire of "Big Chief De Sota" to the slapstick of "The Joint Is Jumpin'" to the melancholy of "My Very Good Friend The Milkman" to the gentle brilliance of "Jitterbug Waltz." During the 1930s Waller rose steadily in public profile to become one of the most well-known entertainers on radio and a constant presence in the charts. He toured constantly, sometimes sticking on the West Coast for a time, or in Chicago, but always using New York as his base. By mid-decade he was hearing the siren call of Hollywood, appearing in films until 1938 when he was one of the stars in *Stormy Weather*, with Lena Horne. Waller died in that winter on the trans-American railway en route to New York from a long engagement in Los Angeles, succumbing to pneumonia after registering symptoms prior to his trip. Waller is remembered for his ready burlesquing wit, but he had higher aspirations: in London in 1938 he recorded his *London Suite*, a set of six "impressions" of parts of the capital, on solo piano. Had he lived, it is conceivable he would have produced considerably more such instrumental compositions.

fact file

BORN 1904

DIED 1943

MUSICAL SELECTION

London Suite

"Honeysuckle Rose"

"Ain't Misbehavin'"

Jitterbug Waltz"

Fats Waller's career as a pianist and composer brought his music to the Broadway stage, to radio and even to film in the 1940s

SEE ALSO: James P. Johnson

Weather Report

fact file

FORMED 1970

DISBANDED 1986

MUSICAL SELECTION
Weather Report
I Sing The Body Electric
Heavy Weather

The fusion supergroup Weather Report featured original members Joe Zawinul, Wayne Shorter, Miroslav Vitous, Alphonse Mouzon and Airto Moreira

The fusion group Weather Report was founded in late 1970, the brainchild of keyboardist Joe Zawinul and saxophonist Wayne Shorter. The original line-up, in addition to the two leaders, was Miroslav Vitous on bass, Alphonse Mouzon on drums, and Airto Moreira on percussion. Their initial albums, the eponymous debut (1971) and the follow-up *I Sing The Body Electric* (1972), gathered the immediate past of jazz, funk, and progressive rock and fused it into an imaginative, often untidy hybrid bristling with ideas and multifaceted personality. The compositional honors were fairly evenly shared at first between Zawinul and Shorter, with Vitous contributing from time to time as the group evolved their ideas on collective music-making and removed themselves almost completely from standard jazz improvisatory practice of everyone sitting back and listening to a string of solos. The point with this group was always the group interaction within any given composition. This interaction changed its character greatly as personnel changes brought in extremely diverse personalities, perhaps the biggest change coming with the arrival of bassist Jaco Pastorius in 1976. A latter-day concentration of the compositions of Zawinul also changed the musical picture considerably.

Weather Report, along with Return to Forever and the Mahavishnu Orchestra, were the heavyweights of the jazz-rock fusion scene; it is their overall contribution, too, which has lasted longest in terms of influence and popularity. By the mid-1970s the group had embraced a number of the principles of rock and funk, including the energy and drive, not to mention the compositional unity, an insistent beat can give a band of determined explorers. Although stuffed with virtuoso improvisers, Weather Report was never merely a vehicle for blowing, at however an exalted level. With its elevation to pop chart success in 1977–78 through the single "Birdland" (a set of lyrics were later supplied by Manhattan Transfer) and the album from which it came, *Heavy Weather*, the band became ever more conscious of the need to keep to tight structures, however wild and imaginative the sounds, synthesized, electric, or plain amplified, were getting.

By the end of the 1980s a Weather Report world tour was a major musical event, reported in music magazines, newspapers, and other media. In 1982 Jaco Pastorius left, replaced by Victor Bailey. By 1986 founder member Shorter felt it was time to explore other musical avenues; his departure led to the break-up of the band, with keyboardist Zawinul quickly forming a short-lived successor, Weather Update, before moving on to other projects. To date the two founders have shown no inclination to resurrect the band.

SEE ALSO: Joe Zawinul, Wayne Shorter, Jaco Pastorius

Chick Webb

fact file

BORN 1909

DIED 1939

MUSICAL SELECTION
"A-Tisket, A-Tasket"

Chick Webb not only supported a big band with his stylish drumming style, he drove any group with which he performed

Drummer Webb was, by common consent, the most dynamic and gifted big-band drummer of the 1930s. Born in Baltimore, Webb suffered from progressive deterioration of the spine which left him a hunchback in adult life. This proved no curb on his ambitions to be a drummer: on his arrival in New York in 1924, just 15, he began working as a professional with various leaders. By 1926 he was, by dint of his talent and his driving personality, leading his own groups in clubs and dance halls around New York, featuring in his bands some of the best New York freelance talent, including a pre-Ellington Johnny Hodges and Bobby Stark, who would stay with him and experience the glory years. By early 1927 Webb had landed a spot at the Savoy Ballroom in Harlem; gradually he built up a powerful and swinging aggregation, short on star soloists but working brilliantly as a team.

Webb's band began recording for Brunswick in 1931; he soon drafted in Edgar Sampson to provide top-flight arrangements and to give his band an individuality to add to its impeccable swing. He also recruited trumpeter Taft Jordan to add a dash of color to his brass section. By the mid-1930s Webb's band was the unchallenged king of the Savoy, often rising to the challenge of visiting bands (the huge room had a number of bandstands) and seeing them off by audience acclamation. Webb, unremittingly competitive, made it a point of honor to swing harder and with more precision, flair, and style than any other group. Yet Webb's band would surely have remained something of a local phenomenon had it not been for his recruiting of the teenaged Ella Fitzgerald in 1934. Her voice, heard on records from 1935 onwards, gave them an unmistakable presence on record and on radio broadcasts, as well as in person. She also gave Webb the opportunity to unashamedly pander to the pop sensibilities of the day without descending to out-and-out crassness: the million-selling "A-Tisket, A-Tasket," after all, was just a rather twee souped-up nursery rhyme rescued by Fitzgerald's grace and verve. By the time that record made Webb and Fitzgerald household names, the drummer was already seriously suffering from tuberculosis of the spine and resorting to the use of stand-in drummers. He died in June 1939. Fitzgerald took over the band, retaining the name in his honor until 1942, when it was disbanded.

SEE ALSO: Johnny Hodges, Ella Fitzgerald

Eberhard Weber

Eberhard Weber created an entirely new sound for jazz during the 1970s with his "electrobass"

fact file

BORN 1940

MUSICAL SELECTION
Solstice
Pendulum
Colours of Chloë

Bassist Weber was instrumental in ushering in a completely new sound to jazz in the 1970s when, with a bass made to his own design and which he dubbed the "electrobass," he began making albums for ECM during the early 1970s such as *Colours of Chloë*, where his winding and hugely sustained melodic bass lines snaked through the sustained arabesques and repeating figures being articulated by piano, keyboards, and wind instruments. Although he has since gone on to all manner of instrumental and musical accomplishments, this remains his most defining contribution to date.

Weber was born in Stuttgart into a musical family, being taught cello by his father from early boyhood. In his mid-teens, around 1956, Weber switched to double bass after taking a marked interest in jazz. After initial adjustment to the larger instrument and the different tuning, he was quickly finding local work in dance bands and jazz groups. His involvement in jazz gradually deepened: in 1963 he met the pianist Wolfgang Dauner at a festival in Germany and they began playing together in various groups, but his main employment was completely removed from jazz. By 1970 Dauner had started a band, Et Cetera, of which Weber became a member and which concentrated on exploring the fusion between rock and jazz. By 1972 Weber, now investigating new adaptations of the double bass including a fifth string and amplification, joined the Dave Pike Set, moving on in 1973 to Volker Kriegel's band, Spectrum, in which he played more heavily rock-oriented music. It was after this that Weber decided to strike out in his own direction, using compositional techniques not far removed from those of minimalists Steve Reich and Phillip Glass; including the crucial ingredients of improvisation and a love of sweeping melody, Weber began his long relationship with the "atmospheric jazz" often associated with the ECM label.

Within this ambit, Weber was extraordinary in his diversification, playing in bands with Ralph Towner (*Solstice*), Gary Burton (*Ring*) and later Jan Garbarek on a number of projects. At the end of the 1970s he also formed the influential group, Colours, whose members included pianist Rainer Brüninghaus and saxophonist Charlie Mariano and who molded jazz with influences from many countries. A member of the occasional group, the United Jazz and Rock Ensemble, up to 1987, Weber has continued to pursue many musical paths. Most recently he has been making a number of stunningly virtuosic and beautiful solo bass albums (with subtle augmentations), of which *Pendulum* (ECM, 1993) could well be the pick. Weber remains a true giant of the European and international jazz scene.

SEE ALSO: Ralph Towner, Gary Burton, Jan Garbarek

Ben Webster

Ben Webster, universally acknowledged as the king of tenor balladry in his lifetime, seen here in Europe during the 1960s

fact file

BORN 1909

DIED 1973

MUSICAL SELECTION
"Just a Settin' and a Rockin'"
"All Too Soon"
"Cottontail"

Saxophonist Ben Webster was thought of in the 1930s as a follower of the Coleman Hawkins school of tenor saxophonists, but his revelatory stint with Duke Ellington (1940–43) not only showed the inadequacy of that summation, but also proved fundamentally influential for a generation of saxophonists who followed, from Gene Ammons to Flip Phillips, when trying to combine the sinuosity of Lester Young's rhythm and melody with Hawkins's weight of tone and emotional impetus.

Webster was born in Kansas City and, as a boy, put in study on the violin and piano with private teachers. His piano playing was helped along by Pete Johnson, who taught him how to play piano blues, but he was attracted to the saxophone playing of Frankie Trumbauer, as evidenced on "Singin' The Blues," and got Budd Johnson to show him the basic fingering on a saxophone. Teaching himself from there on in, Webster joined the family band of Lester Young's father in the latter 1920s, moving on eventually to a string of territory bands, including Jap Allen and Blanche Calloway. A sometime member of the Bennie Moten band from 1931 onward, he arrived in New York with that band in 1932, fixing up work quickly with Benny Carter and Fletcher Henderson. All through the 1930s Webster was a stylish and often vivid section man, soloist, or accompanist (he appeared on Teddy Wilson's dates and some of Wilson's Billie Holiday sessions); he even briefly played with Duke Ellington in mid-decade. But his mature style was not fully revealed until his permanent hiring by Ellington in 1940. As with so many others of his sidemen, Ellington knew exactly how to construct vehicles so as to display the tenor player's optimum abilities. Webster responded with playing, whether relaxed ("Just a Settin' and a Rockin'"), smoochy ("All Too Soon") or supercharged ("Cottontail"), which never fell below the inspired. In turn, Webster inspired the Ellington band and its leader's imagination.

Webster, a man who was charming when sober, often uncontrollable when drunk, left Ellington in 1943 after failing to cope with the long-term demands of a big-band regimen; from then on he concentrated on freelance work, but by the end of the 1940s, out of fashion at the peak of bebop, he was struggling for work and often having to play in R&B settings. Rescued by Norman Granz, he began touring with the JATP troupe in the 1950s and made a remarkable series of classic small-group albums for Granz, plus two artful ballad albums accompanied by strings. By the end of the 1950s Webster was universally acknowledged as the king of the ballad, his sensuous tone and elegant phrasing as unabashedly romantic as a Rachmaninov prelude. Webster quit the US in 1964, his family ties ended with the death of his mother and his taste for second-rate venues quite sated. In Europe he found willing audiences and respectful rhythm sections, and this state of affairs suited him to perfection for the rest of his career. Happy to hang out with visiting US colleagues, play at the best European clubs and festivals, and record virtually at will, Webster finally died in his favorite adopted country, Sweden, in 1973.

SEE ALSO: Coleman Hawkins, Duke Ellington, Gene Ammons, Flip Phillips, Lester Young, Pete Johnson, Budd Johnson

Lee Wiley

fact file

BORN 1915

DIED 1975

MUSICAL SELECTION
Night In Manhattan

Vocalist Lee Wiley took elements of popular theatre styles and combined them with a solid appreciation for jazz to win a loyal fan base

Singer Wiley was one of the first popular female singers to develop a style which combined elements of Broadway with the intimacy of jazz and blues phraseology and expression. Her style, which was already mature by the onset of the 1930s, was a considerable influence on all who followed, as she showed the way ahead to a generation of singers still wondering how to match the might of Bessie Smith with the chutzpah of Sophie Tucker.

Wiley, always a very self-willed person, abandoned her home in Port Gibson, Oklahoma, to become a pianist and professional singer in St Louis at the age of 15. Arriving in New York in 1930, she landed a singing job at the Central Park Casino. This club had a radio link-up and she quickly became popular, appearing in both New York and Chicago. Wiley began an association on radio with Leo Reisman and his orchestra in 1931, then hitched up with Victor Young, with whom she had a major affair. Young arranged for her to have her own radio show and to appear with Paul Whiteman and his orchestra as well as sign a record deal with Jack Kapp at Decca. Some of her performances featured orchestrations by the black classical composer, William Grant Still.

Her voice and her style were becoming highly fashionable in early-1930s America, but a series of illnesses saw the waning of her public star just as the swing era was getting under way. By the end of the decade Wiley had abandoned all attempts to restart a career in popular vocals; in 1939 she met pianist Jess Stacey, with whom she started an affair which led to marriage. This romantic relationship quickly extended to her professional life, for she began appearing with the Eddie Condon crowd known to Stacey, on radio, and at concerts, especially the Town Hall series of the 1940s which did so much to revive interest in Dixieland and associated styles. Her marriage with Stacey was over by the mid-1940s.

Wiley's remarkable honesty of expression and openness continued to win her fiercely loyal fans, and in 1950 they were rewarded with her classic album, *Night In Manhattan* (Columbia), featuring Joe Bushkin and Bobby Hackett. Still, she worked infrequently during the 1950s, despite two further albums, for RCA, one with arrangements by André Previn, the other a mixture of charts by Ralph Burns, Billy Butterfield, and others. The last two decades of her life saw little professional engagement, although a TV documentary, *Something About Lee Wiley*, was made in 1963. Virtually silent in public, she made one final album a couple of years before her death and appeared at the 1972 Newport Jazz Festival, accompanied by Teddy Wilson, but her best and most influential work – surprisingly small in quantity – was made between 1930 and the mid-1950s.

SEE ALSO: Eddie Condon, Teddy Wilson

Clarence Williams

fact file

BORN 1893

DIED 1965

MUSICAL SELECTION
"Royal Garden Blues"
"Brownskin, What You For?"

Clarence Williams, at the piano with singer Sara Martin, was influential in the jazz scene as a businessman trying to build the music's credibility

Williams was not an important instrumentalist or even a particularly gifted songwriter, but he was a key part of the early jazz scene in 1920s New York, where he ran his own management and publishing business and worked as an A&R man and talent scout for Okeh records. Like many of the time, he was not above copyright theft and other underhand tactics to further his own career and bank account, and this side of his activities occasionally led to violent confrontations (for example, with Bessie Smith's husband, Jack Gee, who threatened to punch him out over some typical cutting of legal corners), but on balance his activities did more good than harm in the development of the music.

Williams was born in Plaquemine, Louisiana, his family in the hotel business. He moved to New Orleans at the age of 13 in 1906, then in 1911 went out on the road as a traveling entertainer with a minstrel show, moving around Texas and Louisiana. He was back in New Orleans by 1913, by which time he was also active as a songwriter, often teaming up with others to turn out songs like "Gulf Coast Blues," "Royal Garden Blues," and, in 1916, "Brownskin, What You For?" By this latter date he was running a publishing house in tandem with A.J. Piron and earning considerable royalties. Most of his activities to this date were tangential to jazz's development, but before the end of the decade he had moved to New York (via a short stay in Chicago) and began moving among the best black talent that city currently had to offer.

In New York he married singer Eva Taylor in 1921, and set up a new publishing house and a number of music stores. By late 1922 he was also working for Okeh as a talent scout, some of his first sessions occurring in February 1923 involving Sidney Bechet and a young Bessie Smith. During the course of that year Williams set up a recording group with interchangeable personnel called Clarence Williams's Blue Five. Key members were Bechet and, later, Armstrong, who used the informal formats to expound on their ideas for jazz's future. Later, after Bechet's departure, other players such as Buster Bailey and Coleman Hawkins were used, while Bubber Miley, famous for his work elsewhere for Ellington, became a Blue Five regular for a while after 1927.

In the new decade Williams found the lure of Broadway and associated publishing deals irresistible and his jazz work began tapering off, helped along by the quick eclipse of his preferred jazz styles. In terms of recording, Williams found a new lease of life by moving into the washboard-band field, an area in which he was a front-runner for almost the entire decade. By the 1940s Williams was sufficiently financially secure to virtually retire to live off the money he had made, but he decided to make good on his assets, selling to Decca in 1943 for a princely sum and then contenting himself with a shopfront in Harlem unconnected with music. Williams lived in comfort and contentment but in slowly failing health until 1965, when he was hit by a New York taxi and killed.

SEE ALSO: Sidney Bechet, Coleman Hawkins

Mary Lou Williams

born Mary Elfrieda Scruggs in Atlanta, Georgia, Mary Lou grew up in Pittsburgh, where she made her (amateur) public debut on piano at the age of six. She became immersed in music and determined to make it her profession, playing around Pittsburgh in her early teens as Mary Lou Burley (her stepfather's surname) before leaving town with Seymour and Jeanette, a vaudeville act, at the age of 15 in 1925. That same year she joined a carnival band run by John Williams, whom she subsequently married at the age of 16. The couple moved to Memphis and joined Terrence Holder's band, which subsequently metamorphosed into Andy Kirk's band when the ex-sax player joined in 1929 and took the group over. Williams stuck with Kirk, being promoted in 1930 to first-choice pianist and a key supplier of material and arrangements to the band, especially as they had now begun a recording career. Throughout the 1930s Williams became the fountainhead of the Andy Kirk band's original sound, material, and image as well as supplying fine freelance arrangements to many of the emergent swing bands, Benny Goodman's included. The longevity of much of the Kirk band's material on record is chiefly down to Williams's outstanding work, which includes the song bearing the famous title, "What's Your Story, Morning Glory?"

In 1942 she left the band and formed her own small group, which at one time featured the young drummer Art Blakey. Now settled in New York, she had divorced Williams and married Harold "Shorty" Baker, who in the 1940s became a member of Duke Ellington's band. For Ellington she wrote the superb "Trumpets No End," a reworking of "Blue Skies," in 1946, while also continuing to concentrate on her own material, which at that time included the long-term composition of her *Zodiac Suite*, portions of which were premiered in a Town Hall concert. In the mid-1940s Williams was also an assiduous supporter of the young bop artists, contributing charts to Dizzy Gillespie's band as well as hiring young boppers for her own units. The influence was also felt in reverse, as she updated her own previously swing-based style in the face of the innovations of Monk and Powell. Williams had a quiet time of it in the late 1940s and moved to Europe for the first half of the 1950s; by the time she returned to the US she had begun to be involved in religious activities. One of the highlights of the 1950s for her was the performance of her *Zodiac Suite* at the 1957 Newport Jazz Festival by the Dizzy Gillespie big band: the performance was taped by Norman Granz and subsequently released on LP, and it has recently been reissued on CD. By the end of the 1950s, Williams was a long way off the pace of the music, but had turned her attention to its history and its preservation, giving many concerts, demonstrations, talks, and lectures on the development of a great many jazz styles and mannerisms, especially those which applied to the piano.

She continued to become further immersed in her religious practice, although this did not curtail her activities right into the 1970s. In 1979 she embarked on a brave venture, playing a season of duets with Cecil Taylor, some of which were recorded and released on the Pablo label. Two years before that she had been appointed to the teaching staff of Duke University in North Carolina. She taught and played until shortly before her death, in 1981, by then easily the most honored and decorated female instrumentalist and a major figure in her own right in jazz history.

fact file

BORN 1910

DIED 1981

MUSICAL SELECTION
Zodiac Suite

Mary Lou Williams, among the most decorated and celebrated women in jazz

SEE ALSO: Andy Kirk, Benny Goodman, Art Blakey, Duke Ellington, Dizzy Gillespie, Cecil Taylor

Tony Williams

fact file

BORN 1945

DIED 1997

MUSICAL SELECTION
Life Time
Emergency!
Turn It Over

Taking jazz drumming in a new and highly-influential direction, Tony Williams enjoys a place in jazz history as an innovator and creator

Drummer/bandleader Williams, born in Chicago, became with Elvin Jones the fountainhead of modern jazz drumming as still practiced all over the world today. Williams moved with his family to near Boston when he was in his infancy; born into a musical family he started learning drums at the age of 10, taking private lessons from the great teacher Alan Dawson. Within a year or so he was sitting in with Art Blakey and Max Roach. Just a handful of years later he was freelancing all over Boston, often working with saxophonist Sam Rivers, who gave Williams a grounding in music theory as well as improvisation and drumming. By 1962 word had spread about his talents, provoking Jackie McLean to invite him to play in New York. McLean was bowled over by the 16-year-old's talent and made him a permanent member of his group. McLean told his old friend, Miles Davis, about his discovery. By spring 1963 he was Miles Davis's 17-year-old drummer and shortly after he was recording albums as a leader for Blue Note, as well as appearing freelance on any number of albums for them.

The drummer became a vital part of the new Miles Davis quintet, at one point attempting to get Sam Rivers the job as the trumpeter's saxophonist, but the post finally went to Wayne Shorter. For the next five years Williams constantly astonished the jazz world with his drum accompaniment of Davis's music.

By 1969, the drummer felt ready for new challenges. Immersed in the huge changes gripping the rock world and seeing jazz losing out at the cutting edge, he formed a trio with John McLaughlin and organist Larry Young which became Life Time – in effect, the first great fusion band, before anyone had invented the term. As often happens with originators, their music met with stiff resistance from many sides; after three albums of varying quality Life Time broke up. Williams persevered with the power-trio format with Allan Holdsworth on guitar. However, the band's radical improvisatory nature counted against a major breakthrough into popularity. As Williams began to become increasingly desperate for a fusion quantum leap, he withdrew from public performing, emerging again when he became involved in the Herbie Hancock–Wayne Shorter project for the revival of the old Miles Davis band without Miles. VSOP was born in the late 1970s, with Williams in the drum chair. The band toured repeatedly during the 1970s and 1980s to wildly enthusiastic receptions worldwide, with Freddie Hubbard usually on trumpet.

By the mid-1980s, Williams had formed his own band, again recording for a revitalized Blue Note record company. Williams continued to stoke the fires under his return to acoustic jazz right through the 1990s, his drumming now reaching its full maturity. In early 1997 he entered hospital for what seemed a routine operation. Post-surgery complications set in resulting in a fatal heart attack.

SEE ALSO: Elvin Jones, Art Blakey, Max Roach, Jackie McLean, Miles Davis, Eric Dolphy, John McLaughlin

Teddy Wilson

fact file

BORN 1912

DIED 1986

MUSICAL SELECTION
"Blues in C Sharp Mincr"
"My First Impression of You"

Teddy Wilson was one jazz pianist whose influence was felt subtly, as evinced by Erroll Garner, or Dodo Marmarosa

One of the most urbane and accomplished pianist/leaders to come to prominence in the 1930s, Wilson was born in Austin, Texas, but grew up in Tuskegee, Alabama, where his father was English master and his mother librarian at Tuskegee University. Young Theodore learned violin and piano as a youth, discovering jazz from 78rpm records while he was studying for a music major at Talladega College. After a move to Detroit in 1929 Wilson began playing with local bands, including Speed Webb, for whom he made many arrangements, staying until 1931, when he moved via Toledo to Chicago, initially working with Erskine Tate before also playing with Louis Armstrong and Jimmie Noone.

Wilson's arrival in New York in 1933 to play with Benny Carter presaged the beginning of his larger reputation. Recording with the Chocolate Dandies for John Hammond (who had arranged his transfer from Chicago), Wilson was quickly appreciated among New York musicians for his rock-steady left hand, his harmonic sophistication, and his immaculate right-hand technique. He was also an inspired arranger, whether for small or large groups, and he was the perfect musical coordinator for the decade-long series of recordings undertaken by Brunswick and featuring assorted personnel, often with singer Billie Holiday as the focal point. These recordings, especially those featuring Holiday in tandem with Lester Young, have justly become regarded as some of the crown jewels of jazz recording.

By 1935 Wilson had been inducted into the Benny Goodman setup, initially as part of his Trio (one of the first racially mixed groups of the swing era), recording and touring with the leader as a separate musical unit to his big band. Wilson's superb left hand, providing accurate rhythmic and harmonic support, knitted the group's efforts together while his right-hand counterpoint added the dimension of musical conversation which led Goodman's group to be termed the first exponents of "chamber jazz." In 1936 Lionel Hampton's arrival made it a quartet and one of the most popular small groups in jazz history.

Wilson left in 1939 to form his own short-lived big band. After its demise in 1940 he formed a sextet, which appeared regularly at Café Society in New York and recorded for a number of labels, especially Musicraft, where he led his own sessions and arranged dates featuring Maxine Sullivan and, from 1946 onward, Sarah Vaughan. By the mid-1940s Wilson was reappearing with Goodman's small groups for short stints, but the rest of the decade was largely taken up with teaching and broadcasting work. Wilson spent most of the latter part of his career involved in teaching and in various music capacities for the broadcaster CBS, interspersing this with appearances at major festivals with hand-picked groups (he was with one such band at the 1957 Newport Jazz Festival) or brief reunions with Benny Goodman. The original quartet made a last record together in 1963 and played occasional concerts. Wilson continued to make records up to the time of his death.

SEE ALSO: Louis Armstrong, Jimmie Noone, John Hammond, Billie Holiday, Lester Young, Benny Goodman

Lester Young

Born in Woodville, Mississippi, into a highly musical family (his college-trained father led a family band while his younger brother Lee later became a successful drummer and record producer), saxophonist Lester Young would grow into the first tenor saxophonist to offer a viable musical alternative to the jazz orthodoxy devised in the 1920s by Coleman Hawkins. As one of the major influences on Charlie Parker, let alone the "cool" school in postwar jazz, Young has been one of the most significant players in jazz history.

Young, who moved in infancy with the family to New Orleans, initially chose drums, but also took lessons from his father on violin, trumpet, and alto sax. After playing drums with the family band, at 13 and now based with his family in Minneapolis, he decided to switch to saxophone. Parting ways with the family band in 1929 when they traveled to California, Young stayed around the Midwest, playing with many groups around Minnesota, the Dakotas, Kansas, Oklahoma, and Nebraska and spending brief periods with both "King" Oliver and Walter Page's Blue Devils in the opening years of the 1930s. Young was evolving a style of playing which combined a light, agile tone with driving rhythm and an emphasis on melodic construction.

By 1933–34 Young was based mostly in Kansas City and enjoying his first brief stint in a band organized by Count Basie, but in 1934 he was called to New York to join Fletcher Henderson as a replacement for the departing Coleman Hawkins. This short tenure was a disaster for all concerned and Young left after three months. A stint with Andy Kirk and other jobs as well as an unsuccessful attempt to join Earl Hines in 1936 was the unpromising prelude to Young finally joining Basie permanently in KC in 1936. Within months Basie was "discovered" by John Hammond and his best players, Young included, were making records prior to a move to New York. From that point on Young made an enormous impact and he was a frequent guest in all sorts of musical situations, from Benny Goodman big-band and small-group sessions to the immortal Teddy Wilson–Billie Holiday series where Young, an old friend of Holiday's, gave her instrumental accompaniment which has to be heard to be believed.

Young stayed with Basie, making scores of classic recordings as well as live performances, until December 1940, when he decided to form his own small group. Not gifted as a leader, he failed to secure solid work for the band or a recording contract, finally drafting in his brother Lee as drummer and band organizer, but the group folded in 1943 and Young worked as a sideman for Al Sears and then, once again, Basie in early 1944. At this stage the US Army draft caught up with him: already an habitual drinker and marijuana user, he spent 18 miserable months in training, mostly in detention barracks, his lifestyle and personality utterly at odds with Army life and conventions.

On his release in 1946 he alternated between running his own small groups, usually with much younger players (trumpeter Jesse Drakes acted as the group's road manager), or touring with JATP. Young's recordings up to the beginning of the 1950s show a markedly different approach from that of his days with Basie, but his creative fertility was largely unaffected.

During the course of the 1950s Young's life began to become unraveled as alcoholism began to take its toll, as evidenced in the 1957 television show, *The Stars of Jazz*. Young died in New York in March 1959.

fact file

BORN 1909

DIED 1959

MUSICAL SELECTION
"Lady, Be Cool"
Lester Young Trio
"Taxi War Dance"
"Just You, Just Me"

Lester Young is an undeniable influence on the jazz scene, particularly that of the postwar period, a key player in the development of the 1950s "cool" jazz style

SEE ALSO: Charlie Parker, Coleman Hawkins, "King" Oliver, Frankie Trumbauer, Count Basie, Fletcher Henderson, Andy Kirk, John Hammond, Benny Goodman

Joe Zawinul

fact file

BORN 1932

MUSICAL SELECTION
Zawinul
World Tour

Joe Zawinul, keyboardist, band leader and co-founder of Weather Report, pictured here preparing for a gig

Pianist/keyboardist/leader Zawinul started life in Vienna, beginning his lifelong love affair with music virtually from birth. By early boyhood he was playing the piano accordion and by his seventh year he was studying music at Vienna Conservatory. Dedicated to becoming a classical pianist, Zawinul discovered jazz through the film *Stormy Weather*, starring Lena Horne and Fats Waller, in postwar Vienna. This led him toward jazz and popular dance music and for 10 years he made a living through playing in studio bands and at clubs with top Austrian musicians such as Friedrich Gulda and Hans Koller. In 1959 he arranged emigration to the USA, where after a brief flirtation with Berklee College he joined the Maynard Ferguson band, after which he became part of the wider jazz fraternity, working with a number of top artists, including Dinah Washington from 1959 to 1961.

Leaving Washington for Cannonball Adderley, he stayed with the altoist's band until 1970, learning much about the art of pleasing one's own artistic inclinations and the public at the same time. During his stay with Adderley he supplied his leader with a number of successful tunes, the biggest being the jazz-funk-drenched "Mercy, Mercy, Mercy," which was a chart-topper around the world in 1966. Zawinul toured widely with Adderley, including Japan, and also arranged some of Adderley's big-band efforts for his label, Capitol, before going out as a single in 1970.

His composition "In a Silent Way," which appears on his Atlantic album *Zawinul* (1969), was taken up by Miles Davis, then moving into his electric-jazz phase, and restructured to become a formative piece for the coming fusion revolution. Zawinul was invited to participate in Davis's recordings after the departure of Herbie Hancock, the keyboardist making telling contributions to *Bitches Brew* and *Live-Evil*. Stimulated by what he saw as a viable future for the music, in 1971 Zawinul teamed up with Davis saxophonist Wayne Shorter and founded Weather Report. By the time that group came to its natural end in 1986 Zawinul was one of the best-known names in contemporary music and a man with the means and ambition to run his own groups (Zawinul Syndicate, Weather Update) concentrating on his own compositions and keyboard work. He was also keen to write extended compositions for orchestras and other instrumental combinations. Zawinul still leads a highly active career, his album with the Zawinul Syndicate, called *World Tour* (Escapade, 1998), taken from music played on his band's 1997 world tour.

SEE ALSO: Maynard Ferguson, Dinah Washington, Cannonball Adderley, Miles Davis, Herbie Hancock, Wayne Shorter

John Zorn

fact file

BORN 1953

MUSICAL SELECTION
The Big Gundown
Masada
Cobra

John Zorn, altoist and avant-garde pop culture theorist par excellence

Avant-garde saxophonist/composer/leader Zorn, born in New York, has pursued a creative course in music which is only partially covered by his jazz activities, but has brought crucial new life to a new music scene in New York which was beginning to become somewhat threadbare in the 1980s as neo-bop classicism threatened to take over once more.

Zorn started his musical education as a child, beginning on piano, then taking on flute and guitar in late boyhood. Attracted to contemporary classical music in early adolescence, he became interested especially in the theories of composer/theorist John Cage, from whom he derived many ideas about chance music and pre-arranged (or pre-disrupted) concertized "occurrences." He also became a major fan of the quality end of the film music genre. Studying at college in St Louis, Zorn for the first time began making connections between classical and jazz avant-garde ideas, especially those of the Chicago-based AACM players such as Roscoe Mitchell and Anthony Braxton.

On his return to New York in the late 1970s Zorn, now principally on alto sax, began assembling like-minded musicians to play a very wide range of music, including rock, scored compositions and wild free blow-outs with an unusually wide instrumentation, including electronic instruments. Zorn by the early 1980s was also becoming increasingly interested in musical and artistic creeds emanating from Far Eastern disciplines. By the middle of the decade Zorn's ideas had begun to coalesce in a series of scintillating performances and albums, some under his own name (*The Big Gundown*, 1986, where Zorn reworked the film music of Ennio Morricone) and some under the group Naked City (*Spillane*, Nonesuch 1987). Of the moving cast associated with this band, guitarist Bill Frisell was a regular participant. By the end of the decade Zorn paid the first of a number of recorded tributes to Ornette Coleman on *Spy vs. Spy* (Nonesuch, 1989), where Coleman's compositions were viewed through the perspective of thrash metal, played at incredible speed and with maximum violence by two saxophonists (Zorn and Tim Berne), bassist Mark Dresser, and two drummers, Joey Baron and Michael Vatcher.

In the 1990s Zorn has continued to widen and diversify his efforts, getting involved in tributes to an incredible range of subjects, from Grand Guignol to Japanese bondage photography (all on his own label, Avant). He has also successfully led a trio, News For Lulu (a tribute to the silent-film star Louise Brooks), with trombonist George Lewis and guitarist Bill Frisell, which in 1990–92 made two albums for Art records and toured Europe. His most ambitious project is the 15-volume series, *Masada*, on Japanese DIW records, which entwines mystical and philosophical Jewish tradition with the musical legacy of the original Ornette Coleman Quartet. In this he is aided by trumpeter Dave Douglas, bassist Greg Cohen and drummer Joey Baron. Zorn has also recently been making off-center organ-sax records with Big John Patton. His career continues apace.

SEE ALSO: Ornette Coleman, Bill Frisell, Big John Patton

Index

Abrams, Muhal Richard 8
Adderley, Julian "Cannonball" 9
Akiyoshi, Toshiko 10
Allen, Henry "Red" 11
Ayler, Albert 13
Ammons, Gene 14
Anderson, Ray, 15
Armstrong, Louis 17
Art Ensemble of Chicago 18
Bailey, Mildred 19
Baker, Chet 21
Barber, Chris 22
Barnet, Charlie 23
Basie, "Count" 25
Beiderbecke, Bix 26
Benson, George 27
Berigan, Bunny 30
Berry, Leon "Chu" 31
Blakey, Art 32
Blanton, Jimmy 33
Bley, Carla 34
Bley, Paul 35
Bolden, Buddy 36
Bowie, Lester 37
Braff, Ruby 38
Braxton, Anthony 39
Brecker, Michael 40
Brookmeyer, Bob 41
Brown, Clifford 42
Brown, Marion 43
Brown, Ray 44
Brubeck, Dave 47
Burrell, Kenny 45
Burton, Gary 48
Byard, Jaki 49
Byas, Don 50
Byrd, Donald, 51
Calloway, Cab 52
Carter, Benny 55
Carter, Betty 53
Carter, James 56
Catherine, Philip 57
Catlett, Big Sid 58
Chaloff, Serge 59
Charles, Ray 60
Cherry, Don 61
Christian, Charlie 62
Christy, June 63
Clarke, Kenny 64
Clarke, Stanley 65
Clayton, Buck 66
Cobb, Arnett 67
Cole, Cozy 68
Cole, Nat King 69
Coleman, Ornette 71
Coleman, Steve 72
Coltrane, John 75
Condon, Eddie 73
Connor, Chris 76
Corea, Chick 77
Coryell, Larry 78
Crispell, Marilyn 79
Criss, Sonny 80
Crosby, Bob 81
Dameron, Tadd 82
Davis, Eddie "Lockjaw" 83
Davis, Miles 85
Davison, Wild Bill 86
DeFranco, Buddy 87
DeJohnette, Jack 88
Desmond, Paul 89
Dickenson, Vic 90
Dodds, Johnny 91
Dolphy, Eric 92
Donaldson, Lou 93
Dorham, Kenny 94
Dorsey, Tommy 97
Eckstine, Billy 95
Edison, Harry "Sweets" 98
Eldridge, Roy 99
Ellington, "Duke" 101
Ellis, Don 102
Ervin, Booker 103
Eubanks, Kevin 104
Evans, Bill 107
Evans, Gil 105
Farmer, Art 108
Ferguson, Maynard 109
Fitzgerald, Ella 111
Foster, George "Pops" 112
Freeman, Bud 113
Freeman, Chico 114
Frisell, Bill 115
Fuller, Curtis 116
Gaillard, Slim 117
Garbarek, Jan 118
Garner, Erroll 119
Getz, Stan 121
Gillespie, Dizzy 125
Giuffre, Jimmy 122
Gonsalves, Paul 123
Goodman, Benny 129
Gordon, Dexter 126
Grace, Teddy 127
Grappelli, Stephane 130
Graves, Milford 131
Gray, Wardell 132
Green, Grant 133
Griffin, Johnny 134
Guaraldi, Vince 135
Hackett, Bobby 136
Haden, Charlie 137
Hall, Edmond 138
Hall, Jim 139
Hamilton, Chico 140
Hamilton, Scott 141
Hampton, Lionel 143
Hancock, Herbie 144
Handy, John 145
Harrell, Tom 146
Harris, Bill 147
Harris, Eddie 148
Harrison, Jimmy 149
Hawes, Hampton 150
Hawkins, Coleman 151
Haynes, Roy 152
Henderson, Fletcher 155
Henderson, Joe 153
Hendricks, Jon 156
Herman, Woody 159
Higginbotham, J.C. 157
Hill, Andrew 160
Hines, Earl 161
Hodges, Johnny 162
Holiday, Billie 165
Holland, Dave 163
Hubbard, Freddie 166
Hutcherson, Bobby 167
Ibrahim, Abdullah 168
Jackson, Milt 169
Jacquet, Illinois 171
Jamal, Ahmad 172
James, Harry 170
Jarman, Joseph 173
Jarrett, Keith 175
Jefferson, Eddie 176
Johnson, Budd 177
Johnson, Bunk 178
Johnson, J.J. 179
Johnson, James P. 180
Jones, Elvin 181
Jones, Jo 182
Jones, Quincy 183
Jones, Thad 184
Jordan, Louis 187
Kenton, Stan 191
Keppard, Freddie 185
Kirk, Rahsaan Roland 188
Knepper, Jimmy 189
Konitz, Lee 192
Krupa, Gene 195
Lacy, Steve 193
Ladnier, Tommy 196
LaFaro, Scott 197
Lake, Oliver 198
Land, Harold 199
Lang, Eddie 200
Lateef, Yusef 201
Lewis, George 202
Lewis, John 203
Lewis, Meade "Lux" 204
Lewis, Ramsey 205
Lincoln, Abbey 206
Little, Booker 207
Lloyd, Charles 208
Lovano, Joe 209
Lunceford, Jimmie 210
Mann, Herbie 211
Manne, Shelly 212
Manone, Wingy 213
Marmarosa, Dodo 214
Marsalis, Branford 215
Marsalis, Wynton 217
McCann, Les 218
McDuff, Jack 219
McFarland, Gary 220
McFerrin, Bobby 221
McGhee, Howard 222
McKinney, William 223
McLaughlin, John 224
McLean, Jackie 225
McRae, Carmen 226
Merrill, Helen 227
Metheny, Pat 228
Miller, Glenn 229
Millinder, Lucky 230
Mingus, Charles 233
Mitchell, Roscoe 231
Modern Jazz Quartet, the 234
Monk, Thelonious 237
Montgomery, Wes 235
Morgan, Lee 238
Morton, Jelly Roll 241
Motian, Paul 239
Mulligan, Gerry 245
Murray, David 242
Navarro, Fats 243
Nelson, Oliver 246
Nichols, Herbie 247
Nichols, Red 248
Noone, Jimmy 249
Norvo, Red 250
O'Day, Anita 251
Oliver, Joe "King" 253
Original Dixieland Jazz Band 252
Ory, Edward "Kid" 254
Osby, Greg 255
Page, Oran "Hot Lips" 256
Parker, Charlie 259
Pass, Joe 257
Pastorius, Jaco 260
Patton, Big John 261
Pearson, Duke 262
Pepper, Art 263
Peterson, Oscar 264
Petrucciani, Michel 265
Pettiford, Oscar 266
Phillips, Joe "Flip" 267
Powell, Bud 269
Pullen, Don 270
Quebec, Ike 271
Raeburn, Boyd 272
Redman, Don 273
Redman, Joshua 274
Reinhardt, Django 275
Remler, Emily 276
Rich, Buddy 277
Roach, Max 279
Rogers, Shorty 280
Rollini, Adrian 281
Rollins, Sonny 283
Roney, Wallace 284
Roppolo, Leon 285
Rudd, Roswell, 286
Rushing, Jimmy 287
Russell, George 289
Russell, Pee Wee 290
Sanders, Pharoah 291
Scofield, John 292
Shaw, Artie 295
Shaw, Woody 293
Shearing, George 296
Shepp, Archie 299
Shorter, Wayne 297
Silver, Horace 300
Simone, Nina 303
Sims, Zoot 301
Smith, Jimmy 304
Smith, Stuff 305
Smith, Willie 306
Smith, Willie "The Lion" 307
South, Eddie 308
Spanier, Muggsy 309
Stern, Mike 310
Stewart, Rex 311
Stitt, Sonny 312
Strayhorn, Billy 313
Sun Ra 315
Surman, John 316
Tatum, Art 317
Taylor, Cecil 319
Teagarden, Jack 320
Teschemacher, Frank 321
Threadgill, Henry 322
Timmons, Bobby 323
Tjader, Cal 324
Towner, Ralph 325
Tristano, Lennie 326
Trumbauer, Frankie 327
Turner, "Big" Joe 328
Turrentine, Stanley 329
Tyner, McCoy 330
Vaughan, Sarah 333
Venuti, Joe 331
Waldron, Mal 334
Waller, Fats 337
Washington, Dinah 335
Weather Report 338
Webb, Chick 339
Weber, Eberhard 340
Webster, Ben 341
Wiley, Lee 342
Williams, Clarence 343
Williams, Mary Lou 345
Williams, Tony 346
Wilson, Teddy 347
Young, Lester 349
Zawinul, Joe 350
Zorn, John 351